THE DEATH AND LIFE
OF BISHOP PIKE

By William Stringfellow

AN ETHIC FOR CHRISTIANS
  AND OTHER ALIENS IN A STRANGE LAND
A SECOND BIRTHDAY
  A Personal Confrontation with Illness, Pain, and Death
MY PEOPLE IS THE ENEMY:
  An Autobiographical Polemic
COUNT IT ALL JOY:
  Reflections on Faith, Doubt, and Temptation
DISSENTER IN A GREAT SOCIETY:
  A Christian View of America in Crisis
FREE IN OBEDIENCE:
  The Radical Christian Life
A PRIVATE AND PUBLIC FAITH

By Anthony Towne
EXCERPTS FROM THE DIARIES OF THE LATE GOD

By William Stringfellow and Anthony Towne
SUSPECT TENDERNESS: The Ethics of the Berrigan Witness
THE BISHOP PIKE AFFAIR

THE DEATH AND LIFE
OF BISHOP PIKE

*William Stringfellow
and Anthony Towne*

1976
DOUBLEDAY & COMPANY, INC.
GARDEN CITY, NEW YORK

Some material used in this book is from *The Other Side* by James A. Pike with Diane Kennedy, copyright © 1968 by Diane Kennedy Pike, and *Search* by Diane Kennedy Pike, copyright © 1969, 1970 by Diane Kennedy Pike. Both books were published by Doubleday & Company, Inc., Garden City, New York.

"Capernaum" by Anthony Towne appeared in the January 1974 issue of *Anglican Theological Review*. Reprinted by permission of *Anglican Theological Review*.

Article of September 15, 1969, from the New York *Post*, reprinted by permission of the Associated Press.

Excerpts from THE PSYCHIC WORLD OF BISHOP PIKE by Hans Holzer. Copyright © 1970 by Hans Holzer. Used by permission of Crown Publishers, Inc.

"Thank God for one less pike," February 5, 1966, issue of the New York *Journal-American*. Copyright © The Hearst Corporation 1966. Reprinted by permission of the Hearst Corporation.

"All the Mediums Say He's Dying" by Abraham Rabinovich appeared on January 22, 1970, in the Jerusalem *Post*. Reprinted by permission of the Jerusalem *Post*.

Excerpt from ARTHUR FORD: THE MAN WHO TALKED WITH THE DEAD by Allen Spraggett. Copyright © 1973 by Allen Spraggett. By arrangement with The New American Library and Mary Yost Associates.

Excerpts from articles by James Feron, September 8, 1975, and September 9, 1975, issues of the New York *Times*, copyright © 1975 by The New York Times Company; excerpts from article of June 16, 1967, of the New York *Times*. Copyright © 1967 by The New York Times Company. Reprinted by permission of The New York Times.

Excerpt from THE BISHOP PIKE STORY by Allen Spraggett. Reprinted by permission of Mary Yost Associates.

Library of Congress Cataloging in Publication Data
Stringfellow, William.
    The death and life of Bishop Pike.
    1. Pike, James Albert, Bp., 1913–1969.
I. Towne, Anthony, joint author. II. Title.
BX5995.P54S83   283′.092′4 [B]
ISBN 0-385-07455-7
Library of Congress Catalog Card Number 75-32721

FOR
Scott Kennedy

On the Status of This Book as Biography

The body of James Albert Pike was found, dead, in the wilderness in Judea on September 7, 1969.

During his lifetime, Pike was thought so controversial that the term became as much a prefix to his name as his title as bishop. The media consistently depicted him as "the controversial Bishop Pike" and that is how he was regarded both by those who knew him personally—and loved or hated him—and by those multitudes, inside and outside the Church, who beheld him as a celebrity and who were often attracted and sometimes provoked by his public role.

Bishop Pike's reputation as controversial rests, in part, upon the passion and persistence of his participation in public issues—birth control, the liberation of women, the racial crisis, McCarthyism, capital punishment, abortion, fair housing, the plight of farm workers, censorship, civil liberties, the Vietnam war, resistance to illegitimate authority, among a host of others. In an era in which most ecclesiastics of high rank were devoting their energies to churchly housekeeping, the nurture of religiosity, and miscellaneous soothsaying, Pike's involvement in disputes such as these was deemed controversial *per se*.

The bishop's concern for matters of the Church often rendered them publicly controversial, too, where they might otherwise have remained of pedantic or esoteric interest to churchpeople only. Thus, the recovery of Christian origins, studies of the historical Jesus, the reform of ecclesiastical due process, the ordination of women, ecumenical renewal of the Church, the credibility of traditional dogmas, the semantics of apologetics were among the issues within the Church which, because of Bishop Pike's articulation and advocacy, evoked widespread public interest and argument. This happened, over and over again during Pike's career, because of the way in which such controversies became personified in Pike, as in the repeated accusations of heresy against him, or in the censure he suffered in the House of Bishops, or, earlier, when he was barely confirmed in his election to the episcopacy, or, later on, when he was ecclesiastically ostracized. Simultaneously, the same gifts, through which Pike attracted great public attention to the Church and to the Church's controversies, agitated the concern of many Christians for social and political issues.

Controversy also attended more private aspects of Bishop Pike's life—sometimes with heavy imputations of scandal—in his various marriages, in his alcoholism, in his sexuality, in the suicides of his eldest son and of a mistress, in his parapsychological inquiries, in speculations about his mental health. The circumstances of his death became immediately notorious throughout the world. And, in death, his name and his influence virtually haunt the Church and continue to incite controversy.

If in life and in death, and in memory, Bishop Pike remains controversial—even though some of the issues with which he became associated have quieted—that points, we think, more to the personality and character of James A. Pike than it does to any particular causes or controversies or to the tides of opinion. This person possessed truly catholic interests and extraordinarily variegated talents. This was a man who did not tire of his mind and of the use of it: of asking questions, of seeking more knowledge of every sort, of changing, of growing, of listening, of thinking, of learning about everything and about anything. He had a restless, relentless, questing, insatiable curiosity for living. His was an open, intuitive, risking, audacious spirit. Bishop Pike has been frequently called a prophet; we consider that not quite precise; we think his genre is pioneer.

Some say that Pike was mad. They conclude, specifically, that in the latter years of his life, after expending himself so extravagantly in so many ways for so long, he was rendered insane. While working on this book, we have encountered such opinions—commonly volunteered with a certain eagerness—many times. If no more, this is one way of coping with the phenomenon of Bishop

Pike. In instances, his madness is alleged with condescension, as if to assert the stability or the reasonableness of those making the accusation more than either to diagnose or to defame Pike. Others no doubt use similar terms about the bishop's state of being as a way of evading or equivocating or dismissing views which Pike articulated. There are survivors who harbor such hostility toward Pike that, though he be dead, they propagate his madness as if to persecute or to kill his memory. In this book, attention is given to the matter of madness; it is sufficient for now to notice from the frequency with which the subject is mentioned in post-mortems of Bishop Pike that Pike's existence and Pike's life-style and Pike's pioneering facility have been profoundly threatening to very many persons, and they still are. We are, in this connection, of course, deliberate in invoking as introits to the sections of this book passages from the Corinthian correspondence attributed to an earlier controversial Apostle, in which St. Paul explicates his vocation for the edification of those who, among other things, thought him mad.

This is a way of saying that the very quality of his person which occasioned Bishop Pike's repute as controversial, and which since his death in the wilderness has convenienced gossip concerning his sanity—that characteristic of Pike which we identify as the spirit and capacity of the pioneer—make him a fresh and a contemporary figure. If some of the specific issues which were incarnated in his witness have by now been bypassed or concluded that does not make Pike passé. His life was something more than a brilliant, transient flash. To write today of James A. Pike involves more than reconstructing a chronicle, more than nostalgia, more than biographical recall. To read of Pike now means a risk of being exposed again to the vitality of his humanity and, thus, a risk of being challenged in one's own humanity because of that exposure.

We have written before of Bishop Pike in occasional articles and, at length, in *The Bishop Pike Affair*, the book about the so-called heresy charges against the bishop and the attendant scandal in the Church. These matters are treated in this book, with the vantage of some additional facts and a knowledge of the disposition of the case, if not the controversy, which the previous book, written in 1967 in the midst of the tumult, could not have.

It was while *The Bishop Pike Affair* was being written that Pike asked us if we would one day write his biography, a suggestion to which we gladly agreed. We supposed, at the time, that it was a distant task, one which we would undertake years hence, assuming we survived Pike. Comparing his energies with our own, we entertained doubts about that, but the commission was accepted nonetheless.

Those doubts were not facetious. Little more than a year later, Bishop Pike, accompanied by Diane Kennedy, who was presently to become his third wife, canceled other commitments to visit the Columbia Presbyterian Medical Center in New York City and there administer unction to one of us then in profound illness. With the pastoral intercession of Bishop Pike, among other happenings, that crisis passed and Stringfellow lived, but in less than another year, Pike had died while lost in the Judean desert.

We received the news that Jim and Diane were missing on September 2, 1969, at our home on Block Island. Stringfellow was still slowly recuperating, adjusting laboriously to changes in diet and exercise, work and rest requisite for survival. Since his medical regime made it necessary for him to have nourishment every few hours, around the clock, he could sleep only in intervals, and would be awake periodically each night. Perforce, Towne adapted to this schedule. It had become a habit in the household during the years of illness and convalescence to leave a radio turned on to a twenty-four-hour news broadcast, so that when waked intermittently during the night one was instantaneously informed of events. (This is dubious practice, and probably pernicious, since the news is being relayed during episodic sleep. We have found it sometimes has a confusing impact upon dreams, rendering their recollection more difficult and their interpretation impracticable. And this custom may make perception of the news ambiguous. One wakes up, and listens to the latest reports, but finds the news already vaguely familiar.) So it was, subliminally, as if part of a dream, though later plainly, that word reached us through the radio that the Pikes were lost in the wilderness in Israel. When morning broke, we used the Book of Common Prayer to intercede for Jim and Diane, and for those who were searching for them. In the days that followed, along with millions of other persons throughout the world, we attended the search: waiting and hoping, praying, and comforting one another with recollections of the lore of Bishop Pike. Diane made her way to safety on September 2, and, despite her own ordeal, marshaled the effort to locate Jim. Scott Kennedy, her brother, who had assisted Jim in the research in Christian origins which had so obsessed Pike in his last few years, flew later in the week to Israel to participate in the search and to be with Diane. We were in contact by telephone with Diane and Scott during that week.

Our vigil ended the morning of September 7. About three o'clock we woke simultaneously. "I think he's dead," one of us said. "Yes, he's dead," the other replied. Then, after a while, the silence between us was interrupted by the radio carrying the same news.

Some months after that, when Diane and Scott had returned to the United States, they came to Block Island. It was during that visit that Diane ratified and renewed Jim's request to us to write this biography, and to urge that we begin the work right away.

And so we did. Towne went promptly to Israel, together with Diane and Scott, and with the bishop's mother and his aunt, to survey the scene where the Pikes had become lost and where Jim's body had been found. The work of interviewing countless surviving friends and enemies and assorted acquaintances began. Pike's letters, papers, and diaries were retrieved and the prodigious task of arranging and auditing them was started. But these efforts were soon overtaken by certain other events. One was the interruption occasioned by the seizure of Daniel Berrigan, S.J., at our Block Island home by the federal authorities and by the subsequent indictment of us for allegedly harboring a fugitive. In due course, the indictment was dismissed by the court, but defending ourselves against this political prosecution hindered concentration on the Pike biography for almost two years. We do not begrudge that time, for we are confident that Bishop Pike would have supported us in this involvement most heartily, specifically so since he had entered a special appearance as a defense counsel in the trial of the Catonsville Nine, and since he had publicly committed himself to resistance to illegitimate political authority.

Then there have been problems directly related to the subject of this book, those having to do with the personality and history of James A. Pike. This man was so versatile in his interests—his concerns were multifarious and ecumenical and, somehow, simul-

taneously pursued—that any attempt to treat his life chrono-
logically would be too prosaic to furnish an accurate impression
and would be apt to give a sense of diffusion that would be misleading. At the same time, there is heavy redundancy in the life
and death of Bishop Pike. Again and again, similar themes are
sounded; over and over, he returns to the same queries; repeatedly, he reopens issues. Weighing both elements—diffusion and
redundancy—caused us to reject a chronological principle as a distortion of Pike's story. Taking both as clues, however, we tell of
Bishop Pike by focusing upon themes recurrent in his death and
throughout his life, relating particular episodes within that frame-
work as they seem to us to pertain particularly to his death and to
his life. Thus this book has two sections only, each divided into
many mini-chapters, one part about the death of Bishop Pike and
things portending or otherwise pertaining to his death, the other
concerning his life, that is, his public career, personal relationships, work and activity, thought and belief.

A risk inherent in this arrangement of the biographical material
is that what may be gained in coherence is lost in oversimplifica-
tion, that the ambiguous or contradictory aspects of the subject's
life may be minimized by the emphasis upon the main topics,
that the thematic schema may be self-serving. About all we can
say now is that we have been aware throughout this work of such
risk, that we have sought conscientiously to avoid arbitrary or
artificial interpretations, that we have tried hard to be loyal to the
factual truth. In doing so, we give tribute to Bishop Pike in the
biographical method we have adopted because if there was anything central to Pike's very being as a person it was his passion for
the truth empirically related and verified.

Of course, we recognize that we do not put down here the
whole truth about Bishop Pike, despite the diligence of our
inquiries and research. There are a number of living persons who
retain an interest in spreading particular versions of Pike as a person or prejudicial views of certain of Pike's involvements and activities. That is, we suppose, the case to some extent with anyone
who dies, so far as some relatives or friends or enemies are concerned, and is all the more so where the one who dies has great celebrity. There are, as well, certain people who are dead now, and
whose knowledge of Pike, or of significant happenings in Pike's

life, has been buried with them. That is a limitation for any biography.

Recognizing factors affecting this book such as these does not, however, address what has been our most serious problem in writing of James A. Pike. *That* is the event of our affection for him. We have wondered, from time to time, whether our own long-standing friendship with Jim, dating back to the mid-1950s, constitutes a basic disqualification for our writing his biography. We have not been especially worried that our love for Pike would cause us to romanticize his memory in this book. Our esteem for him, as has already been intimated, includes a sufficient regard for the truth to safeguard against that. Quite the contrary, a romanticized version of Pike's life would only dishonor him as a person. The problem has been how to tell the full story of Bishop Pike, insofar as circumstances avail that, without furnishing titillation to those who steadfastly remain Pike's detractors and enemies. We have not been tempted to exaggerate Pike as a hero, pure and undefiled, but we have been tempted at some junctures while writing this biography to rationalize some of Pike's moral ambiguities, or what some might label his scandals, because they are matters which we had, long since, comprehended and accepted within our affirmation of Pike as a human being. We have not wanted to suppress anything, it would be an ironic disservice to the memory of this friend—of all people—to do so, we trust we have not done so, but, at the same time, we are sensitive because of our affection for Pike to how he is, in his death as, at times, he was in his life, a target of ridicule and condescension, and we have not wanted either gratuitously or inadvertently to nourish such sentiments.

Our effort to cope with these matters has concluded, as we trust this book verifies, that the truth furnishes its own perspective and proportion, and that Bishop Pike, as we have all along been acquainted with him, would want neither more nor less than that in the recounting of his biography, knowing that no human being has judgment over him. As for the petty, as for the jealous, as for the pietistic, as for the judgmental, we notice that those eager to throw stones betray their own moral vulnerability, as Jesus once mentioned.

A bibliography of Pike's writings is appended here, and there are photographs of his life included. The official autopsy of James Pike is reproduced, that being the only available information about his death and the manner of his death and the source from which one can surmise the final experience of Pike in the time in which he was alone in the wilderness. The medical authorities who examined the body have told us that Bishop Pike was so radically dehydrated that it is likely he suffered remarkable hallucinations in the time immediately before he died: sights terrible and marvelous, comparable, perhaps, to those the lore of Christianity attributes to St. Jerome's experience in the wilderness. To anyone so much discomfited because Bishop Pike was a pioneer or to anyone so amazed by his acceptance of himself that he needs to conclude that Pike was insane let it be published that, in those last hours in the wilderness in Judea, Bishop Pike was, indeed, mad.

A straightforward account of our sentiments concerning Bishop Pike is included in the epilogue, in the form of a homily delivered at a requiem for the bishop celebrated at St. Clement's Church in New York City one week after his body had been found in the desert.

William Longfellow
Anthony Towne

Maundy Thursday, 1975
Eschaton
Block Island, Rhode Island

Therefore, knowing the fear of the Lord, we
persuade men; but what we are is known to God, and
I hope it is known also to your conscience. We
are not commending ourselves to you again but
giving you cause to be proud of us, so that you
may be able to answer those who pride themselves
on a man's position and not on his heart. For if
we are beside ourselves, it is for God; if we are
in our right mind, it is for you.

II Corinthians 5.11–13

ACKNOWLEDGMENTS

The authors acknowledge, with gratitude, the assistance and cooperation they have received during their work upon this book from very many persons.

Especially, in this connection, they wish to name Diane Kennedy Pike, Scott Kennedy, Pearl Chambers, Ethyl Larkey, Esther (Pike) Fuller, Gertrude Platt, Philip Adams, Darby Betts, Dean Julian Bartlett, Trevor Hoy, Armand Quiros, David Baar, Bishop John A. T. Robinson, Robert Cromey, John Riley, Bishop and Mrs. George Barrett, Bishop Stuart Wetmore, Canon Edward West, Robert Hutchins, Harry Ashmore, Justice William O. Douglas, Frank and Barbara Kelly, John Cogley, Prof. David Flusser, Prof. Amos Wilder, Dr. Eugene Carson Blake, Alex Liepa, John Orth, William Stemper, Bishop Edward Welles, Bishop John Krumm, James Feron, Dr. Ian Stevenson, Major Enosh Givati, Jane Kingman-Brundage, Ena and Harry Twigg, Mrs. Hannah Tillich, Prof. William H. Hensey, Jr., Moshe Decter, Gerald Gilmore, Will Maslow, Rabbi Arthur J. Lelyveld, Harlan Spore.

They desire also to express thanks to the staff of the George Arents Manuscript Library at Syracuse University which accomplished the inventory and preservation of Bishop Pike's letters and papers pursuant to his testamentary gift.

CONTENTS

LIST OF ILLUSTRATIONS

(following page 88)

James Pike, age five.
On the golf course, 1926.
As a Naval Intelligence officer, World War II.
The future bishop with his mother.
James Pike, his wife Esther, and their children.
Columbia chaplain James Pike with Columbia president Dwight
  D. Eisenhower.
With Francis Cardinal Spellman.
Installation ceremony, Cathedral of St. John the Divine, New
  York City.
At the altar of Grace Cathedral, San Francisco.

(following page 160)

Grace Cathedral.
A visit from Geoffrey Fisher, 99th Archbishop of Canterbury,
  1964.
Officiating at a baptism.
With Supreme Court Justice William O. Douglas.
With Presiding Bishop John Hines and Dean Julian Bartlett.
Martin Luther King, Jr., visiting after the Selma march, 1965.
In England with Bishop John A. T. Robinson.
At Cambridge University.
The Bishop's Office, Grace Cathedral.

(following page 256)

James A. Pike, Jr.
The Pike family en route to the requiem mass for Jim, Jr.
A close-up, James A. Pike.
The final sermon at Grace Cathedral.
Bishop Pike's resignation.
Press conference, April 1967.

(following page 328)

At the Center for the Study of Democratic Institutions.
Wearing the resistance button.
With Mrs. Diane Kennedy Pike.
At Qumrân, Israeli-occupied Jordan.
Wife and mother at the grave of Bishop Pike.
The gravestone of Bishop James A. Pike.
R. Scott Kennedy.

CHRONOLOGY

1913   James Albert Pike is born in Oklahoma City, Oklahoma, on February 14 to James Albert and Pearl Agatha Wimsatt Pike.

1915   His father dies of tuberculosis.

1921   Pearl moves to California with her son.

1924   Pearl is remarried to Claude McFadden, an attorney.

1925–30   Attends Hollywood High School, Hollywood, California.

1930–32   Attends (Jesuit) University of Santa Clara, Santa Clara, California; drops out of Roman Catholic Church and Santa Clara (1932).

1932–36   Attends (one year) University of California and (three years) University of Southern California, Los Angeles, California; completes undergraduate arts program and graduates from law school.

1937–38   Attends Yale Law School, New Haven, Connecticut; earns doctorate in law; moves to Washington, D.C., as an attorney with the Securities and Exchange Commission; establishes law firm of Pike and Fischer; marries (1938) Jane Alvies.

1940   Divorces Jane Alvies Pike.

1941–45   Serves during war in Washington, D.C., first in Naval Intelligence and later as an attorney with the U. S. Maritime Commission; marries (1942) Esther Yanovsky; is ordained a deacon of the Episcopal Church (1944).

1946   Jim Jr., second of Jim and Esther's four children, is born; is ordained priest by Bishop Angus Dun in Washington, D.C.

1947   Earns degree in divinity from Union Theological Seminary, New York City.

1948   Pearl marries her third husband, C. B. Chambers, a retired railway employee.

1947–49   Rector of Christ Church and Episcopal Chaplain at Vassar College, Poughkeepsie, New York.

1949–52   Chaplain and Chairman of Religion Department, Columbia University, New York City.

1952–58   Dean of the Cathedral of St. John the Divine, New York City.

1958–66   Episcopal Bishop of California, San Francisco, California.

1966   Suicide of Jim Jr. (February); returns from five-month sabbatical in Cambridge, England (March); resigns as Bishop of California (May); joins Center for the Study of Democratic Institutions, Santa Barbara, California (August); accused of heresy by Bishop Louttit and others (September); censured by the House of Bishops (October).

1967   Suicide of Maren Bergrud (June): divorced by Esther Pike (July); Toronto television séance with Arthur Ford (September); vindicated at General Convention, ending heresy battle (September).

1968   Attempted suicide of his daughter (February); marries Diane Kennedy (December).

1969   Announces intention to leave institutional church (April); forms the Foundation for Religious Transition, Santa Barbara, California (April); is severed from the Center for the Study of Democratic Institutions (June); dies in the Judean desert, Israeli-occupied Jordan (probably on September 2); is buried in the Protestant Cemetery in Jaffa, Israel (September 8).

INTRODUCTION

Jim Pike was an event. To know him was to be deeply affected by him in one way or another. Even to be in the same room with him was to be touched in a personal way by him—to be stimulated into a response.

Jim Pike was fully, dynamically, energetically alive. His rhythm of being was much faster than most people's. He lived in double-time, and thus accomplished twice as much, had twice as many experiences, felt twice as deeply, risked twice as often as most people would in the same number of years.

Images flood in for me whenever I turn my attention to him. During the last week of his life, we were in Paris together. We had spent two days in the Louvre, walking, absorbing, appreciating. I was wrestling with "traveler's trots," visiting every public rest room and feeling more and more tired and weak as the day wore on. It was midafternoon when Jim saw a museum map which described the Museum of Man as an anthropological history of human evolution, with an emphasis on the cultures people have developed over the ages. "We have to see that museum," Jim said with great excitement.

So we caught a taxi and rushed across the city to the Museum of Man—with one stop along the way so I could explore yet another public facility. There was less than an hour left before museum closing time, but that did not deter Jim. He was just like a kid turned loose at a circus. He took hold of my arm, dragging me from one display case to another with enormous excitement and curiosity. "Look at this," he would exude, pointing out and commenting on nearly every item in each case.

At the end of the first room, I was too tired to feel like going on. Spotting a chair, I said, "I'll wait for you here." "OK," he said, not pausing for a moment in his exuberant exploration. Two minutes later, he was gesturing to me wildly from the display case he had moved on to. "Diane, you can't miss this," he called. I dragged myself off the chair and over to where he was. He poured out in a stream of enthusiastic recounting all he had just learned about *this* culture, *this* phase of human evolution. I agreed with what energy I had left that it was indeed fascinating, and went back to my chair. Only moments later he was at my side, taking me by the arm to show me his next discovery. *Everything* was exciting. No matter how tired I was, in his enthusiasm he couldn't imagine that I would want to miss *this*.

As the guard ushered us out of the museum that day so they could lock it up, Jim said to me, "Next time we're in Europe we'll come to Paris just to see this museum. We'll spend an entire day here. We'll hire an English-speaking museum guide to tell us all about each display. Imagine," he said, almost ecstatic at his discovery, "the entire history of the human race is here in summary form, with actual replicas of the costumes and artifacts of each culture and age! Why, you could get a complete education from this one museum!"

Such was his response to life in every new moment. It was as though he had never before been exposed to the history of humanity. He was as a child, humbled and delighted by the magnitude of all there was to learn. And he wanted to know it *all*, to experience everything.

His curiosity was insatiable. Perhaps that's why he had read both the dictionary and the phone book from cover to cover by the time he was five, and a whole set of the Encyclopaedia Britannica before he was ten. He rushed at life, embraced it, experienced it fully, and welcomed the new whenever and however it presented itself.

So vigorous was his interaction with life that most persons experienced him as a whirlwind of energy. Some were delightfully stimulated by that, others were threatened; some stood in awe, others were overwhelmed; some felt their lives to be transformed and made new by a simple encounter with him, others found him too much to take—exhausting or frustrating because he was never still.

I delighted in his strength and forcefulness of energy. I found it stimulating and challenging. It kept me on my toes, growing every moment, but it did not overwhelm me. I *could* absorb it, and did. And I could match it in strength if I needed to. Moreover, I experienced him in his stillness on many occasions.

The last week of our life at home in Santa Barbara was typical of his way of engaging with life. Jim had determined he would catch up with all his correspondence before we left on our trip to Europe and Israel. He was also finishing research on the book on the historical Jesus which he, my brother Scott, and I were to write, and gathering reference materials to take with us on our trip. Five secretaries had been working full time for several weeks: Jim gave them dictation in tandem and they took turns at our various typewriters, preparing letters for his review.

In the midst of the rush of the last day, when all five secretaries were making one final effort to finish their work and Scott and I were rushing about packing and readying reference materials, Jim kept an appointment he had made several weeks before. The man who came to see him felt Jim to be his last resort. He was convinced there was a plot by government agents to drive him crazy. He was an Austrian baron who had fled from his country during the Second World War. Through a series of events which he recounted at length, since coming to our country he had lost all of his money, several jobs, and eventually his wife, finally ending up in various institutions. Jim had agreed to see him because he had said that no one was ever willing to listen to his story; people kept dismissing him as insane.

Jim sat with him in the living room, giving him his full and undivided attention for at least three hours, while around them swirled a veritable whirlwind of last-minute activity. We were astonished that anyone could concentrate in the midst of the turmoil, but Jim was so totally focused on the baron that he seemed unaware that the rest of us were around. As far as he was concerned, when he was talking with someone, especially in a counseling situation, no one else *was* around.

At length, he and the baron rose and came into the kitchen, where about four of us were waiting to consult with Jim about one matter or another. Jim introduced the baron all around, exclaiming, in the perfect calm of that quiet energy which many people never experienced in him, what a fine conversation they had had. Then he turned to the baron to tell him goodbye. He reached out and embraced him fully. The baron's eyes filled with tears and his whole being softened.

After Jim's death, which came only eleven days later, I received a letter from the baron. He said Jim had saved his life. Everything had begun to change for him after that afternoon's conversation. He had recovered his health, had new employment, and was well on his way to a life of fulfillment and joy again.

Such was the impact Jim had on many, even in the midst of a bustling rush of activity, *because* of the intensity of his energy and because of his single-minded focus on whatever he gave his attention to.

From the time I first met Jim, which was only three short years before he died, I was challenged and inspired most by his aliveness. I was impressed that at fifty-three he was willing to give up his successful, powerful, and influential position as Bishop of California and to launch out on a new life. He was a sign of hope for me that persons can remain fully alive and growing at all ages and in all periods of their lives. In an age of such rapid change, it was refreshing to know someone who not only did not fear change, but actually welcomed it.

In the short time we shared together, I was to see that willingness to change and grow manifest over and over again as Jim found himself in new circumstances and made responses to them. Life was, as he used to say, a process of growth through encounter.

Most persons who heard Jim speak in person or on television knew well his brilliant mind, and certainly that was one of his most powerful and formative personal attributes. But only those who actually approached him in person to shake his hand or speak to him touched that childlike quality which I feel made him so alive and so able and eager to grow. The ingenuous little boy in him was the aspect that responded to each person as a friend, totally open to whatever interaction ensued. He was spontaneous, forgiving, full of humor, and insatiably curious. People would often be caught completely off guard, and thus be disarmed, by his complete lack of guile and his totally straightforward openness. The free child within him was incredibly resilient and enabled Jim to live almost totally in the here and now.

The Chinese philosopher Mencius said, in 372 B.C., "A great

man is he who never loses the heart of a child." If that is so, then Jim Pike was a great man. He grew to eschew the other values usually associated with greatness: accomplishments, power, position, wealth, and fame. He gained those things and found them hollow. It was life itself that fascinated him, and increasingly he gave value only to the quality and style of life he felt Jesus to exemplify—that of a "man for others," fully human, giving of himself in selfless love to other persons that they might discover fullness of life as well.

I have been amazed many times over, since Jim's death, at the vast numbers of persons all over the country and in other parts of the world who have written or spoken to me about the impact Jim had on their lives. While I knew he was famous, I hadn't realized how deeply and personally he had touched the lives of so many—even people who had never met him or seen him in person. For many people he became a symbol of hope, freedom, openness, fearlessness, and courage. By his own willingness to risk growth and to challenge what he viewed as illegitimate or unjustly exercised authority, he inspired them to dare to be a little more fully who *they* were and are.

It is difficult to capture that quality so often called "charisma" in a book *about* Jim. I observed it over and over again as he engaged with people in the privacy of our home, in his office, in small groups, or in huge stadiums and gymnasiums filled with thousands of people. It was a quality that often brought a hush to the room when he entered and then sent forth rushes of excitement and bubbling delight the moment he opened his mouth to speak. It was the quality which so captured people's hearts that they hung on his every word for hours at a time, even when I was sure they could not be understanding all he was saying. It was the quality that made one of his fellow bishops say to him at the end of one of those many struggles in the House of Bishops, "Jim, the thing that makes me the angriest about you is that I can't stay mad at you and I can't dislike you." To know that quality fully, you really had to experience Jim directly, either in person or through his books.

However, this biography partakes of something of the essence of Jim's charisma, in the rhythm and structure of its format as well as in its content. It is sensitively written and assembled by

Anthony Towne and Bill Stringfellow, friends of Jim's who knew, understood, appreciated, and loved him as fully as any I have met. For those who knew Jim, the book will reawaken their sense of his energy and person. For those who did not, here is a glimpse of a uniquely creative and energetic man, who in Mencius's terms was indeed great.

I am deeply grateful that the patterns of our individual lives were such that I had the joy and the privilege of knowing Jim Pike the last three years of his life. When people ask me what he was like, I always feel inadequate to describe him. He was an event which I wish I could share. This biography now provides a vehicle for such sharing, and it has been my joy to cooperate with the authors while they were writing it.

I commend Jim Pike's spirit of aliveness to you. May it quicken in you that quality of all-encompassing eagerness to be, to do, and to know, which is of the nature of being fully and magnificently human.

Diane Kennedy Pike

PART ONE

Sojourn in the Wilderness

For we do not want you to be ignorant, brethren, of the affliction we experienced in Asia; for we were so utterly, unbearably crushed that we despaired of life itself. Why, we felt that we had received the sentence of death; but that was to make us rely not on ourselves but on God who raises the dead; he delivered us; on him we have set our hope that he will deliver us again.

II Corinthians 1.8–10

Jim and Diane Pike drove out into the Judean desert in the late summer of 1969 to continue what amounted to their honeymoon.

Diane was driving the white Ford Cortina roadster they had rented two days earlier upon their arrival at Lod airport in Tel Aviv, and Jim was charting their course from a crude map they had been given by Avis at the same time. Before heading out into the wilderness they had stopped near their hotel on the Mount of Olives to pick up two Coca-Colas. They had nothing else with them except the clothes on their backs and the usual tourist paraphernalia.

It was not a prudent safari. Their intention was to pursue what the map indicated to be tertiary roadbeds winding deep into the desert up the backside of cliffs overlooking Qumrân on the Dead Sea and joining up eventually with the road to Jericho. In terms of distance this was a manageable undertaking. They had started out from Jerusalem just after noon and had they been able to proceed routinely at a moderate pace they could have expected to be back at their hotel readily by late afternoon. There would even have been time to pause now and then to take pictures and to savor the atmosphere of the wilderness.

Unsafe at any speed, the Ford Cortina is not a vehicle Ralph Nader would have chosen to navigate a tertiary road in the Judean desert, and harder though they may try, Avis is not the place most of us would have turned to for a reliable map of a wilderness. Two Coca-Colas might refresh a honeymoon at Niagara Falls but for a nuptial adventure in a barren canyon hard by the Dead Sea a five-gallon jug of water would seem more like it.

What in the world were they doing out there? That is the question many people were to ask at the time. Part of the answer is that few of us would care to attempt an answer to the same question in relation to a fair number of experiences into which we have somehow calamitously blundered. That we have nevertheless survived to ponder the question proves that grace is multifarious. And that leads us to another part of the answer, which is that Jim and Diane Pike were not most folks. They *would* honeymoon in the wilderness of Judea. Were that not the case we would not have occasion to write this book, nor you to read it.

The Gospels tell us that Jesus spent forty days praying, fasting, and meditating in the same wilderness and that he suffered there three remarkable temptations at the hands of Satan. That is notorious. We have all heard about that, but how many of us have stopped to wonder what in the world Jesus was doing out there? Bishop Pike did wonder about that. He had a hunch, supported by some recent scholarship, that Jesus might have gotten into the desert from the Essene community at Qumrân where he could have been a member or a guest as a young man. That is why the bishop wanted so badly to venture out into the desert and up behind the spectacular cliffs overlooking the excavations of Qumrân. He wanted to see for himself and to share something of the environment in which Jesus may have undergone his notorious wilderness experience.

Jim and Diane Pike, passionately drawn to one another, in love, were passionately drawn into their desert ordeal, now also notorious, by a consuming curiosity about the person of Jesus and the origins of the Christian faith. Their safari into Judea was neither capricious nor frivolous. It was a quest more compelling and hazardous than the quest which is the substance of every honeymoon.

For the quest of true love, the quest of one another, Jim and Diane were superbly equipped, but for the quest of Jesus in the Qumrân wasteland they could not have been more inadequately outfitted.

The Community of Qumrân

In the spring of 1947 two Bedouin shepherds discovered in a small cave, high up the face of a cliff overlooking Qumrân on the Dead Sea, nine jars, eight of them empty but the ninth of which contained three sheepskin scrolls, one more than twenty feet long and destined to be identified as the Scroll of Isaiah. The scrolls were sold in Bethlehem for almost nothing. Parts of them were later resold to Hebrew University and the rest to the Syrian Superior of St. Mark's in Jerusalem. Early in 1949 the small cave

(Cave I) was excavated by scholars, who found other scroll fragments, much pottery, and some linen which was dated, on the basis of a carbon 14 test, as A.D. 33 plus or minus 200 years.

In 1951 excavation of the Qumrân ruins was begun, and in the first room to be cleared jars of the type found in Cave I were unearthed, and a coin of A.D. 10. That same year in another nearby cave (Cave II) more fragments of scrolls were discovered. This led to a systematic search of thirty-seven other caves, in one of which (Cave III) rolls of copper with clear Hebrew characters were found. In the fall of 1952 Bedouin made the largest discovery of all, innumerable scroll fragments, in a cave (Cave IV) on the face of a spur not more than a hundred yards from the Qumrân excavations.

The scrolls and fragments of scrolls discovered in and around Qumrân have come to be known collectively as the Dead Sea Scrolls.

Excavation of the Qumrân ruins was completed in 1956. What it disclosed was a primitive stone habitation, but with an elaborate water system dependent upon rainfall, designed to accommodate an ascetic religious community. Scholars of the matter seem of a consensus that the inhabitants of the place were Essenes, a sect of Jews who flourished, if ascetics do flourish, for a century or so B.C. and another century or so A.D. There were several communities of Essenes. They were distinguished by a taste for communal organization, severe discipline, and a theology dualistic though exempt from gnosticism. The Qumrân community seems to have been in placid residence for about a century when it was dispersed by a great earthquake in 31 B.C. In 4 B.C. the sect returned and restored the place. There ensued a second placid interval disrupted in A.D. 68 or 69 by Roman legions which sacked the buildings and massacred the community. Except for occasional squatters the ruins appear to have been undisturbed from that time until the recent excavations.

The Essenes of Qumrân had a remarkable library. They cherished it. When the Roman legions descended upon them the Essenes hurriedly hid what they could of that library in nearby caves. Besides the virtually complete Scroll of Isaiah fragments of nearly every other Old Testament book have been recovered from Caves I through IV and the ruins themselves. Those scrolls antedate by a millennium the earliest previously known substantial Hebrew manuscripts of the Old Testament. The significance of their discovery for Old Testament studies is incalculable, and efforts to calculate it will be going on for a long time to come.

Other manuscripts and fragments have been recovered, commentaries and tracts produced by the Essenes themselves, which illuminate hitherto obscure background of New Testament literature. Many of the esoteric passages of the New Testament are prefigured in Essene texts, and our understanding of the New Testament is being enhanced by scholarly work directed at the influence of Essene theology on the early Christians. Historical research into the origins of Christianity has been profoundly enriched by the recovery of the Dead Sea Scrolls.

The ruins at Qumrân are not much to look at unless one has a thing about ruins. To be excited by them, as Bishop Pike was, one would need to bring to them, as he did, knowledge of what had gone on there and imagination to reconstruct the scene as it must have been when the community eked out its Spartan career and suffered its terrible calamities. Bishop Pike visited the ruins more than once, exploring them with exuberance and delighting in every detail of what must have been for the most part a tedious endurance. He had scrambled up to peer into the caves overlooking the ruins. He was familiar with the recovered scrolls and the scholarly works about them, and he was in conversation with some of the ablest of the scholars. For Bishop Pike Qumrân was a decisive eschatological event not only in its historical posture but also in his personal spiritual biography.

Fascination with the Qumrân event is what tempted him to undertake that improvident wilderness sojourn.

An Interview in Tiberias

Late one rain-swept afternoon in January 1970, several months after Bishop Pike had been found dead in the Judean desert, his mother, Mrs. Pearl Chambers, an intrepid octogenarian, who had survived three husbands and one son, her only child, settled wearily into a beige armchair in the lounge of a hotel in Tiberias, glowered balefully out a window at the Sea of Galilee, glanced at a nearby tape recorder as though it might transmit some loathsome disease, poured ritualistically two cups of a pungent tea, and consented to reminisce. Her delivery was persistent, impeccably precise, and disarmingly flirtatious. To have interrupted her reverie would have been to have committed a gratuity. To utter the past was to utter a gospel. Mrs. Chambers recollected that past with authority suggesting that she had sensibly allowed herself to forget whatever no longer mattered.

Ethyl, she announced, rhyming her sister's name with *lethal*, would be unavailable that afternoon. The Mount of the Beatitudes had exhausted her. Mrs. Larkey, Ethyl, Bishop Pike's favorite aunt, a lady then in her late seventies, alert, spry, and diffident, had been Mrs. Chambers' companion off and on, especially at times of misfortune, throughout her long life and had joined her once more in that capacity for a pilgrimage to the Holy Land and to the bishop's grave in Jaffa. Mrs. Larkey had more likely been refreshed by the Mount of the Beatitudes. It was Ethyl's habit to defer to her elder sister, and she may have had an intuition that Mrs. Chambers preferred, that afternoon, to hold a solitary court.

Mrs. Chambers had told the story of her life more than once, and it was a fascinating story. "When I lived in San Francisco," she began, "there was a friend of mine that always wanted to— she kept after me to write my life because I would tell her so many things about James." (Bishop Pike's mother invariably called him "James," never "the bishop," and never, as most people close to him did, "Jim.") "She was interested, of course, in that. I had had some very interesting things happen in my lifetime. I told James that this friend wanted to write my life story. He said, 'Write it yourself.' Of course, I never did." It is a pity she did not.

Pearl Agatha Wimsatt and James Albert Pike were married in 1907 in Kentucky, where they had both been born and raised, and they moved almost immediately to Oklahoma to claim forty acres of land he had purchased from the government and which they proposed to homestead. He had just graduated from college and it was his plan, once the claim had been proved up, which would take a year, to enter medical school. He wanted to be a doctor. She had done some teaching before their marriage and intended to return to it while her husband pursued his medical education.

To prove up their claim a house had to be built, the property fenced, and the forty acres of land cultivated. Neither of the newlyweds had ever lived on a farm. The ground turned out to be full of mesquite, a tenacious woody shrub with cantankerous roots. It would be necessary to engage a hired man in order to clear the land. There was no money for that so Pearl secured a position as teacher in a school some miles away, and in a matter of months she had connived to have her husband named principal of the place. "I told him what to do, of course," Mrs. Chambers confided *sotto voce*. Between them they collected salaries totaling $125 a month, which to them seemed for the times a "princely sum." The house got built, the property fenced, the land cleared, and in due time a crop of cotton was planted.

James Pike's health, meanwhile, had begun to fail. His illness was certainly tuberculosis, though Mrs. Chambers chose not to identify it, perhaps because she could remember when TB was so feared that people did not care to mention it. The couple, on recommendation of his doctor, went to Alamogordo, New Mexico, where they lived in a one-room shack made half of pine boards and half of canvas. She supported them by playing piano with a dance orchestra. She also played background music for silent films in the local movie house, becoming one of the earliest practitioners of that quaint and fugitive art. His health responded enough to the climate that they were able to return to Oklahoma, arriving with ten cents to their name, "enough in those days for two cups of coffee and two doughnuts." Fortunately, the cotton was ready to be harvested.

Their obligations under the Homestead Law were now fulfilled, and they were able to prove up the claim. He was too ill to work, so they sold the homestead and bought a home in Oklahoma City. Despite a prohibition against married teachers in the city schools she persisted in applying for such a job and eventually got one. Several months later she discovered she was pregnant. Her mother came from Kentucky to help out, and early one morning in February of 1913 Pearl Agatha Pike went into prolonged, difficult labor. A doctor was summoned. His attentions were immediately required by James Pike, who collapsed and had to be put to bed and sedated. Pearl's mother, who had borne five children of her own, took a dim view of the doctor's handling of her daughter's condition. The infant, she insisted, was "stuck" and would have to be forcibly extracted. Throughout the long day and into the evening the doctor stubbornly demurred.

Finally, just after midnight, at the breach of February 14, 1913, the doctor did intervene, and the fifth Episcopal Bishop of California was yanked from the reluctant entrails of his mother into a fallen world. He was promptly endowed with the name of his stricken father. Nearly sixty years later Mrs. Chambers remained adamant in the conviction that only the malingering of the doctor had made of James Albert Pike a Valentine baby.

"When he was one year old," Mrs. Chambers recalled, "I entered him in the Better Babies Contest at the State Fair, and he received the First Prize, the highest score out of four-hundred babies, and when he was two years old he won it again, both years. I thought you would like that. He started out a winner." But his father was not so favored, and ended up a loser. In 1915, when the boy was two, James Pike died and Pearl was left with young James. She would stay a widow for the next nine years.

Not long after her husband's death Pearl brought her mother and her sister Ethyl to Oklahoma City, and the three women established a household, the center of which was Pearl's son. The two sisters worked as teachers, and the mother took care of young James. One day in 1915, some months after his father's death, the boy would inquire of Pearl, "You're to Granny; I'm to you; you're to Ethyl—who's to me?" Somebody was missing.

"He always wanted a sister."

Mrs. Chambers wanted a nap before dinner.

Descent into Wadi Mashash

JERUSALEM, Wednesday, Sept. 3—Dr. James A. Pike, former Episcopal Bishop of California, was reported missing last night in the Judean wilderness west of the Dead Sea.

Dr. Pike's wife, Diane,

walked into a work camp
this morning at Ein
Feshka, on the north-
western shore of the
Dead Sea, after an all-
night trek to seek help
when their car broke
down.

Israeli police and army
authorities mounted an
intensive search for the
controversial 56-year-old
churchman but had to
postpone it at sundown.

So began James Feron's front-page story for the New York
Times of September 4, 1969. Bishop Pike, who had been front-
page news off and on for two decades, churned up headlines on
front pages the world over for the better part of a week during
most of which he lay dead in the Judean desert. Death is nothing
if not solicitous. The anonymous die anonymously and the celebrated with celebrity. There is no way Bishop Pike could have
slipped unnoticed into oblivion. He died as he had lived, in an el-
egant, flamboyant disarray.

Dr. Pike has been to
Israel on several occa-
sions, a prominent Jeru-
salem churchman said,
adding that he rarely
made contact with
church people when he
came.

The area of the search
is rich in Biblical history.
It is just north of the
sites of Sodom and Go-
morrah and across the
Dead Sea from the hills
of Moab, where Moses
finally viewed the Prom-
ised Land before he died.

Ein Feshka is close to

> Qumrân, where the Dead
> Sea scrolls were found.
> The area is riddled with
> caves.

Death in such circumstances, as James Feron in the *Times* seemed to convey, cannot be ordinary. But the progress of Jim and Diane Pike out into that wilderness in their Ford Cortina had had a strangely ordinary aura about it. They did not seem to feel that they were doing anything unusual, and they had no idea at all of the extraordinary catastrophe that lay ahead. To them it was another day, another adventure—as all the days of their time together had been. Nothing more sinister lay ahead of them, so far as they could see, than what lay behind them.

The narrative of the drive out into the desert, the getting stuck of the Ford Cortina, the abortive efforts to free it, the decision to proceed on foot toward the Dead Sea, the collapse of the bishop, Diane's decision to go on alone through the night, her astonishing ordeal and miraculous survival, the search for the bishop, and the discovery six days later of his body in the depths of Wadi Mashash have been definitively rendered in Diane's book *Search*.* Her book, written in the very aftermath of the events of that dire and dreadful week and completed within two months of the bishop's death, is thorough, straightforward, vivid and urgent, and humanly engrossing. To her account little need be added save some details here and there, recollections of others who played some part in the search, the crude contents of official records, and the ambiguous perspective afforded by relative detachment.

> The scenery was beautiful. There were Arab villages on both sides of the road on hillsides, and a very dry riverbed off to our left, which we believed to be the Valley of Kidron. We commented about the strange beauty and I took some pictures. Each time I stopped to take a picture Jim made a comment manifesting minor impatience. "I don't see what that really shows," he would say. He never liked taking pictures while traveling, but he loved sharing them with friends when we got home.
>
> "It helps capture the mood," I responded. "It shows what the houses look like and gives you a feeling for the desert." We both sensed that feeling—an indescribable sense of elation

---

* Garden City, N.Y. Doubleday, 1970.

which the clear air and expansiveness create, unlike anything I have ever experienced before.

They might have been two classic American tourists passing a casual afternoon exploring alien exotica. Unfortunately they were not. Bishop Pike would *not* have seen the point of random snapshots (and he *would* have delighted in them later). "I don't see what that shows," sums up an intellectual attitude he cultivated all his life. He had a lively distaste for the jejune, and was impatient always to get on with whatever was the business at hand.

> Once we came to a place where the road seemed literally to end. Jim jumped out of the car and ran down to the right and across the wadi, quite a deep riverbed, and called back, "It's all right. It is a road."
>
> I felt extremely anxious. "Oh no, sweetheart," I called. "Let's don't go." As I stepped out of the car, planning to join Jim where I could see what was ahead, I suddenly got sick to my stomach. I leaned over the side of the road and called to Jim. By the time he reached me the momentary sickness passed, but I had soiled my dress, my legs and my hands.
>
> Since there was no water available, Jim got out one of our two Coca-Cola bottles and opened it on the bumper of the car, insisting that I wash myself with it.
>
> "No, I won't do it," I said emphatically. "We only have two with us."
>
> His response was equally emphatic. "You certainly *will*."

There was no water available. *That* is what this wretched episode ought to have made emphatic. The folly of being in a desert without any water had been demonstrated for them, but they did not get the message. The bishop's stern solicitude for Diane's physical manifestation of anxiety was characteristic of him, and so was his disinclination to understand it as a suggestion that they turn back. His pertinacity was awesome.

On they went for more than an hour ever deeper into the wilderness along a dubious roadbed that was sometimes barely passable.

> Once or twice I said rather nervously, "Sweetheart, it looks like endless desert, just endless desert."
>
> But Jim replied, "It can't be endless desert. The map doesn't show endless desert."

I could see nothing but mountains, so I tried again: "Darling, look. Just endless desert. Endless."

Jim's logic dominated. "It can't be endless desert. The map doesn't show endless desert."

Bishop Pike was not being logical. He was being stubborn. He was also being wrong because where he thought they were in terms of that questionable Avis map they were not. He thought they were near Qumrân, but Qumrân was miles to the north and somewhat east of them. Diane was right. Ahead of them lay miles of desert, and though it was not endless it was nearly so as she would discover during the long night to come. The road Jim thought they were on they had turned off, and they were on another that persisted ineluctably to the southeast and canyon Wadi Mashash.

A Grievous Transfiguration

The morning after her interview that lugubrious afternoon in Tiberias Mrs. Chambers found herself crumpled into the back seat of a Mercedes-Benz taxicab as it rutted crazily up a narrow winding tarmac to the summit of Mount Tabor. Her son the bishop was to blame. It was he who had planned this tour of the Holy Land in which she was now entrapped, and though he had not lived to share it, it had been with her particularly in mind that he painstakingly worked out its itinerary. No tour bus could manage such an ascent; it would be necessary to mount Tabor on foot, he had been told. Impossible, he had replied; his mother would never make it. Hence: the small flotilla of battered taxicabs grinding themselves up the face of the sacred mountain, and in the back seat of one a bewildered Mrs. Chambers and her sister Ethyl.

It was on—or above—the ample chunked crest of Tabor, as tradition has it, that the Transfiguration of Jesus took place. Luke and Matthew tell us Jesus was joined in apparition by Moses and Elijah, and that "Peter and John and James," though they may have slept through some of it, were witnesses to the phenomenon. Let us assume they were awake when a great cloud came and overshadowed them. "And a voice came out of the cloud, saying,

'This is my Son, my Chosen; listen to him!' And when the voice had spoken, Jesus was found alone." Luke indicates there had been conversation among the apparitions about Jesus' "departure, which he was to accomplish at Jerusalem," a reference presumably to the events commemorated during Holy Week.

In the midst of the rapture of the miracle Peter had proposed, we are told, that three "booths" be constructed to shelter the apparitions, but then the great cloud had come and suddenly it was all over. No booths got built. But both before the episode of the Transfiguration and off and on ever since there has been no end of construction, destruction, and reconstruction on Mount Tabor. The place is an archaeologist's paradise, and for those who may be turned off by archaeology there is the option of an exhilarating and historically nourished view.

Mrs. Chambers and Mrs. Larkey and their party, which included Diane Pike, so lately wooed and widowed, having achieved the summit of Tabor by way of *Bab el Hawwa*, the Wind Gate, stumbled from their caravan onto the gaily-gardened esplanade of a pseudo-Roman-Syrian basilica and were enthusiastically greeted by a delegation of Franciscan monks who had prepared in their honor an oddly poignant agenda. From a bell tower done up in a sort of medieval style (but with a clock in it) there rang out the tender strains of "Home on the Range." Nearby, in a plot of winter-dormant shrubbery the image of Pope Paul VI, almost life-size, faintly smiled benevolence.

The chief of the delegation, or head monk, so it seemed, a man of irrepressible jollity, ushered the three bereaved women and other residue of the late bishop through an ornately sculptured narthex into the holy basilica. Beyond an ancient, sunken crypt there loomed up in a fustian of stained glass the three transfigured apparitions who did not seem to notice the intrusions taking place beneath them. The three women were encouraged to kneel together on the bench of a regal, oaken *prie-dieu*. The jolly monk, ecstatically grinning, sank into the recesses of an immense, cobwebbed organ and the sanctuary erupted in crescendos of "Ave Maria."

Tears flowed down like righteousness, and the three women had for themselves a mighty weeping. That was the catharsis. There remained some amenities. Ushered back out of the basilica, purged of all passion, the women of the bishop and the others were escorted into a refectory so low of portal that many heads were bashed to the utter merriment of the monks. A collation of tea and cookies had been spread out, and precious memorabilia. There were shards and bits of sculptures, blurred inscriptions, and for coin freaks and parchment fetishists the components of an orgy. There was a post-funereal atmosphere Bishop Pike would have known how to banish.

The refectory gave onto a narrow balcony overhanging a panorama of the plain of Esdrelon which gave in turn onto the Samarian mountains, and much farther in the distance in another direction the snow-capped pinnacle of Mount Hermon. It was enchanting. Much history had crisscrossed that sprawling valley, and from Tabor holy men and some not so holy had looked down on it. From the bell tower, meanwhile, issued, scratchily, a melancholical "Auld Lang Syne."

"Over there," the jolly Franciscan giggled matter-of-factly, "Armageddon will be fought."

Precognitions and Premonitions

Major Enosh Givati of the Bethlehem police, whose eyes took in everything and communicated nothing, a meticulous man, alert to pretty secretaries and fond of strong coffee, was dissatisfied with the English a translator had made of his Hebrew. "I did not say," he said in English, "that *Mrs. Pike* could not have driven a Ford Cortina so far into the wilderness. I said *nobody* could have done it." Major Givati had supervised many searches in the Judean desert for persons lost or presumed to be lost in it. It was part of his job. He wanted it understood that the elaborate search he had mounted for Bishop Pike was no more and no less than what he would have done for anybody else. "He was a human being lost in the desert," he said. "That is a terrible thing."

> The right rear wheel was in a rut so deep that it did not touch bottom. We put some rocks underneath it and I tried driving it out again. The wheel spun. "You're just wearing the rubber down," Jim called out, his voice strained. "We're really in trouble."

"I know," I murmured. I began to get a sick feeling in the pit of my stomach. Surely, there must be a way to get out.

It was about 2:45 in the afternoon.

That they would sooner or later get stuck was a certitude. They had, in fact, already been stuck once, perhaps twenty minutes earlier. By quirk or happenstance two Bedouin boys had come along and with their help Jim Pike had managed to push the car free. They would see no more Bedouin, no more anybody. This time they were stuck good and they were going to stay stuck. This time the sick feeling in Diane's stomach was not from apprehension but from reality. They really were in trouble.

> Yet I would not have Jim back. Not now. Not physically. Just as I feel we were both somehow driven by some inner force into that wilderness—seeking the experience, eagerly awaiting what it would bring us by way of insight, understanding and an experience of reality, of God's power—so I feel somehow this portion of Jim's odyssey was finished—his search for Truth at this time on this plane of existence somehow seemed to be completed.
>
> There are so many little things that contribute to that conviction. As I look back over the weeks before we left for Israel, so much that we did points for me to some unconscious realization on Jim's part—or perhaps both our parts—that his journey in this phase was about to end.

During the summer of 1969, preceding their trip to Israel, Jim and Diane Pike had had opportunity to enjoy their bright, cheerful new home in Santa Barbara. In an article for *Look* magazine in April of that year they had disclosed their intention to leave the institutional church, and at the end of June his formal association with the Center for the Study of Democratic Institutions had terminated. For the first time in many years he was relatively free of consuming obligations. He was very happily married. He had the opportunity at last to take account of a crowded life that had, in the last several of its years, burst open in a giddy (and some thought gaudy) display of public scandal and private trauma.

Bishop Pike had had throughout his ministry the habit when confronted with a grave personal problem to make of its solution a vehicle for extending his ministry to others who might share the problem. In that tradition he had now established a Foundation for Religious Transition. He hoped to make of it a many-faceted agency for service to the growing community of clergy and other religious who were suffering personal and vocational turmoil. He was at the same time ever more fascinated with his research into Christian origins, and he contemplated an ambitious series of books based upon that research.

There was even talk of one or more films that might be made.

But Bishop Pike *was* in transition, profoundly. And he *was* in a deep internal, personal, and vocational turmoil.

> We spent one entire Sunday—at a time we could not afford to pause in our work—talking about his life in terms of his spiritual growth. He took me all the way back to his childhood to share each deep experience with me, interpreting its significance for me in terms of his growth toward personal—spiritual —freedom.

With a wife like Diane who would give up a whole Sunday to a biographical regurgitation it is no wonder Jim Pike was happily married. Perhaps he had finally found that sister his mother said he always wanted.

> Just before we left, he withdrew his offer to waive his right regarding a hearing for his deposition, thereby ensuring that he would remain a bishop of the Church until after we had completed our trip to Israel and Europe.
>
> We spent time with his children before we left for Israel, having to make a special trip to Sacramento and San Francisco to make it possible. Jim said he felt it was "important" we have time with them, and I felt, even at the time, that it had a deeper significance than any fulfillment of a "fatherly obligation" would have implied.
>
> We spent a great deal of time with Jim's mother during the summer and he often spoke of feeling that our love had made it possible for his mother to be restored to him.

During that menacingly halcyon summer Bishop Pike does seem to have been making those amends and tidyings up which harbinger redemption in the terminally ill. Despite the chaos by which he seemed ever about to be engulfed he was at the center of it a very tidy man. And now as the longed-for month of vacation and research in Israel and Europe began chaos and tidiness conspired dismaying portents.

> For the first time—in spite of all the traveling we did—we took out accident insurance on our lives before leaving.
>
> Jim mentioned many times that he had never looked forward to a trip so much and that he knew a big breakthrough was coming in Israel.
>
> When we arrived in Israel Jim said, "Dear, I didn't kiss the ground, but this is holy land, and I have come home."
>
> Our second night in Jerusalem we stayed up nearly all night rejoicing in the detailed memories of our relationship.
>
> The day before we went out into the wilderness, Jim had a precognition (we thought) of his mother's death, which caused us to talk at length and in detail about the meaning of death, our feelings about it, what kind of burial and requiem he felt were appropriate, etc. Thus, when I had to make those decisions about his death, I knew exactly how he would feel. And, oddly enough, he had "seen" his mother fall and felt that the fall might cause her death. I feel now it was a kind of premonition of his own manner of dying.
>
> That same day, at lunch, Jim chose a title for his autobiography: *Nothing to Hide*. It was the first time I ever remember his considering an autobiography; he had always insisted it was "too early" for that. He outlined its content for me that day.

Did Bishop Pike sense he was about to die? Had he sensed it he *would* have taken out airline insurance on his life. He *would* have done what he could to prepare his wife for the death. He *would* have found occasion to tell her of his wishes with respect to the "kind of burial and requiem he felt were appropriate, etc." He *would* have done all in his power to reassure her of his love for her and of the great joy their time together had been for him. And above all he *would not have failed* to disclose the title for his autobiography, and to outline the content of it.

Scott Kennedy, Diane's youngest brother, who was twenty years old when his brother-in-law, the bishop, died, had been close to the couple during their courtship and brief marriage. He had accompanied them—together with one of the bishop's two daughters—on an earlier trip to Israel. Diane was to say about Scott in the introduction to *Search* that he "shared Jim's and my search for Truth and knows and appreciates our style of life better than any other single person, I think." One day in the fall of 1972 Scott had a long chat with Bishop Pike's old friend and colleague, George Barrett, the former Episcopal Bishop of Rochester.

Bishop Barrett wondered when Scott had last seen Bishop Pike alive.

> The day they left for Israel. It was one of those typically bizarre scenes. We had a big dinner at our family's in San Jose. It was my brother Jim's wedding—August 19 or 20—and then Jim and Diane left the next day for New York, then Amsterdam, Paris and Israel. It was just a very frantic scene, the wedding scene itself. And Jim was—I don't know how many weddings he had been at where he was not performing the service himself, but not very many, I suspect—and he was just one of the family, really. But he was the real gentleman of the reception. Lots of our friends would approach him. This was mostly Methodist circles, the middle-class San Jose crowd, you know. And people would approach him, but he was very reserved, out of respect for the family, I think. He didn't want to upstage the event. He was very aware, conscious of that, trying not to upstage the wedding. But then he danced. We have pictures of him dancing with my brother's wife. Really nice. Then afterwards we had this big dinner and stuff. And then I remember Jim and Diane were late, of course, rushing up to San Francisco, maybe they were speaking someplace on the way and then catching the plane. I remember carrying their bags out to the car and saying goodbye. That's when I had this really sinking feeling, that I should be going with them, really powerful sort of precognitive feeling that I *really* should be going with them. *But* I canceled it because I thought—well, at that point—well, you just want to be part of that trip, but you'll go again—you don't need to go this time. It would be fun for them. Really, it was their honeymoon. But I had that really strong feeling. Diane remembered that, too, afterwards.

Bishop Pike would probably wonder what *that* shows. It shows affection.

The Via Dolorosa

Mrs. Chambers had somehow survived the expedition to Mount Tabor. She had begun, however, a gradual slip into weariness that would deepen by the end of the two-week pilgrimage into utter exhaustion. The tour bus rumbled south from Galilee toward Jerusalem through raw, inclement weather and a bleak landscape, redeemed by groves of ancient olive trees and now and then a stand of tortured terebinth. Once there was a stop at what purported to be Jacob's Well. Mrs. Chambers made her way slowly down steep, irregular stone steps to sip of the sacred waters. She found herself face to face with a small, framed watercolor of the head of John the Baptist on a platter, looking terribly in need of some freshly chopped parsley. Later there would be another stop at a roadside jewelry concession. Earlier in the tour this would have brought an eager sparkle to her eyes. Now she could barely toy morosely with the far from precious stones.

Early one morning in Jerusalem, leaning heavily on her sister's shoulder, Mrs. Chambers, her swollen feet for the occasion mercifully unshod, shuffled deliberately into the magnificent Dome of the Rock to peer reverently at a large boulder, upon which, Jewish and Christian tradition has it, Abraham came within a hair of dispatching Isaac, and from which, Moslem tradition has it, Muhammad and his horse ascended into heaven leaving behind as imperishable proof the horse's footprint. Bishop Pike had once examined this situation with his usual diligence, and pointing up toward the overarching dome had inquired of a guard, "You mean, he went up through there?" The guard had replied, "Well, the roof wasn't there at the time, of course." The absurdity of the matter had provoked merriment in the bishop, but Mrs. Chambers during her drear vigil did not seem to be amused.

Later that same day the tour bus made its way through intermittent showers to a suburban housing development. A playground and park would be dedicated in Bishop Pike's memory. There were civic dignitaries, the press, a small crowd. Mayor Teddy Kollek uttered the sentiments of the city of Jerusalem. Diane Pike responded, and a marker was unveiled. Mrs. Chambers, draped in a blue coat, edged slowly out of the crowd, studied the marker close up, squared her shoulders, turned, and waited for photographers to record her sad smile. From surrounding balconies and windows sober-faced children stared uncomprehending down. History had invaded their seesaws. It had begun to rain torrentially. An umbrella opened over Mrs. Chambers as she was led out of the playground back to the bus.

Despite the drenching rains she was soon to be deposited at Damascus Gate. Her son the bishop had included on his itinerary for the tour a stroll along the Via Dolorosa. By then able to walk at all only assisted on one side by Ethyl and on the other by Diane she had not got far into Jerusalem's Old City when she slipped on wet cobblestones.

Mrs. Chambers—as Bishop Pike had fore "seen"—fell.

Falling into Nothingness

"I feel myself sinking now . . . falling through the column . . . Oh, God . . . everything is black, empty, hollow . . . God . . . I'm falling and there's nothing at the bottom . . . no bottom . . . I'm falling into nothingness . . . blackness . . . no way to grab hold, nothing to catch onto . . . save me, save me . . . what can save me . . . falling . . . nothingness . . ."

I listened to Jim's distress with more than empathy. I was experiencing vicariously his terror.*

Bishop Pike was watching the older of his two sons and his namesake freaked out on a cough medicine. It was not the first time. He and Jim Jr. had been sharing a flat in Carlton Court in Cambridge for several months while the bishop pursued a sabbatical in England and the young man studied at Cambridgeshire College. Jim Jr. was a very mixed-up guy, so mixed up in that January of 1966 that within a month he would be dead. He was only twenty years old. A tall, lank, good-looking fellow, average of intelligence, Jim had been finding it increasingly painful to relate to young women and young men of his own age. The drugs in which he sought surcease served him badly.

"Now wait a minute," I tried to interrupt. "Wait just a minute. You can't possibly be serious about this. You can't live that way —without friends, without love, without people—"

"Like hell I can't. A cool cat doesn't communicate, he only hides and protects himself. And that's why drugs are really cool. I mean like you take off into a world all your own where nobody can intrude. I mean like that's *your* world, and it's really cool. You just take off . . . and float . . . and nuthin' can touch you —nuthin'. No sir, I'm nobody's fool. If you think I give a damn

* James A. Pike, *The Other Side*. Garden City, N.Y. Doubleday, 1968.

about anybody or anything you got another long think comin'.
No sir, it's Number One all the way—and if that's all the way
on drugs, well . . ."

And it *would* be all the way on drugs, but the way would be
short. The two Jims happened to have that colloquy over lunch
the bishop had fixed for himself and breakfast he had fixed for
Jim Jr. the day after an earlier "trip" the son had suffered through
while the father tried clumsily to soothe, to comfort, to bring the
boy "down." These were experiences the two men had been sharing, and a conversation they had been having with each other,
since they arrived in Cambridge, and the pattern would continue
up to a day in early February of 1966 when the bishop flew off to
San Francisco and Jim Jr., after a hassle over his passport, flew to
New York City to die.

Jim Jr.'s biggest problem may have *been* his father. The sons of
clergymen notoriously have a tough time of it. Bishop Pike was
not only a clergyman but a bishop, and not only a bishop but a
celebrity, and not only a celebrity but a man in many, many ways
to be reckoned with. It cannot have been easy to be Bishop Pike's
son. It must have been a ball-breaker to bear his name. The struggle to stake out an identity all one's own is what it's all about. Jim
Jr. was terribly torn between the need to be his own man and the
temptation to be swallowed up in his father's kaleidoscopic
image. Those months lived together intimately in that Cambridge
flat were for both Jims a disturbing, warming, ambivalent, threatening experiment with love.

One evening Jim asked if he could bring a college friend, Peter,
home for dinner. He would like to have me meet him, he said.
I was delighted.

"Tomorrow night?" I asked. Jim said he would check.

The next evening when the two of them arrived we sat in the
living room for a while chatting over coffee. His haircut and
clothes halfway between Mod and conventional, our guest was
both intelligent and articulate. He intended to go on the next
year to pursue a degree in philosophy at a university in the Mid-
lands. After dinner, in our by now familiar bachelor style, we all
joined in cleaning up, while continuing what was for me—and
seemingly for them—most interesting dialogue on the pros and
cons of dualism and monism. As they started for the living room,

I excused myself, saying I had some work to do (no white lie), and settled down at the dinette table with papers and typewriter. A couple of hours later his friend left and Jim opened the door close to where I was sitting. I looked up from my work.

"I think he's great," I began, "and he threw some interesting light on—"

"Then why did you cut out?" he interrupted. I could see from his expression that it mattered to him.

"Oh," I said disconcertedly, "I thought you two would be wanting to talk and play records, and I didn't want to be in the way."

"You wouldn't have been. It seemed you weren't really interested," he countered.

"I'm sorry. I *was* interested. Let's have him again."

We did. This time after supper and tidying up I followed them into the living room and sat down with them. Then Jim said, "Well, Dad, I think we'll be running along."

Bishop Pike always did have difficulty grasping that for most of us "the pros and cons of dualism and monism" are *not* what it's all about.

"Yell 'Help Me' All the Way Along"

"Professor Flusser will just have to understand," he said sadly.

Jim Pike had begun to grasp the seriousness of the predicament into which he and Diane had blundered that desolate afternoon in the Judean desert. It was about 4 P.M. They had frivolously drained their energies for more than an hour in desperate, vain efforts to free the stuck Ford Cortina. The temperature was approximately 130 degrees Fahrenheit with a negligible humidity factor. He was about to use the bumper of the car to force open their one remaining Coca-Cola, and he would lose some of that in the process. There was no way they were going to keep a 7:30 P.M. dinner appointment with David Flusser and his wife in Jerusalem.

Flusser and Pike were good friends. They enjoyed one another. A New Testament scholar at Hebrew University, short, orotund, dynamic, a practicing Jew but with an ardent interest in the historical Jesus, David Flusser shared Bishop Pike's preoccupation with research into Christian origins and especially with the implications in that regard of the Dead Sea Scrolls. What really drew the two men together, however, was their common gift for animated, brilliant, witty conversation. Professor Flusser would later recall how much he had been looking forward to that aborted dinner and evening with Bishop Pike.

"Bishop Pike was my friend, my dear friend! It was my honor to know him! It was my joy to know him! How that man could talk! His enthusiasm was like wildfire!" Professor Flusser spoke in exclamations, and his own enthusiasm, no matter what the subject, seemed also unquenchable. So, on Friday evening of the week their friend was lost in the desert the Flussers had walked a great distance, so as not to violate their Sabbath, in order to be present for a hastily arranged mass the Anglican Archbishop of Jerusalem had consented to offer for Bishop Pike. Professor Flusser, enthusiastic even in compassion, *had* understood.

"This reminds me of the movie *Lawrence of Arabia*," I commented.

"What?" Jim sounded puzzled.

"Did you ever see it?"

"Yes," he replied.

"Well, I was thinking of those incredible desert scenes with the blinding sun beating on the sand. I remember how thirsty I was at intermission." The comment was almost small talk, but it reflected my growing realization that, though there was no sand in this desert, the sun was beating down on our heads and backs and dehydrating our bodies. And we had just begun to walk.

Jim and Diane had decided to abandon the Ford Cortina and to set out on foot toward the Dead Sea. They believed themselves to be near Qumrân, where they knew there would be water. And they reasoned that the distance back toward Bethlehem was much greater than the distance ahead toward the Dead Sea. Had they decided to walk back the way they had come they would have been likely to encounter Bedouin tribesmen or possibly Israeli militia. But their fixation on Qumrân, and Jim's sureness from the map that they were near to it, displaced other fairly obvious contraindications and their peril was to be compounded. They did not, in fact, give any thought to alternatives.

They were, when they started walking, not more than ten miles in a straight line from Bethlehem, and less than that from villages east of Bethlehem, and they were roughly four miles in a straight line from the Dead Sea. The terrain through which they had driven was far from hospitable but the terrain into which they elected to walk would deteriorate steadily into unimaginable wilderness. The effects of dehydration in desert conditions are rapidly dreadful. They had already suffered dangerous loss of fluid during the strenuous, prolonged struggle with the recalcitrant Ford. Walking, stumbling over rocks, and at times climbing up or down in the tortuous ravine could only aggravate their distress.

In 1972 a team of experts in consultation with Alonzo W. Pond, former Chief of Desert Branch, Air University, Maxwell Air Force Base, produced a manual for desert survival based upon some two thousand case studies. One of the cases was that of Bishop Pike.*

They worked about an hour, until 4 P.M., in an attempt to free the tires. One hour of hard work in that temperature would produce the following:

	Est. Weight	Est. Water Loss	Lbs. Equiv.	% of Total Weight
Bishop Pike	180	4.2 qts.	7.2 lbs.	3.9%
Mrs. Pike	120	4.2 qts.	7.2 lbs.	5.9%

By 4 P.M. both Bishop and Mrs. Pike experienced dizziness and exhaustion which probably led to the following:
A. They could not figure out how to use the jack from the auto's trunk. They thought it wasn't all there, although later investigation proved it was there.
B. They left the car and the sources of signaling and protection.
  1. Did not take rear view mirror.
  2. Did not take water from radiator.
  3. Did not use gasoline or tires to create a smoke signal or fire at night.

After briefly resting at 4 P.M., the Bishop and his wife began walking. They walked until 6 P.M. over difficult terrain which necessitated climbing and walking. Bishop Pike had removed

* J. Clayton Lafferty, Patrick M. Eady, John M. Elmers, *The Manual for the Desert Survival Problem*. Human Synergistics, 1972, pp. 39-40.

some of his clothing in the now 125 degree F temperature and the increased dehydration caused by the Bishop's removal of his clothing would have caused a significant water loss.

	Water Loss	Lbs.	% of Body Weight
Bishop Pike	11.2 qts.	17 lbs.	9%
Mrs. Pike	11.2 qts.	17 lbs.	14%

(NOTE: 10% to 15% of body weight loss will produce severe symptoms. 20% is usually fatal.)

When they began to walk away from the car Bishop Pike led in the purposeful stride that was his customary locomotion and Diane had trouble keeping up with him, but within a half hour she was in the lead and he was straggling. Dehydration made speech difficult and they communicated only occasionally and he would sometimes fail to respond to her remarks. Once they spotted pipes ahead of them, suggesting possibly water, but the pipes proved to be broken bits of fencing. Diane for a time was persuaded that a cliff in the distance was the cliff backside of Qumrân. It was not. Down upon them beat the pitiless sun.

Remarkably, Diane paused several times to take pictures. Bishop Pike did not bother to wonder what they showed. Some showed him. He had removed his trousers. He should not have done that. Bedouins in the desert wear a lot of heavy clothing covering themselves as totally as possible. The layers of cloth help keep the sun out and the moisture in. By 5 P.M. they had walked an hour and gotten essentially nowhere. Jim's heart was pounding and his weariness was utter. He pleaded a rest. So, in the shadow of an overhanging rock they lay side by side covered with flies they had not the strength to brush away.

> Suddenly Jim put his hand on my lips and I felt the cooling touch of water. I realized that he had urinated just a little bit on his hand and was giving me the first moisture. I licked it off and swallowed it, grateful for anything wet. Then I heard Jim wash some around in his mouth and spit it out. When he gave me more, I drank it—drank it because it was wet. The taste seemed irrelevant. He took more in his mouth and again spit it out.
>
> Then he let his urine flow and we both took it and washed it all over our faces and arms. It was unbelievably refreshing. And

even though immediately afterward the flies covered our bodies again, the feeling of relief from the intense dehydration persisted for some time.

When Jim's heart had slowed they dragged themselves up out of the shade of the rock and stumbled on. Suddenly, Diane was seized again with the chimera of Qumrân. This sustained them for a time. From a different vantage it became clear it was not Qumrân and that before them lay bare cliffs and twisted canyons interminably contending for the horizon. It had become too much for Bishop Pike. He pleaded sleep. Once again they lay side by side. This time they were on a flat rock unprotected from the sun. Happily, the sun would soon sink behind the hills west of them into the Mediterranean Sea beside which within a week the bishop's bones would be buried. The withdrawal of the sun would bring a sensation of relief, but the intense heat and the dehydration would continue almost unabated.

Diane was restless. She sat up once and tried to brush flies off Jim but it was too difficult. Then she decided to go on alone. Jim did not object. "Tell them to bring lots of water. Tell them I'm feeling faint—to bring something for that. Tell them to bring whisky; I'd even try whisky." She had no idea which way to go. She began trying to climb up out of the canyon they were in. It was just too hard for her. She returned and lay down again beside her husband glad just to be in contact with him.

I said, "Sweetheart, if we're going to die in the desert, I want to die here beside you." For the first time death seemed the most likely possibility.

"OK," was his only reply. We lay for a long time in the silence. Then I had a sudden flash of memory of several lengthy conversations Jim and I had just a few weeks before about our inability to comprehend why a person with any degree of rational control in a crisis situation would not do everything possible to save the life of another.

"Diane," I thought. "If you were to stay here to die beside Jim it would be purely selfish. It would be only because you wanted to be with him, to be beside him when you die. If you get up and go, there is a possibility, a slight possibility, that you might be able to get help. You have to go on."

I also had another brief flash, a momentary one but an impor-

tant one, I think. If I were to stay there and we were both to
die on that rock in the desert and someone were to find us in
the future, they might think it was suicide.

That was an odd intuition for her to have had. Why would anybody in the future think it had been suicide? It would have to
have been the strangest double suicide on record. Whatever its
provenance it seems to have been decisive in persuading Diane to
go on alone, that and the conversations the two had lately had
about appropriate behavior in crisis situations. It was probably the
wrong decision. His chances for survival were better if she remained with him. Logically speaking so were hers. But as things
turned out—by what has to be accounted a near miracle—the decision enabled her to survive. It might in the same way have saved
him. But near miracles are seldom vouchsafed. He would perish.

> "Sweetheart, I'm going for help." I sensed either decision was
> all right with him.
> "OK," Jim said. "Tell them to bring lots of water."
> "If I die in the desert, you'll know that I went because I love
> you and I was trying to get help for you," I said.
> "I know that," Jim responded. "I love you, too, and if I die
> here"—his voice broke slightly—"I am at peace, and I have no
> regrets."

The passivity with which Bishop Pike accepted Diane's decision
was not characteristic of him. He may have decided to feign
greater exhaustion than he actually felt in order to persuade
Diane that she had no choice but to leave him. He may have
come to the conclusion that her only chance for survival was to go
on without him. In that context his passivity would make more
sense to us.

Diane told him she would climb down the canyon to the very
bottom until she reached the Dead Sea. He indicated that after
sleeping awhile he might be able to follow. He suggested she leave
what she had been carrying so that her hands would be free for
climbing. She did leave her cosmetics case, her camera and sunglasses, and that absurd map. She had gone only a short distance
when he called after her.

> "Tell them to bring lots of water—and yell 'help me' all the
> way along."

His last words were pastoral.

It was 6:10 P.M.

An Extraordinary Woman

"Help me, Mother; help me."

These are the first words Bishop Pike uttered from the other side, according to Harry Twigg, who heard them. Harry was, at that time, a morose Englishmen of late middle years who managed to seem simultaneously deferential, respectable, sober, and bewildered. Harry's wife was Mrs. Ena Twigg, the gifted and famed medium and psychic communicator, and it was in their comfortable, cluttered home in East Acton in the west of London that Harry and Canon John D. Pearce-Higgins, Vice-Provost of Southwark Cathedral, sat during the evening of September 4, 1969, in emotional séance with Mrs. Twigg. The bishop was still missing in the Judean desert. "I have never heard anything like it before," Harry would later report. Mrs. Twigg heard nothing. She was in a trance.

The séance was taped. Roy Stemman, who had listened to the tape, rendered this account of it in the September 13, 1969, issue of *Psychic News*, "The Spiritualist Newspaper With The World's Largest Circulation," which is published out of London.

> The canon asked who was speaking and was told, "You know who I am."
>
> Pike said he was lost, adding: "I'm not a coward about death. I'm nowhere and I don't belong anywhere."
>
> He went on to say, "If I believed before, now I must believe even more."
>
> The entranced medium grasped her throat, then thumped her chest. Pike said there were many people around him but he could not see anyone. He felt lonely. Asked how he had died, he replied, "Choked."
>
> The canon comforted him and reminded him that it took Jesus three days to come back. Pike could not expect to communicate easily so soon after his passing.
>
> Pike asked for prayers to be said, "for us . . . pray for my darling . . . such hopes." The couple married in December last year. The exbishop complained that he was surrounded by a mist. He hadn't expected this.

Referring to his disappearance, he said, "I don't think they'll find what's left of me."

The canon asked, "Did the Arabs get it?" The reply was, "No, the sand got it." Trying to elicit more information, Pearce-Higgins asked if he had walked away from the car. Pike said he had.

"Did you choke in the sand?" the canon continued. "I don't know!" Pike cried.

Then he said to the canon: "God bless you. This is the second time you have helped me." This was a reference to Pearce-Higgins' introduction of the bishop to Ena Twigg in 1966.

Pike continued to complain about the other world conditions in which he found himself. "I want to see you all. I can't see you. You would have thought they'd have opened my eyes a bit."

The canon told him he hadn't read his Crookall (author of astral projection books) and that it took three days before the "vehicle of vitality" is shed. Pike's retort was, "Baloney!"

Some months and a year later Mrs. Twigg and Harry served tea with crumpets from a tiny, movable tea cart that seemed too delicate for its burden. Their guests were Diane Pike and her brother Scott and two writers who happened along. It was a dull, chilly London afternoon in February of 1971 and the tea was welcomed. Once again the proceedings were taped. (They were twice-taped, in fact, since the writers made one tape and Harry Twigg another.) Mrs. Twigg had agreed beforehand to talk about her recollections of Bishop Pike, and she would do so in an artful, gay, ingratiating, insistent monologue which glanced enticingly at many other matters and lasted the better part of two hours. Now and then laconic questions were interposed. Her responses were candid and her evasions adroit.

Ena Twigg was by that time the most famous medium in the world. This was by no means entirely on account of her sittings with Bishop Pike, both before *and* after his death, but association with Bishop Pike had certainly embellished her reputation. She seemed disarmingly vain about that and about the opportunities and the responsibilities her prominence in an arcane profession conferred upon her. Born of a Church of England family and educated for a time in a Roman Catholic convent in France, she was informed on church affairs, alert to theology, and knowledgeable of the Bible. She had lived abroad off and on especially in

Mediterranean countries, including Israel. To be in her considerable presence for even a short interval would compel the conclusion that Ena Twigg was nobody's fool.

Bishop Pike had respected Mrs. Twigg as a medium, and he had been fond of her as a person. She felt the same way about him. Following their first meeting, within a month of Jim Jr.'s death in 1966, she would tell Harry, "He's *right* on *my* wave-length! He's *right* on *my* wave-length!" Later, at the close of a séance in which Jim Jr. had "come through" in a reassuring way, the bishop had impulsively embraced the lately entranced medium. "I said, 'My goodness!' and he gave me *such* a kiss. I said, 'It's the first time in my life I've ever had *that* done by a bishop.' We've often laughed about that." Mrs. Twigg was careful to add that it had not, of course, been for her that the bishop had delivered his kiss. It had been because "he was so thrilled to think the boy had managed it." Jim Jr. *had* "managed to come through" in startling ways in two séances Bishop Pike had had with Mrs. Twigg just after the young man's death. He would subsequently "come through" in other séances with mediums in the United States.

Ena and Harry Twigg had vivid memories of their experiences during the week Bishop Pike had been missing in the Judean desert and the whole world awaited the outcome of the massive search Major Givati had mounted for him.

"We were in the kitchen Monday night, weren't we? We got the news on, and they said Bishop Pike was lost in the desert."

"Am I going to worry you, Diane?"

"Pardon me?"

"Are we going to worry you?"

"Heavens no . . . no, no, no . . . not at all . . . of course not."

"Remember these words, Diane? 'You can't die for the life of you'?"

"Yes, I remember your saying that."

"I came in to dinner. My instinctive thought was—reaching out to Jim Jr. And I couldn't get *anything!* Tuesday. I tried all day long to make a contact with Jim Jr. I tried to reach my father to get to Jim Jr. *Nothing! Just nothing!* On Wednesday I got up in the morning—I was covered in gray mist. Everything I looked at was entirely gray mist. And on and off all day Wednesday—it was a very busy week, wasn't it?—I kept trying to get a

link, to get a link. And in between—first somebody would call
from here, then somebody would call from there. Somebody
called from the *cathedral*. Somebody called from the *abbey*. I
thought, 'What the *dickens?* Can't somebody else look for Jim
Pike?' We thought, 'Why *me* all the time?' *Not* me. I *can't* do it.
It's the other side who do it."

"On Thursday morning Scott rang from the airport, didn't you?
And you just added to it. You said, 'Have you found Jim yet?'
Do you remember? You *really* put the cat in the mouse, the pi-
geons, you know. We'd had this all week. *Find* Jim!"

"*Well*. I asked you, 'Did you *get* anything yet?'"

"Yes. Well, I got to the point, you know, of—why am I tied
up in this? How have I got so involved with America? My job's
been here and on the Continent and different places. I said, 'No,
I haven't been able to get anything.' I think I told you how this
had been happening. I was going over to a hospital to visit
somebody who was dying. I said, 'I can't do anything today. I
shall have to be with this person most of the day.' Do you remember? I told you that, didn't I?"

"I asked if anything at all had come through from Jim. You
said, 'No,' but that there had been a mist. And that it was very
—that the impression you had, though it wasn't anything very
specific, was a *bad*."

"I didn't remember saying that."

"Anyway, I went over and stayed with this person—dying of
cancer, as a matter of fact. This is part of my job. It was a
person I liked very much, a sweet woman. And when I got back
Diane had rung. I said to Harry, 'Did you tell her we were going
to sit *specifically* for this tonight?' I rang John P-H up. 'What
you got on, John?' He said, 'I'm at a conference.' I said, 'Well,
you jolly well better find a way out of it.' And he came out
here. When we managed to get together it was eight-thirty on
the Thursday night. I was sitting here. John was there. Harry
was there. The tape recorder—thank God we put it on—it was
on the floor. And we sat in quietude just waiting—for Jim *Jr.*
You see? Instead of which I just went *out-like-a-light*. Didn't I?
When I came back—I've *never* felt like it in my life. I *never* in
all the years I've been a medium. I was shaking inside and outside, and everything in my body was quivering—you know?—
every organ, every muscle. I've never felt that way before. *I* was
as white as death. Poor John and Harry—*they* were as white as
death. I said, 'For God's sake, what *is* happening?' And they said,
'Well, Jim's been talking.' When we'd had a cup of tea and

pulled ourselves together a bit, I rang Oliver Hunkin—the BBC-TV religion man—and I said, 'Oliver, you've got the program on tomorrow night of Jim and Dr. Ian Stevenson, talking on, my mediumship. What're you going to do? Jim's been *talking* to us.' And Oliver Hunkin said, 'Oh, you *are* an extraordinary woman!' *Dear* Oliver! *Poor* Oliver!

"Then, in the morning I put a call through to Diane—at half past seven. They lost my number. I don't know what happened. Anyway, I waited from half past seven until half past nine. We rang again, but Diane had gone off to join the search. I had this *ghastly* day. Diane, you'll *never* know what that day was like. Wondering what I was going to *tell* her. Eventually, it was five o'clock, wasn't it?"

"In Israel, yes."

"She greeted me and said she'd just come in. And do you know what you said to me? Do you know what you said?"

"Well, I think I know what I said, but go ahead."

"*I'll* tell you what you said. You said, 'Everybody's ringing me up from everywhere giving me messages. Jim's in a cave. Jim's safe here. Jim's safe there. The Bedouins have got him.' Do you remember saying that?"

"Well, I could have said that because it was true."

"So, there was this girl saying that to me. Then she said, 'What's your news?' Can you imagine that? Oh, it was terrible! I never want a job like it again. You tell your husband not to do these things to me! Anyway, Diane said she was going to go on with the search, didn't you? Well, then the program went on at eight o'clock. Then I got the final break. I was sitting here. An assistant editor of one of the papers was sitting right there. I said, 'I've got the end of the story. Jim's climbed somewhere and fallen.' Then the program came on. Then the telephone went mad. Then we got to bed. About half past twelve we'd just gotten to sleep when New York rang up. Then Dr. Ian Stevenson rang up. Then everybody rang up. We could have wrung the necks of everybody in New York. I ended up saying, 'Will you stop ringing in the middle of the night?' They don't realize the time change."

"The time differences, yes."

"But, you see, they were all reputable people, reliable people who were told these things before Jim's body was found on Sunday. And they would call and tell me what they had been told."

"What do *you* make of the cave business? I know you didn't

get such a message, but apparently many people did. Why do
you think that should be?"

"Well, I think—I'm not taking this up psychically or anything
—but knowing the terrain, knowing the country and knowing the
sort of biblical image people get in their minds—this could well
be that they were *wishing* he was safe in a cave. Do you see
what I mean? I'm not being unkind about anybody. Don't you
think this could very well have happened? They wanted him to
be safe. They wanted him to be secure. And this was something
that they could envisage, something that was part of the terrain
there. Don't you feel that, Harry?"

"I feel that."

"And I don't for a minute think . . . Then we got a phone
call—it was after three o'clock—from somebody to do with
Arthur Ford. Now Arthur Ford was in hospital and wanted me
to ring him and tell him the latest news. I said, 'Let *him* ring
me.' By this time I thought, 'This *is* the limit.' Poor man. He's
gone on to the other world now, too, hasn't he? Poor man. He's
probably a lot better off over there. He wasn't well."

Suddenly, Mrs. Twigg interrupted herself.

"He's got a mother in the spirit world, haven't you?"

Mrs. Twigg's guest was startled. A poet, he was used to being
ignored or to being treated with deference. At that moment, in
fact, he had been trying to picture *Arthur Ford* in the spirit
world. Arthur Ford and the poet had spent an evening together
in Philadelphia eight days after Bishop Pike was found dead in
Judea. The poet remembered the medium as a man ensconced in
the flesh. How Arthur Ford would look as a spirit he lacked imagination to conjure.

"A mother?"

"Yes."

"No. My mother is living."

"Somebody's calling 'Mother' over there. Can you hear them?
Can you hear that voice?"

"No."

"Can you hear that, Diane?"

"No."

"That's extraordinary! There, she's calling again. No, I'm not
going to tune in. I dare not."

Extraordinary things happen in the lives—and in the deaths—
of extraordinary people.

An Honest Man Is Candid

> "She talked about my mother in the next world, but as you
> can see my mother is in the next room right now by the fire."

Bishop Robinson's elderly mother was indeed sitting by a roar-
ing fire in his converted farm house in a village outside London. It
was an early afternoon in February of 1971, a sunny, cheerful day,
but chilly. Only the day before the bishop's two guests had been
entertained at tea by Ena and Harry Twigg. It was their account
of that visit which had prompted the bishop to recall the one occasion when he had been in Mrs. Twigg's company.

His guests had not come to talk about Mrs. Twigg. They had
come to talk about Bishop Pike. Bishop Robinson had seated
them comfortably in his study, an addition to the old farmhouse,
a bright, colorful room in the contemporary manner and with
large picture windows giving onto an ordinary English country-
side. There were bird feeders scattered among the shrubs and
winter-barren trees. No voices from the spirit world would interrupt Bishop Robinson, but during pauses in his recollections his
guests would welcome the reassuring chatter of finches and
chickadees.

John A. T. Robinson, sometime Bishop of Woolwich, and author, among other books, of *Honest to God*, a best seller on both
sides of the Atlantic in the mid-1960s, had been a friend of
Bishop Pike's, and the two bishops had met many times throughout that decade in England and in the United States to discuss
theology and to have good times together. *What Is This Treasure*,
which Bishop Pike published in 1966, included a dedication to the
Bishop of Woolwich.

✠ JOHN A. T. ROBINSON
GOOD FRIEND AND
COMPANION-SPIRIT ALONG
THE WAY

Toward the end of September of 1969 Bishop Robinson was to relinquish his duties in Woolwich, and for the occasion he "laid
on" some festivities. Jim and Diane Pike had been expected to
stop in England on their way back from Israel especially for those
festivities, but their desert ordeal and his death had intervened.

During the summer of 1962, which he spent in Wellfleet on
Cape Cod, Bishop Pike had begun to write, under the working
title "I Believe," a book on doctrine. His intention had been to
consider particular traditional Christian beliefs, as set forth in the
Creeds, in terms of their applications to daily living in the modern
world. He wrote an initial chapter on the nature of belief, but
after fussing with several further chapters on specific doctrines, he
found he could not go on and set the book aside. In the spring of
1963 Bishop Robinson sent him an advance copy of *Honest to
God*. That book had a powerful impact on Bishop Pike.

> I admired his courage; I felt he was getting somehow closer to
> the point. And it gave me the courage to throw away all the
> chapters I had written except the one on belief, and to write
> an entirely different kind of book, which is quite iconoclastic.
>
> In other words, by then I really had moved on further, even
> beyond the place where I was, and I decided not to try to come
> out smelling like a rose on orthodoxy.

"I Believe" was jettisoned, and Bishop Pike proceeded to write a
controversial study of the Creeds which was published, in 1964, as
A Time for Christian Candor.

Honest to God and *A Time for Christian Candor* came to be
lumped together as precursors within the Anglican communion of
a development in theology that some found subversive of funda-
mental Christian doctrine. Reread a decade later, however, neither book would seem to have seriously challenged any of the essential teachings of the Church, and neither Bishop Robinson nor
Bishop Pike would seem to have advanced a theological position
that was new or even novel. Both works had importance because
they raised questions about the efficacy of antique and inaccessible magisterial creedal formulations. *Honest to God* was a
searching approach to that problem limited by its caution. *A
Time for Christian Candor* was bolder in its argument but unfor-

tunately the argument had not been nearly as carefully thought through as it deserved to be.

Bishop Robinson would later feel some regret that his work had been so frequently associated with Bishop Pike's.

Theologically, I've always been twinned with him by *Time* magazine and that sort of thing. I'm not quite sure I'm really happy about that. I don't know whether he was either, for that matter. But this is the way the press deals with people. I find it difficult to assess him theologically. He was essentially a popularizer, and a brilliant one. He was essentially still a legal mind rather than a theologian. He was brilliant, of course, in the sort of "p.r." field. You always felt when he was talking to you that he was giving you a press interview. You felt it was all for the tape. I found this disconcerting. You felt there was this sort of spiel coming out and whoever was there . . . well, it didn't seem to make much difference. To that extent I did feel a certain unease with the fact that he never seemed *really* to listen.

This doesn't mean, of course, that he wasn't always himself . . . absolutely disarming and very charming . . . such a warm person that one wanted to expand with him . . . and one felt entirely at ease with him in *that* way. But having watched him at work . . . the way he sort of switched on a press interview at a moment's notice . . . and the way it didn't make much difference whether he talked to you or to them . . . it just sort of all spilled out . . . *this* was the thing that was so distinctive about him. It was the fact that he was able to communicate to that kind of audience which was his great gift, I think. He was obviously a person who could . . . with a very competent theological training without being in any sense a scholar . . . a person who could get over the language barrier that so often makes communication between theologians and others impossible.

Now I felt that in some ways the title of his book A *Time for Christian Candor* compared with my *Honest to God* perhaps put the finger on something of the difference between us. I think that basically what made Jim tick in all this *was* the need for candor. In other words, for heaven's sake say what you really believe, and if you don't believe it don't say it. It was with the *saying*, I suspect, that he was *really* concerned. It was this . . . and being truthful in the way you were prepared to put across what you believed . . . *that* was for him the nub of the problem.

And so many of the things the Church says in its Creeds and
its sort of official doctrines just don't mean anything . . . so why
not say so?

Now this was, I think, a slightly different exercise than the
one I was concerned about . . . which was not *primarily* a matter of communication. That did come into it because the two
are so interconnected as to be almost inseparable. But I was *more*
concerned not with what you say . . . or the candor with which
you express it . . . but with how you can re-express your beliefs
so that they actually do correspond with what you think. These
are, of course, very closely related exercises. But I do think there
is a difference between candor and honesty. Honesty in a way
cuts a bit deeper. Honesty is prepared always to go to the roots
. . . and that for me is what it means to be a radical. I was
trying to dig pretty deep down . . . to get at the roots of the
problem of beliefs . . . and to re-express what some of the other
formulations had been trying to say. I would *now* agree that the
Creeds and so on don't really say it . . . or say it in ways you
really can't make meaningful . . . or truthful . . . to yourself
much less to other people.

There is a difference of emphasis here. I was more concerned
with digging down than he was. How you communicated this
was obviously one part of the whole thing. Jim's image of "the
package" which comes in in his stuff very often has to do with
that. Let's throw away the packaging, he would say, and get at the
treasure under the earthen vessels. That seemed to me to be
simplistic. The idea was basically that it was the packaging that
was getting in the way. So, if you could give to people what's
inside, shorn of all these other things, then they would take it
. . . or at least it would be more intelligible . . . and they could
eat it . . . or something. Whereas I am not sure the exercise
doesn't need to get a bit deeper than that.

Bishop Robinson's regard for Bishop Pike was rooted deep down
in honest affection. It was the treasure within that Bishop Robinson delighted in, and not that dazzling earthen vessel the world
knew as Bishop Pike, that glitter of packaging which for so long
captivated the press and the demimonde of the media. Once, in
the spring of 1968, the two bishops had been together at Princeton University for "one of those star-studded conferences that
drone on for days and accomplish nothing whatsoever." One afternoon, weary of it all, the two old friends stumbled out of the

Princeton Inn into a breathtaking display of flowering cherry and dogwood. An especially lovely pink cherry at the peak of its bloom enchanted Bishop Robinson.

> I said to Jim, "Isn't that a gorgeous sight?"
> And he said, "What's that?"
> You know, he really didn't know what I was looking at.

Make Way for Dorothy Day

"Where am I?"

It was past midnight on a rain-drenched night early in November of 1968 in the deserted lobby of Friendship International Airport. Bishop Pike was told that he was in Baltimore. "H. L. Mencken liked Baltimore," he said as he darted off toward a newsstand, "so I guess it can't be all bad." He gathered up indiscriminately, it seemed, half a dozen newspapers and as many magazines, including *Playboy*, the centerfold of which he ceremoniously displayed to a friend and then to a blind man waiting behind the cash register for some payment. Pinned to the lapel of the bishop's clericals was a large button urging DEFROCK CARDINAL SPELLMAN. When this was commented upon he turned the lapel inside out, disclosing other buttons with messages then in vogue among counterculturists and the proponents of one liberation or another.

Bishop Pike had come to Baltimore because he had been asked to attend the trial of the Catonsville Nine. He had little idea what the trial was all about, and only the sketchiest notion who the defendants were. He made inquiries as a taxi navigated through the downpour from the airport to a downtown hotel near the courthouse. "Aren't two of these people priests?" he demanded. "We don't put priests in jail in America." He was reminded that the defendants had burned draft records as a protest against the war in Vietnam. "I don't think I approve of that," he said. "It's illegal." He asked a number of questions about the specific charges. His training as a lawyer led him to weigh—one against the other—several possible defenses. Told that the case was being handled by William Kunstler he decided he would try

to have lunch with him the next day. Kunstler was a brilliant attorney but he might not have thought of everything. "We'll get
them off. There's no doubt of that. *Imagine* bringing criminal
charges against priests!" Bishop Pike was silent, unusual for him,
until the taxi reached the hotel.

The taxi drove away into the rain. Huddled into the hotel entrance the bishop seemed suddenly spent, the animation of the
airport having dissipated. "I'm not sure what to make of all this,"
he said. "But I *am* sure of one thing. There are priests in trouble
with the law. They've asked for my help. What kind of a bishop
would I be if I didn't do what I could to help them?" That lapel
button seemed somehow drained of its frivolity. It took on a pastoral import. Would it be possible to come by early in the morning to wake him? "I am *incredibly* tired!" It might be a good idea
to find out where the trial would take place. He had known a lawyer once who lost a case because he could not find the court-
house.

Six hours later it was 8 A.M. "Hi!" The raspy tremolo was un-
mistakable. "Come on up. I'll send for coffee." Bishop Pike was
naked as the day he had been yanked from his mother's womb.
His episcopal garments were strewn all about the room. On the
floor by the bed there was a litter of newspapers, and on top of
them *Playboy* magazine, the centerfold extended crazily. On a
bed table opened with both covers face up lay S. G. F. Brandon's
Jesus and the Zealots. A bellboy arrived, did a double take, and
turning his back inched a tray of coffee onto the dresser. Bishop
Pike insisted on a tip. His back still turned the bellboy extended a
palm backward, received the tip, and fled. "What in the world is
the matter with that young man?" the bishop demanded. "Well,
Jim, you don't have any clothes on." There was a pause. "Aha! I
see. He's never seen a naked bishop before."

He remained naked. For the next hour he dashed about the
room, pouring coffee, brushing his teeth, shaving, combing his
hair, and talking incessantly in his rapid, staccato way about Jesus
and the zealotic thesis of S. G. F. Brandon. It was an astonishing,
brilliant performance, laced with witty asides and giddy excur-
sions into obscure scholarly disputations and personal remarks
about the disputants. His toilet accomplished he swooped down
upon yesterday's shirt, sniffed vigorously at both armpits, discarded it in favor of a fresh one, and proceeded to get dressed. His

lecture continued without abatement until at about 10 A.M. the two men pressed breathlessly through a mob outside the court-house and made their way to the trial.

"No more room in there." The marshal was adamant. So was the bishop. "I am of counsel in this matter. You can't deprive these people of counsel. And this is my chaplain. I can't function without my chaplain." The two men were admitted to Judge Thomsen's court. Bishop Pike's entrance into the packed court-room generated a commotion to which he appeared oblivious. He made straight for the defense table, greeted William Kunstler and his associates, and launched into a discussion of "strategy." The nine defendants filed in and took seats side by side on a long bench.

Bishop Pike wanted to greet each defendant. He moved down the line, shaking hands, telling jokes, asking questions. Judge Thomsen took his place on the bench. William Kunstler requested the courtesies of the court for the bishop, whose creden-tials in the law he recited. The judge said "Dr. Pike" would be welcome to sit with counsel for the defense. He did sit with them throughout the day. He listened intently and made notes on a yel-low legal pad. Now and then he would mutter suggestions to William Kunstler. A film was shown which had been taken at the scene of the crime. He watched the two Berrigans and their friends burn draft records in a metal basket. He watched solemnly as they gathered around the conflagration and with hands joined uttered the Lord's Prayer. He watched them as they were led away and loaded into a van. Bishop Pike began to comprehend what this case was all about.

During the lunch recess the bishop emerged from the court-house to great applause from a large crowd of young supporters of the Nine. Reporters and TV cameras closed in upon him. He was in his element. To his "chaplain" he said, "Oh yes! Oh yes! This is where it's at! This is where the action is!" To the delight of the crowd he raced across the street to parry with a small group of pro-war demonstrators confined there by the police. "What are you doing here?" one of them asked. "I'm here because I'm against that dirty, stinking war," he replied. Spotting some flowers growing near a fountain he picked a bunch and presented each demonstrator with one flower. The pro-war people were visibly disarmed.

William Kunstler and Bishop Pike were joined for lunch in a
crowded, noisy hotel dining room by other defense counsel, theologian Harvey Cox, the bishop's "chaplain," and several hang-
ers-on who happened by. Kunstler explained that the defense
"strategy" would be to offer no defense. The "crimes" would be
conceded. Every opportunity the court permitted would be taken
to bring an indictment against the war itself. The jury would be
asked, in effect, to ignore Judge Thomsen's certain charge that the
"higher motives" of the defendants had no standing. The defense
would attempt to appeal to each juror to be bound solely by his
own unfettered conscience. It was a novel defense and would earn
for William Kunstler a singular place in the history of American
criminal law procedure.

Bishop Pike was bemused. "You can't do that. Everything I
know about the law tells me that won't work." He noted that
Jesus hadn't offered any defense either. He reminded Kunstler
how that case had turned out. "But that's the point, isn't it? The
lawyer in me says you can't do it, but the bishop in me says you
must do it." On the way back to the courthouse Bishop Pike
would say to his "chaplain," "They've asked me to speak at some
kind of a rally tonight. I didn't know what in the world I could
say. But, you know, I think I'm getting my head together about
that." He stopped to drop some coins into a beggar's cup. "My
God!" he said. "Those crazy people are trying to act like Christians!" He dashed two steps at a time up the courthouse stairs.

That night hundreds of people, most of them young, some
nuns, a few clergy, gathered in a Catholic church about a mile
from the courthouse for what was intended to be a combination
of vigil and rally in support of the Catonsville Nine. Bishop Pike
arrived early for the potluck supper. "No sense eating in the hotel.
The kids will have better food." He commented on the number of
nuns and the paucity of priests in the crowd. "Find me at least
one Episcopal priest, if you can," he said. It wasn't easy. But one
was finally found. "Bishop Pike, meet Tom Pike, an Episcopal
priest." The bishop's countenance lit up. "Not only a priest, but a
Pike!" he said. "I knew everything would turn out right." He was
eating macaroni and cheese off a paper plate using a raw carrot as
a fork.

He had found a new button for his lapel. SUPPORT THE
NINE, it read. Somebody handed him an arm band. It read,

SUPPORT THE MILWAUKEE FOURTEEN. He put it on. "Who the hell are the Milwaukee Fourteen?" he asked. But there was no time to explain. Suddenly, he was off for the platform where he was at once the center of attention. He listened attentively as somebody reported to the crowd what had transpired in the court that day. Twice he interrupted to correct the speaker. Then, without waiting for an introduction he took the microphone and began to speak. It was one of his more colorful extemporaneous utterances.

> I supported that damned war in the beginning because I believed the lies we were told about it . . . but *I* was wrong and *you* were right! . . . I opposed burning draft cards when that started to happen because I thought it was childish . . . but *I* was wrong and *you* were right! . . . I declined to support Benjamin Spock and Bill Coffin and the others when they were on trial for conspiracy to incite draft refusal because I thought they were being irresponsible . . . but *I* was wrong and *they* were right! . . . and I came to Baltimore last night certain in my own mind that the Catonsville Nine should not have burned draft records because it was illegal . . . but *I* was wrong and *they* were right! . . . and I am here tonight . . . and proud of it . . . because *I* was wrong and *they* were right! . . . and because . . . mark my words . . . because *you* are right!

Bishop Pike was drowned out and forced to pause as the hall filled with the mighty roar of a standing ovation and the crowd threw up at him a sea of peace signs. But he had only just begun. He returned the peace sign and would do so again and again as he went on. Artfully, he drew up his own indictment on charges of incitement to draft resistance and refusal. ("I don't trust the Justice Department to do it. I can do it better myself.") He flailed the clergy and especially the bishops for their silence on the war. "I say to my good friend Patrick O'Boyle . . . the Cardinal Archbishop of Washington . . . tell me, sir, where you stand on that war . . . where you stand on the trial of these priests . . . or don't you dare tell me . . . don't you dare *try* to tell me . . . what kind of a pill I can give to my wife!" His arms thrown up in a characteristic arch above his head he thundered into peroration.

> I urge . . . I direct . . . I *abjure* . . . every young man in America of draft age . . . who cannot in conscience support that

abominable war in Vietnam . . . to refuse the draft . . . to refuse
to serve in the military forces!

There was pandemonium as Bishop Pike sat down. He resorted
to one of his favorite platform devices. Several times he darted
back to the microphone, slapping it vigorously with his hands to
quiet the crowd, and added, by way of encores, a few choice
phrases or a joke. Two young men appeared on the stage with
their draft cards held aloft. Bishop Pike supplied the light and the
cards went up in smoke. "Where's the FBI?" the bishop wondered. The FBI did not choose to notice.

Suddenly, Bishop Pike spotted in the audience Dorothy Day,
the venerable matriarch of the Catholic Worker movement.
"Let's hear from Dorothy Day," he shouted. But Miss Day would
not be moved from her seat. The bishop raced from the platform
and made his way through the crowd to greet her. She rose as
though the Pope had appeared. Leading her by the hand Bishop
Pike insisted that she come to the platform. "Make way for Dorothy Day! Make way for Dorothy Day!" As she moved slowly across
the stage the crowd hushed. Dorothy Day could do that to a
crowd. She consented to speak a few words. Movingly, she recalled
Roger LaPorte, a young Catholic Worker who had burned himself
to death in front of the United Nations building in New York City
in one of the earliest protests against the war. Miss Day seemed to
want to remind that young throng of the terrible seriousness of
the enterprise upon which they were so enthusiastically engaged.

"Did you notice how the young people greeted one another last
night?" the bishop wondered. He was stepping into a bus the next
afternoon that would take him to the airport. "Peace." And he was
gone.

This Woman Must Be a Sabra

"Help me," I called desperately. "Shalom!"
A cry came back. "Shalom!"

It was 4 A.M. Ten hours had passed since Diane left Jim Pike
on a rock in Wadi Mashash. She had walked and climbed, up

cliffs and down cliffs, stumbling and falling, and finally rolling, through terrain so rugged and so parched and so desolate, it resembled the surface of the moon by which it was illumined. She had had no water save her own urine. Her body was bruised and battered and horribly cut. Her sense of time and of place was shattered. She was in utter exhaustion. Nobody should have been able to do what she had done.*

She had rolled at last to rest beside a roadbed under construction next to the Dead Sea. She could move herself no farther. She cried out one final, desperate call for help. By the wildest chance it was heard. Her odyssey had come to its end not fifty feet from an Arab work camp. It housed a small crew who were building the road. The foreman of the camp, Wasffy Dahu, according to testimony given later that week to Jericho police, was informed that a "foreign lady" near the camp was calling for help.

> I told them "don't go to her" as we have our orders concerning such matters, and fear patrols. One of them came back and said, "She came to the camp." I asked, "Who brought her?" They said, "Esmail Baraka."

Moussa Kuskeibat also gave his account to the Jericho police.

> I was sleeping in my tent and I heard a scream in English, "Help me." Me and my friend Esmail Baraka went to the foreign lady. She stood up, but fell down. Esmail held her, and I helped him. We carried her to the tent. She sat on the ground, and we gave her a little water to drink. A moment later we called the foreman, and he came and took her to his tent. We gave her first aid. She asked for tea with lemon. We gave it to her, and afterwards I went back to my tent as the foreman was taking care of her. I testify that I saw the lady injured on her arms and legs, and I saw her clothing torn on the shoulder and from behind.
>
> She was exhausted, and signs of fear and terror were on her face. I asked her in English where she came from, and she said, "Qumrân, and my husband was with me." I asked her about her husband, and she said he could not walk and stayed near a big boulder to rest. I asked her where it was—to give him some help. But she said it was very distant.
>
> This is the end of my testimony.

* For a detailed, harrowing, definitive account of Diane Kennedy Pike's incredible ordeal during that awful night see her book *Search*, pp. 33–54.

Ha'ader Moussa remembered asking the foreign lady what had happened.

> She said the car was broken, and they left it and walked to a great distance from the car. Her husband could not walk anymore, and he fell asleep. He put his hand under his head, as he was an old man. He was also very thirsty.
>
> I asked her about her husband, and she said she left him at a distant point and came to look for help. She asked us if we had a phone to call the police. But I told her we did not have a phone. She stayed with us until a car arrived. We went in this car to Mas'ulia where we left her and went to work.
>
> I testify that the American woman was exhausted, very tired and thirsty and injured in her arms and legs. Her clothes were torn from the backside. We asked her how old she was, and she said she was thirty-two. She said she came from the United States to rest and relax, and she also said she was writing books.

Not only was there no phone in the camp, there was no radio and no vehicle of any kind, not so much as an animal that might be ridden. Diane had no choice but to wait until 6 A.M. when other workmen would arrive. At 5:45 A.M., a few minutes early, a truck appeared and in that she was driven to Mas'ulia, which proved to be another, larger construction camp. She got there at about 6:15 A.M. There was no telephone. Nothing could be done until the foreman arrived. He turned up at 6:45 A.M. She would be driven to Nahal Kalia, an Israeli army kibbutz where definitely there would be a radiotelephone. Nahal Kalia was an hour's drive north along the western shore of the Dead Sea. It was close by the seductively elusive Qumrân.

Diane stepped from the truck at the gate to Nahal Kalia a little before 8 A.M. An Israeli officer drove up. She told her terrible tale to him and then to other officers. A helicopter would be dispatched. By then she was so exhausted she could no longer stand. The officers arranged for a cot in an air-conditioned room. It was 8:30 A.M. Diane lay on the cot listening intently to the buzz of activity outside her room. She was confident that any minute she would hear Jim's voice. About 9 A.M. she was brought a light breakfast and a medic came to treat her wounds.

At 10:15 A.M. she was summoned to the radiotelephone. The helicopter crew had found nothing. They asked her to repeat her description of the spot where the Ford Cortina had been abandoned and the spot where she had left her husband. She insisted that if she could only be with them she could show them where he was. It was decided that she would be driven to Bethlehem, out of which a search was being organized. At 10:30 A.M. she was driven from Nahal Kalia in a jeep. She could think of nothing but Jim still somewhere out in that desert and once again under that parching, searing, pitiless sun.

The official log of the Bethlehem police had begun to reflect the drama which would preoccupy most of its constabulary and its commander, Major Enosh Givati, for the balance of that week.

> On Tuesday 9–2–69 10:30 A.M. we received a phone call from the army that an American tourist had arrived at Nahal Kalia and said that she and her husband had been in the Judea desert, their car was stuck and they continued on foot—to a place where her husband stayed and she continued.
>
> At 11:30 A.M. she arrived and identified herself as Mrs. Diane Pike and said that on Monday 9–1–69 1:30 P.M. she left Herod's mountain in a rented car together with her husband. She had a road map and they wanted to go to Kumeran. She said that they lost their way and took the wrong way—a southern road—instead of a northern one—which leads to the center of the Judea desert and crosses the new road Ein Fashka—Ein Gedi.
>
> Around 4 P.M. when they were about four miles west of the Dead Sea the car sank in the little stones of a dry riverbed. They left the car—and thought it was easier to go to the Dead Sea than to go back twenty-four miles. They started walking and after ninety minutes (1.5 miles) Dr. James said he was tired and wanted to sleep. It was about 6 P.M. They found an area in the riverbed where they rested fifteen minutes until Mrs. Pike suggested that she should try to go to find help—as she thought she was not far from Kalia. She left her husband resting and walked in the *wadi* all night—until 4 A.M. on 9–2–69 she arrived at a workers' camp on the road Ein Fashka—Ein Gedi—located twenty-five miles north of Ein Gedi. At the camp she was given first aid—as she was injured all over. For lack of vehicle or communication she waits till 6 A.M. when a vehicle arrived and took her to Kalia and on to Bethlehem.
>
> Upon receiving the message forces of the police and border police were prepared and later went out with her to the area where the car was found locked. Also, some Bedouins were seen there—

the same people who, a day earlier, had helped the couple to push the car and move it from another, nearby spot. They were asked if they saw the man once more the same day—but they didn't. Also—they were asked to join the search, which they did.

Diane reached Bethlehem police headquarters about 11:30 A.M. The army helicopter was waiting for her at army headquarters, she was told. She was quickly driven there but the helicopter was gone. There is a mystery about what became of it. No records can be found as to its further activities. It is probable that a decision had been taken to withdraw it from the search in favor of a ground search by jeep and on foot. Diane returned to police headquarters.

She was kept waiting for some time in the office of Sergeant Major Shaul. There was a great bustle of activity all about her, but she could not understand what was happening because most of the conversation was in Hebrew or in Arabic. She got the impression people were saying Jim was probably dead.

> I began to moan and cry, quietly. Immediately the men asked what was wrong. I said, "My husband will be dead. He will be dead."
>
> "No," they explained, "not necessarily. If he has found a humid cave, he will be all right. Men have been known to survive for as long as seven days without any water or food when they are in a humid cave."
>
> "Are you certain?" I pressed. They nodded assurance. Those words were to be repeated to me over and over in the course of the week. I took solace in them, even when the possibility seemed remote.

About 12:45 P.M. Diane set forth again, this time in a convoy of two trucks and two jeeps. She sat in the front seat of the lead jeep. Remembering Jim's injunction to bring plenty of water she inquired about that, and was assured there was lots of water in the trucks. She directed the party out into the desert on the route she and Jim had followed almost exactly twenty-four hours earlier. The men were amazed at her memory for the route. Frequently she would warn them of some especially difficult hazard in the roadway. They were even more amazed that she could have driven a Ford Cortina through such obstacles.

They found the Ford Cortina just as it had been when she and Jim left it. It was by then about 2 P.M. She slipped the keys out of her bra. They had rusted as though left for days in the rain. A soldier took them and got in the car on the driver's side. He started the motor without trouble. Other men pushed and the car was readily freed.

Henry Albala of Jerusalem would give testimony about the car later in the week to Sergeant Ben-Haim of the Bethlehem police.

> I work at the Jerusalem branch of Avis whose Lod branch checked out a car to the tourist James Pike on 8–29–69. Last Thursday I got a message from Bethlehem police (Mr. Almar) that this car was found in the desert. On Friday 9–5–69 I went to the place where the car was found and together with the border police I used a truck to tow it out from the *wadi*, then started it myself and drove to Jerusalem with no mechanical problem. The car was a little damaged on the bottom probably from rocks.

The soldiers and police who were with Diane when the car was found were incredulous that it could be in good working condition. One officer said, "This woman must be a Sabra; only a Sabra can drive over these roads." Diane had been paid a compliment. A sabra is the edible prickly fruit of certain cacti found on the coastal plains of Israel. But in the lexicon of modern Israel, a Sabra is a native-born Israeli.

Our Freedom as a Glorious Winding-sheet

Jerusalem had been "done." Mrs. Chambers had tottered to the Mount of Olives and through the Garden of Gethsemane. She had visited two tombs which competed for the honor of having housed, temporarily, Jesus. She had been to the stone pavilion—with its own eternal flame—erected by the Jews of America in memory of John Fitzgerald Kennedy, and to a handsome medical center high in the hills outside the city where she marveled at a room vibrant with glorious color from stained glass windows by Marc Chagall. At sundown on the Friday she had shared with Orthodox and Hasidic Jews the woe and the joy of the Wailing Wall, and had she been a Jew and not a Christian she might have wailed and even danced a bit herself. Her son the bishop had specified a tarry in the austere precincts of a museum built specially for display of the impressive fragility of the Dead Sea Scrolls. She had gone shopping—a "free afternoon" had been decreed—among the enchanted bazaars of the exotically aged Old City.

One day she had been conveyed to Bethlehem. In the Basilica of the Nativity she had dragged herself down through the bowels of crypts into a dank grotto where it was alleged the manger of Jesus once lay. Jesus certainly did not wet his first diaper there. Layer upon layer of holy edifice had nevertheless been constructed over it. Buried under all that historical junk the sacred grotto was fetid with the stench of suffocation. Herod's massacre of the infants had by the attenuation through centuries of grotesque reverence at last achieved its intended victim. Jesus had been expunged. He was not there and he never had been. Mrs. Chambers had nearly been expunged herself. She was too weary to accompany Diane across the plaza from the basilica to Bethlehem police headquarters to greet Major Givati and his constables.

Now Mrs. Chambers was back in the bus. She had been more or less lifted in and sat slumped as usual just inside the front door next to her sister Ethyl, who rhymed with *lethal* but shouldn't have because she *wasn't* lethal. Both women were exhausted, and Mrs. Chambers was wretched from lung congestion that would worsen and almost take her life some weeks later when she was back home in California. The bus was bound for Qumrân on the Dead Sea. It would not follow the route Jim and Diane had chosen four months earlier. But it *would* turn off on that route in order to give Mrs. Chambers a "feel" for the desert. It went only a short way and in trying to turn around got stuck. Fortunately, there were enough hands to push it free. Mrs. Chambers seemed relieved when the bus resumed a conventional road and made its way down, down 1,300 feet below sea level to the Dead Sea and Qumrân.

By nightfall Mrs. Chambers found herself in Beersheba, an oasis far to the south of Qumrân and in a desert that had sand in it and seemed more like a desert and less like a wilderness. The night would be spent in a new motel that seemed entirely out of place and forlorn. It was Diane's birthday and there would be an unbearably painful celebration. Diane would sleep that night in the same room she had shared with Jim on an earlier trip to Israel. Tomorrow they would go to Masada. Masada had a very special meaning and intoxication for Jim Pike. He had wanted his mother to see it and to share his joy and jubilance about it. But Mrs. Chambers was too weak and too sick to go. Ethyl would go and tell her all about it later.

Masada is an enormous freestanding rock at the eastern edge of the Judean desert with sheer drops on all its sides tumbling more than 1,300 feet onto the western shores of the Dead Sea. The summit—a barren rhomboid plateau, prowed at the north and somewhat at the south—measures 1,900 feet north to south and 650 feet east to west across its middle. By a quirk of geography the summit is barely above mean sea level despite its spectacular survey of the Dead Sea 1,300 feet beneath it. To the west of it the vast tangled mass of the cliffs and canyons of the Judean desert stretches interminably. Beyond the Dead Sea to the east loom up the forbidding mountains of Moab and to the south on desiccated salt plains the sites of Sodom and Gomorrah, wasted and parched, debauch and shrivel in arid sunlight. Somewhere down there are presumably the remnants of that pillar of salt which was once Lot's wife.

How is it that utter desolation can be so improbably exhilarating? What is the fascination of Masada? Why had Bishop Pike climbed so many times to its summit and been on each occasion so deeply, enthusiastically transported? What moved his Aunt Ethyl to tears when at last she stood in her high-heeled shoes where he had stood and saw with her own eyes the wonder he had so often described for her? Later she would try to explain the matter to her sister, but she would not be able to find the words. She would be reduced to exclamations of awe. The experience of Masada is in part mystical and ineffable. Photographs of the place suggest extraordinary topographies, but they do not capture what Masada is all about.

Herod the Great had been fascinated with Masada. Fearful that Cleopatra might one day carry out her threat to drive him from the Kingdom of Judea, he took the precaution to have built as a refuge not one but two palaces on the summit of the rock. Cleopatra, preoccupied perhaps with Antony, never did turn up and Herod never used either palace. Two palaces were built, one for use in summer and one for use in winter, primarily to get maximum advantage from what few, insipid breezes might chance to wander by depending on the season. Rainfall was seldom but torrential when it came. Mammoth cisterns were dug out of the rock to save the water and an aqueduct was built leading down from the cliffs in the Judean desert into a cistern system dug into the rock halfway up its face. Donkeys and slaves would have carried that water up to the palaces along a narrow winding path.

Flavius Josephus, a turncoat Jew and Roman historian, writing in the latter part of the first century after Christ, described the larger palace-villa Herod had built to the north and west of the precipice with three tiers of terrace tumbled over the side.

> He built a palace, too, on the western slope, below the fortifications on the crest and inclining in a northerly direction. The palace wall was of great height and strongly built, with ninety-foot towers at the four corners. The design of the apartments within, the colonnades, and bathrooms, was varied and magnificent, the supporting pillars cut from a single block in every case, the partition walls and floors of the rooms paved with stones of many hues. At every spot where people lived, whether on the plateau, round the palace, or before the wall, he had cut out in the rock numbers of great tanks to hold water, ensuring a supply as great as where spring water can be used. A sunken road led from the palace to the hilltop, invisible from outside.

Herod never used his Masada palaces, which were built toward the end of the first century B.C., but later, in A.D. 70–73, already falling into desuetude, they would find a use foreign to Herod's intentions. Josephus is the only source of information about this astonishing episode in Jewish history. After the destruction under Titus of the Temple of Jerusalem in A.D. 70 and the crushing of the great Jewish revolt against Roman rule, a remnant of some 960 Zealotic Jews—men, women, and children—fled to Masada and took up refuge in and around the Herodian palaces. Roman legions led by Flavius Silva pursued them there and set siege to the rock.

The Zealots readily repulsed attempts to ascend by way of the "snake path." Stymied, the Romans threw up a circumvallation which completely enclosed Masada and strung out along it pitched a series of encampments. Silva was to sustain urgent siege of the fanatic rebels for three years with an army that numbered at times as many as fifteen thousand men. Eleazar, the leader of the Jews, had brought with him ample food supplies, and he found in the palace storerooms more food, including edible corn that had been in storage since Herod's reign nearly a century earlier. The giant cisterns held plenty of water. Weapons for defense consisted of crude missiles and rocks and these were sufficient to inhibit the Roman legions from ascent.

Silva determined upon a laborious strategy. Stones and earth would be heaped up on the western side of the rock where the aqueduct intersected until it reached a height from which his primitive artillery would be operable. This took a long time. But finally in A.D. 73 he was in position to wreak devastation upon the beleaguered Zealot garrison. Eleazar gathered his people and delivered to them one of the great orations of human history. It was reproduced in full by Josephus in his *The Jewish War*. Where he got the text is a mystery perhaps best left unexamined. The substance of it was that the Zealots would not submit to the humiliations and tortures certain to be visited upon them by the Romans if they surrendered. They would and did slaughter themselves—first the women and children and then by lot the men until the last man fell upon his own sword.

From 1963 to 1965 the Israelis, under the direction of Yigael Yadin, the brilliant archaeologist, undertook to excavate on the summit of Masada the ruins of the Herodian palaces and their ancillary structures, and what remained of the much more primitive Zealotic habitations. The Masada excavations stand among the great achievements of twentieth-century archaeology. Professor Yadin has made of these findings a handsomely illustrated and exciting book. It is called *Masada*.* He and his associates found, as Josephus had reported, that at the end of the siege the Zealots had incinerated nearly every building on the summit so that little survived but what was stone or metal or bone. Bones of men, women, and children were found, all in one place, thrown there, probably, by the incredulous Roman conquerors. Silva had at last taken Masada but the defenders were beyond his grasp.

* Yigael Yadin, *Masada*. London: Weidenfeld & Nicolson, 1966.

Yigael Yadin recalled the most startling discovery turned up by the excavators of Masada.

If, however, I were pressed to single out one discovery more spectacular than any other, I would point to a find which may not be of the greatest importance from the point of view of pure archaeology, but which certainly, when we came upon it, electrified everyone in Masada who was engaged in the dig, professional archaeologist and lay volunteer alike. This find was in one of the most strategic spots on Masada, close to the "water path" and near the square between the storehouses and the administration building where all the northern tracks on the summit meet. The debris on this site was being cleared by a group of volunteers—one of whom, incidentally, is an elephant-tamer in civilian life—when they came across eleven small, strange ostraca, different from any other which have come to light in Masada. Upon each was inscribed a single name, each different from its fellow, though all appeared to be written by the same hand. The names themselves were also odd, rather like nicknames, as for example "Man from the valley" or *Yoav* ("Joab"). ("Joab" may seem perfectly ordinary, but it was extremely rare during the period of the Second Temple, and it was almost certainly applied to a man who was particularly brave.)

As we examined these ostraca, we were struck by the extraordinary thought: "Could it be that we had discovered evidence associated with the death of the very last group of Masada's defenders?" Josephus writes:

They then chose ten men by lot out of them, to slay all the rest; everyone of whom laid himself down by his wife and children on the ground, and threw his arms about them and they offered their necks to the stroke of those who by lot executed that melancholy office; and when these ten had, without fear, slain them all, they made the same rule for casting lots for themselves, that he whose lot it was to first kill the other nine, and after all, should kill himself.

Had we indeed found the very ostraca which had been used in the casting of the lots? We shall never know for certain. But the probability is strengthened by the fact that among these eleven inscribed pieces of pottery was one bearing the name "Ben Ya'ir." The inscription of plain "Ben Ya'ir" on Masada at that particular time could have referred to no other than Eleazar ben Ya'ir. And

it also seems possible that this final group were his ten commanders who had been left to the last, after the decision had been
wholly carried out, and who had then cast lots amongst themselves.

A concluding word about Ben Ya'ir and about a frequent sight
in various parts of Masada throughout our excavations—the remains of the dreadful fires, the fires that accompanied the heroes
of Masada in their death.

It is thanks to Ben Ya'ir and his comrades, to their heroic
stand, to their choice of death over slavery, and to the burning of
their humble chattels as a final act of defiance to the enemy, that
they elevated Masada to an undying symbol of desperate courage,
a symbol which has stirred hearts throughout the last nineteen
centuries. It is this which has moved scholars and laymen to make
the ascent to Masada.

Not long after Yadin had completed his excavations toward the
end of 1965 Bishop Pike interrupted his sabbatical in Cambridge
in order to spend the Christmas holidays in Israel with his son,
Jim Jr. On the advice of scholars in Jerusalem they decided to
spend a day at Masada ("each of us felt that it was the most impressive twenty-four hours ever experienced") and they became
among the very first "civilians" to make the ascent following the
excavations. It was the first of Bishop Pike's many visits to the
rock.

> Standing at the top of the plateau and looking out over the vast,
> barren desert, I somehow felt caught up in the courage which
> must have enabled those 960 to stand till the very end against
> 10,000 Roman soldiers. So much so that I felt I too could almost
> believe—as they did to the end (as a recently discovered frag-
> mentary farewell note shows)—that God *would* break into his-
> tory, through the Son of Man and his angels, to bring victory to
> his people Israel if I would wait there long enough. I felt trans-
> ported into a plane of hope where time is no longer significant
> and courage is the motivating force. It was a kind of psychedelic
> experience without drugs.
>
> Jim felt that special spirit too, and as we followed the Snake
> Path (as Flavius Josephus called it) to the Dead Sea below we
> both sensed that a new dimension had been added to our already
> deep relationship—one which tied us to a heritage of courage
> and hope.

Six weeks later Jim Jr. would lie dead, shot through the head, in a nondescript hotel room in New York City. Four years later Bishop Pike would lie dead on a rocky spur in Wadi Mashash. His body would bloat and blacken and feed maggots some five days in the intense heat. He would die and his body would rot close by the western shore of the Dead Sea near the twin fascinations of his latter days—Qumrân to the north and Masada to the south. The cliffs surrounding Wadi Mashash are within sight of the summit of Masada.

Eleazar ben Ya'ir, as recorded by Josephus, having exhorted his loyal followers to remember that "long ago we resolved to serve neither the Romans nor anyone else but only God," proceeded to utter an anathema which frustrated the Romans, served God, and inspired Bishop Pike.

> For [our] wrongs let us pay the penalty not to our bitterest enemies, the Romans, but to God—by our own hands. It will be easier to bear. Let our wives die unabused, our children without knowledge of slavery: after that, let us do each other an ungrudging kindness, preserving our freedom as a glorious winding-sheet.

An Adult, White Female, 5′3″ in Length

SANTA BARBARA, Calif., June 15—The police said in an autopsy report today that Miss Maren Bergrud, 43 years old, operator of a literary agency here and employee of the Right Rev. James A. Pike, Auxiliary Bishop of California, died of acute barbiturate poisoning yesterday.

Miss Bergrud died at Cottage Hospital an hour after telephoning Bishop Pike, who lives in the same apartment building, that she had swallowed a large number of sleeping pills.

Bishop Pike, who resigned as Episcopal Bishop of California last summer to become a staff consultant with the Center for the Study of Democratic Institutions here, went to her apartment and called an ambulance.

An empty pill bottle was found beside the bed of Miss Bergrud, who was a divorcee. A note addressed to her three grandchildren in San Rafael, Calif., was found in the apartment. The police said that a portion of the note appeared to be missing.

The police said she had established the New Focus Lecture and Literary Agency and was employed in a literary capacity for Bishop Pike since last July.

Dr. Stanley Ostern, Miss Bergrud's physician, reported he had treated her for about a year and that she had been despondent about her health, the police said.

Maren Bergrud had no grandchildren. She had no children. Her note—the part that wasn't missing—was addressed to three *step*children by way of an unhappy marriage from which she was divorced. Bergrud was her maiden name. Bishop Pike did not call an ambulance. He called Dr. Ostern and it was Dr. Ostern who called an ambulance. Otherwise the New York *Times* of June 16, 1967, was fairly accurate about the events, but as its story implies there was more to Maren's death than appeared in the newspapers.

Bishop Pike met Maren Bergrud in the summer of 1964, the summer he had gone dry. She came to his office one day on an errand for a parish in Marin County. He found her attractive. His marriage with Esther Pike was falling apart. He had anyhow a wandering eye and not infrequently wandered with it. Unfortunately for this situation Bishop Pike was scheduled to spend much of that summer in New York City as preacher at Trinity Church, Wall Street. He would need to defer any attentions to Maren until fall. During the summer he received one letter from her which he interpreted as a "come-on." It was not unusual for Bishop Pike to receive such letters but not all of them came from women he considered attractive.

People who knew Maren during her time with Bishop Pike have different recollections of her physical attributes. During that same time she was to suffer serious illness and major surgery. Even so it is hard to believe she can have been "rather tall" *and* "very short," "plump" *and* "scrawny," "flat-chested" *and* "busty," "blond" *and* "chestnut-headed" *and* "frowzy-haired." By the time she reached the coroner she was, of course, dead. Taking that into account and allowing for the odd perspective a coroner brings to observations, Maren's coroner found before him the body of a woman normally developed, rather slender, short, small-breasted, and with straight, yellowish hair. The hair, he callously added, was darker at the roots. It does not matter how she looked to others or to her coroner. Bishop Pike found what he saw attractive and he also found Maren to be intelligent and intellectually alert.

During the fall of 1964 Bishop Pike and Maren spent occasional evenings together. He found comforts in those evenings which he felt were no longer available to him at home. During the Christmas holidays of that year the marital crisis of Jim and Esther Pike deepened. She threatened to move out of the house and to take the children with her. It was decided on the advice of

Phil Adams, a family friend, that instead he would move out. Bishop Pike moved in with Phil Adams early in January of 1965.

Meanwhile, Maren had come under suspicion of uterine cancer, and also in January she suffered a hysterectomy and the removal of her gall bladder. The cancer was stopped in time. But her recovery would be prolonged. Bishop Pike formed the habit of visiting her daily in the hospital. He also paid the hospital and other medical bills. It turned out that Maren was flat broke. In fact, as time passed he became aware that she had accumulated many debts in Marin County by the device of moving and changing her name frequently. As he learned of these debts he also paid them. It would appear that he generally used his episcopal discretionary funds for that purpose.

In the spring of 1965 Maren was released from the hospital and took an apartment in the Mission District of San Francisco. Bishop Pike paid the rent. He continued his habit of daily visits and did those errands that would be necessary for a convalescent. As she got stronger Maren began to attend to certain of his personal needs. She did his laundry, for example. Sometimes she would cook although this does not seem to have been one of her gifts. In due course Bishop Pike moved out of Phil Adams's house and into Maren's apartment. It only made sense in the circumstances. Maren had by this time begun to interest herself in the bishop's work, and she would assist him with typing and sometimes with research.

To Bishop Pike these arrangements seem to have been primarily a matter of mutual convenience. He later insisted that at no time did he contemplate eventual marriage with Maren and that he had, on the contrary, repeatedly gone out of his way to make it clear to her that regardless of the outcome of his marriage with Esther he had no intentions to marry Maren. She does not seem to have accepted his understanding of the arrangements. Somewhere along the line, in fact, she came to a determination that sooner or later she would be Bishop Pike's third wife.

During the summer of 1965 the bishop decided upon a sabbatical and asked leave of the diocese to spend that fall and winter in Cambridge, England, in pursuance of scholarly reflections and study. He proposed to Esther that she accompany him as a means

perhaps of repairing their marriage. She was not interested. It was
at that point that he decided to ask Jim Jr. to accompany him.
Jim Jr. *was* interested. So was Maren. When she learned of the
plans she announced that she would make a trip to Europe that
fall as well. She would visit relatives in Norway. She would go by
freighter as that would be cheaper. She would stop in England on
her way to Norway to spend a few days with Jim Sr. and Jim Jr.

Maren reached England some weeks after the bishop and his
son had settled into what was to have been a bachelor flat in
Cambridge. She moved in and she stayed. She never did visit her
relatives in Norway. She began to assume a role in relation to the
disturbed younger man. She told the bishop she thought she
could be of help to the boy. Jim Jr. did seem to like Maren.
Bishop Pike persuaded himself that a relationship with an older
woman might be good for Jim Jr. He himself was ambivalent
about having Maren around. It was convenient in that it kept
him from becoming involved with other women. It was awkward
in that he could not decide how to present this woman not his
wife to scholars and clergy and other friends in England.

Maren began to be known as Bishop Pike's secretary. She did
concern herself somewhat with his work but her talents as secretary were scant. She was at least as disorganized as the bishop.
The apartment gradually became a dreadful mess. There was a
housekeeper who tidied up but she was not a secretary. Unat-
tended mail accumulated. Books and periodicals which had served
a fleeting purpose drifted under beds. Everywhere from the bathroom floor to the top of the refrigerator became a scholarly litter.
Maren was often unwell and she consumed assorted medications
that left her dazed and vague much of the time. Her sole and relentless preoccupation was to entrench herself however she could
in the midst of Bishop Pike's varied affairs.

The two Jims went off to Israel for the Christmas holidays and
Maren went with them. She was left behind, however, when the
two men returned to the States early in February. She was still in
Cambridge when Bishop Pike came back after Jim Jr.'s death to
finish out the remainder of his sabbatical. That took about a
month and in the middle of March the bishop and his secretary
made their way by stages back to California. He moved back into
his official residence, Esther having agreed to this on condition

that he occupy a separate bedroom. During the spring of 1966 Bishop Pike made a determined effort to sever his relationship with Maren, aware that it had gotten out of hand, and he saw her on only a few rather brusque occasions.

In the summer of 1966 the bishop announced his resignation as Bishop of California and his decision to accept an invitation from Robert Hutchins to become a resident fellow with the Center for the Study of Democratic Institutions in Santa Barbara. Esther flatly refused to move to Santa Barbara and the couple publicly stated their intention henceforth to maintain what they called "dual residences." Bishop Pike would, in fact, occasionally stay a weekend at the San Francisco residence in order to visit with the children. Esther, however, came to Santa Barbara only twice for family matters and stayed both times in a hotel. In these circumstances the bishop decided to bring his mother to Santa Barbara. Mrs. Chambers would share for a time his Santa Barbara apartment.

Maren reintroduced herself into this situation. Bishop Pike was still a bishop but his resignation as diocesan had divested him of the considerable staff upon which he had been accustomed to rely. He persuaded his personal secretary of many years, Myrtle Goodwin, to move to Santa Barbara and become his secretary at the Center. He felt it would be improper, however, to conduct other business from that office. He would need separate facilities and staff to handle his writing commitments and his outside lecture engagements. He was also worried that a heavy schedule of such lectures in the year ahead would leave Mrs. Chambers too much alone. Maren suggested herself as the solution to these multiple woes.

The New Focus Lecture and Literary Agency was created. This was in part a financial and tax convenience for Bishop Pike but it was primarily a vehicle for Maren Bergrud and her intended activities. Another apartment in the same building where the bishop and his mother lived was rented as combination residence for Maren and office for New Focus. In due course two other women were engaged to assist Maren. They *were* secretaries. It all made a certain sort of sense but it would prove to be a disastrous arrangement.

Mrs. Chambers and Maren Bergrud quickly detested one an-

other. Within a matter of months Mrs. Chambers chose to leave
and moved into a nearby retired teachers' residence. Maren
moved herself into the bishop's apartment. He came back from a
trip one day and there she was in his bed and her clothes in his
closets. By this time the great heresy ruckus had commenced.
Bishop Pike was too busy and too harassed to confront the problem posed by Maren. He was unaware that much of the work he
assumed Maren was doing for him was undone. Later, drawers
full of unanswered mail would be discovered. Their personal relations had also deteriorated into an incessant quarrel about his refusal to divorce Esther and his endlessly reiterated disinclination
to elevate Maren to episcopal matrimony.

Throughout the winter and spring of 1967 Maren grew increasingly distraught. Her consumption of medications—stimulants by
day and sedatives by night—achieved epic proportions. The
bishop does not seem to have paid much attention to this and
may have been unaware of it. The two women in the New Focus
office were quite aware of it. Frequently they would spend the better part of a morning rousing Maren so that she could become
semi-functional for some hours of the day. They attempted several
times to communicate their concern to the bishop and their ap-
prehensions about the virtual collapse of orderly procedure within
the office. He had neither the time nor the emotional stamina to
be responsive. The women gave up.

In May of 1967 Bishop Pike went to Geneva for the *Pacem in
Terris* conference sponsored by the Center. Maren insisted on
going with him. He refused to have her present for the meetings
and she spent that part of the trip somewhere in Spain. On their
way back to California they stopped overnight in Dayton, Ohio.
The bishop prudently arranged separate hotel rooms on different
floors of the hotel. During the night she telephoned his room to
report that her room was on fire. He raced up two flights of stairs
and found that she had dropped a cigarette into her mattress and
the room was indeed on fire. He dragged the mattress into the
bathtub and somehow got the rest of the fire out. She was overcome and sick from smoke. He called a doctor.

Maren professed to be too ill to continue to California the following day, so the bishop left her in the hotel in the care of the
doctor. She took four days to pull herself together and make the
return flight to Santa Barbara. Within a day or two of her return

the bishop's younger son was to graduate from high school and the family, including Esther, would gather in Santa Barbara for appropriate celebration. The bishop directed Maren to remove her personal effects from his apartment. She refused. With the assistance of a maid he did it himself. There ensued a tantrum and Maren's temporary disappearance from the scene. She was not gone long. When she returned she seemed to the women in the office to have reached the edge of breakdown. One day she placed on the office coffee table an enormous bottle of sleeping pills. Efforts to elicit some concern from the bishop were unavailing. He simply could not face the matter. Nor could he prevent Maren from moving her clothes and her personal effects back into his apartment. There was an impasse.

On the evening of June 13, 1967, the bishop entertained at dinner in his apartment a guest of the Center. Maren was present. After dinner he drove the guest to his place of stay in another section of Santa Barbara. Finding that this brought him near the home of a lady friend who was in some domestic difficulties he decided to pay a pastoral call. He was also in no hurry to return to Maren. He got home after midnight to find Maren in a state of rage. She upbraided and she excoriated. She would kill herself, she said. He went to a bedroom to which he had by then managed to consign her and found the large bottle of sleeping pills. He took the pills and announced he would go to sleep in his own bedroom.

About 2 A.M. Maren entered his bedroom and turned on a light. She renewed her denunciations and continued for some time in hysterical diatribe. Bishop Pike could stand it no longer. He got up and fetched the bottle of sleeping pills. "Take your pills and go," he said. She did. About 5 A.M. Maren again entered his bedroom. She said she had taken fifty-five sleeping pills. She was strangely composed. "Use your head," she said, "and get me back to my own apartment before anything happens. And use your head when the police come." The bishop could discern from her demeanor that she was being deadly earnest. He rose and started with her down the hall toward her putative apartment. She collapsed. He dragged her into the apartment. Then he called her physician, Dr. Ostern, informed him of the situation, and asked the doctor to summon an ambulance.

He thereupon began to race frantically back and forth between the two apartments. He brought sheets from his apartment and made up Maren's bed. He lifted her into it. He brought her clothes from his closets and hung them in hers. He brought the bottle from which she had taken the pills and placed it on a table by her bed. He got dressed. In the bedroom she had been using in his apartment he found two notes. One was addressed to him and he placed that among some papers on his desk. The other was addressed to her three stepchildren. He read it. The last lines of it contained references to him. He tore that part of the note off. Later he could not remember what he had done with it. But he put the rest of the note next to the pill bottle in her apartment. All of this he somehow managed to do before the ambulance and then the police arrived.

Attempts to revive Maren with oxygen failed and she was rushed to Cottage Hospital. Dr. Ostern was there and pronounced her dead at 6:17 A.M. An autopsy later in the day confirmed that her death resulted from "acute barbiturate poisoning." Dr. Ostern informed the coroner's office that he had been treating Maren for about a year, that at times she had been despondent, but that when he last saw her about ten days earlier she appeared in good spirits. The coroner identified the type of death as: "Accident, Suicide or Homicide: Over-dose sleeping tablets." He certified the death to have been: "*Suicidal*."

When Sergeant Correa of the Santa Barbara police department arrived at Maren's apartment at 5:45 A.M. he found the ambulance crew had taken charge of the dying woman. He went to Bishop Pike's apartment. The bishop told him he had received a telephone call from Maren at 5:30 A.M. Maren said she had taken fifty-five or sixty-five sleeping pills. The bishop had dressed and gone to her apartment. The door was open. Maren was standing but soon sat down on the bed. She lapsed into unconsciousness. The bishop had noticed the empty pill bottle. Dr. Ostern's name was on the bottle so he had called him. He had slapped Maren's face in an effort to revive her but this had been to no avail. He thought Maren had been despondent on account of her health.

Detective Bowie arrived, representing the coroner's office. The two policemen went to Maren's apartment. They noted that it seemed more like an office than a residence. Her clothes were hanging in the closet, but they were puzzled to find no personal items such as "stockings, panties, undergarments, etc." They thought it odd that there were no blankets on the bed or in the apartment. Next to an empty pill bottle they found a hand-written note. Part of it had been torn off. Search of the apartment did not turn up the missing fragment. No purse could be found. Detective Bowie returned to Bishop Pike's apartment. The bishop had the purse. He explained that he had brought it to his apartment in order to examine it to see if the missing part of the note might be in it. It was not. What survived of the note consisted of a few lines difficult to decipher. The substance was of love for the stepchildren.

The note Maren had written specifically for Bishop Pike was disturbing. He could not bring himself to destroy it. He was fearful it might somehow be inadvertently discovered. So, for many months he carried it on his person at all times. Nearly a year later he decided to share the true story—as he knew it—of Maren's death with Diane. By that time his relationship with Diane had matured and deepened into total trust. (Later, in the last days in Israel, when the bishop confided to Diane the title he had chosen for his autobiography, he also told her he intended to tell the whole story about Maren's death in the autobiography.) When he had finished telling her about the suicide and his part in it the bishop handed Maren's note to Diane and asked her to keep it for him. The note, he remarked, told it pretty much the way it had been.

Jim—The ease (five minutes of psychology?) with which you consented to this makes it obvious that it will be a basic relief to you. Sorry about the extra twinges it will produce—to explain the reasons for my death are tiresome and would be out of your depth anyway. Let's just say that I have finally accepted the fact that you do not love me. For a long time now that's all that has been important to me. Both of our inadequacies (a) I am unlovable and (b) you are unloving. Anyway the one you really want is Esther (the Roman Catholic in you?) and a blood sacrifice will probably effect a reconciliation. Now to business: 1. Use your head about the coroner and the publicity. 2. My last wish is that even though my will which is in my safe deposit box leaves all to you please see that the kids (*mine*) get something. They have loved me unreservedly. I've loved you I guess in a way you haven't wanted or understood. I needed hope. You never offered it— never once offered it.—MAREN.

At 12:10 P.M. on June 14, 1967, the residue of Maren Bergrud lay on a slab in the offices of the coroner of Santa Barbara County.

"This is the embalmed body of a normally developed, rather slender, adult, white female, 5′3″ in length."

Open Letter to Bishop Pike

November 3d 68
there is no reason why Bishop Pike should not conjure out of the rabbit hole of his consciousness (or unconsciousness) the thought-image of Dr. Tillich (how incomplete it may prove,) with whom he has conferred many times during Dr. Tillich's lifetime. I am mildly surprised, though for which reason he did not turn to the spiritual emanations of Dr. Tillich (his books) instead of being lured into the difficulties of spiritualistic jabber. The scene seems a bit like Alice through the looking glass-scene, Bishop Pike assuming the role of the rabbit. Bishop Pike, a very educated man indeed, would have found in those books the clearest expression of Dr. Tillich's not incomplex personality . . . If Bishop Pike's memory of his confrontations with Dr. Tillich were as meager as the interruptions of a poltergeist "Tillich," I would be very sad indeed. I definitely feel, it is not worth the trouble to try to listen to the voice or voices out of the rabbit hole . . .

I remember students who had read Dr. Tillich's books or had known him, who had confessed to me, that Dr. Tillich's utterances in book or life, had changed their lives, given new insights, erected new road signs, pointing to the small crossway, which had led to their "facing themselves" to their own daimon and Kairos. Bishop Pike's daimon, seems to have assumed the voice of a poltergeist, which lures him straight down the abyss, where the big black trapdoor opens to illusions without end . . . where the broken pieces of a sometime many-faceted noble crystal mirrors in the splinters the spiritualistic "Fata Morgana" instead of spiritual depth.

I would be happy, if Bishop Pike could turn his back to the

magic-mirror-game (we all know about it, to be sure). The pit-falls to the road to peace are many, so are the pitfalls to the road of self-realization. Bishop Pike tried one of the detours coura-geously but the order of the day is: "Face thy Self." At this point, even the fate of his son has nothing to do with Bishop Pike's struggle. His son worked out his own fate and nothing is left for debate but "acceptance." For Bishop Pike, regarding his own fate, nothing is left either but acceptance, without softening or de-facing guilt-feelings. "Guilt" may be nothing but the poor man's (the confused man's) consolation for not facing himself . . . If he would face himself, "guilt" would dissolve into necessity to act as a "new" man.

Bishop Pike has always been a brave man, full of inside and out-side challenge. I wish him luck to new insights and new fights and he may be sure, that men of good will, good intellect and spiritual awareness will stand by his side.

East Hampton Long Island, New York 11937
> (signed) Hannah Tillich
> (and in her hand) Copy to LOOK with the
> request to print—

November 27, 1968

My dear Hannah:

Because it was a carbon and not addressed directly to me your letter got among the second-class matter by mistake and I have just now reached it.

I was interested in your comments.

Rather than seeking to deal with the various matters which you have raised elliptically (and pejoratively, in some cases), I am sending you a copy of the book, *The Other Side*, of which the articles in *Look* are simply a small portion. There you will find, for example, reference to the fact that I had dedicated *What Is This Treasure* (Harper & Row, 1966) to Paul with the words "principal mentor," hence no doubt is left that I was cognizant of Paul's writings.

You need not burden yourself to read this, but I think doing so would make it possible for you to have a somewhat more open view to the phenomena (which I did not seek) and the various alternative explanations (in line with the scientific works on the subject) which I have tried to set forth in the book.

Whatever explanations one finds most plausible, I was touched by the fact that it seemed that Paul had a concern for the "new-

comer," my son, and also continued interest in me. If in fact Paul
were not the source of these communications, it still has done no
harm that, under one hypothesis, he seemed to be.

I hope this letter finds you well and that our paths cross again
some time.

With affectionate regards,

Sincerely,

Rt. Rev. James A. Pike

A Deceased Friend with a German Accent

Then, unmistakably, Mrs. Twigg spoke for herself. "Someone
with a foreign accent—German, I think—is speaking. Wait . . .
Paul, there is a Paul here. He says, 'Don't worry about the boy.
He's in safekeeping. He is surrounded by our love.' And he says to
tell you, Bishop, to be a rebel with a cause, for a rebel without a
cause is ineffective. He says he's still working—that nothing de-
stroys his faith. He sends you his love, and shares a common bond.
He says, 'Thank you for dedicating your new book to me.'"

It was midafternoon of March 2, 1966. Jim Jr. had been dead
less than a month. Bishop Pike, having resumed his sabbatical in
England (which was to expire March 15), found himself in the
East Acton sitting room of Mrs. Ena Twigg. There had begun
what was to become a series of the more celebrated séances of the
century. Harry Twigg sat soberly to his wife's left. Canon John
Pearce-Higgins, Vice-Provost of Southwark Cathedral, and an old
hand in these affairs, was serving as scribe of the occasion. He
took notes. It was Pearce-Higgins who had arranged for the sitting.

Maren Bergrud was also present. This will come as something
of a surprise to readers of *The Other Side*. Bishop Pike's account
of the March 2 séance tells us Jim Jr. mentioned Maren's birthday
but it does not tell us Maren was in the room at the time. (Later
on in the book there *is* a reference, in passing, to her presence at
the March 2 séance.) There are other omissions and some gross
distortions of fact in *The Other Side* with respect to Maren
Bergrud's role in these bizarre events. We are told, for example,
that at the time of Jim Jr.'s death Maren was on an extended voy-

age by freighter to Europe and the Scandinavian countries. She was indeed in Europe but she never went to any country in Scandinavia. She had, in fact, been for months with the bishop and his son in their Cambridge flat. She was still there when the bishop's chaplain, David Baar, arrived in mid-February to be followed a few days later by the bereaved bishop.

Maren Bergrud posed a problem for Bishop Pike when he undertook to write *The Other Side*. He could not exclude her from his narrative because she had played a central part in the events he was seeking to explicate. On the other hand, his relations with his (estranged) wife, Esther, were such that he was disinclined to expose to her the degree of his intimacy with Maren. He was probably also concerned about the impact such disclosures might have upon Jim Jr.'s surviving brother and sisters. The bishop's bad conscience led him to serious breaches of truth which blur the integrity of what is otherwise perhaps his finest book. Maren's behavior during the Cambridge experience is not fully told in *The Other Side*. It was even more extraordinary than would appear from the book. What is more damaging, however, is that insofar as her behavior *is* recorded it does not ring true because the context for it has been partially suppressed.

Bishop Pike was not particularly surprised when his son manifested himself in Mrs. Twigg's salon. That is, after all, Mrs. Twigg's business. When a famous bishop goes to a famous medium one month after his son's death something is likely to happen. It did. What did surprise the bishop was the sudden intrusion into the scenario of his old friend and esteemed mentor, Paul Tillich. Tillich, who had died the previous fall, had been one of Bishop Pike's favorite people. He was both a man of great intellectual accomplishments and a man of the world. Bishop Pike liked that sort of man. He admired Tillich so much that he had installed him in stained glass in one of the windows in Grace Cathedral. Tillich liked *that*. Jim Jr. had met the old theologian, casually, during one of several visits Tillich had paid the bishop in California. So, while it was perhaps plausible that Tillich would turn up for the bishop's first séance it was nevertheless an unexpected bonus.

The late great American monologist Ruth Draper had a remarkable gift for so conducting herself during a monologue that by the time it was over her audience was persuaded that she was not alone on the stage but was at the center of a roomful of people who were the characters in the story she was unfolding. Mrs. Twigg has a similar gift. Whether or not persons from "the other side" actually do enter her sitting room Ena Twigg behaves persuasively as though they must have done so. Her technique is professionally superb. It may be that her guests from the other side seldom have much to say that is compelling but the way in which their messages are conveyed is invariably dramatic and usually seductive. Thus, Jim Jr. would commonly speak directly using Mrs. Twigg's voice as though it were his own instrument. According to Mrs. Twigg, when that happens she does not know what is being said. It is as though she had been taken possession of, as though she had been displaced by another spirit. Tillich's intervention was of a different order. Mrs. Twigg announced his presence. "Someone with a foreign accent—German, I think—is speaking. Wait . . . *Paul*, there is a Paul here." She then reports what Paul is saying to her. Paul is not heard by others in the room. He is reported to be saying reassuring things. "Don't worry about the boy. He's in safekeeping." He is reported to go on to say things which are described in spiritualist literature as "evidentiary." "He says, 'Thank you for dedicating your new book to me.'"

That latter observation was, of course, startling to Bishop Pike. Here we have old Tillich—himself dead only a few months—apparently telling Mrs. Twigg—in a *German* accent—to convey to Bishop Pike his thanks for the bishop's dedication of a new book to him. It was startling because it was true. Bishop Pike *had* dedicated *What Is This Treasure* to Paul Tillich (and to Bishop John Robinson). What is more the book was only then coming on the market in America and was not available in England. How could Mrs. Twigg possibly have known about the dedication? Since it was unlikely (though not impossible) that she could have known the conclusion is inescapable that Tillich told her, as she said he did. And if Tillich was really there, why not Jim Jr.? He, after all, had far more reason to be there.

(There is another hypothesis sometimes advanced in discussions of these matters. Perhaps Mrs. Twigg can read other people's minds? By that reasoning she might have somehow gleaned from Bishop Pike's mind—he certainly *did* know about the dedication—the fact of the dedication. We find that hypothesis hopelessly farfetched. It places upon Mrs. Twigg a burden of gifts too heavy for any mortal to bear. She already has Jim Jr. making utterances through her larynx. Now she must simultaneously rummage about the vast accumulation of information that was Bishop Pike's head and ferret out the fact of the dedication. That fact must thereupon be transposed into an expression of gratitude—in a German accent—from an imaginary Paul Tillich *for* the dedication. It just won't wash.)

There is no particular reason why we should dismiss the possibility that Jim Jr. really was there. Who are we to say the medium *was* the message? There is no question whatever that Bishop Pike thought Jim Jr. was there. He had even had a sense of such a presence before the séance formally got under way. As was her custom with new clients Mrs. Twigg had engaged Bishop Pike at the outset in idle conversation. The purpose of this was to create an atmosphere of normalcy and warmth and ease. But Bishop Pike was not at all comfortable with this artificial chitchat and was impatient to get to the business that had brought him there. He terminated Mrs. Twigg's amenities by excusing himself to use her w.c.

> Away from the others, I suddenly felt rather ridiculous for having been swept by a series of events into such a new situation without too much thought. The burden of work had been enormous. There had been deadlines for each segment hanging over the scene like swords of Damocles and an overarching ultimate deadline: the end of this marvelous, tragic, illuminating, somber, joyous sabbatical. In the midst of it all, I had had too little time for reflection. I now wished that, in regard to this matter, I had been less precipitous in my responses.
>
> Then, as I put my hand on the doorknob to re-enter the hallway, I had a distinct awareness that my son was there; at that moment it would not have surprised me if as I came out I had met him in the hall smiling at me. That was the life-sized picture which flashed through my mind as I opened the door. Not replacing this image, but sort of superimposed on it like a gloss, was a flashback to that other beautiful moment of meeting back early in January in Herzliya, Israel, when I opened a door, he smiled like that and then we embraced in joy.

That embrace in Herzliya, one month *before* Jim Jr.'s death, had been very important to Bishop Pike. His months in Cambridge and then over the Christmas holidays in Israel with his son had been painful and frustrating, but they had also been on his part (and on Jim Jr.'s part) profound efforts to get through to one another, to communicate to each other their love. The joyful encounter in a hotel hallway in Herzliya had seemed a real breakthrough in their relationship. He had felt they were at last beginning to make it as father and son, and as friends. Might not that breakthrough, achieved out of so much pain and alienation, be the warrant now for another breakthrough that would tear asunder the most terrible of all alienations?

"I love you very much," the medium's voice went on. "So much love and no means of giving it." How true, I thought, how true. True in one sense now, true in another sense before he died. He was a loving person, yet he seemed incapable of breaking free to express his love. He had come to be able to express his love for me in words now and again during the last three or four months. But still I had the feeling he was blocked—generally not able to tell anyone freely what he really felt.

Mrs. Twigg went on, still quoting in the first person. "I'm tied to my regrets. Yet they are showing me the way out, and we must make progress together. I have to live my way and you yours."

Later, near the end of the séance, the matter becomes explicit.

"I'm breaking down the last enemy—death—so I suppose I have overcome."

Reminiscences of the Bishop's Mother

"He always wanted a father."

There was nothing Mrs. Chambers would rather do than talk about her son the bishop, and as is often the case with elderly people she remembered best and most enjoyed talking about the early days, the years when young James was growing up and she, widowed, had devoted herself utterly to the education and future of her only child.

He always felt out of it because the other boys had fathers and he didn't have. Every night he'd pray at my knee and he'd pray for a good father. I had a banker friend in Oklahoma City who had a friend in California, and he wrote a letter and said I was coming to California and had a little money to invest. This friend in California was a widower at the time, and I was rather young and wasn't too bad to look at. He immediately wanted to start taking me places. And I would take the whole family. Or if he came I would always bring in the whole family. After a while I noticed that James had quit praying for a good daddy. I said to him, "Son, you haven't prayed lately for a good daddy. What's the matter?" And he said, "I was afraid I might get one with a lot of white skin on his neck." He was quite a bit older than I was, this man was.

This old man was quite persistent. He wanted to get a new car, and he wanted me to decide on what one I'd like. I said, "Well, that's up to you." I had no serious intentions whatever. One day he brought a handful of diamonds around that had been his late wife's. He said, "I'll have these remounted for you. We will go to Europe on our honeymoon." Finally, I just had to tell him I wasn't interested. About two weeks later he drove up in that new car with a young woman in the seat next to him—she was about my age—and of course she was wearing all the diamonds.

I was a widow nine years. I had lots of friends, went with a lot of men, and had opportunities to marry. But it was one thing to marry for a husband, and quite another to marry a good father for my son. I didn't want anything to happen that would change James's life or thwart him in any way. When I married again in 1924 I married an attorney in Los Angeles. James was eleven at the time. My new husband, Claude McFadden, didn't want me to continue to teach but I insisted on keeping that position. I didn't know how things might turn out, and I didn't want to take any step that would jeopardize James's future in any way.

James and Claude got along wonderfully. He was a fine father. He was very proud of James, and he was the influence that caused James later on to study law. My whole family had been Catholic and James's father had been Catholic but Claude McFadden was not. When the time came to send James to college Claude and I nearly separated over the matter. I wanted to send James to a Catholic college because so many young people would lose their faith in a non-Catholic school. Claude said, "Why send the boy to an inferior college when you have a superior college right in your front yard for free?" That was UCLA. But I was insistent and we sent James to Santa Clara. And that was where he did lose his faith.

Up until then James had wanted to be a priest. As a student in

Hollywood High School he went to mass and communion every morning at Blessed Sacrament Church on Sunset Boulevard. He had a regular daily routine. You see, after I married Claude my sister—Ethyl—and my mother established their own home just across from Hollywood High, and each morning James would go to mass and then to Ethyl's for breakfast and so to school. And in the afternoon on his way home he would stop often at the church to talk with a very fine elderly priest. I found out later that even then he was having doubts about some of his faith. That fine old priest would tell him just to pray and he'd be guided.

When he went off to Santa Clara he fully intended to go on from there to study for the priesthood. He wasn't happy at Santa Clara. He didn't like it. When he would come home for vacations—Christmas and Easter an so on—he would say, "I'm going to go over the hill." There was a seminary just over the hill from Santa Clara. When a boy would drop out of Santa Clara to go to the seminary the other boys would say he had gone over the hill. And when James would say that I would weep. I spent most of those vacations crying. I didn't want him to go over the hill. He was too young. I would say, "No, you must finish college first. You are too young to make a decision that serious." He was only sixteen when he entered Santa Clara.

James would say, "Well, Mommy, if I go over the hill, they will educate me, and you won't have that expense." I would say, "Son, I don't want anybody to educate you. I will educate you myself. That's why I'm teaching." You see, I didn't want my husband to feel that he had inherited a responsibility, and I wanted to be completely independent in what James and I did in that regard. So, he stayed at Santa Clara and by the end of two years he had lost his faith. He stopped going to church. He had nothing to do with any kind of church for about four years. And at the end of two years he decided he would have to leave Santa Clara even if he couldn't go over the hill.

He transferred for his third year of college to UCLA. It was during that year—influenced, as I say, by Claude—that he decided he wanted to study the law. In those days there was no law program at UCLA and he knew that for the law he would have to switch to the University of Southern California. So, for his fourth year of college he transferred again and he took his B.A. degree at USC. He was allowed to select certain of his courses for the fourth year and chose courses that would apply to his law degree, thereby saving one year of law school. He got his LL.B. at USC, and then went on to Yale University, where he earned his doctorate in law.

When he was finished at Yale I wanted him to come on back to Los Angeles to begin his practice, but Claude advised that he should go first to Washington, D.C., and get some experience there. So he did. He did very well but he was so lonely. That was when he married for the first time. He married a girl he had gone to school with back in Hollywood, Jane Alvies. They had also been classmates in college, and she had gone to Yale the same year he did to study. You have to understand that he was very lonely in Washington—there all by himself. He really wanted to come home. I wish he had.

Mrs. Chambers interrupted herself at this point. She was not sure, she indicated, that she ought to talk about that first marriage. James had never in his life had an unkind word to say about anybody. He could not bear to hurt anybody. Mrs. Chambers would never forgive herself if she should say a word about somebody in James's life that might be hurtful. She decided that she *would* talk about the first marriage but she was pretty sure she would not be telling all she knew. She wanted to make one other point. James had not been an alcoholic. Nobody should say that he was. There were some things you just did not say about other people. She knew that James himself had called himself an alcoholic. He had even told *her* that. He had only said that so that he would be better able—when he had stopped drinking—to help other people who *were* alcoholics.

Jane was a highly intelligent girl. She was Phi Beta Kappa. But she was an extremely nervous person. She was not emotionally stable. I realized that and my husband did, too. We liked her, personally, but we knew that she was just not for James. She was unstable. And you know it wasn't only with James. She has been unhappily married twice since then. They were married about two years, she and James. Then, they came home for a visit. Both families met them at the train, her mother and my family. We were so happy to see them. It was the first time since their marriage that either one of them had been home. When they arrived I knew there was something very definitely wrong. She stepped out away from James and went home with her mother. It was like the chains had clanked to the floor. There was no turning to say goodbye to him or anything. She just went home with her mother. And he went home with us. They hadn't been home long when he went over to see her one afternoon. He came back as white as that napkin. He said, "Jane and I are getting a divorce." Just like that! I don't want to say much more. I think she had kept some connections she had had before their marriage. Of course, James couldn't have *that*. And it seemed she wanted to be with this other man while they were there in California. James told her, "Just go right ahead." She did. He knew about it, and that was it. He had felt all along that there was some disturbance in their marriage, and as I say she was emotionally unstable.

James went right to the bishop. They had been married in the Episcopal Church. He went right straight to the bishop, and told him the whole thing. He wanted to make it clear that it was not because *he* had met someone else. There had been no complications on his part. And the bishop annulled the marriage. It was an Episcopal thing. At that time James was a very unhappy ex-Catholic, so to speak. He had been received into the Episcopal Church while he was married to Jane. She joined the Church, too, at the same time. I was in Washington when it took place. But in her case it didn't seem to take. She had no inclination to live up to it. She was unstable—didn't know what she wanted to do. They went to communion service together that Christmas, and when the communion was to be served she jumped up and ran out of the church, screaming. You can imagine what it would be like to live with that sort of thing. James couldn't live with it.

But James never lost a friend. He never cut loose from Jane. He didn't feel like she had done him a wrong. He didn't feel like this thing had come between them, and he should hold it against her. He never held anything against anybody. Never. And after he was married again he had Esther—and later Diane, too—meet Jane. He always held on to a friend. And over the years he continued on occasion to see Jane—never, of course, on the *side*, but openly. His wife would always know about it. And when Jane had troubles he would do what he could to help her out. She was still living up in San Francisco the last I knew. She was a nice girl, but she was not for James.

The Girl Who Was for James

FROM HERE TO ETER-
NITY: When he needed
a lift from Berkeley to

San Francisco, controversial teacher-preacher Bishop James A. Pike asked if anyone in his summer-session seminar was going that way. A blue-eyed blonde offered her services and off they went. That was 1966 and soon Pike began noticing other things about Miss Diane Kennedy of Palo Alto. Her term papers, he recalled were "exceptionally good." Pike, 55, arranged to work with Miss Kennedy, 31, on his latest book, "The Other Side," about psychic phenomena. The two claimed to have contacted Pike's late son, James, and last week they announced that the boy's spirit had given hearty approval to their weekend wedding, his third, her first. Since they agree on the survival of the soul, Pike and Miss Kennedy insisted on the omission in their marriage ceremony of the words "till death do us part."
—*Newsweek* magazine, December 30, 1968

Diane Kennedy met her future husband for the first time at the Pacific School of Religion, Berkeley, California, in June of 1966. She knew little of him other than what she had read in the newspapers. She did know about the death of his son four months earlier. She did not know that his marriage to Esther Pike was in

disorder and that efforts to reconcile it were in progress. Nor did
she know of the relationship that then existed between Bishop
Pike and Maren Bergrud. Finding herself (she was actually
twenty-eight then) somewhat at loose ends, she had thought to
pass that summer studying theology. Two courses being offered by
Bishop Pike, one on "The New Morality" and the other on "The
New Theology," appealed to her and she enrolled for them.

Raised in a close-knit Methodist family, Middle-Western in origin but settled in San Jose, California, Diane took her religion
seriously. That was the sort of Methodist family she was part of.
She had spent several years in South America as a missionary-
teacher under Methodist sponsorship, and she was, when she met
Bishop Pike, employed in the education program of First United
Methodist Church in Palo Alto. Though she had been looking
earnestly for some time she had not found the man she wanted to
marry and to share with the interests and concerns she felt so
deeply. Her decision to enroll for courses in theology during the
summer of 1966 had not been governed entirely by the prospects
for intellectual enrichment.

> My principal interest had been to make one final effort to find
> myself a man who was eligible, concerned about ultimate ques-
> tions, and committed to service in the Church. I had long been
> all three, and at twenty-eight was trying to decide whether to
> finally give up my hope that I could share in such depth with a
> man and marry someone who I loved and with whom I was most
> compatible—but who was outside the Church.
>
> My dilemma had always been that in spite of my inner dedica-
> tion and conviction, I was attracted more to men unrelated to the
> Church than to what I began to call "ministerial types." And
> though I loved the Church in the deepest way, I was most impa-
> tient with her, finding the institution inflexible, all too slow to
> change, and lacking in compassion and true love and concern for
> individual persons. So much within me responded to the secular,
> where it seemed there were often more genuine acts of justice and
> love done than in churches, yet I considered myself a deeply spir-
> itual person.
>
> So as a last-ditch effort I enrolled in summer school at that
> Berkeley seminary. True to past experience, however, I met many
> interesting persons but found no one both eligible and interesting
> in the classes.
>
> I was intrigued by the professor, however.

Bishop Pike, for his part, ever mindful of the benefits which accrue to the early bird, wasted no time. There were to be only three weeks of seminars, meeting twice in each week for six-hour sessions. By the afternoon break of the first session the bishop had become aware of a bright, vivacious, blond and blue-eyed young woman, somewhat on the plumpish side. (Bishop Pike liked his women on the plump side, he confided more than once to close friends.) Would anybody be driving back to San Francisco after the class? Hands shot up. Diane Kennedy was chosen to serve as episcopal chauffeur.

As things turned out Diane drove the bishop back to San Francisco after five of the six seminar sessions. The conversation during these forty-five-minute interludes was not personal, certainly not intimate. They talked of what had gone on in class and of what was going on in the world. On the surface the communication between them was unremarkable, but for both of them these encounters were charged with an extraordinary empathy. Had they been adolescents it might be said of them that they were suffering love at first sight.

> I knew nothing about his personal life (except that he was married and was "too old" for me anyway), but in spite of all (and the lack of any personal exchange of words between us) I went home after the second ride across the bridge and said to my roommate: "Shirley, this is going to sound very strange, but when I am with Bishop Pike I feel as though we're already married. It's like, literally, a 'marriage made in heaven'—a full-blown relationship which has just dropped down over us without our doing a thing to make it be."

There was the sense that they already knew one another, that perhaps they had been married in a previous incarnation. The three weeks of seminars whirled around them as around the eye of a storm, leaving in their wake illuminations of "The New Theology" and "The New Morality." During the months that followed pretexts were easily found for occasional rendezvous—a cup of coffee, lunch, a few minutes or a few hours torn out of the bishop's crowded days and nights. A bond was forged. Matters would fall into place accordingly. There would come a time for Diane to write to say the intimacy between them must go no further. He would indulge a two-week interruption of the inevitable.

She would go up into the mountains to face alone her moment of truth. Then—it was by now November of 1966—he would telephone to suggest dinner.

I had shared on that occasion—the first time Jim had had an entire Saturday evening free since I'd met him—a "devil" I'd been wrestling with and had finally conquered: the temptation to put Jim at the center of my life, to let all meaning flow through and from him, to focus my thoughts on him, to wait in animated suspension between our meetings—in effect, to make him "god" of my life.

Jim's comprehension was complete. "The problem of idolatry," he said. "Of course, that would be a big mistake for either of us. But you could not do that any more than I could. 'Hear O Israel, the Lord thy God is *one* God and thou shalt have no other gods before Him!' That is the great commandment in the light of which all other ethical claims fall into their proper places. Neither of us could live any differently."

It was settled between us. We reflected on it many times but the reality never faltered. Our individual centers were made one in a common dedication of will and in a common act of faith in the One who is above, below, within, through, before, and beyond all else—who is no thing and no person, but who is all and is certainly no less than personal—the One, the Ground of all Being, *The* Life, God. Ours was/is a monotheistic marriage— idolatry of even the beloved "other" had fallen by the wayside and we were free to be fully united in serving God, in quest of the Truth, together.

In other words, on that fateful Saturday night in November, Jim and Diane, by grace of the new morality and the old absolutes, had sex. It was obviously no ordinary coupling. Diane Kennedy had ceased to be a virgin. James Pike may astonishingly have become one. Two Novembers later, in the coffee shop of the Columbia Presbyterian Medical Center in New York City, Jim and Diane would share with an old friend the news that just before Christmas of that year they would be married. "You understand, of course, that we've been married right along, but there are always the formalities." The friend remembers thinking to himself that Bishop Pike was an inexhaustible source of delightful surprises.

Jim and Diane Pike were formally married on December 20, 1968.

The Bishop's Fifty-fifth Birthday Party

PILLS FELL
DAUGHTER
OF PIKE

The daughter of Bishop James A. Pike was hospitalized today, apparently after taking an overdose of pills, as family misfortune continued to haunt the controversial churchman.

Santa Barbara, Cal., police rushed unconscious Constance Ann Pike, 19, from her suburban Montecito apartment to St. Francis Hospital last night.

The hospital reported she had taken an overdose of barbiturates and was in fair condition today.

Police said they entered Miss Pike's apartment after Pike's secretary called them, saying that a neighbor of Miss Pike's had told her the girl was "in trouble."

New York *Post*,
February 15, 1968

The apartment where this near-tragedy took place was not Constance Pike's apartment. She did not live in Santa Barbara. She had, in fact, come down from San Francisco to spend a few days with her father in *his* apartment. February 14, 1968, the bishop's fifty-fifth birthday, happened to fall during Connie's visit. On the morning of that day Connie and Diane had planned a party for the evening. A few friends were invited, a menu was decided upon, gifts were considered. Connie went off to shop and came back in the early afternoon with two gifts. She and Diane wrapped the gifts and straightened up the apartment. Diane then left the girl, seemingly in good spirits, and went down the hall to a smaller apartment (once Maren Bergrud's putative abode) which served as office for New Focus, the bishop's agency for personal business, lecture engagements, and the like.

About 4 P.M. the bishop called Diane from his "other office" at the Center for the Study of Democratic Institutions. Connie had called him and asked that he come right home. He was busy but would come home in about an hour. Would Diane meanwhile investigate? She returned at once to the bishop's apartment and found Connie in bed in the room she was using during her visit. She said she had taken twelve Seconal tablets. There was a bottle of the bishop's sleeping pills on the dresser. But the young lady seemed so calm Diane did not at first believe her. She started to question her further when Connie suddenly lost consciousness. Efforts to wake her did not avail. Diane rushed to a phone and called the bishop. He said to call an ambulance and he would be home right away.

The ambulance and the bishop arrived together. The stretcher would not fit into the elevator and Connie was carried down the steps to the waiting ambulance. The bishop and Diane followed by car. There was an interval of several hours while the girl's life hung in the balance. She did recover. She told Diane that she had not really wanted to kill herself. She spoke of a traumatic personal experience she had suffered the preceding fall. She said she had been very tired and wanted to sleep a very long time. The next day Esther Pike flew down from San Francisco, and a few days later she took Connie back with her.

So passed Bishop Pike's fifty-fifth birthday. It had been two years and ten days since Jim Jr.'s death. It had been twenty months to the day since Maren Bergrud's death. It had been nineteen months since Jim and Esther had consented to divorce. And it was nine months before Jim and Diane were (formally) married. Nineteen months later he would himself lie dead in the Judean desert.

"Dead?"

As we rose above the canyon, I began to feel sick all over. I was directing the pilot, "Move to the right. Yes, it was here I left him. There, that's the spot. Oh, we've gone too far. It's back that way."

But inside I could see it was hopeless. "My God," I thought. "Could that possibly be the canyon I walked through? How *could* I have walked through such a canyon? It is impossible."

It was no wonder Diane felt sick. She had had no sleep worth mentioning since the ordeal of the desert began. It was 2:30 P.M. Tuesday, September 2, 1969, more than twenty-four hours after she and Jim had driven out into the desert. Following her uncannily accurate directions the search party had located the Ford Cortina. They had proceeded to the point at which it would be necessary to descend into Wadi Mashash, that deep and interminably treacherous canyon leading, eventually, to the Dead Sea. It was not possible for the jeeps to make that descent. Searchers tumbled from the jeeps and started down in a direction indicated by Diane. She was too weary to go with them.

A helicopter had landed near Diane's jeep. She raced toward it, at some jeopardy from its whirling propellers, and prevailed upon the crew to take her up over the canyon. For the first time she fully comprehended the enormity of the desert and the utter improbability that she could have walked out of it through the long, harrowing night. Beneath her now Wadi Mashash tumbled out of sight among sheer cliffs rising hundreds of feet in a chaos of desolation. Somewhere down in the awesome entrails of that canyon Bishop Pike almost certainly lay dead.

There was, however, a sufficient possibility of his survival to warrant prolonging the massive search Major Givati had set in motion. Bedouin tribesmen might have come upon him. He might have found water. From the helicopter Diane would see far down in the canyon a small pool of water. It was such sparsely scattered watering holes that enabled the Bedouin to survive in the desert. But the Bedouin knew where the water was. Bishop

Pike did not. He did not even know there *was* water in that desert. The temperature was 140 degrees Fahrenheit. If Jim Pike had not by then found water he was surely dead. The search continued until 4:30 P.M. when Major Givati called it off for the day.

No trace whatever had been found of Bishop Pike. It would be much too dangerous to proceed at night. Major Givati directed that the search was to resume at 4:30 A.M. the next morning with fresh troops. Diane was driven to the Dead Sea along a road that led over the top of the desert cliffs and proved to be the road she had rolled down at the end of her night-long trek. She was briefly reunited with the Arab workmen who had found her when she cried out at the foot of the road. They told her that when she first cried out they had dismissed her cries because they assumed she was a hyena.

The trip back to Jerusalem, by helicopter, took, surprisingly, only a few minutes. By 6:30 P.M. Diane was back at the Intercontinental Hotel for the first time since she and Jim had left it about noon the day before. In her room and alone her composure collapsed and she fell into tears. Even then, however, she was unable to pay heed to the numerous lacerations and bruises that covered much of her body. She suddenly recalled that she and Jim were expected for dinner at 7:30 P.M. by Professor Shlomo Pines of Hebrew University and that they had been expected for dinner at the same hour the previous night by Professor David Flusser and his wife. She placed a telephone call to Professor Pines. He was bewildered by her news. He would call Professor Flusser and explain. He and his wife would be available if there was anything at all they could do.

> "Dead?" Mother's voice registered her astonishment. "Honey, what happened?"
> "He's lost in the desert," I sobbed. "We can't find him." I thought my heart would break and I could no longer hold back the frantic sobs and the flood of tears. I must have given an explanation of sorts. I remember Mother asking if she and Dad should come to Israel. I said no, there was nothing they could do and that I would be coming home immediately. The police would go on with the search but it was hopeless.

Diane and her mother agreed upon procedures to pass the grim news on to Mrs. Chambers and the bishop's children so that word would not come to them by radio or on the evening TV news. Mrs. Kennedy suggested her daughter should see a doctor. For the first time Diane became aware of the fearful way her body had been abused by the desert. She did go to a doctor, who was astonished at the multiplicity of her wounds. He used a full bottle of Mercurochrome and part of another treating them. Her left foot, badly sprained, required an elastic bandage, but her other injuries, though numerous, were medically superficial. He gave her appropriate injections and a sedative to enable the sleep she so obviously badly needed.

She did sleep, restlessly. At 7:30 A.M. the next morning Major Givati sent an officer to bring her to his headquarters in Bethlehem.

"I thought it would be easier for you to be here than to wait in your hotel room," he explained. I was very grateful.

"The American embassy has called several times already this morning," the major commented.

"My husband is a very famous man in the United States," I tried to explain.

"What we're doing to try to find your husband we would do for any human being. It is a man's life that is at stake," the major said simply.

I was afraid he thought I was criticizing the police for not doing enough or suggesting that they should do more because my husband was a famous man. "I only meant that that was undoubtedly why the embassy was calling," I replied apologetically. "And I'm sure that all the news media will soon be here. My husband is very well known and the press always follows his activities closely."

By 10:30 A.M. Diane had given four interviews to reporters. She did not feel much like talking about the ordeal but it helped pass the time and it spared Major Givati having to talk to the press. Diane also remembered that Jim had always been accommodating to journalists. She would try to be the same. Her few years with the bishop had taught her that accommodation is the most comfortable way to endure the glare of publicity. She even assented to be photographed despite her wounds and despite the way the ordeal had ravaged her face. The newsphotos which resulted were cruel.

At ten-thirty that morning Major Givati reported that the searchers had found a map. A piece had been torn from it. Had they had a map with them? She disclosed the wretched Avis map. In that case, Major Givati wanted her to go back to the desert. He wanted her to show the searchers the rock where she had left her husband. She was driven back out into Judea—her third such excursion in as many days. When the jeep could go no farther she had to walk on her swollen feet along the same route she and Jim had taken until finally—much farther than she had remembered it to be—she was back at the rock where she had left Jim. The searchers only then told her that that was where they had earlier found the map. She was assisted back to the jeep and waited with Major Givati through the afternoon. At 4:30 P.M. the searchers climbed back out of the canyon. Nothing had been found.

She was driven again to the workers' camp by the Dead Sea. On the way one of the other jeeps had overturned. Several men were hurt, and one suffered a broken leg. At the camp there was a light supper. Diane could manage only a few bites of a tomato and generous draughts of tea. By this time she had conceived the idea that whenever she drank liquids she was somehow sharing the nourishment with Jim. That evening she was driven back to Jerusalem and was not in her room at the Intercontinental Hotel until about 10:30 P.M. Encouraged by the discovery of the map, and still hoping the bishop might be in the care of some Bedouin, Major Givati had ordered another day for the search.

Messages had begun to pour into the hotel, many of them from spiritualists and mediums. One message was from Arthur Ford, the celebrated American medium with whom Jim had had two sittings. Ford, suffering at the time from a heart condition, was in a New York City hospital. He had nevertheless had a vision. Bishop Pike, he said, was alive but sick in a cave not far from where Mrs. Pike had left him. There were many caves in canyon Wadi Mashash, hundreds of them, maybe thousands. Ford's vision seized him at 8 A.M. (Israel time) on Tuesday, September 2, or early in the morning after Diane had left Jim on the rock. Bishop Pike may well have been still alive at that time and if he was he was surely sick and could have been in a cave. But Ford's information was not much use unless he could locate the cave more exactly. Diane—through her family—asked the old medium

to try to be more specific. Ford did try but could not "get" anything beyond the initial vision.

Diane also attempted that evening to reach Ena Twigg in London to ask whether she had had any communications concerning
Jim. Mrs. Twigg could not be reached. As things turned out it was
the next evening (London time) that the Twiggs and Canon
Pearce-Higgins held the séance during which Bishop Pike was to
make the first purported manifestation of himself from the other
side. But news of this would not come to Diane until the end of
the week. It was very late when Diane finally got to bed. She had
been comforted by word that her younger brother, Scott Kennedy,
was on his way to Jerusalem.

The next morning, Thursday, September 4, Diane was driven
once again to police headquarters in Bethlehem. She reported
Arthur Ford's vision to Major Givati and Chief Schmauel. Both
men said at once that they did not believe in such things.

> "But," Chief Schmauel said, "if you can get some specific di-
> rections or instructions, we will search there. Or if you can get
> someone who has these talents, we will send men with him to
> look."

Diane did not go out to the desert that day. She passed the
time in conversation with reporters, by now a considerable throng
from newspapers, radio, and television. She doggedly continued to
express hope that Jim would be found. There was something
about the atmosphere of busy search and widening interest and
concern that offset the dire pessimism she had felt at the end of
the first day of the search. The finding of the map was some concrete progress. The word from Arthur Ford had been reassuring.
And she was by that time numb from shock and exhaustion. She
grasped at straws.

The day's search was wholly unproductive. She returned to
Jerusalem. More press were gathered at the hotel. She consented
to a general interview.

> The press interview was over at about 6 P.M. and I had been
> back in my room only a few minutes when there was a knock at
> the door and I heard Scott's voice.
> "Diane?"

An Altered State of Consciousness

On March 14, 1973, Scott Kennedy would find himself in the offices of David Baar (at that time co-partner of Excelsior Incense, a business located in San Francisco), who had been Bishop Pike's last chaplain and executive assistant. He was somewhat surprised to find the former priest, also a young man, casually dressed and with hair that fell several inches below his shoulders. Scott had come to see Baar at our request to tape an interview about his recollections of the bishop.

Reluctant at first to be interviewed, Baar had sought for some time to avoid or evade it. Scott persisted and finally just went to Excelsior Incense and waited until Baar agreed to see him. The two men warmed quickly to one another, however, and the interview itself, after initial tension, proceeded fluently and in an open, candid way. Baar's life-style had clearly changed in the years since he had served the bishop. His idiom would have found greater favor in an Esalen Institute than in Grace Cathedral. He reviewed with Scott some of his experiences with the bishop. He had obviously been very fond of his former boss, was loyal to him, and was at pains not to breach the confidentiality of a relationship he had valued.

Not long after Jim Jr.'s death Bishop Pike had sent Baar to Cambridge to prepare the way for his own return there to wind up his sabbatical. Baar was to try to get the bishop's assorted projects in order and to assemble Jim Jr.'s personal effects and correspondence. He was also to look after Maren Bergrud, who might be expected to have suffered some trauma on account of the junior Pike's violent passing. The bishop may well have felt, perhaps unconsciously, that it would be comforting to have another younger man in the flat he had been sharing with his son. And it seems likely the bishop did not relish sharing that flat alone with Maren Bergrud.

> In England I became aware of Jimmy's conflict around the person of his mother. There was a dream I had the first night I was in England—after I had been packed off to clean things up and stay with Maren. There was no place to sleep. I mean the first

Early snapshots show James Pike,
above left, at age five during summer
of 1918;
above right, on a golf course in 1926;
below, as a Naval Intelligence
officer 1942–43.

Two pictures from the 1950s: *above*, the future bishop and his mother, and, *below*, Dean James A. Pike and his wife Esther and their children, left to right, James Jr., Christopher, Constance Ann, and Catherine Hope.

While chaplain of Columbia University, 1949–52, Pike met with, *above left*, President (then of the University) Dwight D. Eisenhower; *above right*, Francis Cardinal Spellman, Roman Catholic Archbishop of New York. *Below*, in 1952, Pike was installed as Dean of the Cathedral of St. John the Divine, New York.

The first two published pictures of the bishop at the altar, above, and in front of Grace Cathedral, San Francisco, below.

night there was only one place for me to sleep and that was in
Jimmy's bed, so I climbed in and proceeded to have the most incredible half-asleep, half-awake dream. It was a waking dream.
There was the feature of a woman who I—in a moment—interpreted to be Jimmy's mother. I proceeded to have a very clear,
lucid dream with a lot of fear and a sense of massiveness about
the mother—domination and that sort of thing—which really
meant a freaky trip around women. Suddenly I popped out of it.
Those were new thoughts for me. And I wondered, "Where in
the hell did that come from?" Then I went off to sleep.

When Jim came back about a week later I happened to mention this dream to him and started laying out some of the details
to him, and he got this shocked look on his face, and said, "My
God, that's exactly the sort of stuff that came out in Jimmy's sessions with the psychoanalyst, Dr. Perry, in San Francisco."

That was one of the first psychic phenomena that occurred
while we were in Cambridge. That stuff came to me out of the
clear blue sky.

YOU DON'T FEEL THAT YOU HAD SUFFICIENT EXPERIENCE WITH THE
FAMILY THAT YOU HAD BEEN GATHERING THAT IMPRESSION?

No, absolutely. I did not have that at all. I *did* know something
about Jim's own feelings about Esther. Oddly enough they were
reflected in Jimmy. Both shared some . . . certain feelings. There
was a definite ambivalence on the part of both of them about
Esther. Her strength and dominance is the only way I can put it.
Jim once related to me a lot of feeling about Esther's being intimidating. I picked that up in the dream too, quite strongly. I really didn't know a hell of a lot about Jimmy Pike. I learned a lot
more posthumously than I had known before.

IN ENGLAND, WAS IT TO TAKE CARE OF BUSINESS OR TO TAKE CARE OF
MAREN?

I have never really talked about this. I don't know how much
of this I would like to see come out in print.

I THINK IT WOULD BE HELPFUL FOR BILL AND ANTHONY TO HEAR
WHAT YOUR EXPERIENCE WAS.

You see, I was assigned as Jim's executive assistant and I was
theoretically his chaplain. The bishop's chaplain happens to be
his confessor. Jim had a way of maintaining . . . He was a doctor
of jurisprudence. The guy was always looking at that line of pro-
priety and whether it was the confessional or the ethics of the
legal profession or whatever handle he happened to use, Jim was
always concerned about an individual's right to be protected from

his own mistakes, his admissions or whatever. So there are lots of things that he told me and there are lots of things that he told me to do that I feel fall into the area of . . . There are things Jim never wanted dealt with or revealed. And I've never dealt with them or revealed them to anybody. I kind of weave my way through that.

But this was a personal experience of mine which I will relate because it happened to me. I was there. This was not something Jim told me or that Jim asked me to deal with in complete confidentiality. One of the things that infuriated Jim was instances of priests in the diocese breaching the confessional. He once issued a directive to all his priests saying he would depose anybody on the spot if he ever heard they had breached the confessional. As Jim's chaplain . . . As Jim's executive assistant I took care of his papers, and I took care of a lot of the things he wrote. I would frequently draft out his memoranda . . . etc. . . . As his chaplain frequently I would handle things for him which were strictly personal business, including his bank account and his discretionary funds.

Now. The trip to England . . . When Jimmy killed himself, there I was. I had a passport and I was ready to go if I was needed. When Howard Freeman came to me with the news story that Jimmy Pike was in New York and that he'd shot himself in his hotel room, I said, "I don't know if that's true, but I'll find out." He said, "Well, how can you find out?" I said, "I don't know that, but I'll find out." I went back to Jim's office and got on the phone—his private line—and I called Maren in England. I said, "Is Jimmy there?" She said, "My God, there are reporters here. I don't know what to do. They say he shot himself. There's a story he's in New York. I don't know where he is. I only know he set off from here yesterday to follow Jim back to the States."

Maren told me Jimmy was into eating Romilar. The kids in England . . . Romilar is a cough medicine. There's a tablet form of it. Jimmy was into this. Maren told me (later) who his connection was in London, the guy he used to buy his hash from and things like that. He was definitely using drugs. One of the favorite trips of that time was eating these Romilar tablets which gave a sort of delirium effect . . . It's a very strong hallucinogenic . . . a delirium kind of thing where you felt your head was cooking. Apparently it was behind Romilar that Jimmy shot himself. I think this is what Maren told me. Maren told me it was not LSD. It would have been Romilar.

Maren was a very excitable person. Also she was riding a very thin line in terms of her own metabolism being intact. She had had surgery several times. I think she had a hysterectomy, and I believe there were various other malignancies at one time or another. She was taking quite a few drugs to balance . . . to keep her system in balance. In fact, that was one thing I did . . . I brought a series of prescriptions for her . . . It turned out the English wouldn't observe American prescriptions. She was using a lot of drugs. She took a lot of codeine. She was using a lot of opiates.

When she met me at Heathrow Airport, down at London . . . Well, by the time we were onto the train she was ill . . . She was physically sick . . . Really riding a very fine edge when I got there. We went up to Cambridge and got installed in the apartment. I looked around and got a picture of what it was like. It was a total mess from one end to the other. There was the same situation there that there had been in the States. Jim had piles and piles of correspondence that hadn't been answered. He was working on the book. There was not much housekeeping being done. They did have a housekeeper and she did all that *was* being done. Maren . . . Apparently while he was gone . . . It was just sort of quietly falling apart. I spent several days there with her trying to figure out how to drive the car . . . Trying to get accustomed to England. At the same time I was going through daily freaks with Maren . . . Which were really pretty intense.

You asked me earlier whether there was some indication that Maren had manipulated some of the psychic phenomena. I can perhaps answer that best by pointing out that in my estimation the quantity of drugs Maren was taking, for whatever reason, had to have a pretty profound impact. She was an extremely alert, high-strung, hypertensive person. In combination with Jim the synergism was incredible. Those two could make each other so hyped! At times I would have to look at both of them and say, "Hey, knock it off!"

This whole psychic phenomena thing began as I recall . . . That month in England in that apartment is like a month inside some pressure cooker somewhere. I had never taken any psychedelic drug at that time in my life. The number of hallucinations during that experience . . . or whatever they were . . . The kinds of things that were going on were so intense . . . And I had had no experience whatever. It was an altered state of consciousness . . . We were involved collectively in an altered state of consciousness . . . And I didn't even know what that was. But after having had some drug experiences I was able to look back at that and say, "My God! There is no question about that being an altered state of consciousness." Coupled with that was the fact that it was similar to being in a delirium or in a fever . . . Like being on the approach curve to a really sound flu. It was very difficult to find the ground . . . To find any sense of "I am standing here. I physically feel alive relative to this place. I understand what's going on. My day makes sense." Those kinds of feelings were absent most of the time.

We were like refugees. We must have consumed among the three of us ten packs of cigarettes a day, easily. We would smoke and smoke . . . Eat butts, you know? We would normally work until two or three in the morning . . . Typing, discussing. We ate out. We would have breakfast in the apartment, but lunch and dinner were eaten out. Laundry was sent out. It was like a camp . . . A camp in a very straight modern apartment house in England. We did have a car. We were somewhat isolated from the various colleges so that we always had to take the car in . . . Other than that we were in an isolation camp. We would sit there for eight to sixteen hours at a shot. And it flew by pretty fast.

When I arrived Maren was in very bad shape. Psychologically she was ill. I think it was a combination of enormous anxiety—overload—coupled with her frail physical condition to begin with. Maren had what some people would think are demons. She was really a driven person. I've only met one other person like her since . . . She was undone by the event of Jimmy's death. She was undone partially because of Jimmy's transference to her . . . Jimmy (according to Maren) wanted to relate to her somewhat as to a mother. I think he wanted to relate to her—to attempt to relate to her—as a lover. I can't lay that on him because I really don't know . . . But I remember Maren saying that Jimmy wanted to be close to her but he didn't know how.

Apparently he had talked with Jim sr. about his frustration at his incapacity to really relate to a woman.

That was obviously reflected in his relationship with Maren. And oddly enough it was reflected back into Maren's relationship to me. When I got there she used me—to some degree—as a replacement for Jim *and* Jimmy—and/or—and it was very difficult at times to get sorted out exactly how she was relating to me. There were times when she would come on to me in the same

way she would to Jim. Other times . . . I woke up the first morning . . . The first morning I woke up in England . . . The reason
I'm gaping at you is because I suddenly went back to the room
. . . There I was looking at the room with the Venetian blinds
and the sun coming through . . . There was a glass of orange
juice being stuck in my hand and Maren was kissing me . . . She
leaned over and I was waking up . . . And she was kissing me on
the mouth . . . There was her face looking benevolent as a
mother . . . Really soft . . . I wondered—in a flash at that moment: "Pop, what is going on? What's happening?" I really
didn't know and I don't think she knew either. It was somehow
good for me to be there. There I was in Jimmy's bed. The roles
were interfacing.

We spent that first day just trying to dig what had happened. I
tried to clean up some of Jimmy's things . . . I went through
what few letters he had—he had very few, all from the States—
and I found a few he had written which he had never sent. I
collected all his stuff for Jim to look at and then I forgot about it.
I just sort of put the whole thing together and that was it. Maren
began to detail out for me her trauma . . . Her conflict about the
different roles Jimmy was trying to work out with her . . . She
had a lot of guilt about him going off and leaving and then committing suicide . . . Apparently there had been some rejection
thing that had happened there between her and him.

PRECIPITATING HIS LEAVING?

Here's a point where I don't want to get into projecting . . .
But my recollection is that Maren told me that the combination
of his wanting to follow Jim back plus some unsuccessful attempt
at relating to Maren directly caused . . . not the suicide certainly
but a tremendous sense of guilt in Maren *over* the suicide. That
is the sort of stage in which this is set. Plus she talked to me at
the same time about going down to London . . . Scoring hash
down in Soho with some guy who was Jimmy's connection down
there.

WAS SHE DOING HASH?

I don't know. I believe so. Maren was into smoking dope. I
know that because when I first met her back in San Francisco
. . . one of the first things she did was show me her stash.

I feel that by the time Jim got back to Cambridge we were
ready for anything to happen. I really feel that. I had that weird
dream which to me was *very* weird. Jim was trying to maintain
. . . He wasn't accepting the shock of Jimmy's death. That was
pretty clear.

YOU MEAN, SORT OF BUSINESS AS USUAL?

Absolutely. It was back to business as usual . . . Back to the book . . . Back to research . . . Back to appointments he had made . . . Back to speaking engagements. It was "press on," you know? But it was really rolling off him. He would sit and chain-smoke cigarettes—more than I had ever seen him smoke. He had quit at one point in England but by then he was really back into it. Sometimes he would begin to reflect. I remember him discussing the fact that they had only found half a bullet or something like that. He would review these things and wonder about them. Maren would try to calm him down a bit. Then it would all go away and we would go back to work.

This was all fine and good until Maren, as I recall, came in the room one day and her hair had burned around her forehead. Now, I didn't think a thing about it . . . The way they smoked it wouldn't have surprised me if she had a bunch of cigarettes sticking out of her mouth when she fell asleep in bed . . . Jim too. But it seemed to make a big difference to her. She felt it was an attack of some sort. Then other odd things began to happen . . . Such as safety pins being strewn all over the place. Now I had noticed that Jim—when he got his laundry which he constantly did —would simply rip the bands off the shirts and pins would be thrown all over . . . And he would just put the shirt on and walk out. Jim never cleaned up after himself. It was evident to me that one reason pins were lying around all over the place was because of the way Jim did this.

Other things happened. I don't remember the order of things. One thing that happened . . . We were sitting in the living room and I commented on the fact that the hands on the clock— which had stopped—were set in a way that suggested an open safety pin. I may have precipitated that one. I don't know. That started us off. I began telling Jim about that weird dream. That really blew his mind.

BECAUSE OF THE ACCURACY OF IT?

Yeah. Right. Because I told him it was a very strange dream . . . That I had never felt anything like that about women before. It had been very odd. I mean that there were feelings added . . . There were feelings about women that I had never experienced. It was a very strange thing for me.

IT WAS AN EXPERIENCE OTHER THAN YOUR OWN?

Yeah. Quite. All that fear and I had never felt that way before. The personality involved was distinctly Esther . . . Esther . . . Esther-esque . . . Whatever.

That was when we began to keep the log. Jim decided we would keep a journal of anything odd that we noted. And boy, I'll *tell* you, in the first couple of days we found more damn things to note than you could shake a stick at.

WHAT WAS THE IMPULSE BEHIND THAT LOG?

Partially Jim's Sherlock Holmes-esque personality. Get it all down, you know? Did you ever see his notes from college? When Jim was in law school he had all his notes typed up by a secretary and bound in volumes. All of his class notes were outlined . . . The whole shot . . . Beautifully done . . . *Typed up* . . . Amazing. His sense of organization if a task arose . . . Like with his research material. I mean, if Jim wanted—by God—to know about the Dead Sea Scrolls he would go up to Manchester to see John Marc Allegro. He would go to look at the scrolls himself . . . He couldn't read them . . . He had no more than a layman's concept of what was involved in taking a scroll apart . . . But nevertheless Jim wanted to be there. He wanted to see it for himself . . . To get to the source. Taking notes was just his way . . .

The psychic phenomena . . . whatever they were . . . There were only two which involved me actually. I think those are spelled out in *The Other Side*. There was one where I knew some pictures were missing from the mirror in Jimmy's bedroom . . . And I knew where they were. They were underneath everything in the bottom of the closet and I just *knew* where they were. They were underneath everything in the bottom of the closet and I knew that. There was a pile of shit in the closet and I said, "They're under that pile of shit." Well. I didn't put them there. But the instant I saw they were missing I knew where they were. That was just too much for me.

Other than the dream and the pictures . . . those were the only two things where I felt that I myself could not explain in some way what was going on. So far as the books being thrown around in their room . . . So far as the cigarette burns . . . So far as the milk turning sour . . . I didn't pay much attention to all that.

HOW ABOUT THE MIRROR SLIDING OFF THE CLOSET SHELF?

I don't recall that at all. But that doesn't mean a damn thing. As I said, we were in a state of altered consciousness. I considered it a sort of group psychosis. I don't use "psychosis" in a pejorative sense. I just recognize it as a place that we were in. These things occur. I'm not sure that psychic communication was going on. But also I'm not sure that poltergeists weren't going on. I'm not so sure that I wasn't out there putting photographs under things. But boy, if I did *that* I have blocked it out as thoroughly as anything in my life. Because I have no memory of it. I remember being shocked the moment I realized I knew where those pictures were.

We didn't know what in hell we were doing. And then at the point they went down to see Ena Twigg . . . Well, that was that. Jim and Maren came back from that with a whole new attitude.

WHICH WAS "COMMUNICATION"?

Yes. Exactly. From that point on they were on that and they were seeking anything that would support it.

IS THIS ANOTHER EXAMPLE OF WHERE JIM'S AND MAREN'S ENERGY WAS FEEDING OFF EACH OTHER?

They did that. But so did I.

I thought they were no longer waiting for something to happen. They were definitely jumping right ahead. They were generators of the experiences . . . Not in any manipulative sense at all . . . Or even consciously. I attribute it more to Jim than to Maren. But Maren reflected Jim in a lot of ways. She was a very, very bright woman. I would also say she had a few screws loose.

DID JIM DEAL AT ALL WITH HIS GRIEF?

He never dealt with it in the sense that I would or in the sense that I have seen other people deal with it.

I call it shock because Jim looked as if he had been hit in the face when I told him about Jimmy. And then in England when I told him about that dream he looked the same way. That's all he registered when Jimmy went other than conventional grief.

I never saw him break down. I never saw him get sick or any of the things a normal person might do.

David Baar's account of the events in Cambridge following Jim Jr.'s death does not depart substantively from the account given by Bishop Pike in *The Other Side*. His recollection of the experience is, of course, the only one possible after the passage of some years since both Bishop Pike and Maren Bergrud are dead. He was also the least emotionally involved either in Jim Jr.'s death or in the strange interactions that ensued from it. He was to have no part in the séances with Mrs. Twigg and later with other mediums. His estimate that the three of them—the bishop, Maren, himself—were, in fact, in what he calls an "altered state of consciousness" is not implausible when all of the circumstances are weighed. That he was himself to some extent caught up in that atmosphere is not surprising since he makes it evident that he found himself at the time in over his head in more ways than one. Fortunately he had a good head to be in over.

There were actually many more so-called poltergeist phenomena during that experience than David has alluded to (or than turn up in Bishop Pike's account, for that matter). When the bishop and Diane came to write *The Other Side*—roughly two years after the events in Cambridge—many of those phenomena (of which Maren had made a complete record) were excluded from the book on the ground that Maren might have fabricated them or on the ground that they were unconvincing as poltergeist phenomena. Most of those phenomena—included or excluded—had to do with objects having been mysteriously (as it seemed) moved from one place to another in the flat. As David points out, once the log was established there was a disposition to look for such phenomena in order to fill out the record. Most of those items could have been moved by Maren. David was obviously little impressed by that aspect of the experience. Nor does the souring of the milk really add up to much. Assuming that poltergeists do exist we can concede them power to move objects about but need we concede them the power to sour fresh milk? Milk does sometimes go sour and there is no reason to think that is not what took place in Cambridge.

Several of the psychic events, however, are more troubling. Maren's burned bangs, for example. (This happened twice, on successive days, according to *The Other Side*, and on the third day an even more macabre scene is described which involved Maren's fingernails.) Were these authentic poltergeist phenomena? One of the exasperating features of such things is that it is really not possible to prove they weren't. Alternatives, however, may be suggested. Much is made in *The Other Side* of the fact that the bangs appeared to have been burned *as though* they had been cut. Burning seems to have been adduced the cause because the ends of her (blond) hair were black where the apparent cut was. But as the coroner of Santa Barbara County has indiscreetly revealed to us Maren's hair was dyed and was dark near the roots. Might not this account for the "burned" look?

> The next morning, much to our discomfort, the same phenomenon repeated itself. Another third of Maren's bangs had strangely disappeared, seemingly burned off in a straight line. We

were extremely puzzled—even disturbed. Yet we had no explanation. After much discussion Maren said—trying to make light of the whole matter—"Well, some people didn't like my hair in bangs anyway, so maybe it's better this way."

Her words jarred, for I recalled Jim having commented to me in San Francisco, after dropping off some work at her place for me one time, that he didn't like Maren's bangs and that he had told her (in his "say it like it is" spirit!) he thought she should cut them off.

Jim Jr. may well have been instrumental in the severing of Maren's bangs, but that doesn't necessarily mean he did it.

David Baar's telling of the incident of the pictures that had gone from the mirror in Jimmy's room and were found, by his instant knowing where to look, under the "pile of shit" in the closet is also troubling. We have pressed him rather hard about this by way of follow-up to the taped interview and he has stuck by his guns. (According to *The Other Side* it was Maren—not David—who first noticed that the pictures were missing from the mirror.) Perhaps the only way—short of poltergeists—to explain David's conviction at the time and long afterward that he did inexplicably know where the pictures were is to take refuge in an altered state of consciousness.

There is also David's deeply affecting weird dream on his first night in Cambridge (antecedent to his even weirder encounter with Maren the next morning). But do we need to posit a poltergeist to account for it? Surely the circumstances were bizarre enough to have engendered the details of that dream as David has related them. (In *The Other Side* the same dream is virtually unrecognizable. Esther has been scrupulously expunged from it and we are left with so much stuff and nothing to hang it on. Esther's "dominance" seems to have been so awesome that Bishop Pike feared to include her in a dream she *had*, in fact, dominated.) David had just completed the long, exhausting journey from California to Cambridge. Memories of a family (including Esther) in deep grief and shock accompanied him. He was plunged into the company of a very distraught woman who obviously had designs upon him. He was consigned to sleep in Jim Jr.'s bed. The intervention of a freaky dream would seem to have been a moral certainty.

There cannot be many nights in the odyssey of a bishop's chaplain when he is going to wake to find a woman not his wife (and nearly old enough to be his mother) seducing him with orange juice and a kiss on the mouth.

Sucking on That Weed

New Year's, 1970
Dear Mister William Stringfellow and Anthony Towne,

I seen in the New York review (of books) where you are authorized and want stuff about Pike. Well, I recall I was personally watching when the bishop was on Mr. Joe Pines TV show and was nervous and smoked a lot and couldnt answer very good when Mr Pine said did that look good with his collar and all—him dressed up like that and sucking on that weed and agin America in Vietnam and like that. So I guess you can use it in your writing but this is all I specially remember on his subject. You don't have to return this original unless you just want to.

pleased to be of service,
Harlan Spore

February 14, 1970
Dear Mr. Spore,

William Stringfellow and I would like to thank you for your letter about Bishop Pike.

You will be glad to know that not long after his appearance on Joe Pine's TV show Bishop Pike gave up smoking and did not smoke again before his death.

Sincerely,
Anthony Towne

February 14, 1970, would have been Bishop Pike's fifty-seventh birthday.

The Memorial Forest near Yatir

THE KEREN KAYEMETH LEISRAEL
(JEWISH NATIONAL FUND)
cordially invites you to attend
the dedication ceremony of the

FOREST
in memory of
BISHOP JAMES A. PIKE
SANTA BARBARA, CALIF., U.S.A.
Sunday, January 25th 1970 at 2:00 P.M.
at YATIR
with the participation of
MRS. DIANE K. PIKE

Mrs. Chambers spent the morning of January 25 in bed in her room in the improbable motel in the oasis of Beersheba. She was too exhausted to go with Ethyl and the others for the ascent to Masada. Two weeks' wandering about the Holy Land had done her in. She had an incipient pleurisy. She was bitterly disappointed not to visit Masada because she knew how much it had meant to James. But she took comfort from the invitation that lay on her bed table. That afternoon she would be driven out into the Negev desert to attend the dedication of the Bishop James A. Pike Memorial Forest.

She would regret it. When her car turned off the highway onto a crude winding wilderness roadbed the driving rain began. At first she would see an occasional primitive Bedouin encampment. She felt sorry for the camels which stood forlornly in the mud. Soon there would be no sign of life at all save for a few frantic birds resembling, sparsely, quail. She could not imagine how a forest could be expected to prosper in such a place. She did not know that the Israelis had diverted water from the Sea of Galilee in order to irrigate vast stretches of the Negev. The soil would not support farming but it would support a forest. The Pike Memorial Forest would consist of some ten thousand Jerusalem pines, but it would be only a fraction of a projected fifteen-million-tree woodland extending all along what had been the southern border of Israel prior to the Six-Day War.

Having been driven perhaps an hour into the wilderness Mrs. Chambers was reunited with Ethyl and Diane and the others. The official party had taken shelter from the winter storm in a woodsmen's watchtower at the edge of the nascent forest. The ceremonies would be abbreviated owing to the weather. Mrs. Chambers was unhappy about that. She liked ceremony. Sipping hot, bitter coffee and slumped into a folding chair, she listened intently as Professor David Flusser, Bishop Pike's good friend and colleague, proclaimed that like the forest they were about to dedicate Jim Pike had had his roots in Israel. Diane Pike responded, tears running down her cheeks, overcome by gratitude that Professor Flusser had made the long drive from Jerusalem to pay tribute to the bishop. Jim would have been very proud.

There was a surcease in the storm and even a shaft of sunlight. It was decided to proceed with the original plan. The party left the cramped watchtower and made its way on foot down into the newly planted pines and gathered around a marker that identified the Bishop Pike Memorial Forest. Mrs. Chambers was driven precariously through the mud and sat gloomily in the front seat staring out at the unlikely scene. Diane planted a tree to the marker's right and Mrs. Larkey, Ethyl, planted another to its left. It seemed certain from her devotion to the task that Ethyl's tree was meant to flourish for a thousand years. Professor Flusser and his wife planted another tree, and then, movingly, Scott Kennedy and two young Israelis, who had been with him when Bishop Pike was found dead in Judea, added three more. The rains had resumed. There was a scramble through the mud back to the watchtower. Mrs. Chambers was sure the new trees would all be washed away.

The ceremonies were concluded by a rabbi who recited the prayer which is customary on the planting of trees in Israel.

> Heavenly Father
> Thou who buildest Zion and Jerusalem
> And hast set up anew the sovereignty of Israel:
> Look down from thy holy habitation, from heaven,
> And bless thy people Israel,
> And the land which thou hast given us
> As thou hast sworn unto our fathers.
> Take pleasure, O Lord, in thy land
> And bestow upon it of thy goodness and grace.
> Give dew for a blessing
> And cause beneficent rains to fall in their season,
> And satiate the mountains of Israel and her valleys,
> And to water thereon every plant and tree,
> And these saplings
> Which we plant before thee this day.
> Make deep their roots and wide their crown,
> That they may blossom forth in grace

Amongst all the trees in Israel,
For good and for beauty.
And strengthen the hands of all our brethren,
Who toil to revive the sacred soil
And make fruitful its wastes.
Bless, O Lord, their might,
And may the work of their hands
Find favor before thee. Amen.

One year later, in January of 1971, Diane and Scott returned to the forest. To their delight nearly all of the pines planted on that somber, rain-swept day had survived and had more than doubled in size. Many more trees had by then been planted and there was already the sense of forest stretching far out of sight to the north and east. There was even a merry melody of songbirds and here and there a wildflower.

On Behalf of "the Jews of Silence"

Conference on The Status of Soviet Jews
16 East 85th Street
New York, N.Y. 10028

Moshe Decter, Executive Secretary   January 30, 1970

The Bishop Pike Foundation
P. O. Box 5146
Santa Barbara, California 93103

Gentlemen:
  I would very much like you to know that Jim Pike's tragic death represents a profound loss not only to the many just causes of which you may already be aware, but not least to the cause of Soviet Jewry, to which he was faithfully and unremittingly dedicated.
  I brought him into this work in 1963, when this Conference was organized. He chaired a session then, and also spoke. And since that time, he was ever ready to do whatever he was called upon to do on behalf of "the Jews of Silence." And he did many things . . .
  With warm wishes for success in your endeavors,
                                        Sincerely yours,
                                        Moshe Decter

Moshe Decter's letter is representative of dozens of letters which emanated from the Jewish community in this country and in Israel following Bishop Pike's death and attesting to an astonishing variety of contributions which he had made to Jewish organizations and concerns. He had been a frequent speaker at dinners undertaken to raise funds for Jewish causes and for the state of Israel. His enthusiasm about Israel was translated into many activities for which it is difficult to see how he found the time. Some of the letters were of a more personal nature and indicative of the remarkable impact he had upon people who were with him only for the briefest of encounters.

American Jewish Congress
15 East 84th Street
New York 28, N.Y.

Office of the Executive Director   December 19, 1969

Dear Mr. Stringfellow:

I am not sure the evening I spent with Bishop Pike some ten years ago would be useful to you; nevertheless, I will tell you my story.

In the winter of 1954 I was giving a course on civil liberties at the New School in New York. The course consisted of a series of guest lectures. I had invited Dean Pike to lecture and had dinner with him and his wife. I believe her name was Esther. We had a leisurely dinner before the lecture was to begin during which Pike told me of his early life.

He noted in passing that when he met a comparable dean in England, I think it was Dean Hewlett, the latter said that he was known in England as the "Red Dean." Pike's retort was that he was known in America as the "Green Dean." I knew that he had worked for a governmental agency in Washington and, indeed, had written a very useful manual on administrative law which was still being published with his name being listed as one of the editors. He explained that this was purely a business arrangement and that he had not looked at the material in years.

I was curious about his conversion from Catholicism to Protestantism. He told me that during World War II he had been assigned to some intelligence work in Washington which gave him many leisure hours during the night. He used these to think deeply about religious matters and decided to convert.

I believe he told me, however, that his marriage with Esther, a

Jewess, was celebrated as a civilian, secular marriage without Catholic, Protestant or Jewish blessing.

That was the only time I met him although he maintained a friendly interest in the American Jewish Congress and we had routine correspondence over the years.

Sincerely,
Will Maslow

Another letter recalled Bishop Pike in a provocative attitude.

Mr. Anthony Towne
Mr. William Stringfellow
Block Island, R.I. 02807

Gentlemen:

You ask for "appropriate" recollections of the late Bishop Pike. This one may be "inappropriate" but serves to illuminate his irrepressible élan.

In 1966 (?) at a Freedom Fund dinner of the NAACP here in Cleveland (at which I was toastmaster and publicly announced for the first time that Carl Stokes would be Mayor of Cleveland) the Bishop told us that we had misunderstood the Free Speech movement at the University of California. He said that the posters the students were carrying simply stood for "Freedom Under Clark Kerr." All he got from that antediluvian audience was an audible gasp—

Very truly,
Rabbi Arthur J. Lelyveld
Fairmont Temple
Cleveland, Ohio

"Not That He Was Any Saint . . . Far from It!"

Darby Betts had been closely associated with Bishop Pike professionally and personally from 1946 until the latter's death. He had served his friend as assistant chaplain at Columbia University and as Canon for Community Relations and Canon Precentor at the Cathedral of St. John the Divine. When Pike left New York to become Bishop of California Betts accepted a call to be dean of the cathedral in Providence, Rhode Island, but the two men were in frequent communication by telephone and letter and occasional visits. The bishop missed his valued confidant, nonetheless, and persuaded him to move to California, where he became executive assistant to the bishop. Toward the middle of Bishop Pike's reign in Grace Cathedral Betts elected to accept another call and became rector of St. Paul's Church, Oakland, California.

On March 3, 1973, Darby Betts, still rector of St. Paul's, consented to an interview with Scott Kennedy. Scott supplied him with a list of themes—in the form of questions—for this book, and Betts used the list as the basis for a fascinating portrait of a man few had known so long and intimately. The tape of that interview is relaxed and informal, occasionally interrupted by laughter. Darby Betts had understood Bishop Pike. He had never made the mistake so many made of taking the great man too seriously. That was something the bishop had respected, and it explains how Betts had been able to serve him so well and so durably.

"What were your impressions at the time of his death, and what did his manner of dying say about his manner of living?" . . . The Episcopal Church General Convention was in progress at Notre Dame when Jim died. I remember being startled that even in dying he was managing to cop the headlines from the rest of the Church. He knocked that General Convention right off the front pages without even attending it. The manner of his death was typical of his manner of living. It was pretty much full steam ahead and not preparing too well. I understand he had read the maps he had with him wrong and that would be typical. He did things on the spur of the moment without really thinking about the consequences. There was also, of course, the unique fact of his dying in the wilderness the way he did. You could draw all kinds of allegories from that and everybody has so I won't repeat it now. The requiems that were celebrated regarding him were a late recognition of his true contribution, even though at the end he had separated himself from the Church pretty much.

"Would you say he had a passion for Jesus?" . . . That was always a part of his life. He was constantly struggling to get to the bottom of things. When there were things he wanted to find out about he went in every direction imaginable to find answers. He didn't care how bizarre or how strange his methods seemed to others. Usually—given time enough—he would refine his ideas and get some scholarship about them. But his eagerness to solve the riddles sometimes hindered others from understanding that eventually he really would put discipline into eagerness. He al-

ways did—*in* time and *given* time. But it was pretty hectic while
he was in the process. This had something to do with his problems with the Church. At base he was really very orthodox but he
had to thrash around an awful lot before coming back to the
same conclusions orthodoxy has. And when he got back to those
conclusions, of course, he would not necessarily express them in
the traditional doctrinal forms.

"What will be his impact on the Church's future?" . . . He
did away with the idea of heresy in the Church as a viable concept. Heretics in the past were—like Jim—people who were investigating, but usually the heretics—unlike Jim—got frozen halfway
to their destination. If a doctrine is true and truly considered it
may well be that to comprehend it we have got to go through a
process of heresy on the way. Certainly that was the case with
Jim. He couldn't take some doctrine and tell himself that it was
true because the Council-of-something-or-other said it was. He
had to investigate the doctrine—take it apart, break it down, and
examine all its parts. *Then*, he would put it all back together
again in his own words and say the doctrine was true because he
had studied it and found it to be true. That seemed to some
other bishops to be heretical—or they said it did—but all he was
doing was investigating doctrine. If he hadn't done it so publicly
and so flamboyantly nobody, of course, would have paid any attention to him. But when all that fuss was over about his so-
called heresy I think the Church as a whole was pretty well convinced that the idea of heresy has no place in the Church today
or in the future of the Church. That was probably his greatest
impact on the Church and its future.

"What were the origins, personal and political, of his conflict
with the church?" . . . The origins of his conflict with—and of
his impact on the future of—the Church were in his pioneering.
And Jim's pioneering was often pretty crass because of his instinctive desire to be heard. For Jim "being heard" meant getting
the attention of the press and the media. Media was to him a
way to evangelism and not a way to personal aggrandizement.
That is what so many people didn't understand about him. His
nose for news was just another way of preaching. His nose for
news was a tool he used to spread *his* idea of the gospel. He
loved the gospel and he loved the Church. Had he lived I think
he would have come back to the Church. He would have come
back to it when he saw it shrinking and sloughing off a lot of
people who were only peripheral anyway. The Church's *need*
would have drawn him back. Its *distress* would have drawn him

back. He couldn't have stayed outside it. The Church was already
on the way down, of course, when he left it. Some people used
him as a way to hurt the Church then in its discomfort. But
when it really began to fall into deep distress I think he would
have come back to it. And I think the Church would have been
glad to have him back.

Jim was politically and personally naïve. This was due primarily
to a basic inability to understand the meanness of people.
MEANNESS?

Yes. Their smallness. Not that he was any saint . . . far from
it! But he was a large-minded person and really had no tools to
gauge smallness. I don't think he did. He was always taken advantage of by littler people, and he rightly got into trouble because
it's a failing not to be able to comprehend the littleness in people. Sometimes you can't understand the greatness in people until
you *have* understood their littleness. It's a constant paradox when
you talk about Jim. I had known him and worked with him and
suffered with him since 1946 when he was first going into seminary. I had been through his agonies at Columbia and the cathedral in New York and then out here. But somehow the paradox
of the man remained impenetrable to me. He just wasn't *aware* of
smallness. Maybe that was it. It was no virtue. It was a blind spot
in him. He would realize later oftentimes that he had not been
aware of somebody's smallness and he would always be puzzled
about it. I think he would have been a greater man without that
blind spot. Strangely, it made him appealing. But it also weakened him. It made him subject to all kinds of attack and abuse.
He never knew how to fight back in such circumstances. It was a
lack in his character—a pleasant lack—but a lack nevertheless.
SOME PEOPLE SPEAK OF HIS INTUITIVE ABILITY TO DISTINGUISH BE-
TWEEN A PERSON AND AN ISSUE.

Yes. He had that. It sprang from a basic Christian belief which
he often talked about. "You hate the sin but not the sinner."
"You differ with the belief but not with the believer." This was
related to his not seeing what he didn't like in people. He simply
overlooked—was unaware of—the meanness in other people. He
really was never for an instant on guard. Now that did make him
very appealing but it also got him into all sorts of trouble.

"What about the burden of celebrity? Was he a natural celebrity?" . . . His celebrity came from his passion to spread the
word in the deepest sense. He had a brilliant mind, a gifted
tongue, a nose for news, and an eagerness to share that combina-

tion. That's what made him a celebrity. Yes. He *was* a natural celebrity. He was like Winston Churchill in that sense. Both men
had a determination to plow ahead, a zest to get to the bottom of
things, and the habit of ignoring the smallness of other people.
Churchill was more aware of himself than Jim was. He was by far
the more astute politician. But the two were alike in being natural celebrities. They appealed not only to mass interest but also to
mass affection. Maybe that's what makes up celebrity—mass interest and mass affection. Jim certainly did interest and excite all
sorts of people in and out of the Church.

"Was his spontaneous quality toward his own celebrity a form
of humility?" . . . His humility was immense. Some people
thought him vain but they were very wrong. His humility was a
detriment to him. Here again there was an inability to see the
way people were using him and taking advantage, really, *of* his humility. Many times it was the last person who had seen him
whose words would come tumbling out in some press conference.
If you wanted to be sure your idea got out you would be the last
person to talk to him before he went on the air.

BOB CROMEY TOLD ME THAT WHEN JIM CAME BACK FROM ENG-
LAND HE HAD PREPARED A STRONG DEFENSE OF THE VIETNAM WAR
AND HE AND BAAR AND A BUNCH OF HIS STAFF GOT TO HIM JUST
BEFORE HE WENT INTO THE PULPIT AND GOT HIM TO TEMPER HIS
VIEWS SOMEWHAT.

This is right. There were many times when I wished I had gotten to him before he said some of the things he did. During my
last months as his executive assistant—Cromey succeeded me—
my whole effort was to keep him out of the press. Howard
Freeman and I conspired to keep him out of the news. His celebrity needed a rest. He needed not to be heard for a while. We did
manage to keep him quiet for about three months—*publicly*. People wanted to know if he was sick. He joined in the effort. He
knew he had to stop talking. I was always fussing at him about
running dry. Nobody can constantly give out and never take time
to replenish. Oh, he would pick things up immediately with his
photographic mind and his photographic ear, you might say. But
he would run out of ideas and start to respin old ones. There
were some lectures that he gave—the law lectures at North-
western, I think—and they were terrible. He was just rehashing old
stuff. Awful! That was when Howard and I decided to build a
wall around him. He agreed. He knew he had to shut up for a
while. The man had a compulsion to answer every question that

was put to him—at *length*. No man can pour out so much without refilling. And as to contemplation and meditation—well, he
never had the time for stuff like that.

"What prevented him from getting across on Christian origins?" . . . I'm not sure. I think he jumped in too far too fast on
Christian origins. He bought Allegro a bit too much. There's no
harm in being way out *provided* you make it clear that you are
proposing an hypothesis and *not* an ultimate conclusion. But Jim
would go way overboard on something and leave people with the
notion that that was his final opinion on the matter. It very seldom *was*, but the way he came on about things made it seem so.
The last time I saw him—at a motel near the airport here—he
spent more than an hour agonizing with me about his need to
refine and to dig deeper concerning Christian origins. He was really overwhelmed by all the new discoveries and never got time to
come to a balanced view about them. Had he had time to do
this—as we are all doing now in regard to the Dead Sea Scrolls—
I'm sure he would have struck a balance eventually.

"How do you relate his accessibility—pastoral and otherwise—
to his vulnerability?" . . . He was terribly vulnerable. He had no
care for the proper way to be interviewed. He had no strategy
about this. He was so full of ideas that he would just let them
rush out at random. He would put things all out of context in his
enthusiasm to share whatever happened to come bubbling to the
surface. People took advantage of this—especially the press and
the media people. He was never on guard and that made him vulnerable. Now as to his pastoring the same vulnerability served
him better. He was a great pastor. His contributions to pastoralia
were much greater than his contributions to theology. I wish he
had written more pastoral books and fewer on theology. The procession of clergy and others through his office day after day with
every sort of problem imaginable was simply astonishing. He was
not professional in his pastoring. That may be why he was
so good at it. That's where his vulnerability came in. He would
get personally involved in every problem he handled. A professional pastor would avoid that like the plague. Not Jim. That
deep involvement in pastoral situations was *very* destructive to
him, but it was incredibly helpful to most of those who sought
him out.

"Why was his ambition to be a scholar never fulfilled?" . . .
He never found time to think anything through deeply enough.
He would get some wonderful idea and he would ride it hard.

Then another wonderful idea would hit him and he would be off after that. A real scholar is one who stays with one idea for a very long time—maybe a lifetime. Jim never stayed with anything long. His mind was too vulnerable to whatever new idea came along. I would make him mad by saying he was a great apologist but he was no scholar. This was true. He could put into words— very colorful words, usually—exciting ideas he had photographically and immediately apprehended. But when it came to digging down he just wasn't that kind. He had so many ideas and he would get caught up—*ground* up—in them, and sometimes he ended up on the side he started out fighting.

He had no discipline about him. He was too effervescent. He should never have been a bishop. My wife and I fought that for all we were worth. His great podium was the Cathedral of St. John the Divine. He should never have left it. He didn't have to worry there about money or power. He had a perfect spot to be heard and to be seen. He used it magnificently. I *begged* him not to accept California.

WHY DID HE?

It's a strange thing in the Episcopal Church that practically all the clergy share. I'm now close enough to retirement to be free of it, but I wasn't when I was a little younger. Every clergyman feels that if he isn't a bishop he hasn't *really* made it. Yet nearly every bishop comes to feel that the office and the honor aren't worth the price. Jim didn't think they were either after a while. But at that time he felt that to be bishop would increase his power to tell what he had to tell. It didn't. It diminished his power to be heard. The problem was he could not be himself—speak his mind —and not hurt his diocese. And that's the real reason he eventually gave it up. He saw that he was wrecking the diocese.

He simply could not be anybody except Jim Pike. You cannot be a bishop *and* a prophet. That is even truer if you are without any strategy. He had no strategy whatever. It was just run on from this to that to whatever came along. The office of bishop is as necessary as the office of prophet but the two jobs take different men. They cannot be combined. You cannot be a basic critic of the Church and a basic defender of the Church. No one man can do that. And if you *are* a bishop any criticism you may have of the Church has got to be subordinated to your obligation to defend the Church. Jim couldn't do that. His message was basically prophetic. There is nothing wrong with that, of course. But he just should not have been a bishop. I don't mean to say he didn't do some great things as a bishop. He did. He was very effective sometimes in the House of Bishops.

HOW MUCH DO YOU THINK HIS DECISION TO MOVE TO SAN FRANCISCO WAS AFFECTED BY HIS FAMILY SITUATION?

Well. At heart he was a Californian. He had grown up with the idea that San Francisco was it. The idea of being bishop there had an overwhelming fascination for him. There were other things, I suppose. But he was obsessed with the idea of being Bishop of California. Nothing in heaven or hell could have stopped him. Maybe there was nothing wrong with that but it destroyed him. His prophetic voice was too much for this diocese. The people were hurt. They felt he had betrayed them. He was too frank and he was too hard on them. That was all very necessary but he shouldn't have done it here. He should have stayed at St. John the Divine. I used to argue with him about it even after he became bishop. Sometimes I could get him to tone down his remarks but they didn't stay down long. Another cause would come along and "slam-bang" he would be off on that. The price he paid for that was the end of his official ministry.

"We he a popularizer?" . . . Yes. That's what I mean by an apologist. And it was his great gift. Jim himself never held that to be a popularizer was the whole story. It was his longing to be a scholar that showed he was never satisfied with being a popularizer. But he couldn't help it. He put things into the vernacular, *truly*. He had a clear mind and he could organize it. He had a sense for the dramatic and he could dramatize things. He could put the Christian religion in story form so that almost anybody could understand it. Anybody could understand him provided he talked slowly enough—which often was not the case.

"What frustrated his ambition to be a scholar?" . . . He couldn't stay with any idea long enough. And we live in an age when ideas are multitudinous. A scholar is one who often cloisters himself from the temptation of different ideas so that he can focus on one idea. Jim was too much in the world to do that. A new idea would come along and "bang" there he was. He had no time for scholarship, really. Oh, he used scholarly phrases and he did take that sabbatical. I had a lot to do with making him take that sabbatical. I'm not sure I should have, looking back, but I did.

"Did his generosity and vulnerability when it came to pastoral concerns precipitate crises in his own household or did his personal problems qualify his sensitivity to the problems of others?" . . . I was so close to both Esther and Jim that my response to that has to be that the whole thing was a tragedy. It was a tragedy that could not have been avoided given the two people. He loved his family very much but the situation was hopeless. It couldn't be avoided. He sacrificed his family to his job. I worked all the time to try to save their marriage. I know Diane wouldn't mind my saying so, but I was so long related to them that I still always think of Esther as his wife. I know how much Diane helped Jim and how much she meant to him and he to her. She was very *much* his wife. But Esther was Jim's wife and still is in my mind. Esther's strengths and Jim's strengths were destructively oriented to one another. It was something neither of them could save and both of them wanted to. It was a tragedy.

"Did his personal problems qualify his sensitivity to the problems of others?" . . . Yes. Yes they did. In spite of his immense pastoral gifts he moved so fast he would often miss some of the finer points. He was always gravely stricken when he would realize he had done that. He would give bad advice sometimes because he hadn't been paying close attention. Then later he would think back on it and recognize what he had done and be horrified. Often it would be too late to correct the mistake. His extraordinary ability to evaluate people didn't keep up with his haste to talk to them about themselves. He talked so much he seldom heard. What he knew of a person he got mostly from his very unusual gift for instant divination. He didn't get much from what they told him because he didn't listen. That was his one pastoral weakness. He wouldn't listen. His clergy knew that, most of them. So they fought to be heard and *were* heard. But you had to *fight* to be heard with Jim. Not that he wanted to blot people out but his mind raced so fast even his tongue couldn't keep up with it. I guess you could say that many of his pastoral successes—and they were myriad—happened because people *forced* him to help, fought for it.

I remember when the Archbishop of Canterbury visited the diocese. It wasn't Ramsey but the one before him—Fisher, I think. Jim had him for dinner one night and as usual was talking lickety-split at the table. The archbishop interrupted him. "Shut up," he said. "*Will* you be *quiet.*" Jim was abashed. He was routed and agonized and almost weeping to realize that he had dominated the conversation. He didn't mean to do it. He simply couldn't help it. And the same thing happened the next morning in Jim's office. He was talking at ninety miles an hour and the archbishop suddenly began beating him on the knee. *"Can't* you be *quiet?"* Jim's response was a deep *"Ouch!"* Two minutes later he was off on another monologue. Not even someone as imposing as the Archbishop of Canterbury could reduce him to silence.

"What about his care for enemies?" . . . It was immense. This was largely because he seldom saw the enmity. He forgave people too soon. Forgiveness is absolutely necessary but only after the offender has reached the point where he can receive it. He wasted his forgiveness quite often. He never gave people time. Maybe his greatest enemy *was* time. He barely recognized its existence.

HIS CHRONOLOGY WAS OUT OF JOINT WITH EVERYBODY ELSE'S?

Right. He was a genius. A genius is the next thing to a nut. He was usually on the edge of being out of communication with whomever he happened to be with. He was very much *in communication* in the mass but if you wanted to be in communication with him *personally* that was pretty much up to you. You had to fight for his attention—bang him on the knee or something. Those who really knew and loved him took that responsibility upon themselves. It was the only way to get to him and therefore the only way for him to get to you.

"His alcoholism and his problems with women?" . . . He overcame his alcoholism. His problems with women were high speed just like everything else. He was a very whole person. Everything he did was at high speed—intense, absorbing, dominating—and his way with women was that way, too. He was a great lover of women. He never used women just to use them, so far as I know, but sometimes his absorption, while genuine, was short. He had much to be forgiven for there and I'm sure he has been forgiven by most. This was used against him.

WAS IT EVER BROUGHT OUT PUBLICLY?

No, not publicly, but it might have been better if it had been. It was a constant whisper in the diocese, in the House of Bishops, and everywhere he went. You can't combat whispers. And he couldn't have combated it anyway. As with other things he had no discipline when it came to women either. He didn't *have* to be undisciplined. That was proved when he *did* overcome his alcoholism and later when he gave up smoking. But when he was being undisciplined he was intensely so. I used to hide his bottles from him. He would hide them in his office in the most extraordinary places. I would find them and hide them in other places. He had sunk that low in his drinking. But when he finally did see that alcohol was preventing him from doing his work and was interfering with his ability to think clearly he called a halt to it. So he *could* be disciplined if he saw that he had to be in order to pursue his first love, which was the proclamation of the gospel as he understood it. The truth is that in Jim's life everything in the end was subservient to his vocation. Perhaps he should have been celibate. He sacrificed everything to his work—his family, his friends, his own welfare, and even in the long run his tastes for alcohol and tobacco and women. But he *had* to experience everything. That in itself would have ruled out celibacy. It would be difficult to imagine a celibate Jim Pike.

"Rumors of madness?" . . . Some people thought his interest in extrasensory perception and so on indicated madness. I didn't think it was madness. It was another example of his total absorption in whatever subject came along. His experiences with psychic phenomena most people thought strange and that strangeness was sometimes interpreted as a sign of madness. I didn't see it that way. He told me on more than one occasion that he was not through investigating that subject. He was by no means satisfied that he had gone into it thoroughly enough that he could be sure his communication with his son had been real.

One day he came into his office in the cathedral shaken. His face was the color of putty. It was during his great battle with the tongue-speaking people. He told me he had waked up in the night reciting a psalm in a language he didn't understand. "My God," he said, "I've been speaking in tongues!" He had immediately put the psalm onto a tape. He and I together were able to find it. It was in archaic Latin. I forget which psalm it was and unfortunately he destroyed the tape lest it be misused. But it was definitely in archaic Latin, which he had never studied. Well, we were able to figure out what had happened. Remember that Jim had a photographic memory. We found in his study a book of psalms in archaic Latin and the psalm he had recited—which related to some stress he was under at the time—was in that book. Sometime or another he had been looking at that book and had read through that psalm. He had no recollection of doing it but he agreed that he must have. And his mind picked that psalm out of his memory—the mind is the greatest of all computers—and played it back for him. Now that incident took place well before he got involved with psychic phenomena. Maybe later he would have interpreted the experience differently. I don't know.

Jim was such a rational man that he would go overboard to deny the miraculous. He said to me many times, "Everything that is miraculous God understands, and we who are created in his image have the potential of understanding it." That's true, of course, but the trouble is when you put it that way you tend to erase for yourself the possibility of making use of what is *seemingly* miraculous. Had he told the tongue-speakers of his archaic Latin psalm they would have broken out in hymns of joy. But he didn't. He said, "There's an answer to this and *I'm* going to find it." And he did. It took him several months but eventually he did find the answer. You see, I think he was fighting tongue-speaking—or the *abuse* of tongue-speaking—so hard that this experience came along to tempt him. God was playing a trick on him —or his mind was. God develops us sometimes, it seems to me, by having a little fun at our expense.

"Rumors of madness?" . . . Well, when is a genius *not* mad? The two are so close together and there is a fluctuation. A mind like his up against so many lesser minds strikes out now and then in frustration and in hysterics, you might say. He would try so hard sometimes to get something across that what he was saying didn't make sense. That might be a form of speaking in tongues. Maybe his madness was more a matter of speaking in tongues, though *he* would never have admitted to *either*, of course.

Jim Pike was a gift of God to the Church. I have to add that because he was so undisciplined he somewhat wasted that gift. But it was a great gift nevertheless. It could have been much more. Humanity either wastes or perverts most of its gifts and he was no exception to that.

IS THERE AN ANECDOTE ABOUT JIM THAT YOU SHARED THAT CAPTURES HIS PERSONALITY ESPECIALLY WELL?

Just after the Blake-Pike proposals here in the cathedral—back in the early sixties—he had to go to New York to be on the radio about the proposals. I went with him. Our plane couldn't land in New York because of a snowstorm and we ended up in Boston. The last night train down to New York—the Owl—had already left and the airline put us on a very uncomfortable bus. We wandered all over Massachusetts and Connecticut in the damn thing. It was bitterly cold. Jim had a half-pint flask of Bourbon with him. He usually did in those days. He passed that around but it didn't help much. He got colder and colder. Finally I got out my pajamas and he put those on over his clothes and under his overcoat. The bus eventually stalled near Norwalk.

We sat there stalled until Jim noticed we were alongside the New Haven railroad line. "Let me out!" he shouted. "You're mad," the bus driver said. Jim dashed up front, tore his clothes

open exposing his purple vest, and began waving his pectoral
cross. The driver—a good Roman Catholic, no doubt—opened
the door and let him out. He raced down an embankment onto
the railroad tracks. A train soon came along and he flagged it
down. He stood there in the *middle* of the tracks waving that
pectoral cross. There was a screeching of brakes and a whistle
blowing frantically and sand and snow flying all over. But the
train *did* stop and we all got off the bus and boarded the train.
Jim was delighted that he was on time for the radio broadcast. I
don't suppose I will ever forget that.

The Psychic World of Hans Holzer

The exploitation of Bishop Pike by smallness and meanness did
not terminate with his death. He had no more than stretched out
in his grave hard by the Mediterranean Sea than Crown Publishers of New York saw fit to publish (1970) *The Psychic World
of Bishop Pike* by Hans Holzer, who was identified on the jacket
as "the country's most notable parapsychologist." The book is
truly without redeeming social value. Unfortunately, Bishop Pike
was partially responsible for this posthumous insult. Holzer, who
seems to have made a career out of flitting from poltergeist to poltergeist, turned up on the bishop's doorstep one day with the proposal that he make a documentary film about him. Was he told
to go fly a kite? No. He was warmly received and in no time the
bishop was a captive of Holzer's tape recorder.

Hans Holzer had authored over the years sixteen books on extrasensory perception and psychic subjects. Some of the titles will
convey the wide range of his interests: *ESP and You, Ghost
Hunter, The Truth About Witchcraft, Psychic Photography:
Threshold of a New Science?* and so on. He has lectured in
universities and appeared on television. That seems to be the sum
and substance of his professional accomplishments. Dr. Ian
Stevenson, Carlson Professor of Psychiatry in the University of
Virginia School of Medicine, who may *be* "the country's most notable parapsychologist," does not hold Holzer in high regard.

> No, you did not really need to ask my opinion about Hans
> Holzer. His reputation among scientifically trained parapsychol-
> ogists could not be lower. What we particularly complain about
> in Holzer is not that he is a bad journalist, but that he pretends

to be a scientific parapsychologist, which he is not. I think I once glanced briefly at Holzer's book *The Psychic World of Bishop Pike,* and put it down quickly. Is it the book in which he made some near libelous statements about Diane Pike? I think it may be. Are you quite sure that Jim Pike allowed Holzer to tape an interview with him?

I suppose you have checked this out with Diane Pike, who might know. It seems probable also that in the earlier periods of his interest in mediumship, Jim came into contact with a good many persons working in and around parapsychology and accepted them at face value before he knew better.

Holzer's talent for invention is considerable but he did not invent his conversation with Bishop Pike. That conversation is reproduced in his book verbatim. It occupies several pages. Another several pages are given over to a conversation with Canon West of the Cathedral of St. John the Divine. Bishop Pike had personally written Canon West authorizing the interview. Those two conversations and Holzer's interviews with Ena Twigg and George Daisley, mediums Bishop Pike had consulted, are the fundaments of reality in an otherwise surreal document. Big chunks of the book have to do with meandering gibberish coughed up by female mediums Holzer corralled into the Pike situation.

One of these females is Betty Dye. She is said to be a "non-professional medium . . . who makes her home in the Deep South." According to Holzer, Mrs. Dye had forecast to him several months before it happened (and in "great detail") the murder of Martin Luther King, Jr. He says he tried to alert the nation to the impending tragedy in a radio address but to no avail. During the fall of 1969—just after Bishop Pike's death—Betty Dye supplied Holzer with a stream of messages concerning the bishop. Some of them would require an expert in coded language to decipher.

> Received this message: "Cabana anaac." Later, "Pike alfirsha in cabana."

That striking bit of news "came through" on December 16, 1969. (Holzer is meticulous about dates, which may be the basis for his publisher's assertion that he is "a scientifically trained investigator.") On December 18 Betty Dye (who is apparently sometimes meticulous herself) speculated that "anaac" in her December 16 message might mean "anak." She explained that "anak . . . is the meaning given to giants in Numbers 13:33." Holzer seemed pleased to have *that* mystery cleared up.

On October 31, 1969, less obfuscated, Betty Dye had reported Bishop Pike's murder. She *saw* it. He had been struck on the head with a weapon sixteen to eighteen inches in length and one and a half to two inches in diameter. The blow caused some difficulty in his right eye.

> There were *two men and one woman* indicated in this episode, Pike's elimination. One of these three persons owns a small dog. It was a white or light blond colored dog, long curly ears that hung downward. It had a small, dainty, almost childlike quality to its face. It was looking down at the three people—the two men and the woman—so I was not able to determine which one of them was its master.

Betty Dye would make a superb witness at a murder trial. Her recollection of detail is as awesome as it is gruesome. Even so, Hans Holzer, "scientifically trained investigator," knows better than to propound a murder based upon the testimony of only one witness, however persuasive.

On December 5, 1969, Holzer's "good friend" Sybil Leek, a semi-celebrated "sensitive," having come to New York from her Florida home, stretched herself out on a couch in the investigator's office and filled him in on *her* news of the episcopal murder. Two days after Bishop Pike disappeared in the desert she had given Holzer a statement—in "the presence of Gail Benedict, a public relations director and friend of both Sybil Leek and myself" (witnesses upon witnesses)—and Holzer had carefully preserved it.

> The Bishop is still alive and in the hands of Bedouins, and being held for political reasons. He will show up. Two people are involved in his disappearance. They are dark people in loose garments which are tan colored. Not everything has been revealed about this.

On Holzer's couch on December 5 she rambled on, according to his book, for some time without being very precise about anything. The investigator found himself obliged to pin her down.

> "Is it your intuitive feeling that there was foul play?"
> "Yes. Definitely."

"Is it your feeling that there was just one person involved, or more than one person?"

"Intuitively, I feel there are three people. Logically I feel there's only one, but I no longer try to bring logic into this. Everything I'm saying to you is intuitive, because I am deliberately not thinking about this."

"The three people—are they men or women?"

"One woman and two men."

"Who are the two men? What background?"

"The background was not the same race as the Bishop."

Murder will out. Now we have—thanks to our intrepid investigator—two material (or possibly *immaterial*) witnesses to the elimination of Bishop Pike. There were minor discrepancies in testimony. Sybil Leek didn't mention the dainty-faced dog. Betty Dye didn't mention the tan-colored loose garments. Robert Browning and others have pointed out for us that no two witnesses to a crime will have *identical* recollections about it. Dye and Leek did agree where it counted. A foul deed had been done by two men and one woman.

Holzer was not finished. He wanted a motive. To that end he led Sybil Leek through inconclusive speculations. She toyed with the possibility of "an *apparently* motiveless murder" but rejected that and settled for something political. She suggested that Bishop Pike himself would provide the motive once he got settled down on the "Other Side." The two men were presumably Arabs. But who was that woman? Holzer leaves us with the fantastic inference that it must have been Diane Pike. Was she a *witting* accomplice to the murder? That is the one loose end Holzer is content to leave dangling.

Sybil Leek, who sometimes identifies herself as a witch, also had a bit of prognosticatory gossip about Mrs. Pike.

"What will happen with Mrs. Pike?" I asked now.

"I feel that Mrs. Pike will marry soon, someone she's known for a long time. I feel that within eighteen months she will announce marriage."

Would you believe it? Betty Dye had made a similar (though more guarded) prediction.

On November 14, Betty again wrote to me. She said that her communicator had mentioned something about his teeth, which she didn't understand; also that he wanted to reaffirm the information about an injection he was given. Finally, Betty wrote that he said, "Before the snow falls Mrs. P. is to remarry." To which Betty herself added, "The trouble is I am not sure *which* snow of which year."

Diane Pike has not remarried. She lives in Southern California and may have to wait some time for that imprecise snowfall. In fairness to the tandem Dye and Leek, however, be it noted that neither used a Christian name in forecasting remarriage for "Mrs. Pike." *Esther* Pike—who lives in San Francisco, where snow *has* occasionally fallen—*has* remarried. Hans Holzer is not the nation's *only* scientifically trained investigator.

The few pages of Holzer's book which are given over to verbatim excerpts from taped conversations with Bishop Pike and Canon West are of some interest. Bishop Pike *sounds* like Bishop Pike. Canon West *sounds* like Canon West. Most of what they say they have said elsewhere and the basic facts are indisputable. Satisfied, therefore, that in those pages of his book Holzer is reliable, we pay him the tribute of adverting to his version of the curious goings-on at Christ Church, Poughkeepsie, and later in the Cathedral of St. John the Divine, New York City. Holzer's conversation with Bishop Pike took place early in April of 1968 and the conversation with Canon West not long afterward.

James Pike's predecessor as Rector of Christ Church, Poughkeepsie, had been Alexander Griswold Cummins, who had served the place forty-six years. Dr. Cummins had been a leader of Low Churchmanship in the Episcopal Church and editor for many years of a publication called *Protestant Episcopal Chronicle*, which espoused Low Church views. Pike and other moderate and High Church types had the habit of referring to Cummins's journal as "Chronic-hell." Cummins had died shortly after Pike was called to succeed him.

> "He moved out of the rectory into a fabulous house he had bought with private means. And he died of a heart attack . . . in anger."
>
> "When did he die?"
>
> "Soon after. People were blaming the Vestry for his death. A terrible feeling came over the place. When I moved into the rectory, which was in late May, having commuted up there from March until May, several things happened, and these are the

things that I'm leading up to. First of all, he had some books he'd never taken from the third-floor attic. And we would hear these books being dragged around—we thought."

"You heard the noise yourself?" I interrupted.

"Yes, all the way to the first floor, it was so noisy. If we'd go to the second floor we'd hear it even more."

"Did you check whether there was anyone up there?"

"There appeared to be no one. We saw nothing."

"Was this during the day or at night?"

"This would seem to be in the evening."

"Can you describe the noises?"

"A dragging sound, a shuffle, rather like boxes of books being dragged. But we could see nobody, and to show you how uninvolved in this kind of thing I was, I never did set a watch, or take a census, of all the boxes up there. We didn't know what we were going to do with these books. But there were no dusty floors that you could see a trace in, unfortunately. I didn't pay too much attention; I didn't bother very much."

The mystery of the dragged books was succeeded by a light that would be switched on and off although there was no one near it. There seemed no way to account for it. But again Pike did not pay much attention. He was busy adding High Church practices to the parish worship. He was determined to put candles on the altar. He made a special trip to New York City to buy two brass candleholders, and hoping to mollify the anti-candle faction in the parish, had them inscribed with a verse from the book of Revelation, referring to heaven, "They need no candle." Delighted with himself, he arrived back in Poughkeepsie late on Advent Sunday night and went at once to the church very anxious to see how the candles would look on the altar.

"I let myself into the church, and underneath the stained glass window was the very plain altar which my predecessor had never allowed to have anything on except empty vases and a cross, nothing else. I put the candles there and lit them. Then I moved back to see what this was going to look like. Suddenly a wind was blasting at them, spattering wax in all directions on either side, spattering, blowing, *trying to blow them out!* I put it anthropomorphically, or psychically, when I say 'trying to blow them out.' All I know is that the effect was of an *attempt* to stop me."

"Was it a cold wind?" I asked, recognizing the symptoms.

"Yes, as a matter of fact it was."

"Was it moist in any way?"

"That I cannot say. But there was this wind, I could feel it—so, I blew them out. Later, to prevent repetition, I ordered these little glass things you put on top that are meant to protect against drafts."

"What did you think it meant?" I asked.

"What it meant I don't know, but it impressed me. I must say, subjectively and intuitively, I was quite aware that *I was defying the old gent.* I had a feeling that he was trying to blow out the candles. I sort of felt kind of funny—I went back to the rectory and said to myself, 'Ha, he did his best.' "

Alexander Cummins failed to prevent his successor from introducing candles and other High Church customs in Christ Church, Poughkeepsie, but it is obvious that his efforts had their impact and that some twenty years later Bishop Pike was still disturbed and puzzled about it. He did not, however, profess to understand what the experience had meant. He reported it because it was vivid in his recollection and seemed pertinent in the context of his encounters with psychic phenomena after Jim Jr.'s death. Dr. Cummins made—or may have made—one last attempt to curb the waywardness of the upstart who seemed to mock a lifetime of austere churchmanship.

Pike had been working late in his rectory one night when a call came requesting that he visit someone dying in a nearby old folks' home. He decided it would be prudent to take with him a reserved sacrament in the event a service of communion and unction seemed appropriate. Dr. Cummins had been dead set against reserving the sacrament for any reason whatever. Pike went to the sacristy and equipped himself with a stole and the reserved sacrament.

"I started back, and I stepped out into this narrow hall. I'm going out into this, and *here is this bat flying at me!* I closed the door quickly, and put the things down, and then I opened the door, and this bat is going back and forth in this narrow space, you know this low-slung place. I had never seen bats there before. I thought, I can't fool around in here, there's no time. But there's no other way out."

"What did you do?" I asked with a measure of doubt in my voice.

"I figured, I can't be stalled by a bat while there's somebody dying, so I went low, and the bat goes down low, too. I don't like bats. I've only seen three or four in my life. I said I'll call over to Dick Corney. I knew one could get at them with a tennis racket. I was going to call Dick Corney and say 'Bring my tennis racket'—but the phone was dead! It had never done that before, and never afterward."

"How did the bat disappear?" I asked the Bishop.

"I don't know," he explained. "I went back into the sacristy and got a brass alms basin. Now there is a hymn called 'St. Patrick's Breastplate,' which has in it the charm used by the ancient Celtic church when they were in dangerous places or walking through woods. 'Christ within me,/ Christ above me,/ Christ around me,/ Christ beneath me,/ Christ . . .' You're protecting yourself against the demons and bogeys, that's what it was. I'm not very superstitious, but I knew about that, it's one of my favorite hymns, so I took this alms basin and I started reciting the charm. I took the basin to protect my hair, and dashed out quickly, went out the back way, closed the door, and went on down."

Dr. Cummins was a persistent rascal but no match for James Pike and his Celtic charm. The next morning Pike had the church searched but no trace of the bat was found, dead or alive. It was the only bat he ever saw in the church and inquiry turned up no one who had ever seen a bat there before. Holzer tried to suggest that the bat had *dissolved*, but the bishop wasn't biting, probably because he didn't know at the time that *dissolve* is a technical term in the psychic world of Hans Holzer employed to indicate that something has vanished, so to speak, into thin air. We prefer to think that Dr. Cummins, bemused by the inspired naïveté of the novice rector with his brass alms basin and "St. Patrick's Breastplate," simply gave up and told the bat to get the "chronichell" out of Christ Church, Poughkeepsie, and go haunt somebody else's sacristy.

Be that as it may, the putative interventions of Alexander Cummins did conclude with a beguiling aftermath to the episode of the bat.

"A friend, Kim Myers, who later succeeded me as Bishop of California, had a pug dog, and he had heard that dogs are sometimes more sensitive to spirits than people.

"So he said, 'I'll bring the dog. I'll be glad of a chance of bringing him.' So up came the dog. Paul Moore, my seminary assistant, came with his wife, Jennie, and we all went out at night, with the dog, into this cloister."*

"Did you have some suspicions already that there was something peculiar?" I interjected.

Dr. Pike nodded and continued. "Well, we came out, it was in the dark, and now we're going along with the dog, and we're chatting; we're not even expecting anything particular, walking along. All of a sudden this dog stiffened, with his tail absolutely vertical to his back—and he stopped cold, wouldn't walk any further."

"Where?" I asked.

"In the cloister, the colonnade of the cloister."

"And then what?"

"Well, this wasn't telling us anything, so we started off. Finally, reluctantly the dog came along with us, and we went inside. We go into this corridor here, and the *same thing happens again.* The dog stiffens. We go into the church. It was dark. I turned on one light. We go right out into the center aisle and, all of a sudden, the same thing: *the dog was literally trembling.*"

There was to be one more psychic event in James Pike's life and then for many years nothing in that realm until the bizarre events in the flat in Cambridge after Jim Jr.'s death. That one further event—much less compelling than the Poughkeepsie phenomena—took place in the Cathedral of St. John the Divine, New York City, in 1953 not long after Pike was appointed its dean. Dean Pike and his family lived on the third floor of a diocesan house in an apartment that had been fixed up for them. The fourth floor was converted into a hostel—it had originally been servants quarters—and it had a small library on it that the dean sometimes used at night when he had work to do and didn't want to disturb the family.

"You lived on the third floor, and the library was on the fourth floor?" I asked, to make sure of my bearings.

"Yes," the Bishop replied. "I was writing a book at that time with Howard Johnson, pulling together more carefully what became dialogue sermons for three. It was a rather good little book, *The Man in the Middle.* We worked up there late evenings."

* In May of 1972 Paul Moore would become Episcopal Bishop of New York.

"It was late at night?" I interrupted.

"Yes. And we were working hard. Now, over at the entrance to this room, *we kept hearing very sharp tappings*. Tap-tap-tap-tap-tap."

"Under your feet?"

"Yes. Tap-tap-tap-tap-tap, on the floor."

"What was above you?"

"The roof."

"What happened next?"

"Ever since moving there, we heard footfalls and shuffles on the stairs, quite frequently. Both above in that room and around there, and on the staircase."

"Both of you?"

"No, Howard Johnson as a canon lived over in that other building. My family and I heard this, frequently. And I checked; there was never anybody there. Finally, I spoke with Edward M. West, the senior canon. 'Oh, that,' he said, 'don't let it bother you, Jim. *That's Bishop Greer.*' I said, 'What do you mean, Bishop Greer?' 'Well, he's been around for a long time, ever since I've been here. He had been given a very expensive, bejeweled pectoral cross by Trinity Parish. It was lost up there *somewhere*, and he's still looking for it.'"

"How was it lost?" I asked, fascinated by the account.

"That's the problem—nobody knows, and Bishop Greer apparently doesn't know: *that's why he's up there.*"

"He lost the cross while he was alive?"

"Yes."

"And how long ago did he die?"

"Well, I think he had preceded Bishop Manning, and perhaps older than that. He's in the records."

"This is quite a while back?"

"Yes. There were oil paintings of him around. But Canon West, who took such things seriously, was very casual about the whole thing. I got quite interested in the pectoral cross. I thought it would be very nice to find it. I looked all around; there is lots of paneling and I tried to move the paneling without success.

"However, I learned, in talking to the rector of Trinity Church, Dr. John Hughes,* that that cross was known and that it had been lost. Title of it still was in Trinity Church, if it were ever found.

---

* Holzer mistranscribed this tape. John *Heuss* was rector of Trinity Church at that time.

"After that I didn't hear the noise for a while, and I thought there was nothing to be gained in our finding it. But soon after we were working upstairs one night, this tapping started up again. It was a nuisance. I would go over there and, say, I'm standing over it and it's going on. I ran downstairs and found that none of the children was bumping a broom or anything like that below."

"You checked right away?"

"Yes, and then I returned upstairs. The tapping continued. Irritated, I went over there, stamped my foot, and said, 'For God's sake, *stop it!*' That stopped him."

"You never heard it again?"

"Never heard it again. And I really feel kind of bad, if it were *he*. Kind of mean, you know? There wasn't any harm in it. It was almost an *exorcistic* remark, though; I used the name of God, and no one could say I wasn't *reverent*, although I'm not sure that was the mood I was in. I said, 'For God's sake, stop it.' "

Holzer, diligent investigator that he is, cross-checked this tale with Canon West, who confirmed the substance of it. He was careful to point out, however, that *he* had never heard the strange tappings. This he accounted for by acknowledging that he had never had occasion to be on the upper floors of that building at night. He also added some interesting information. During the reign of Bishop Manning the bishop and his wife had occupied the rooms later used by Dean Pike and his family. Mrs. Manning often heard Bishop Greer on the staircase to the fourth floor. Canon West recalled that she would often speak of "the Bishop" and it would turn out she meant Bishop Greer and not her husband. Bishop Greer's perambulations in search of the lost cross were, in other words, one of the legendary capers of the cathedral.

"Has the crucifix ever been recovered?" I asked, after the Canon had spoken.

"The crucifix," he replied gravely, "as a matter of fact, has never been recovered. There is still the record of it and the reception of it and all that, but we simply don't know where it is."

"Is there anything in the papers of Bishop Greer to indicate that he might have put the crucifix in some safe place?"

"Bishop Greer actually left no record about it apart from acknowledging the receipt of the crucifix as a gift, but it was my terribly able and distinguished predecessor, Canon Jones, who left a note to the effect that the Bishop had taken it away from the cathedral for some quite adequate reason."

"Bishop Pike was Dean of St. John's and worked in the library upstairs. Did you know the Bishop at the time?"

"I've known Bishop Pike, for years and years. I knew him very well when he was rector in Poughkeepsie, chaplain of Columbia University and of course here as dean of the Cathedral. It was then that I remembered again the things that had gone on in Mrs. Manning's day, because Dean Pike spoke about this with some sort of slight sense of amusement as one more disturbing fact in a world full of disturbing facts."

By the middle of December 1969, three months after Bishop Pike's death, Hans Holzer had most of *his* disturbing facts pulled together. *The Psychic World of Bishop Pike* was simmering away on the front burner. But somehow it lacked an essential ingredient. It needed a communication from the "Other Side." So Holzer made his way—on December 15—to the apartment of Ethel Johnson Meyers on the West Side of New York. Ethel Meyers was another in Holzer's stable of female mediums. She seems to have been his favorite. She had already weaved in and out of his book performing a bewildering array of paranormal chores. Only the choicest chore of all remained for her. And she did not disappoint.

Holzer handed Meyers a letter Pike had written to him some time back—and which Holzer had carefully enclosed in a "neutral" envelope—and the medium barely had time to mutter, "There are three Jameses," when she fell into deep trance, her face contorted into a man's face resembling Bishop Pike's, and she began to deliver, in the late bishop's inimitable inflections, *his* message from the "Other Side." Not surprisingly Bishop Pike confirmed the testimony of the tandem Dye and Leek. He had indeed been murdered. There were indeed two men and one woman. But he was irritatingly vague about the circumstances. He promised to make everything clearer in subsequent manifestations. He professed friendship for Holzer and Meyers and Meyer's "communicator," who is her late first husband, Albert. And so on. Bishop Pike's message waxed philosophical as it moved giddily into peroration.

"One more question, is your son Jim with you?"

"Oh yes."

"In the same sphere, on the same level?"

"He has brought me higher with him. He is working things out as I am working out past conscious, subconscious memories of that which devours one's thinking and makes one respond to the way it has been conditioned, even in the last life. And one is trying to find and seek truth, even though one has been on the evil path to seek hallucination by false means, not within oneself, but from *without*. I am speaking: psychedelic drugs or as I sought escape in liquor. Then all these things have to be dealt with as you would deal with a problem in front of you right here, now. You look at your own problem, and finally erase it."

Oh, there's more—lots more—including a "Master" named "Rodamus," but we wouldn't want to spoil the book for those who haven't read it.

"*Thank God for one less pike.*"

James A. Pike Jr., the oldest son of the nationally-known and hotly controversial Episcopal bishop, aimed a powerful hunting rifle at his mouth yesterday and shot himself to death in a drab, $5-a-day room at the Hudson Hotel, Broadway near 31st st.

Police said the 22-year-old youth fired two shots from the 30-30 rifle. The first missed. The second ripped away the right side of his face and head.

'MIXED UP KID'
A note found on the body ended with "Goodbye, goodbye."

In San Francisco, a spokesman for Bishop James Albert Pike quoted the youth's father as saying:

"I just don't understand it. I have no way of explaining. He seemed reasonably happy."

"This was a mixed up kid," said a detective who read the long rambling note left by the youth.

Bishop Pike said he was "satisfied" the victim was his son and went home to notify his wife.

But The Very Rev. John Butler, a friend of the family and dean of New York's Cathedral of St. John the Divine, was to make the formal identification today. The Bishop had long served in New York before his appointment as California Bishop.

Police said the youth's note "was more like a note book. It rambled on and on." The note contained observations on life and suicide.

LONG HIT OF NAMES [Sic]
On one page there were six drawings, They showed a man, the bird landing on the shoulder, the bird sitting on his shoulder, the man holding a gun as the bird took flight, and the bird falling as if shot.

The note ended with

the words "Goodbye,
Goodbye," and a long
list of men's and wom-
en's first names.

Bishop Pike was called
away from services at
Grace Cathedral on San
Francisco's Nob Hill to
be told of the tragedy.

Young Pike was a stu-
dent at Cambridge and
was transferring to San
Francisco State College.
He was to have registered
there today.

Bishop Pike and James
had made a three-week
pilgrimage to the Holy
Land from England re-
cently and together
walked the length of the
Dead Sea. James stayed
in Jerusalem while Bishop
Pike went to Africa to
protest the new segrega-
tionist government of
Rhodesia.

CAUGHT LATER PLANE

His father last saw him
on Wednesday when
they left London. They
were to have taken the
same flight but the youth
lost his passport and
caught a later plane.

Young Pike arrived in
New York Wednesday
and checked into the
Hotel Hudson—on the
edge of Manhattan's gar-
ment district—tenanted
mainly by pensioners,
about 6:20 p.m.

A hotel spokesman
said no one saw the boy
leave his room and there
were no known visitors.
Young Pike made two
calls to Pan American
Airways in New York
through the hotel switch-
board.

About 3:20 p.m. Fri-
day, police said, young
Pike propped himself
into a sitting position on
his bed, aimed the muz-
zle of the rifle at his
mouth and squeezed the
trigger with his right
thumb.

2D SHOT FATAL

The shot hit the ceil-
ing of the room. He
fired again, this time the
fatal blast. Two hours
later, bellboy Louis Wells
found the body.

Close friends of the
Bishop in San Francisco
said he had been pleased
with his son's progress,
and the youth had good
grades. They could offer
no reason for the suicide.

Young Pike was one of
four children of James
and Esther Pike. He was
born about the time the
Bishop was ordained an
Episcopal deacon in
1944.

The New York *Journal-American* of February 5, 1966, was accurate as to the essential facts if not as to some of the peripheral detail. Jim Jr.'s body was not identified by Dean Butler. That chore

fell to John Krumm, rector, at the time, of the Church of the Ascension, New York City, and an old friend of Bishop Pike's. He qualified for the assignment in that he had attended a party the previous fall also attended by the bishop and Jim Jr. and so had seen the lad within the six-month period required by New York law. Bishop Pike and his son had not walked the length of the Dead Sea (some forty-five miles) during their pilgrimage to the Holy Land but they *had* climbed Masada, which overlooks it. Jim Jr. had stayed in a resort hotel in Herzliya and *not* in Jerusalem while his father went to Rhodesia *not* to protest the segregationist government there but to pay an official visit to the Diocese of Matabeleland, companion diocese to his own California within the Anglican communion. Finally, the two Jims had been scheduled on two different flights out of London on February 2—the bishop to California and Jim Jr. to New York—and *not*, as the *Journal-American* had it, on the same flight.

It had been in Herzliya that Bishop Pike and Jim Jr. had enjoyed one of the warmest moments in their fragile, tentative relationship, that moment, in fact, which the bishop would later recall at the outset of his first séance with Mrs. Twigg and that would so move him as to persuade him that Jim Jr. was really present during the séance. His recollection of that encounter was startlingly sentimental in a man ordinarily too abrupt for sentimentality.

So I flew to Salisbury, leaving Jim in Herzliya. The next day he heard on the radio (on a station which broadcast in English) that I had been arrested. The report said little else, but Jim was able to supply a great deal out of his imagination, for he had read reports of the rising number of persons thrown into concentration camps (unrealistically called "detention centers") for indefinite periods without trial or even specification of offenses, and of the gross treatment of prisoners.

Early in the day I had tried to phone Jim from Nairobi, Kenya, where I had been granted political asylum (having been arrested and then deported from Rhodesia, possibly because of charges against me sent there by Fr. Frank Brunton, a priest of the Diocese of South Florida, who wrote directly to Ian Smith to tell him of my alleged communist connections, racial rabble-rousing tactics and heresy). But I had been unable to get through to Israel.

When after an all-night flight via Teheran, Iran, my feet were finally again on the soil of Israel, I immediately went to a phone booth and called the hotel. There was no answer in the room. Paging produced no results. Impatient to be back with Jim—and for him to know I was all right—I grabbed a cab for the trip to Herzliya. I walked to the south wing of the hotel and then up to the second-floor open-air ramp toward the rooms facing the Mediterranean, and opened the door to the room. No Jim.

I thought I would go down again and look at the outdoor tables in the sun, or out on the beach; but as I opened the door to go out on the ramp, there was Jim walking toward me just five feet away. A beautiful embrace it was, and particularly because for all he knew, by then I was off in some remote part of Rhodesia in one of the detention centers. But here I was. And here he was. All was encompassed within two warm and loving smiles.

The several weeks the bishop and his son passed together in the Holy Land over Christmas of 1965 seem to have been for both of them an idyll of surcease in otherwise deeply troubled lives. There had been their profoundly moving ascent of Masada. They had spent part of a day in the Arab market place in Beersheba where they had themselves photographed together astride a camel. (Was this event so meaningful for them because it was the sort of experience many fathers and sons would have shared when the son was much younger?) Jim Jr. had met socially a pretty Arab girl and they had shared ordinary young man and young woman good times together. They had even gone to church together, which had astonished and pleased the bishop. But in the orbit of Bishop Pike little opportunity was assigned for dalliance and Jim Jr.'s liaison with the Arab girl was unfortunately perfunctory. The two Jims passed Jim Jr.'s last Christmas together in Nazareth.

I had been invited to participate in two services on Christmas Eve—hymns and prayers at the Anglican church (their Eucharist was to be the next morning), and also the opening Mass at the new-rite Catholic basilica. Partly because of being in Israel, with religious history so deeply rooted there; partly because of the haunting beauty, mysterious splendor and unusual music; and partly because of the ecumenical nature of both (in the Anglican service, as well as the Roman one, a Jesuit friend of mine from the United States acted as my chaplain), the two services were particularly meaningful for both Jim and me. In fact, Jim was so moved at the Eucharist at the basilica that for the first time in a long time he came forward to receive Communion. He had long been disenchanted with the Church, but something got to him in a deep way—as it did to me—and his spontaneous response was to come up.

It was my son's last Communion.

Back in the flat in Cambridge (with less than a month to live) Jim Jr. reverted to Romilar and despair. The bishop consulted experts and learned that Romilar was probably more destructive than LSD. He passed this information along to Jim Jr., who said unconvincingly that he would stop using it. In fact, the rapport that had been forged between father and son in Israel collapsed. Jim Jr. displayed mounting anxiety about the impending termination of their interlude in England. He vacillated between staying on to finish the year's schooling in Cambridge or returning for the latter semester to San Francisco State College. Meanwhile, the bishop had decided to interrupt his sabbatical in order to attend the annual diocesan convention in San Francisco. He felt an obligation to report on his visit to the companion Diocese of Matabeleland and his conviction that the Diocese of California should enlarge its support of her beleaguered sister. If Jim Jr. were to return to San Francisco State he would need to register there not later than February 5. Inasmuch as the bishop had to leave on February 2 Jim Jr. elected to do the same. Since there were several days to spare in his case he decided to stop in New York to look up friends he had met there on his way to England.

So it came to pass that on February 2 the two Jims arrived at Heathrow Airport. The bishop intended to put Jim Jr. on a flight to New York and then about an hour later catch his own flight directly to San Francisco. Jim Jr. discovered he had forgotten his passport. (It was later found in the flat in Cambridge.) He was advised to go to the American embassy in London (much nearer than Cambridge), where a temporary passport could be issued. It would be possible for him to catch a New York flight leaving three hours later.

There was little else to do; so I gave Jim money for a taxi into London and back. We embraced and said goodbye. I went up to the second level to pass through immigration and buy some gifts duty-free. As I reached the head of the stairs, I remember looking down to the lobby below just as Jim happened to look up. We both waved and smiled, but I suddenly shivered. I feared his going to New York. In a way it was a free-floating anxiety; in a way it was grounded in the problem of drugs.

Jim Jr. was issued a temporary passport and he did catch that flight to New York three hours later. He checked into the Hotel Hudson at 6:20 P.M. He asked for a room for two days and paid $10.50 in advance. Little is known of his activities—if there were any—between that time and three-twenty or so on Friday afternoon, two days later, when he shot himself to death. He did not look up the friends he had mentioned, nor anybody else, so far as is known. The hotel reported that he had not been seen to leave his room or to leave the hotel and was not known to have had any visitors. He made two phone calls to Pan American Airways. He made no reservations, however, so it must be presumed the calls were for flight information. He did leave the hotel at least once. On Thursday afternoon at about 4 P.M. he purchased a .30-30 rifle in a sporting goods store near the hotel. He told the salesman he intended to go hunting.

He intended, in fact, to become one more wanton casualty of the gun lobby.

The coroner found that Jim Jr. had died of a self-inflicted gunshot wound in the head. He also found that there had been heavy ingestion of a drug—probably Romilar. The drawings and notes found in his hotel room by the police were extensive, incoherent, rambling, and maudlin. He must have spent much of his time in New York in that drab room out of his mind on Romilar composing his dismal legacy of anguish and despair.

He was only twenty years old (*not* twenty-two, as the *Journal-American* had it).

Word of Jim Jr.'s death reached Canon Howard Freeman, diocesan communications officer, at Grace Cathedral moments before Bishop Pike was to join the procession for the opening service of the Diocesan Convention. The canon decided to seek verification of his information before informing the bishop. During the lengthy service Bishop Pike spoke for more than an hour outlining his "five-pronged project" for the Diocese of Matabeleland. He was distracted by an unusual commotion created by newsmen who had arrived to seek his reaction. He had been apprehensive all day about Jim Jr. because he had failed to call from New York as promised to let him know what hotel he was in and what flight that Friday would bring him back to San Francisco. He did not, however, connect the disturbance in the congregation with Jim Jr.'s situation.

When he had concluded his address he turned from the pulpit expecting to find his chaplain, David Baar, bearing his pastoral staff ready to lead him to the cathedral. Instead, Canon Trevor Hoy was holding the staff and he led the perplexed bishop out a side door. David Baar was standing outside and unvested. It was David who told the bishop the grim news. In the cathedral the service continued and was closed by Suffragan Bishop Millard with prayers for the deceased and for the bereaved family. Esther Pike, meanwhile, had left the service directly after the bishop's address in order to be at home should there be some word from Jim Jr. Bishop Pike hurried home himself to break the news first to the mother and then, as they gathered, to the surviving brother and sisters.

Close friends came by to offer condolences. Messages of grief began to pour in by telephone and these were received by clergy wives who were anxious to spare the bishop and his wife additional burden. During the next days hundreds of letters, cards, and telegrams would pile up in the Bishop's House and in the cathedral. Jim Jr. had attracted far more attention in death than he ever had in life. One message came from Fr. Frank Brunton, the same priest who may have precipitated the bishop's expulsion from Rhodesia with his scurrilous letter to Prime Minister Ian Smith. Brunton's "condolence" might have made Jim Jr. even more certain that he wanted *out* of this sorry world. "Thank God for one less pike," the bishop's eldering nemesis had scrawled on a sheet of plain white paper.

Bishop Pike was alone when the depth of his loss finally registered.

> It was not until much later that night that I made my way upstairs for a moment of solitude. As I walked into the bedroom, I was greeted by Jim's warm smile, and for the first time I broke down and cried. I turned the photograph face down on the mantel, unable to look at it, and sank down on the bed, tears flowing in recognition of the reality that Jim was gone—dead. The grief pressed in on me.

"I Have Discovered I Am Not Twins"

Little more than three months after Jim Jr.'s death—in letters dated May 9, 1966—Bishop Pike submitted to his diocesan standing committee and to the presiding bishop his resignation as Bishop of California, effective the following September 15. The standing committee accepted his resignation "with deep regret." (The resignation of a bishop requires the consent of his fellow bishops, but this proved no barrier and was swiftly accomplished, in some cases, no doubt, with more joy than regret.) Bishop Pike's very long letter to the presiding bishop included a summary paragraph giving the reasons for his decision to resign.

> A six months sabbatical, added to some years of studying, writing and communication "on the edges" of one's time, is obviously inadequate to this overall task. Back on the job, I am all the more aware of how difficult it will be for me to continue a dual role of scholar-teacher and administrator-leader. I am not growing any younger and this conflict has in fact been characteristic of me all my adult life in two professions, always keeping me too busy in terms of legitimate allotment of time for family life, rest and reflection. The attempt to fulfill both roles has put great strain on my physical well-being, leaving me feeling exhausted a good deal of the time. My recent sabbatical provided a "laboratory experiment" as to the state of my health while engaged in only one of the two roles; the fact is that I never felt better in my life. In the seven weeks of being back in the dual role, I'm feeling like I did before and it is evident that my health will not endure my going on this way.

When the resignation became public two weeks later the bishop informed the press: "I have discovered I am not twins." He added that during his months in Cambridge: "I experienced the sheer joy of staying with something for more than one disconnected hour." At no time in his letters of resignation or in his press conference did the bishop refer to the death of his son. Few who knew him, however, doubted that Jim Jr.'s suicide had been the body blow that broke the camel's back. Bishop Pike was *not* twins. When he returned from Cambridge that March 15 he plunged with seemingly undiminished ebullience into an array of diocesan and other activities but the old spark and spunk just weren't there any more. He was going through the motions. His staff knew a resignation would come, and they were only surprised that it came so swiftly.

At the time his resignation became public Bishop Pike also disclosed that he had accepted an invitation from Dr. Robert Maynard Hutchins to join the staff of the Center for the Study of Democractic Institutions in Santa Barbara, California. (MIND OVER MITER, headlined the New York *Daily News*.) The Center, founded by Dr. Hutchins—Bishop Pike would come to call him "the Abbot"—was at that time a collection of some twenty scholars and students from many disciplines, who, as the name suggests, brought to bear their various insights upon problems of institutions in a free society. Located in a charming if somewhat run-down villa on Eucalyptus Hill outside Santa Barbara, the staff gathered late each weekday morning for about two hours to consider and discuss a particular problem. Otherwise, members were free to pursue their own studies as they saw fit. Bishop Pike, the first theologian to be a permanent member of the Center's staff, assumed his new position on August 1, 1966.

It should be pointed out—because there has been confusion about it—that Bishop Pike did not *retire* as a bishop. A bishop *must* retire at age seventy-two, but otherwise *may not* retire before age sixty-eight, except for reasons of ill-health or infirmity. Even had he wished to retire—and he did not—Bishop Pike could not have done so. He resigned his *office* as diocesan of California, but he continued as a bishop of the Church in good standing until— and beyond—his death. From the moment his resignation took effect and ever after his formal designation would be the Right Reverend James Albert Pike, the Resigned Bishop of California.

Though he did not shed his status as bishop—he continued until a few months prior to his death to officiate at confirmations and other celebrations upon request—he did shed all income from the Church, and he became totally dependent for his living upon secular sources, his salary at the Center, his writings and lectures—which accounts, in part, for the frequency with which he appeared, during his last years, in print or on the public platform.

Bishop Pike had become, as he himself put it, "a worker priest in the purple."

The two areas of research the bishop contemplated for his work at Santa Barbara were the scholarship then proliferating from the Dead Sea Scrolls, and certain socioeconomic studies of the relationship between church attendance and ethical attitudes and behavior. He used the relative leisure of the summer of 1966 to explore preliminarily both of these fields. His visits to Israel had already involved him rather deeply in the scroll material, which he began to see was likely to revolutionize traditional understanding of the figure of Jesus. "It seemed to me that someone responsible in the churches," he later said, "ought to be getting ready to assess what all this might mean in terms of the future of the Church." In his penultimate sermon in Grace Cathedral on August 7 Bishop Pike spoke to this concern, basing his remarks on an article on the Dead Sea Scrolls by Professor John M. Allegro which had appeared in the August 1966 number of *Harper's* magazine. Among other things the bishop suggested that scholarship such as Professor Allegro's *might* establish that the historical Jesus had not existed, a remark that generated considerable dismay in some quarters. For that same reason Bishop Pike, hedging his bets, perhaps, began the habit, in most public references to Jesus, of using the expression "the servant image of Jesus." That usage didn't go over too well either in conservative circles.

On September 5, 1966, Bishop Pike delivered his farewell sermon as Bishop of California. It was a memorable event well captured by J. Campbell Bruce in the next day's San Francisco *Chronicle.*

> Bishop James A. Pike said farewell as rector of Grace Cathedral to an overflow throng yesterday, and the great gothic pile reverberated with laughter and at the close many an eye glistened.
>
> This was his last sermon as the rector, a post he had occupied since May of 1958. He will appear in the pulpit again September 13, the day a special diocesan convention will elect his successor.
>
> "*That* sermon is not supposed to be loaded," he said; i.e., for any particular candidate.
>
> They started filling the church long before the 11 A.M. service, sliding into the 2200 places among the pews, occupying rows of chairs, standing in the aisles.
>
> Bishop Pike mounted the pulpit, sent glances along the transept and down the nave, shook his head and said:

"It was never like this on Christmas or Easter. I think I should have resigned once a month."

Then his eye took in the worshipers bracing their backs against the walls, and he said:

"I'm concerned about these standees. It's difficult enough to endure one of my sermons when you're comfortably seated."

In a rare if not unprecedented action—the last, perhaps, but certainly not the first in his unpredictable reign as Bishop of California—he suggested that standees move up into the choir loft and chancel, where the clergy sit.

He called for a "minute of soft organ music" to occupy minds while this was going on, but he needn't have, he was distraction enough. In his high jutting pulpit, his arms eloquently beckoning and directing, he seemed an ecclesiastical version of a traffic cop.

"Go ahead," he told a reluctant standee, "you might be sitting in the visiting bishop's seat."

His sermon proper began, as all his subsequent sermons would, not with the customary Episcopal invocation—"In the name of the Father, and of the Son, and of the Holy Ghost, Amen!"—but, the Trinity having fallen from his episcopal vocabulary: "In the name of God, Amen!" The sermon itself was a moving recapitulation of his quest for that which could be conscientiously believed by twentieth-century Christians.

On September 13 the special diocesan convention, after much deliberation and maneuver, elected Chauncey Kilmer Myers, then Suffragan Bishop of the Diocese of Michigan, and an old friend of Bishop Pike's, as the latter's successor and sixth Episcopal Bishop of California. Bishop Myers, while theologically moderate, had a reputation at that time of being more deeply involved than Bishop Pike in social activism, having spent much of his ministry in urban work, and having been in the forefront of the struggle for racial integration.

"It will be nice some day," Bishop Pike observed, "to be remembered as that conservative bishop you had here once."

The Bishop Anoints the Medium, Reviving Her

"You will soon be leaving your post in order to continue your studies." I demurred, since I had not at the time thought of resigning as a diocesan. This evoked, "You will. I'll be in touch with you in August." This entirely puzzled me; but I didn't forget it.

Bishop Pike was in direct "communication" with Jim Jr. It was late in the morning of March 14, 1966. Four hours later he would leave England and fly to Washington, D.C., on his way back to California. The sabbatical was over. Mrs. Twigg had granted a second séance. The bishop had asked for it—not because there had been further poltergeist phenomena since the March 2 séance (there had not)—but because he was leaving and thought Mrs. Twigg might suggest a medium in the United States in the event he found a need for one.

Bishop Pike's recollections of the March 14 séance were exactly that—recollections—since the séance was not recorded and the notes Maren Bergrud made of it at the time were later lost. (Maren did attend the séance although this is not mentioned in *The Other Side*.) Mrs. Twigg, aware the bishop had a plane to catch, dispensed with chitchat and fell promptly into trance. This distinguished the event from the March 2 séance when she had been conscious and her receptions had been "clairaudient," which means—more or less—that *she* heard voices others present didn't hear and she repeated what the voices said. On March 14 she *didn't* hear voices because she *was* the voice of Jim Jr. speaking with his father. *She* was out cold and had no idea what was being uttered through her mouth. The bishop found this perplexing but he didn't for an instant doubt Jim Jr. was, in fact, the source of the communication.

(Later, as indeed with all the séances in which he participated, Bishop Pike would *review* the record and ponder alternative explanations for what seemed to have happened. He concluded that the most probable—though *not* the only—explanation was that Jim Jr. really had communicated with him through Mrs. Twigg and later through George Daisley and Arthur Ford. One consideration that led him to that conclusion was the fact that in every one of his séances with those three mediums he had felt unreservedly that the communications from Jim Jr. *were* genuine. In *The Other Side* Bishop Pike makes a persuasive case for the conclusion which he reached, and the skeptical are urged to read that book and give it a fair hearing.)

Recollections—even when notes have not been lost—are notoriously fallible, as anybody who has ever read a newspaper account of an event he also witnessed will testify. Did Bishop Pike *recall* that Jim Jr. had predicted his resignation only because the resignation *had* meanwhile happened, or did Mrs. Twigg herself *sense* an impending resignation and include news of it on some kind of a hunch, or did mention of the resignation in the séance in itself *precipitate* the resignation? That is an enigma we have no competence to solve. There may be found in parapsychological literature a cornucopia of tortuous wrestlings with similar enigmas. We do know that responsible parapsychologists would give short shrift to the March 14 séance. The evidence for a credible communication is wholly dependent—Mrs. Twigg was out cold, remember—upon recollections set down long after the fact by one far from disinterested participant. Nothing is more impressive among the accomplishments of parapsychology to date than the rules of evidence which have been developed to govern the investigation and evaluation of alleged paranormal phenomena.

Whatever we are to make of it, the fact remains that Bishop Pike *did* later recall that Jim Jr. had predicted his resignation as diocesan in the March 14 séance. He also recalled that he had "demurred" because he had had no thought at that time of resigning. Jim Jr. had again affirmed his prediction and added that he would be with his father in August. That prediction also came true, as we shall see. At the time the bishop found the twin forecasts "puzzling" but not especially impressive, and in any case they did not have to do with the purpose which had led him to seek the second séance.

> Then I turned to something more realistic: "Should I want to be in touch, how would I go about it? I don't know anyone in the States who is a medium."
> "Just a minute," Jim seemed to reply. There was a pause, as if someone were being consulted. Then not a sentence, but four phrases. "Spiritual Frontiers—a Father Rauscher—priest of the Church—in New Jersey."

At the close of the séance, as Mrs. Twigg was making her way back to normalcy, Bishop Pike asked whether she knew anything about the "Spiritual Frontiers" Jim Jr. had mentioned. She looked blank. He had forgotten—or had not yet grasped—that *entranced* Mrs. Twigg *hears not.* Pressed for time the bishop did not pursue the matter. There isn't a Chinaman's chance on the "Other Side" that she *didn't* know about Spiritual Frontiers. She knew Arthur Ford. Arthur Ford knew Father Rauscher. Father Rauscher was president of Spiritual Frontiers. That does not preclude, of course, that whoever it was Jim Jr. paused as if to consult didn't also know about Spiritual Frontiers. We are puzzled, in this connection, why Bishop Pike had asked for a séance if he only wanted to find out the name of a medium in the States. Couldn't he have asked Mrs. Twigg for that information over the phone and saved both of them a lot of trouble? It might be that that is what he did do and that it was Mrs. Twigg who parlayed his inquiry into a séance. That would have given her a little time to reflect upon mediums in the United States who would be suitable for her client.

However that may have been, Bishop Pike had obtained a lead, at least, to a medium and he thanked Jim Jr. for it, noting that he might need it since he was about to go back to the United States.

"I know you are," then came through. "In fact you are going to Virginia."

Bishop Pike was not going to Virginia. He was going to Washington, D.C. He had no plan while in Washington to visit in Virginia. Imagine, then, his astonishment some hours later as his plane descended at Dulles Airport and it dawned on him that the airport *was* in Virginia! How could Jim Jr. have known where his plane would land? We don't know how Jim Jr. could have known (there was no pause for "consultation"), but we *do* know how Mrs. Twigg could have known. It is a likely assumption that when Bishop Pike phoned her and an appointment was made for 10 A.M. March 14 that he also mentioned that he would be flying to Washington at a P.M. that same afternoon. Mrs. Twigg would not have had to go to much trouble to learn that international flights from London to Washington normally landed at Dulles Airport in Virginia. We don't say she *did* do that. We only say she *could* have.

Not too much else, so far as the bishop recalled, "came through" during the March 14 séance. Jim Jr. reported that he hadn't heard "*any*thing about a Jesus." He said he was feeling more at home and that a number of people were helping. Ever curious, Bishop Pike wondered if people were male and female over there and if there was something like "intimate expression."

> The terms of the answer seemed almost to express amusement at my delicacy of expression: it was very much like Jim. Without a pause: "Sex? Yes, there is sex. But it is not like it is there. It is not physical, of course, but actually there is less limitation. It is more obviously like what sex really means. Here you actually can enter the whole person. It is like you are in fact merging—becoming one."

Bishop Pike would have found *that* news reassuring.

> I know that much more came through in the session, but without notes I am not certain of more—except I do recall that several times in the sitting there were the words, "I am beginning to learn." I do remember, though, how it ended. It just sort of "ran down," and Mrs. Twigg lapsed into silence. She was breathing heavily and was showing no signs of coming to consciousness. I began to be somewhat concerned but I was in doubt as to what, if anything, should be done. Not being experienced with persons in trance states I instinctively responded in terms of my years of pastoral calls on the sick: I reached in my pocket for my "oil stock" (a small container of olive oil which is traditionally used in the sacrament of healing—as provided in our Prayer Book), laid my hands firmly on her head and anointed her forehead with the sign of the cross. Mrs. Twigg immediately "revived," saying, "What—what did you do?"
>
> "I used Holy Unction. I hope that was all right to do. I got concerned that you didn't seem to be coming out of it," I explained.
>
> "You did just the right thing," she said, smiling.

It must be said of the March 14 séance that it's hard to decide who was healing whom of what.

There Is a Diversity of Unctions

November of 1968 was a bum month all around. Richard Nixon was elected President of the United States. Early in the month Bishop Pike had gone to Baltimore for the trial of the Catonsville Nine. On November 22, the fifth anniversary of the assassination of John Kennedy, William Stringfellow underwent ten hours of surgery for the relief of near fatal disorders of the pancreas and attendant organs. The following morning, emaciated from long and painful illness and with tubes running into and out of him in all directions, he lay, more dead than alive, in a room high up in the Columbia Presbyterian Medical Center in New York City. In his book, *A Second Birthday*, he has recounted what happened that morning as he struggled back to consciousness and to life.

> When I woke, later, there were three figures in my hospital room. With an effort I focused upon them and recognized James A. Pike and Diane Kennedy and Anthony.
>
> During the vigil, Anthony had received a telephone call from Bishop Pike. I had known, and admired, Bishop Pike since 1955, while he was Dean of New York and I was a student at the Harvard Law School, when we had met and had long conversations about theology and law and about being at once a Christian and a lawyer, as both of us were. Subsequently, when I moved to New York and began my East Harlem practice, we became good friends, and colleagues in some issues in the city and in the churches. After he became Bishop of California, we remained in communication. I usually saw him on his whirlwind trips to New York, and I visited him several times in San Francisco. When heresy proceedings were initiated against the bishop, he asked me to be legal counsel and, during the heresy controversy, Harper & Row commissioned Anthony and myself to write *The Bishop Pike Affair*. At the 1967 Seattle General Convention of the Episcopal Church—at which Bishop Pike won vindication on the heresy issues—Diane Kennedy, who was then aiding the bishop in research and writing, and Anthony and I joined the bishop at an informal caucus concerned with strategy in the debate and disposition of the heresy matter in the House of Bishops. That experience had occasioned our admiration for Diane, and Anthony and I rejoiced to learn later on that Jim and Diane would marry.
>
> The bishop knew that I was ill, that it was serious, that surgery had been considered, but he did not know the extremity that my condition had reached, and he did not know the date that had been set for the operation. Nevertheless, on that day, during the vigil, while the outcome in surgery was dubious, Bishop Pike had

somehow managed to locate Anthony at the hospital by telephone. "I had an overwhelming conviction that I should find out what's happening to Bill," he told Anthony. Anthony reported that the operation was happening, that it was continuing much longer than expected, and that he, and others who were waiting, felt grave and uncertain.

Pike had called from Baltimore where he, accompanied by Diane, had been on a lecture engagement. Their plans to travel elsewhere were canceled and they came instead to New York to the hospital and were present when I revived.

Still traumatized, and heavily sedated, I have but one vivid recollection of their visit. There had been some conversation and then, suddenly, as it seemed to me, Pike exclaimed: "Well, I'm a bishop, I'd better do something." Thereupon he disappeared briefly. He reappeared near the doorway to the room, in the company of my nurse. He had procured from her a large jar of petroleum jelly, which he proceeded to consecrate duly. He admonished the nurse that the substance had now been set apart for uses other than those ordinary and familiar for Vaseline. Taking a thumbful of this freshly made unguent, he came to the bedside and anointed me, signing my forehead with a cross, and saying:

I anoint you, in the name of God; beseeching the mercy of our Lord Jesus Christ, that all your pain and sickness of body being put to flight, the blessing of health may be restored unto you. Amen.

That is, of course, pratically verbatim, the unction of the sick prescribed in the Book of Common Prayer.

The following morning Dr. Porter stopped by and he told me in detail what had happened in surgery and what the prognosis was. He was, I noted, since I was now lucid, pleased and proud about the operation, and properly so, for all that it had been a prolonged and exacting work for him. "I don't know whether or not you realize it," he began, "but your recovery is spectacular!"

"That doesn't surprise me at all," I interrupted him. "I was anointed with Vaseline by Bishop Pike—what else would you expect?"

The reason Stringfellow said the unction used by Bishop Pike was "practically verbatim" from the Book of Common Prayer is that the bishop had, as was by then his custom, omitted the second and third persons of the Trinity in the opening invocation.

Bishop Pike, that morning, had had to wait a long time, though the patient didn't know it, because Stringfellow refused to wake up. The bishop became more and more impatient, dashing in and out of the room to place phone calls or otherwise to make some good use of precious time. "Isn't there something they could give him to *make* him wake up?" he demanded, at one point.

On that same day, in the hospital cafeteria, Jim and Diane told Anthony that one month later they would be (formally) married.

Twenty-three Years of Marriage down the Drain

Thus spake the New York *Times* on Saturday, July 22, 1967:

SAN FRANCISCO (UPI) The Right Rev. James A. Pike and his wife agreed today to end their 23-year marriage. It will be his second divorce.

The Episcopal Bishop resigned last year as leader of the California diocese to join the Center for the Study of Democratic Institutions at Santa Barbara, headed by Robert M. Hutchins.

Bishop Pike's resignation came a few weeks after fellow bishops decided to make a full formal inquiry into charges of heresy and "irresponsibility" brought against him. The charges stemmed from his challenges to the doctrines of virgin birth, incarnation and resurrection.

The divorce suit was initiated by the Bishop's

wife, Esther, on grounds
of mental cruelty. Bishop
Pike, who is 54 years old,
said, through his wife's
attorney, that he would
not contest the suit,
scheduled to be heard
in Superior Court here
Tuesday.

In a statement signed
by the Bishop and his
wife, they said their troubles were "personal" and
both agreed to say noth-
ing beyond the state-
ment. They had been
separated since Jan. 16,
1965.

"It is with regret that
we announce the institu-
tion of legal proceedings
to dissolve our marriage,"
they said in the state-
ment. "This action is not
taken in contemplation
of the remarriage of ei-
ther party; outside factors
beyond the control of
either of us have con-
tributed for some time
to our drifting apart,
though we have ear-
nestly sought a solution
and although we retain
respect and affection for
each other."

The Bishop and his
wife met while he was
lecturing at Catholic
University of America in
Washington, where she
was a student. One of

their four children, James
A. Pike, Jr., 20, com-
mitted suicide last year
in New York. They also
have another son and
two daughters.

Bishop Pike's first di-
vorce was sanctioned by
the Episcopal Church
with a ruling of annul-
ment for the Bishop, a
former Roman Catholic.

On July 25, 1967, Esther Pike was granted an interlocutory
decree of divorce. Bishop Pike was not present in the courtroom.
Esther, in a five-minute appearance, testified that her husband
had remained away from home for periods of time and at times
she had not known where he was. This, she said, had caused her
mental suffering. Custody of the two younger children, Constance, eighteen years old at the time, and Christopher, seventeen
at the time, was granted to Mrs. Pike. The elder daughter,
Catherine, had been previously married, and was, therefore, under
our quaint laws, already in other custody.

The divorce of Jim and Esther Pike took place one month after
the suicide of Maren Bergrud (and seven months before the apparent attempted suicide of young Constance Pike). It had been
one year since the bishop met Diane Kennedy in that classroom
in Berkeley (and ten months since Jim and Diane had become—
"unformally"—married). The formal wedding of Jim and Diane
Pike would take place seventeen months later.

So, as of July 25, 1967, Bishop Pike, having been for some time
unhappily married *and* unhappily mistressed *and* happily mistressed, was happily mistressed *only* and well on his way to
becoming happily married *only*.

Of Maren Bergrud and Miserable Disappointment

"I'll be in touch with you in August."
That is what Jim Jr. told his father, as Bishop Pike later

recalled it, during the March 14, 1966, séance with Mrs. Twigg. August did, of course, come and so, it seemed, did Jim Jr.

Jim Jr.'s apparent manifestation in California launched for Bishop Pike a series of five séances, spread over a year—the first in August of 1966 and the last in August of 1967—with his second medium, George Daisley of Santa Barbara. Taken together the five séances constitute an incredible display of sophisticated effrontery. George Daisley does not suffer trances, or if he does he did not suffer any with Bishop Pike. He is, however, allegedly "clairaudient" and "clairvoyant," which means—more or less—that he both hears and sees apparitions not heard or seen by others present and he is able to repeat what the apparitions say and to describe what they look like. (There is another form of manifestation from elsewhere called "materialization" whereby apparitions are audiovisual—audible and/or visible—to a medium *and* to others who may happen to be on hand. That is one paranormal phenomenon which was never visited upon Bishop Pike.) We are frank to say we do not understand why Bishop Pike took seriously his encounters with George Daisley. The first séance was preposterous. He was nevertheless impressed. The four séances which followed were a sort of deteriorating replay of the first one, and the bishop himself was less than enchanted with the last two.

Maren Bergrud was Bishop Pike's companion for the first Santa Barbara séance.

> Mr. Daisley greeted us at the door of his relatively new, tract-house-style home. He was a man about my age, and in a rather typical British manner of respectful friendliness he ushered us into his living room. His home was attractively decorated with modern furniture. There were many paintings around (I later learned oil painting and tennis were Mr. Daisley's hobbies), and a substantial library of books, primarily in the psi field, was much in evidence. We settled down to a get-acquainted chat in the course of which I learned a great deal about Mr. Daisley himself.
>
> He was born in London's East End, the son of poor parents. His powers emerged at ten, but they only created difficulty in a family which knew nothing of such "nonsense." He began to keep to himself, feeling that he was somehow "different." Finally, in his teens, he happened to meet someone who did know about such

powers and who, in turn, introduced him to a group of sensitives who helped train him. From then on he began to take part in public demonstrations and to give private sittings in the course of which he came to know various well-known mediums and various clergy interested in the field. He had only been in Santa Barbara five years, but already had a fairly full schedule of group meetings, training sessions and appointments for spiritual healing and mediumship.

We confess that we don't know what a "tract-house-style home" is. It must be some sort of exotica (like George Daisley himself) that could only flourish in Southern California. Daisley had indeed gotten to know in London "various well-known mediums"—Ena Twigg and Arthur Ford, to name but two—and "various clergy interested in the field"—Canon John Pearce-Higgins to name one. He also knew other remarkable people on this side *and* the other. He was associated with Spiritual Frontiers. He had moved to Santa Barbara in 1961, and in that mecca of affluence and spiritualism he had prospered—unostentatiously plying his singular trade.

In our correspondence with distinguished parapsychologist Ian Stevenson, who has helped us greatly to understand and evaluate matters for which we have no professional competence, Dr. Stevenson happened to mention that he had once been with Bishop Pike in Santa Barbara. He had gone there, he explained, to investigate startling claims made by a medium who lived in Southern California but who had to remain unidentified as the interview had been confidential. The medium had proved to be fraudulent in his claims. We inquired whether without otherwise identifying the fraudulent medium he could *exclude* George Daisley.

> The medium we investigated at Santa Barbara was *not* George Daisley. Jim Pike *did* attend these sessions with this fraudulent medium and he participated actively in the exposure of the fraud.

We had also asked Dr. Stevenson whether Bishop Pike had been present when the fraudulent medium was exposed. Hence his comment in that regard. In the same letter, in a later paragraph, Dr. Stevenson had additional comment to make concerning George Daisley's mediumship.

I have not had a sitting myself with George Daisley. Jim Pike
spoke enthusiastically about him. Some friends of mine, in whom
I have confidence, had a sitting with George Daisley and felt it
was miserably disappointing.

How did Bishop Pike get involved with George Daisley?

Toward the end of July 1966 the bishop moved to Santa Barbara, where he was officially to begin work at the Center for the
Study of Democratic Institutions on August 1. Esther having refused to join him there, he had persuaded his mother, Mrs.
Chambers, to come and to share an apartment with him. (That
arrangement wouldn't last long because of friction between Mrs.
Chambers and Maren Bergrud.) Maren Bergrud had also come
and moved into the smaller apartment down the hall which
would shortly become also the offices of New Focus. The bishop
was busy unpacking and settling in—both in the apartment and
in his new office at the Center.

On the last day of July Maren and Mrs. Chambers were to have
dinner with the bishop in his apartment. During the day, as he
was unpacking his vast collection of books, he had been brooding
about a problem involving Christian origins. It had occurred to
him that the answer might be found in a certain book he had, but
he despaired of finding it in the general confusion of unpacking.
He did not mention the matter to Maren or did not later recall
that he had. Just before Maren arrived for dinner he sat down to
catch his breath on a sofa in the living room. There before him on
the coffee table lay the book he despaired of finding. Not only
that but there was a postcard inserted in the book (it appeared to
him the card was stuck to a page with a mucilaginous substance)
at just the point in the book which pertained to his problem. The
postcard was of a camel in Beersheba and was of a number he and
Jim Jr. had purchased there.

During dinner he told his mother and Maren about this development. He told them he had a "here we go again" feeling. The
reference, of course, was to the poltergeist phenomena in the flat
in Cambridge. After dinner he and Maren settled down to work
on an article he had promised for *Playboy* magazine. He mentioned to Maren that a point he was striving to make could be
fleshed out if only he could locate a certain UNESCO volume.

That would be hopeless because of the confusion of books so they completed the article without it. He had, meanwhile, placed the found Christian origins book next to his bed in expectation of looking at it before going to sleep. When he did go to bed he reached for that book and up came the very UNESCO volume he had wanted for the *Playboy* article. It was then that he suddenly realized that the next day would be August 1 and recalled Jim Jr.'s "I'll be in touch with you in August" from the March 14 séance with Mrs. Twigg.

Let us pause. The time has come, and we regret it, when we must begin to be a little rough.

How are we to account for these strange happenings? We find only four remotely plausible explanations of which we exclude two. We exclude the possibility of coincidence. The Beersheba postcard stuck to the pertinent page effectively rules out coincidence. We exclude the possibility that Bishop Pike himself invented and/or perpetrated the events. Bishop Pike had many faults but an appetite for chicanery was not among them. We are left with two plausible explanations—each of them, for very different reasons, distasteful to us.

1. Jim Jr., the bishop's loved son, shot through the head, cremated and his ashes scattered six months earlier off Golden Gate Bridge, was nevertheless somehow responsible for what would then have to be accounted two authentic poltergeist phenomena.

2. Maren Bergrud, the bishop's disgruntled mistress, herself sick of mind and body, her faculties distorted by a habit of drugs and destined less than a year later to drug herself to death, had been driven by some wild distraction to perpetrate a cruel hoax.

Take your pick.

Our wonders and our hard choices are, however, by no means ended. The next morning—August 1—Bishop Pike, brooding about what he took to be an effort by Jim Jr. to reach him, bustled into his new office at the Center on Eucalyptus Hill ready for his first day in a new career. He had a brief conversation with one of his Center colleagues. He told the colleague what had happened and discovered that they shared an interest in psychic phenomena. His colleague, however, could not help him locate a

medium or somebody connected with Spiritual Frontiers in Santa
Barbara.

Just then I looked up and saw coming toward me a tall, blue-
eyed fellow with gray hair. "John McConnell!" I called out, extending my hand.

"Bishop Pike! I knew you were coming to the Center, of
course, but I didn't know whether you would be here yet. I'm so
glad I caught you," he responded.

"Come on in." I motioned to my office. "What brings you to
Santa Barbara?"

"We've been having some meetings for persons interested in
Minute for Peace," he explained. John heads a movement which
urges radio stations across the country to set aside a minute for
peace, providing tape-recordings for the brief interlude. (After the
sounding of the United Nations Peace Bell, a public figure says a
word about peace, which is followed by a short meditation period.
The idea is to offer people of all creeds an opportunity to unite,
each in his own way, in thoughts or prayers for world peace.) I
had first met John in San Francisco when he had come to explain
his program to me, to ask for my support and to see if I could
suggest other persons for him to contact.

"Well, how's it going?" I asked with genuine interest. John was
now seated across my desk from me.

"Very well; getting off the ground. I'd certainly be pleased if
you would agree to record a message for us," he said.

I said I'd be happy to and suggested that shortly we could go
down to the seminar room and do the brief recording. In the
meantime I inquired how the meeting he attended in Santa Barbara had been.

"Good group?" I asked.

"Yes. Incidentally, there was a very interesting minister at the
meeting Friday night, the Rev. George Daisley."

"Oh? What church is he with?" I asked—mainly to show
polite interest.

"Well, it's not exactly a church," he answered. "He's affiliated
with Spiritual Frontiers."

"*Spiritual Frontiers*," I repeated. Then: "What's his name
again?"

"George Daisley," John reported, and I quickly jotted down a
note. "A quite remarkable man," he observed.

"He's probably a medium," I commented, not knowing how
much John knew about the subject.

"Yes, he is. In fact, I arranged for a sitting with him," he remarked matter-of-factly. "It was my first experience with a medium. I wish you could meet him."

"I'd like to," I said instantly. "I *will*."

"You'll remember," John continued, "I promised to get you the names and addresses of those I told you had those experiences the night of your son's death. Well, I have them. I brought them along in case I'd catch you either in San Francisco or here."

"Why, thank you, John. I'll want to make notes of this." I remembered that John had come to see me at Diocesan House on what happened to be my last day in office in San Francisco. He had called Myrtle for an appointment. Thinking he was coming about Minute for Peace, and being quite overburdened with last-minute responsibilities, I at first told Myrtle I felt I was too busy to see him.

"He seemed to have something personal to talk over with you, Bishop," Myrtle commented, knowing that I don't turn away persons who seem to want to see me pastorally.

"Then go ahead and set it up," I said. "I'll make time somehow."

I remembered that it turned out that John had come not for help for himself, but to share with me some experiences—both his and others—which occurred in the early morning of the day Jim took his life. John said he had awakened suddenly in the wee hours of Friday morning, February 4, with a terrible sense of dread—as though he were dying, he said. "I struggled in my mind to cling to life and to understand the meaning of the feeling. It then seemed to me that someone—not in my own family —was dying and I should pray for him. I wept and stayed in intercessory prayer for what seemed about two hours."

John McConnell's two hours of intercessory prayers may have been twelve hours premature. Jim Jr.'s suicide did not take place in the wee hours of the morning of February 4. It took place in the middle of the afternoon on that date. That is what the medical examiner found, what was entered in the police blotter, and what all newspaper accounts we have seen reported. This anomaly is not unique to John McConnell's prayers. It runs throughout accounts of Jim Jr.'s death in *The Other Side* and elsewhere in the bishop's private correspondence. There is no doubt Bishop Pike was himself under the impression the death occurred during the night. We don't know where he got that impression. In *The*

Other Side there are numerous reports of persons said to have waked that same night with feelings of dread and the like similar to those John McConnell is said to have experienced.

Two of those persons were the two friends Jim Jr. had said he would look up in New York. Bishop Pike had called one of them, in fact, on February 2 to register his concern about Jim Jr. and to ask if he had turned up. He had not. The two friends had called some thirty hotels in New York—but not, alas, the Hudson Hotel —in an effort to track him down. Early in the morning of February 4, according to *The Other Side*, one of the friends called the other and both were said to have wakened at the same time with a terrible sense of horror and grief which they specifically related to Jim Jr.

We have tried to concoct by speculation some plausible explanation for this rather striking discrepancy. The medical examiner *might*, of course, have been mistaken or he *might* have made a mistaken entry in his records. It is not uncommon, we know, for people to wake in the night with a sense of something wrong and sometimes such experiences are premonitory. Perhaps the accounts in *The Other Side* were of a premonitory nature, but some of them, at least, do not read that way. We have even considered a somewhat far-out possible explanation. The police reported that two shots had been fired and that the first shot missed and entered the ceiling. Is it conceivable that Jim Jr. *did* fire one shot in the middle of the night which missed, and then could not bring himself (perhaps encumbered by intercessory prayers) to fire the second *fatal* shot until the next afternoon? We really don't find any of these explanations, or any combination of them, very persuasive, and we must, therefore, leave it that we find this rather ghoulish matter puzzling.

We are much more troubled, anyway, by other aspects of Bishop Pike's encounter with John McConnell. It is a surprising coincidence that McConnell should have turned up on the bishop's *first* (official) day at the Center (and the first day of the month Jim Jr. had indicated *he* would be with the bishop) bearing news of George Daisley, a medium associated with Spiritual Frontiers. We would accept that much as coincidence, however, were it not also surprising that the same McConnell had also turned up in San Francisco on the bishop's *last* day in office as diocesan and bearing, on that occasion, news of his peculiar experience the night (as he thought) of Jim Jr.'s death. He compounded the surprise of this by going on to inform the bishop that two other persons (one subsequently to become his wife) also had had similar experiences on that same night.

We have no problem understanding that Jim Jr's two friends might have had ominous feelings close to the time he died—especially in light of the call Bishop Pike had made to them on February 2 and the apprehension they were as a consequence already in. But why should McConnell and his wife-to-be and some other friend of his have also had such experiences that night? None of them, we are told, knew Jim Jr. and only McConnell knew the bishop, and that only superficially and in a business way. And that being the case, why in any event should McConnell have made an appointment with the bishop on his last day in office as diocesan for the sole purpose of imparting such information? Bear in mind that at that point the bishop's experiences with psychic phenomena were not on the public record. What on earth did McConnell suppose the bishop would do with such *post facto* news?

We are suspicious.

Bishop Pike, in *The Other Side*, seems to infer (but does not say it in so many words) that McConnell's Santa Barbara visit (and perhaps the San Francisco visit as well) was (were) influenced in some way by Jim Jr. as part of his orchestrated effort to get through to his father. If you buy that you buy it. We do not rule it out. We are more inclined, however, to surmise that John McConnell on both visits was the instrument (witting or unwitting or perhaps *semi*-witting) of others (likely associated one way or another with Spiritual Frontiers) who had their own designs quite independently of any plans Jim Jr. may be conjectured to have had.

So much, however these matters may, in fact, have been, for how Bishop Pike came to get involved with George Daisley. John McConnell was barely out the Center door when the bishop opened a Santa Barbara telephone directory and made note of Daisley's telephone number and address. That evening he was no sooner back in his apartment ("and said hello to my mother") when he headed for the telephone. It rang. There was David

Baar, calling from San Francisco. He and his wife had come home late from a dinner (apparently the previous night) and found safety pins "here and there" open and arranged in patterns recalling (to David) the safety pin incidents in the Cambridge flat. That was the clincher, so far as Bishop Pike was concerned. He telephoned George Daisley. The medium was expecting his call. Jim Jr. had visited him (twice) about two weeks earlier to ask for his help in reaching his father around August 1. Daisley had had to explain to Jim Jr. that it would seem unprofessional for him to do that. "Your father would have to come to me first, Jim." Bishop Pike made an appointment with George Daisley for "a couple of days later" at nine-thirty in the morning.

Let us pause for a short digression on safety pins. Much is made in *The Other Side* of a pattern sometimes described as a 140 degree angle and sometimes as eight-nineteen on the face of a clock. For one thing, the clock in the Cambridge flat was found stopped at eight-nineteen. Books were found arranged in such a pattern. So were postcards. And so were safety pins. The pins would sometimes be open in that angle and sometimes arranged in pairs in that angle. We are frankly embarrassed to have to comment about that. Fortunately, in a letter to us, Ian Stevenson has spared us from having to say what we think about it.

> Jim Pike made a good deal of a pattern of 8:19. I think he goes far beyond the evidence in attributing some special agency to his observations of objects, such as opened books, that he fitted into this pattern. If one opens any safety pin its two parts joined at the spring tend to come approximately to the position of the hands of a clock at 8:20.

What was the significance of the pattern of eight-nineteen? In the midst of the phenomena in Cambridge Bishop Pike (and David and Maren) had become persuaded that eight-nineteen London time would have corresponded with three-twenty New York time, the time Jim Jr. was presumed to have killed himself. (Whether the time was 3:20 P.M. or 3:20 A.M. would seem to make no difference in this regard.) Did Jim Jr. stop that clock at eight-nineteen in order to correct an error of one minute made by the medical examiner? Or did Maren stop the clock at eight-nineteen in order that it not seem to correspond too perfectly to be believed? Whatever may have been the case, that is the significance Bishop Pike came to attach to the pattern of eight-nineteen which was discerned among books and postcards and safety pins.

David Baar, in his interview with Scott Kennedy long after the Cambridge experiences, did not remember having been much impressed by the pattern of eight-nineteen and the related phenomena. He attributed the scattering of safety pins to Bishop Pike's habit of tearing open shirts he had fetched from the laundry and allowing the safety pins to fall where they might. David did not, however, advert to the incident of the safety pins he and his wife found in their home in San Francisco, prompting his telephone call to the bishop on August 1. How are we to account for that? We don't know. But we need not push what we *do* know about the relationship between Maren and David *beyond* what we know to assume that back in San Francisco (post-Cambridge) they had conversations about what had gone on *in* Cambridge. We may also assume Bishop Pike reported to David the substance of his second séance with Mrs. Twigg. So, Maren and David would both have known of Jim Jr.'s "in August" forecast. It is possible that discussion of these matters continued at least until shortly before August 1 when the bishop and Maren moved to Santa Barbara. The power of suggestion is sometimes insidious, and in David Baar's case it may have been rendered more insidious if Maren Bergrud found ways to nourish it. The alternative, of course, is to conclude, as Bishop Pike seems to have done, that Jim Jr. himself accomplished the disposition of safety pins in David's home during the evening preceding August 1.

> "Your son is standing just behind you and slightly to your left," Mr. Daisley asserted. " 'Hello, Dad,' he says. 'I'm so pleased to see you today. I was with you recently when you did not think you could find a book in your library that you really wanted to consult. After you left the room and returned, you were startled to find the book on the desk where I put it in your absence. You know, Dad, I've been trying to bring about a great deal of physical phenomena in your surroundings.' "

Thus commenced Bishop Pike's first séance with George Daisley "a couple of days" after August 1, 1966. The book, as we know, was found on the coffee table and not on the desk. Otherwise the phenomenon of the found book is accurately reported. In the jargon of spiritualism the medium had got things off promisingly with "evidentiary" material. He had made a direct hit. The slight error in the placement of the book somehow or other seems even to enhance the credibility of the communication.

Is there any way at all that George Daisley could have known about that book? We think of five ways he *might* have known about it. Bishop Pike, in *The Other Side*, pondered two of them.

> Either Mr. Daisley pulled the event out of my subconscious by ESP and then attributed a motive to it on Jim's part—and this without knowing about the Cambridge events—or he was in fact in touch in some way with my son who had apparently used physical phenomena to get my attention.

Geoge Daisley may be endowed with ESP but we find no evidence of it in *The Other Side*. Had Bishop Pike professed to have used his *own* ESP to implant the event in George Daisley's *consciousness* we would have found that credible. Nor are we able to share the bishop's assumption that Daisley was ignorant of the Cambridge events. Whether Daisley was "in touch in some way" with Jim Jr. *prior* to the séance (Daisley *said* he had been) seems to us irrelevant. What is at issue is whether he was in touch with him *during* the séance.

How else might Daisley have known about the found book? Mrs. Chambers could have told him about it. She had learned of it at dinner that night. But anybody who knows Mrs. Chambers knows she would do no such thing. Bishop Pike could have told Daisley about it. That is preposterous in the circumstances. Or Maren Bergrud could have told him about it. She also had learned of it at dinner that night if she did not already know about it by virtue of having been responsible for it.

We are back to a familiar dilemma. Common sense *insists* that either Jim Jr. really was "coming through" in that séance or Maren Bergrud and George Daisley were in cahoots.

Another "evidentiary" direct hit ensued.

> "When you missed the street and went on up the hill," Mr. Daisley went on, purporting to speak for my son, "I was afraid you wouldn't get here at all."

While controversy raged in the middle
sixties, James Pike officiated at services
in Grace Cathedral with Archbishop Geoffrey
Fischer of Canterbury in 1964, *above*, and
during a baptism in 1965, *below*.

James Pike the restless crusader during the sixties with, *above left*, Supreme Court Justice William O. Douglas; *above right*, Presiding Bishop John Hines and Dean Julian Bartlett; *below left*, Martin Luther King, Jr., in San Francisco the Sunday after the Selma march in 1965; *below right*, Bishop John Robinson, author of *Honest to God*, in England.

At Cambridge University, England, during the Sad Sabbatical.

In the Bishop's Office at Grace Cathedral.

"How did you know that?" I asked—mainly to see what kind of response I would get.

"Oh, I was along," the answer came back.

On this first visit—in the bishop's case, at least—to Daisley's home he and Maren had driven past the entrance to Daisley's street and had had to turn back to find it. How could George Daisley possibly have known about that? Maren could have told him about it somehow before the séance got under way. More likely, we would think, the incident could have been prearranged. Maren would have been driving. (The bishop seldom drove if there was anybody around to drive for him. His driving was notorious. Some of his friends would flatly refuse to ride in any vehicle of which he was the driver.) Maren could have *deliberately* missed the entrance to Daisley's street.

If Jim Jr. really was "along" then, of course, he really was at the séance and the question is moot. We are bold to wonder, in that event, why Jim Jr. did not see to it that they *didn't* miss the entrance to the street. That would seem to us to have been within the limits of his apparent power to foretell and to influence events and to move objects from one place to another. We have learned, however, that in these matters there are wonders within wonders. It would also have been within the limits of the same apparent power (and this we offer as our final reflection on the missed street) for Jim Jr. to have *caused* them to miss the entrance to the street in order to be able, at the outset of the séance, to *report* that they had missed it, thereby affording evidence that he really was present and communicating in George Daisley's salon.

What next? Well, Jim Jr.'s two grandfathers were somewhat elaborately and vacuously unveiled. They seemed to have little to say. Thereupon the attention shifted from Bishop Pike to Maren Bergrud. This was accomplished by the introduction of a guest celebrity. (Guest celebrities seem to be a feature of séances. You will remember that in *her* first séance with Bishop Pike Mrs. Twigg's guest celebrity was Paul Tillich.) George Daisley is not in Mrs. Twigg's league, by any means, and *his* celebrity was relatively run-of-the-mill. It was the late Edgar Cayce (1877–1945). Edgar Cayce has been turning up in séances for many years. He seems to like them. During his lifetime Cayce had acquired a considerable international reputation ("America's greatest religious seer") by falling asleep and entering into telepathic communication with persons (usually sick people) known to him only by name and address. He is said to have done this some twenty thousand times. His psychic delvings persuaded him of reincarnation and much of his career was devoted to an explication and application of his perceptions in that regard.

What brought Edgar Cayce to this particular séance? It isn't easy to say. He noted that while unpacking books for the bishop Maren had been reading books about him. She confirmed this. He suggested she try a different book which would be not so difficult to understand. He also said he wanted to help Maren develop "spiritual healing." Other than that he didn't have much that was concrete to offer. He *was* remarkably well-informed about odds and ends of goings-on in the bishop's new apartment. He also knew about Maren's loss of bangs back in Cambridge. His interests in Maren and in Bishop Pike seemed to focus on the banalities and trivialities of their daily lives. At one point he noted (correctly, she later told the bishop) that that very morning Maren had trouble choosing among three lipsticks in her bathroom. At about this same point in the proceedings Bishop Pike, who felt the conversation was running down, made an effort to summon up Paul Tillich. He got nowhere with that and shortly thereafter the séance petered to a close.

Either Edgar Cayce really was lurking in Maren Bergrud's bathroom the morning of that séance or Maren was no sooner out of the bathroom than she was on the telephone.

We do not propose to labor through Bishop Pike's other séances with George Daisley. Those which preceded Maren Bergrud's death the following June were similar (though *less* impressive) and susceptible of similar analysis. Two weeks after Maren's death (persons who have gone to the "Other Side" by violence need two weeks to get adjusted, according to Canon John Pearce-Higgins) Bishop Pike went to Daisley in an effort to reach *her*. No luck. Two months after Maren's death he tried again. No luck.

Maren Bergrud seems to have found it easier to communicate with George Daisley on this side than from the other.

". . . *Clearing the Way to Go into the Wilderness*"

Jim and Diane Pike celebrated their marriage on December 20, 1968, in a service for family and close friends in her family church, Willow Glen United Methodist, San Jose, California. The service, while ecumenical in the composition of the participating clergy and congregation, was nonetheless kosher in its conformity to the Episcopal Book of Common Prayer. Negotiations for the marriage had been protracted and complex. Kilmer Myers, Bishop Pike's successor as diocesan in California, had formally declared Jim's marriage to Esther spiritually dead, enabling Jim to remarry within the Episcopal Church, but he had not, in the end, approved the remarriage. He seems to have regarded the fact that it took place without his approval as some kind of personal affront.

Three days after the marriage Bishop Myers uttered a personal request to all his clergy that Bishop Pike no longer be invited to exercise any sacerdotal function—preaching, administering the sacraments, conducting services of worship—in any Episcopal churches within the Diocese of California. Bishop Myers' inhibition in that regard was totally effective. Bishop Pike was shattered. No injury he had ever suffered save the suicide of his son wounded him more deeply. He was still talking to Diane about the hurt of it only days before his death. The anathema Bishop Myers had visited upon his old friend and brother in Christ amounted to a deposition (without due process) from episcopal and sacerdotal office and even to a banishment of Bishop Pike from the community of Episcopal people he had served so long and with such energy and "controversial" devotion.

Bishop Pike brooded for some months over the startling limbo into which he had been abruptly catapulted. He contemplated proceeding canonically for redress of the wrong he felt he had been done. He knew he would get nowhere. No body of authority on earth is more adept than a collective of bishops at washing its hands furiously and weeping copious crocodile tears when attention is directed to the mote in its own eye. Bishop Pike had *had* it. He had *had* it in the sense that his brothers the bishops had exhausted their pastoral resources. They didn't know what to do *about* him and they didn't know what to do *with* him. They wanted him to disappear. They wanted to be left alone to play church together contentedly without being incessantly reminded that they were living in the real world and that it was fallen. And so, in their wisdom and using Bishop Myers as their complaisant instrument, they had, in effect, declared *Bishop Pike* spiritually dead.

It was a blow from which he would never recover.

Bishop Pike had also *had* it in the sense that his confidence in the *institution* of the Episcopal Church had withered away to nothing. He loved it no less (and no bishop ever loved it more), but as he contemplated its shriveling grasp of historical reality and its pathetic adhesion to wreckages of the past he despaired of its future and therefore of his own future in it. In April of 1969 Jim and Diane Pike announced their intention to leave the Church. Few episcopal tears were shed. Had it not been for Bishop Myers's anathema Bishop Pike would not, in our opinion, have bothered to lay out flamboyantly in the April 1969 issue of *Look* magazine his grievance with the Church. He would more likely have agitatedly drifted out of *that* scene into other more or less peripheral pursuits. The personal trauma of the anathema had been terrible, but the calumny of his bride, as he perceived it to be, implicit in the *circumstances* of the anathema is what made it unbearable for him. For all his sometime cavalier promiscuity there lingered in Bishop Pike a vast chivalry. He would sooner shed the remnants of his episcopal panoply than suffer insult to the woman he loved.

> And so with buoyant hearts, with a new 'believing hope' about a future not yet fully born, with the same beliefs we had before (not enough to suit some, too many to suit others), and with a renewed eagerness to minister to clergy and others in transition, we set forth on an unencumbered journey into an open future.

Thus concluded Jim and Diane's passionate forensic in *Look* magazine. Jim Pike informed the press that he no longer desired to use his title of bishop. Since he was denied all opportunity to exercise the functions of bishop the title had become a sham and a mockery so far as he was concerned. How *should* he henceforth be addressed? *Dr.* Pike? *Mr.* Pike? *Jim* Pike would do, he allowed.

He remained, nevertheless, a bishop and *would* remain a bishop the rest of his fleeting days. Formal processes that would depose him from that office were initiated and then were temporarily suspended prior to his terminal journey to Israel. His episcopal dignity survived him as for so long it had survived the extraordinary malice of his enemies.

The pain Jim and Diane Pike experienced in consequence of the brutal way they had been extruded from institutional church life led them to ponder the predicaments of so many others—clergy, clergy families, and laity—who were at that same time in consternation and vocational confusion. It had always been Jim Pike's way to find in any misery he might have an opportunity to serve others who were similarly miserable. So, also in April of 1969, Jim and Diane established a Foundation for Religious Transition in Santa Barbara. The purpose of the Foundation was to organize a ministry (centered around Jim Pike) to those who found themselves on the edges of institutional Christianity—whether just inside or just outside—and who had serious religious (and other) concerns that were being otherwise largely ignored.

Jim Pike saw the Foundation for Religious Transition as a vehicle by which *Bishop* Pike might meaningfully perpetuate his ministry. During the summer of 1969, the last summer he would know, he would be verified in his expectations for the Foundation. There was much interest in it and had he lived on there is little question it would have come to be one of several primary preoccupations of his own transitional ministry. In lighter moments he sometimes spoke of founding some sort of "Church Alumni Association." Just because you'd graduated from the place and gone on to the real business of living didn't mean you wouldn't look back at it with affectionate regard. It was, after all, the place that had nurtured you and prepared you for whatever was to come after. Once in a while it might be fun to go back and see how the old girl was getting on. Maybe a group of classmates could be gotten together to take in, say, a Solemn High Mass for old times' sake. He rather roguishly enjoyed this fantasy.

Coincident with the formation of the Foundation for Religious Transition Jim and Diane had also begun to expand the functions and activities of the New Focus Foundation of which Diane had become director, succeeding Maren Bergrud in that as in other respects. New Focus had been created to attend to Bishop Pike's far-flung interests that were extraneous to his responsibilities at the Center. It handled his lecture engagements and his assorted writing commitments. Now New Focus would assist Jim Pike in his research both as to Christian origins and with regard to psychic phenomena. A modest publication was launched, under the aegis of the Foundation for Religious Transition, called *New Focus* ("For Church Alumni and those on the 'Inside Edge'"), which carried articles and features of interest in both those fields and gave space as well to whatever else might be on Jim Pike's mind at any given moment. It was a zestful and eccentric little journal that was to have all too brief a career.

Thereupon came one last severance of Bishop Pike from institutional life. His tenure at the Center for the Study of Democratic Institutions was suddenly ended. Robert Hutchins, for complicated reasons, had decided to reorganize the Center and the effect of this was to reduce drastically the roster of scholars in residence. Bishop Pike was among those severed. This was in no way a reflection upon his performance at the Center. It was nevertheless, in our opinion, something of a blow to him. He liked the Center. He valued the company of scholars and the esteem of being numbered among them. He may in his latter years have valued this more highly than his ecclesiastical eminence. Having only had time to adjust to being cast adrift from the community of the Church he was now cast adrift from the community of scholars. He really was on his own.

Bishop John Robinson happened to be in California when the Center was reorganized. On the day Bishop Pike learned he was severed he and Bishop Robinson were among the guests invited for dinner at the home of the late Alan Watts in Big Sur. Bishop Robinson remembers that outwardly Bishop Pike did not seem perturbed about leaving the Center and that he made banter about it. Robinson, however, sensed that, in fact, Bishop Pike was distressed and in a way humiliated. Pike described for his good friend the scene in Robert Hutchins's office when he had earlier in the day been summoned there to get the news. The old "Abbot" had been so uncomfortable having to—in effect—*fire* Bishop Pike that the bishop had jumped from his chair and gone around the desk to comfort him. That would be very like Bishop Pike but it would not necessarily mean he was in no need of comfort himself.

On December 19, 1973, some four years later, Scott Kennedy made his way to the Center to discuss Bishop Pike with John Cogley, an associate of the place, a Roman Catholic journalist of note (who would later join the Episcopal Church), and the author, just after Bishop Pike's death, of what might be called an affectionately negative assessment of the bishop's career which appeared in the September 19, 1969, issue of *Life* magazine. (With Cogley's article there also appeared a remarkable photograph of Bishop Pike in his episcopal clerical attire strolling on the beach in Santa Barbara. It was a lovely study of Bishop Pike but it was remarkable because the bishop had seldom been to that or any other beach. He frequently marveled that there seemed to be so many people in the world who had *time* to go to the beach.) John Cogley did not entertain a high estimate of Bishop Pike's intellectual accomplishments.

> Jim Pike was not an original thinker. His strength as well as his weakness was that he was an original man, who had an uncanny ability to make the secondhand look new. He could promote situational ethics as if he had invented the idea. He could propound the new theology as if he had worked his way through to it by immense intellectual effort. When he discovered psychic phenomena, it was as if it had never been heard of. In recent years he went about the study of Christian origins with the same air of fresh discovery, as if the scholars who have worked in the field for years were his research assistants. In earlier days, he was constantly credited with more scholarship, inventiveness, creativity and originality than he actually possessed. He was doomed, then, to be a disappointment to many who looked to him for what he could not give, if only because he was too busy for serious study or prolonged introspection. He finally gained a reputation for glibness and raw publicity-seeking. The result was that his most serious moves, like his trumpeted exit from the institutional church, were not taken very seriously. There had been too many controversies, the publicity releases had become too frequent. If he knew this, he never acknowledged it but carried on as if his latest project would be the greatest breakthrough yet.

Scott Kennedy discussed this and other passages from the *Life* obituary with John Cogley, and then he made his way down the interior corridor of the Center's open courtyard to the lair of the "Abbot" of Eucalyptus Hill, Robert Hutchins. Decades had gone by since Hutchins had headed the University of Chicago and had established a reputation as the boy wonder of the academic world and as something of an innovator in educational practice. He and Mortimer Adler had introduced the Great Books program that was to have such impact on progressive education. (Hutchins also abolished football at the University of Chicago, a brilliant innovation that, unfortunately, did not catch on.) By 1973 Robert Hutchins was a venerable patrician whose austere presence was almost chillingly intimidating although he certainly did not intend it to be. He accorded to Scott Kennedy what surprisingly turned out to be more of a conversation than an interview.

HOW DID YOU FIRST MEET JIM AND WHAT CONTACT DID YOU HAVE WITH HIM AFTER THAT AND WHAT WERE THE CIRCUMSTANCES OF HIS COMING TO THE CENTER?

I first came to know Jim when he was dean in New York. He asked me to be on his radio program or maybe it was television. We kept in touch after that but that was about all. Then, when he had been bishop out here for some years he came down to see me one time, saying only that he would like to talk about his situation. He described his situation to me and said he could see there would be considerable trouble ahead. I said to him that perhaps he should think about getting out of the place he was in and coming to the Center. Some time went by and then he called me one day and said he would like to do that. And that's what happened.

He saw the Center, I think, as a place where he could continue his intellectual work without having to give up his bishopric. He could get around quite a bit though not so much as he had formerly. Our studies are more or less systematic and our meetings are daily during the week. He understood that and fit into it very well. And he continued on here in that capacity until just before he went abroad for the last time.

JOHN COGLEY SEEMED TO THINK JIM HAD ALREADY DECIDED TO GIVE UP AS BISHOP OF CALIFORNIA AND WAS ACTIVELY LOOKING FOR OTHER OPTIONS WHEN YOU INVITED HIM TO COME HERE. WAS THAT YOUR IMPRESSION?

The impression I had when he came to see me was that he really had not decided what he wanted to do. He was restless. He saw many serious problems ahead. But he did not come to me and say, "I've decided to get out of the bishop business, and would like to ask your advice about something else." He said he would like my advice as to *whether* he should get out of the bishop business, and only then what he might do as an alternative to it. My impression is not John's impression. I should add that he is a professional newspaper reporter, and therefore an accurate observer, and I may not be.

I WOULD BE INTERESTED IN YOUR RECOLLECTIONS OF THE WEEK JIM WAS LOST IN THE DESERT AND THEN FOUND DEAD. HOW WAS ALL THAT RECEIVED HERE AT THE CENTER?

Everybody here liked Jim very much. You couldn't help it. The thought that he was in some limbo out there and that something might have happened to him was very distressing to everybody. When we heard about his death we were horrified. During that whole week we were very agitated and we were even more agitated when it ended.

WHILE JIM WAS AT THE CENTER HIS PRIMARY INTEREST IN TERMS OF SCHOLARSHIP HAD TO DO WITH HIS STUDY OF CHRISTIAN ORIGINS AND THE HISTORICAL JESUS. OVER THE YEARS HE HAD GONE FROM WHAT HE HIMSELF CALLED "SMOOTH ORTHODOXY" TO THIS ALMOST OBSESSION WITH THE HISTORICAL JESUS. DID YOU OBSERVE THAT OR DO YOU HAVE ANY THOUGHTS ABOUT IT?

My first connections with Jim were in the area of political problems. We shared an interest in civil liberties. His legal background was very helpful to me in our discussions along those lines. We had gone to the same law school. He also had an interest in communications from a legal point of view. That has perhaps been largely forgotten. We were very much interested in that subject here at the Center. With us he prepared papers and led discussions on the significance of the Dead Sea Scrolls. He was deeply concerned about that. He also wrote a paper and led a fascinating discussion on women in the Church. But as to the development of his thinking in regard to Christianity I am not an authority. John Cogley would know more about that than I do.

MANY PEOPLE OVERLOOK JIM'S TRAINING AS A LAWYER. I'VE LOOKED AT MANY OF THE PAPERS HE WROTE FOR THE CENTER AND AT LEAST AS MANY HAD TO DO WITH LEGAL QUESTIONS AS HAD TO DO WITH THEOLOGY.

Yes. Whenever we had discussions on any subject where legal issues arose he would come into the discussion very actively on the legal side. The question of the relation of church and state from a legal standpoint was up for discussion several times while he was here. He participated vigorously in that conversation.

DID HE EVER RAISE AT THE TABLE OR PRIVATELY WITH YOU HIS INTEREST IN PSYCHIC PHENOMENA?

No. He never raised that at the table. He did talk to me about
his book and something of his experiences that way. But I recall
no extended discussion of that topic with him.

JOHN COGLEY SAID THAT OF ALL HIS BOOKS THAT WAS THE ONLY
ONE NEVER DEALT WITH AT CENTER DISCUSSIONS AND THAT HE DOES
NOT RECALL THAT THE BOOK WAS EVER EVEN DISTRIBUTED IN THE
CENTER.

That would be my recollection also.

JIM ESTEEMED SCHOLARSHIP AND THE ROLE OF THE SCHOLAR.
SOME HAVE SAID HE WAS NOT TEMPERAMENTALLY SUITED TO IT.
HE CAME TO THE CENTER HOPING TO DEVOTE HIMSELF TO SCHOL-
ARSHIP IN A MORE DISCIPLINED WAY. YET IN HIS FIRST YEAR HE
WAS OFTEN ABSENT FOR SPEAKING ENGAGEMENTS AND SO ON. HOW
DO YOU THINK OF HIM AS A SCHOLAR AND DID YOU THINK HIS AM-
BITION FOR THAT WAS IN THE END FRUSTRATED?

Jim was, of course, a very inquisitive man. This led him to
inquire into a great many things where most people would have
said, "I have no time to inquire into that." He would take on
whatever came along. The first year he was here was not characteristic of his whole time with us. He carried out commitments
that he had made but he took on no new ones that could not be
carried out over weekends. After the first year he was very regular
in his attendance at our meetings. I wasn't disturbed about his
absences the first year because I understood the position that he
was in. That was the time of his heresy difficulties. Nobody could
have complained about his attendance thereafter and nobody did.

IN A MAGAZINE ARTICLE AFTER JIM'S DEATH SOME RESIDENT OF
THE CENTER WAS QUOTED AS SAYING JIM PIKE WAS NO INTELLEC-
TUAL AND DIDN'T BELONG UP HERE.

I remember that. I don't know who said it. It certainly was not
true. Scholarship? What does it mean? It has come to mean—
more and more—what is meant by that old definition of a spe-
cialist: "Somebody who knows more and more about less and
less." That is what academic scholarship has come to mean. In
that sense, of course, Jim was not a scholar. And in that sense, in
my opinion, *nobody* should be one. He came in at more points
relevant to our life here than almost anybody I can think of. It
was too much to ask that he *always* come in systematically. His
primary interest, as you say, was in certain historical questions no
one else here was expert about and nobody else here shared his
degree of interest about. Those questions were not the sort of
thing he could discuss with us. A scholar is someone who thinks

about something in a systematic way. It helps if what he thinks about is important. Jim *was* a scholar within that definition.

THE SAME CRITICS WHO DISMISSED JIM AS A SCHOLAR ALSO LIKED TO DISMISS HIM BY DESCRIBING HIM AS A POPULARIZER. I ALWAYS THOUGHT THAT WAS ONE OF HIS GREAT GIFTS BUT THEY USED THE TERM ABOUT HIM IN A NEGATIVE WAY.

I don't know what the ideal bishop would be. He would first of all need great administrative ability. Jim seemed to me to discharge those responsibilities with great skill. He would also need to be able to communicate what he was about and what his institution was about. He would need to reach as many people in that way as could possibly understand it. "Missionary," I would think, is a term of respect and not of reproach. Jim *was* a missionary. I don't know how you could conduct missionary activity without going at it on a popular level. It seemed to me Jim was a fine combination of administrator and missionary.

ANOTHER ASPECT OF THIS WAS THE FACT OF JIM'S CELEBRITY. HE WAS OFTEN IN THE NEWS. HE WAS MUCH CRITICIZED FOR THAT.

Much of that could not be helped. Bishop Crowther was telling me about a meeting of bishops somewhere. Many great dignitaries of the Church were on hand. Jim came in. In thirty seconds everything else was dropped and everybody crowded around to find out what was the latest word with him. He couldn't help that. He was—in spite of himself—a charismatic figure. He attracted attention wherever he went. I don't remember one occasion when he deliberately tried to do this. He didn't make any effort to capture the headlines. He just did.

WASN'T YOUR VISIT WITH JIM ON HIS "DEAN PIKE SHOW" AT THE TIME YOU AND THE FUND FOR THE REPUBLIC WERE UNDER HEAVY ATTACK? HE ALWAYS HAD SUCH A COMMITMENT TO THE SOCIAL GOSPEL AND I WONDER IF THERE WERE OTHER TIMES WHEN YOU AND HE MET AT POINTS OF CONSCIENCE, YOU MIGHT SAY?

We used to be on all the same letterhead committees. You are quite correct about the Fund for the Republic. One reason I was always grateful to Jim was that when we *were* under such serious, vicious attack he invited me to go on the air with him to talk about the problem. That was of great importance to us at that time. Most public forums were closed to us. People were frightened. And over the years after that he and I, in general, followed parallel lines on issues like that.

AS A BISHOP JIM TOOK VERY SERIOUSLY HIS ROLE AS PASTOR PASTORUM. MANY PEOPLE THINK HIS PASTORAL GIFTS WERE HIS

STRONGEST SUIT. DID YOU HAVE INDICATIONS OF THAT DURING HIS
TIME AT THE CENTER?

You could feel that all the time with Jim. He was a teacher,
too. I suppose that is what a *pastor pastorum* does. He tries to
teach. That's what he did with us. He tried to help us learn and
learn himself in the process. That was very much a part of him
and since that is what the Center is all about he was very much
a part of the Center.

DO YOU HAVE ANY RECOLLECTIONS THAT SEEM TO TYPIFY JIM?

I always remember the broad grin and the great good humor
with which he would exterminate opposition. It was wonderful to
watch.

IN HIS LAST YEARS AND ESPECIALLY AFTER PUBLICATION OF *The
Other Side* MANY PEOPLE BEGAN TO SAY HE HAD GONE TOO FAR.
EVEN THOSE CLOSE TO HIM IN THE CHURCH—THE LIBERALS—
WOULD SAY IT WAS ONE THING WHEN HE OPPOSED SEGREGATION OR
MADE A WOMAN DEACON BUT THIS IS TOO MUCH. SOME EVEN SAID
HE HAD LOST HIS BALANCE OR GONE MAD. I WONDER HOW YOU
PERCEIVED HIS STATE OF MIND AND HEALTH IN THE LAST COUPLE
OF YEARS OF HIS LIFE?

I thought both mentally and emotionally he was as good as
ever. And I found his health in every way had always been good.
His experiences with psychic phenomena were things he had experienced and which he reported. It seemed to me it was something that had to be taken seriously. It did not occur to me that
he was doing it for publicity, and it certainly never occurred to
me that he was doing it because he was out of his mind. I never
saw Jim when I thought he was out of his mind.

DO YOU THINK THAT AT THE TIME JIM LEFT THE CENTER—OR
THE CENTER LEFT HIM—THAT HE FORESAW THAT OR ANYHOW
WOULD PROBABLY HAVE BEEN LEAVING THE CENTER EVEN IF THE
REORGANIZATION HADN'T HAPPENED?

I think so. I can't prove it, of course. But I think he got more
and more interested in something that the Center *as* a center by
the nature of things really wasn't much interested in. He wanted
to pursue that. And he would have. So, whether the Center had
been reorganized or not I think he would not have stayed with it
much longer. I think he would have been drawn to forming a
"center" or an institute of his own focused on his own concerns.
He had already begun to do that before he left us.

DID YOU HAVE CONVERSATIONS WITH JIM ABOUT HIS LEAVING THE
CHURCH? DID YOU THINK HE WAS COMFORTABLE OUTSIDE IT? DO

YOU THINK THAT IN TIME HE MIGHT HAVE BEEN RECONCILED WITH IT?

Yes. I had conversations with Jim along those lines. I do think in time he would have gone back to the Church. Time was on Jim's side. He was right, so far as I can see, about what was happening to the churches. That in itself might have led—even by now—to some kind of reconciliation with the Church. He was a bishop until the day he died.

DID JIM EVER TALK WITH YOU ABOUT HIS GREAT LOVE FOR ISRAEL? SOMETIMES HE SPOKE OF RETIRING SOMEDAY TO HAIFA—WHICH HE LOVED—AND I WONDERED IF HE EVER TALKED WITH YOU ABOUT THAT?

He talked with me quite often and enthusiastically about Israel. I don't ever remember his talking about retiring there. I have difficulty imagining Jim Pike retiring to *any* place. He wasn't the retiring sort.

Jim Pike left the Center on June 30, 1969. He had two months to live.

In their April 1969 article for *Look* magazine announcing that they would leave the church, Jim and Diane had quoted (with seeming paranormal prescience) a passage from the ancient *Manual of Discipline* of the Qumrân community.

"This is the time of clearing the way to go into the wilderness."

No More Appropriate Place for Jim to Die

JERUSALEM, Sept. 7— Dr. James A. Pike was found dead today, the victim of a fall, on a rocky ledge in the Judean wilderness two miles from the Dead Sea.

The former Episcopal Bishop of California, missing since last Monday when he and his wife took a wrong turn and drove deep into the desert, was apparently seeking his wife when he died.

Mrs. Pike, who had left her exhausted husband to find help, was with the search party today when the body was discovered by an Israeli border policeman.

Dr. Pike, it was learned, had found a pool of water nearby but had chosen to press on in the apparent belief that his wife, who had passed the same area, might be in trouble.

Police officials said that the 56-year old churchman had left clues behind—a map found Tuesday, undershorts found yesterday and glasses and a contact-lens case found today—to indicate the path he had taken.

He was climbing a steep cliff either to extricate himself from a box canyon or to get better vantage, when he slipped and fell 70 feet. Dr. Pike was found in a kneeling position, fully clothed except for the shorts he had left behind and carrying $700 in cash and some personal papers.

Police officials declined to estimate how long the body had been there, but members of the search team thought Dr. Pike had fallen soon after the search began, or three to four days ago.

Hundreds of soldiers and volunteers had participated in the search in the Israeli-held part of Jordan. Planes and helicopters also had been used the first three days.

A helicopter was called in again today to remove Dr. Pike's body from the perilous cliffside ledge. The body was transferred to a desert vehicle and then to an ambulance for the trip to Tel Aviv, where an autopsy will be performed.

Dr. Pike's 31-year-old wife, Diane, had asked to join the search party this morning. She said she felt her husband had died and she wanted to be with the searchers if they found the body.

Looking pale and still showing the signs of her own 10-hour trip through the same rocky terrain last Monday night, Mrs. Pike said: "There could have been no more appropriate place for Jim to die, if he had to die.

"He died in the country he loved as though it were his own, in the wilderness where Jesus, according to the Gospels, went to pray and meditate."

The desolate region between Bethlehem, revered as the site of the birthplace of Jesus, and the Dead Sea, is said to be the traditional site of the temptation of Jesus.

The book of Matthew in the New Testament recalls in Chapter 4, first verse:

Then Jesus was led by the spirit into the wilderness to be tempted by the devil. And he fasted 40 days and 40 nights, he said, he was afterward hungered. "And when the tempter came and said to him, 'If thou be the Son of God, command that these stones be made bread'." And then Jesus answered, "man shall not live by bread alone."

This was the morose conclusion to a story James Feron had covered for a week in the New York *Times* with competence and colorful restraint. By Monday, September 8, 1969, when Feron's last dispatch entered the *Times*, nobody really supposed Bishop Pike would be discovered alive. Members of the search party, for the most part, had pretty much abandoned hope that his remains would ever be found. The bishop had gone out into the desert on Monday, September 1. Diane had left him at sundown that same day. He had been lost in the sweltering wilderness six days and six nights when at last several intrepid scouts, including Scott Kennedy, smelled and then sighted his body on an overhung rocky ledge deep in canyon Wadi Mashash.

I embraced my brother warmly, blinded by tears, and somehow got him into the room with his bags. Then we both broke down, I sitting on the bed and he on a chair nearby. We sobbed out our grief together for a long, long time. Then as I could, I began slowly to tell him the story. He asked very few questions, listening with a depth of understanding which came from knowing Jim and me well.

"I felt all along I should have been with you," Scott mused. "I felt something was wrong when we said good-bye in San Jose, but because you two were so happy, I pushed the feeling aside. I just sensed I should be along."

"I felt it out there in the desert," I responded. "Once I was out of the canyon and was sure I could somehow get help, I thought, 'If only Scott had been along I could have left him with Jim. I wouldn't have had to leave Jim there alone.' I've thought of it several times since then," I added. "But there's no point in looking back now."

Scott Kennedy had arrived in Jerusalem Thursday evening, September 4, three days after the desert ordeal had begun. He had got word by radio that his brother-in-law was missing and his sister safe while he was driving through Wyoming with friends. By the time he got in touch with his family in San Jose they had already made airline reservations for him to go to Israel via Chicago and London. He was the obvious choice. He had been closest to Jim and Diane. He had been to Israel with them on a previous trip. And he was a very resourceful and plucky young man.

On the way to Israel, his plane had stopped in England. Scott used the opportunity to call Mrs. Twigg to see whether she had any word from her sources in the spirit world. She had had nothing but a gray mist. She was not very optimistic. She had "bad feelings" about the bishop's situation. Scott and Diane decided not to be overly affected by Mrs. Twigg's gloom. So long as the search continued they would hold out hope, and they would do whatever they could to be of help. Scott decided to join the search himself the next morning.

Scott and Diane arrived before 5 A.M. Friday morning at Major Givati's headquarters in Bethlehem. There was no sign of any search. They waited. About 7 A.M. Major Shaul arrived. The search had originated elsewhere, he explained enigmatically. About 8 A.M. Major Givati appeared. The search had not been called off, he said, but the tactics had been changed. Bedouin of the desert would take over. They had been offered a reward. The search had not been called off exactly, but the police and the army and the helicopters had been withdrawn. Major Givati, though he did not say so to Diane and Scott lest he upset them, no longer expected Bishop Pike to be found alive. There was no need for great haste or urgency about locating the body, if indeed it ever would be located.

During the morning Major Givati, a man of singular charm and delicacy, contrived to divert Diane and Scott with an account of the operations of his militia and his personal experiences in police service. He invited them along to witness a ceremony in which he conferred higher ranks upon some of his men. By lunchtime Yitzhak Sover, Israeli Director of the Ministry of Tourism, turned up (having been asked to do so by Major Givati) to take Scott and Diane to lunch. They were joined by two journalists who had been especially kind to Diane during her ordeal. They were able to persuade Scott and Diane that there was no use in their staying in Bethlehem.

Back in the hotel in Jerusalem and trying to rest Diane suddenly thought there should be a mass for Jim. She had had a note from the Anglican Archbishop of Jerusalem offering to do whatever he could. Scott called Archbishop Appleton, who agreed to celebrate a mass at 6:30 P.M. On the shortest of notice a small congregation was gathered in St. George's Cathedral. In a most extraordinary gesture Bishop Pike's esteemed colleagues and friends, Professors David Flusser and Shlomo Pines of Hebrew University, and their wives, observed their own Sabbath and walked (since Orthodox Jews do not drive on the Sabbath) considerable distances in order to attend this Christian solemnity. Bishop Appleton offered an unreformed high Anglican mass. He deviated only once from the fixed liturgy. When serving the Eucharist to Diane he interposed: "Your bodies and souls are one in Christ both now and forever." Diane drew strength and some peace from the service.

Scott and Diane returned to the hotel. London was trying to reach Diane. Mrs. Twigg and Harry had had their remarkable séance with Canon John Pearce-Higgins. They had, Mrs. Twigg said, listened to the tape of it three times and had had it evaluated by a friend with psychic gifts. There could be no doubt. Bishop Pike was already on the "Other Side." He was in transition and was confused. Difficult as the session had been there could be no doubt Bishop Pike had "come through." Mrs. Twigg, in other words, had taken it upon herself to be the first person to tell Diane that her husband was dead.

"But, my dear, I wouldn't tell you unless I was very sure."

"I know," I said. "Thank you."

"Will you be able to stop in London on your way home?" she asked.

"I don't know. How much time would I need in order to see you?" I was thinking how eager I would be to get home once I left there.

"Oh, I should think three or four hours at the least," was her response.

"I see. Well, I'll try to arrange it if I can. In any case, I'm grateful for your call."

"It's all right, my dear. And I am sorry, but I felt you should know."

Let us pause. We have tried to be objective and fair in reporting Bishop Pike's experiences with psychic phenomena. We must suspend our objectivity (though not, we think, our fairness) with respect to this unfortunate episode. Mrs. Twigg had no business making that telephone call. Suppose she had been wrong? You do not tell someone they have lost a loved one unless you know beyond peradventure of a doubt that it is true. Mrs. Twigg had no means of such a certitude. Persons who have listened to the tape of that séance are not persuaded Bishop Pike was anywhere near East Acton at the time. Bishops John Robinson and Mervin Stockwood listened to that tape and they were not impressed. We have listened to that tape and we regard it, despite the fact that Diane herself considers it convincing, as utterly unconvincing.

Mrs. Twigg had parlayed into fact what by the most generous latitude we might concede to have been an informed intuition. She coupled her importunity with the solicitation of a séance with

Diane on her way home from Israel. We understand that the ethics of the psychic world proscribe the solicitation of séances by
mediums. It is true that Diane had telephoned Mrs. Twigg from
Israel, and that Scott had telephoned her during his stopover in
London. To that extent she may have felt authorized to call
Diane. It is not her authority that we challenge; it is her judgment that we deplore.

> "You've got to remember what Jim always said, Diane," Scott
> observed.
> "What do you mean?" I puzzled.
> "Remember Jim always said no medium is infallible—not even
> Mrs. Twigg. And neither is Jim—even if he is on the other side.
> There's no reason for us to accept what has come through Mrs.
> Twigg as any more valid than what has come through the many
> others who have sent messages. We must not give up hope now.
> If he is still alive, we must not give up hope."

Scott's counsel prevailed over Mrs. Twigg's intervention. Had it
not prevailed Bishop Pike's body might well have never been
recovered. Scott prevailed because he was right and because Diane
refused to give up hope even though she sensed Mrs. Twigg
would prove right in saying Jim was dead. She was waiting for her
own "inner confirmation" of his death. Not even Mrs. Twigg
could deliver that.

(The séance Mrs. Twigg attempted to solicit from Diane never
took place. She and Scott did not choose to stop in London on
their way home. About two months later a "proxy" séance was arranged according to which the Reverend Hugh Anwyll joined
Canon Pearce-Higgins in a séance with Harry and Mrs. Twigg.
Diane had provided Hugh Anwyll with a list of questions most of
which had answers she felt only Jim could supply. The séance was
an utter bust. Mrs. Twigg blamed this on the Reverend Anwyll's
alleged skepticism. In February of 1970 Diane and Scott had two
sittings with Mrs. Twigg, neither of which they considered
"evidentiary." Diane has not sat with any other medium since
Jim's death for the purpose of attempting to communicate with
him. She has believed that if Jim wished her to do so he would
somehow let her know. He has not. She has had experiences
where she felt Jim was with her or guiding her in reaching a
difficult decision. These experiences may have been the sort of

comforting reassurance many people have in grief and may or may not have been evidence of Jim's continuing concern for her. We have no opinion whatever one way or the other about that.)

Diane and Scott had scarcely had time to rearrange their composures in the wake of Mrs. Twigg's call when another came. It was Mrs. Margot Klausner, a Tel Aviv sensitive and the president of the Israeli Society for Psychical Research. She reported that the following morning six members of the Society for the Preservation of Nature (a sort of Israeli Sierra Club) proposed to set forth on a three-day expedition into the desert in search of Bishop Pike. They were coordinating their effort with Major Givati. Mrs. Klausner intended to assist the six volunteers (some of whom she knew) by doing "a plumb-line test with a map" and equipping them with the results. This she did. She held a string weighted at one end over two maps and allowed it to sway until coming to rest over some specific spot in the desert. With both maps the result was the same. That spot was presumed to be the location of Bishop Pike.

(Mrs. Klausner also resorted to another of her gifts, which is automatic writing. She held a pencil on a paper and let it write whatever it wished. It wished to write a message from Edgar Cayce, the same Edgar Cayce who had graced Bishop Pike's first séance with George Daisley. Cayce reported the bishop was alive in a cave hard to find because of overhanging bushes. He was wrong.)

Mrs. Klausner's maps would turn out to be of no use. But her call had not been without benefit. For the first time Scott discerned a way he could himself join the search. He decided he would accompany the Preservation of Nature volunteers. Major Givati assented. He also would honor the word he had given earlier in the search to follow up on whatever specific leads might come from psychic sources. He didn't believe in such stuff himself but he was not disposed to disdain those who sincerely did.

Scott and Diane were waked at 4 A.M. the next morning for what would turn out to be the next to last day of the search. Thereupon came another call. It was Dr. Ian Stevenson. It had chanced that during the week Bishop Pike was lost in the desert Dr. Stevenson had been attending a convention of the American Association of Parapsychology. Great had been the agitation of the convened psychics and students of same. Dr. Stevenson had been given one message that did seem specific. He did not know the psychic responsible for it and could not vouch for him. He nevertheless would feel derelict not to pass it along if Diane wanted to have it. She did. It would also turn out to be of no use.

Diane remained that entire Saturday in her room in Jerusalem. Peggy Barnhart of the American consulate stayed with her. Peggy Barnhart had been discreetly helpful the whole week and her company that day was a great comfort to Diane. It was 7 P.M. before Scott returned to the hotel. The day's search had not been unproductive. A pair of boxer undershorts had been found in a pool of water deep in canyon Wadi Mashash.

Major Givati had decided to send a small party of his militia with Scott and the six volunteers. He did this partly to fulfill his promise to check out any specific mediumistic messages and partly because he was fearful for the safety of the civilians, especially the safety of Scott Kennedy, who had no experience of wilderness exploration. It may be said, therefore, that while the messages from mediums did not, in fact, prove accurate, they did have the effect of prolonging the search.

By early afternoon the search party had reached that point in the canyon beyond which previous search parties had not gone. The police were convinced that nobody could have gone farther on foot in the desert heat. Scott pointed out that they had also said Diane could not have walked out of the desert but she had. He was sure Jim would have gone farther in an effort to find Diane. Gideon Mann, one of the volunteers, agreed. The volunteers decided to press on. Scott and the police withdrew to the head of the canyon to wait. About an hour later Gideon Mann discovered one of the rare wilderness water holes, and in it a pair of undershorts, floating.

The shorts were compared with another pair in a drawer of the hotel room in Jerusalem. There could be no question that they were Jim's. Major Givati was summoned to the hotel. He immediately began to lay plans for the next day. The search was on again in force. There was now a tangible clue. And Bishop Pike had found water. He could, therefore, conceivably be alive. Major Givati gave orders that the press should not be informed. All week the demands of the press had burdened the searchers. Scott would be allowed to go again with the Preservation of Nature volunteers. Diane would be welcome to come later to wait with him in his office in Bethlehem.

Next morning, Sunday, September 7, Diane (who insisted on coming early) and Scott arrived in Bethlehem at 4:45 A.M. Upon her promise to remain in the jeep Diane was allowed by the officer in charge to go with the search party. She had with her, at Major Givati's request, a bathrobe and pajamas belonging to Jim. The searchers had with them a dog it was hoped might assist if given Jim's scent. The dog, however, refused to descend into the canyon, having more sense than its trainer. (Earlier in the week two dogs had been taken into the desert on a much hotter day and had collapsed within minutes.) Diane waited restlessly in (and around) the jeep as the searchers made their precarious way deep into the canyon to the water hole.

The pool of water was some twenty feet long, seven or eight feet wide, and varied in depth from three to eight feet. Parts of it extended under boulders. It was a still pool but the water was sweet and potable. Two volunteers stripped and searched the pool thoroughly but found nothing. Jim would also surely have refreshed himself in the pool and drunk of it. And he had left his undershorts floating in it as a clue. He must have then decided to go on after Diane, hoping to find her and bring her to the precious water. She had told him she would go down the canyon to the Dead Sea. She had not because it proved too difficult for her. She had climbed up and over the top of the canyon. But he had no way of knowing that. He would have—and he had—proceeded deeper into the canyon.

Wadi Mashash opened into two separate canyons just beyond the pool. One of the volunteers, Israel Schiller, found sunglasses twenty feet down from the pool and pointed toward the left branch of canyon. The sunglasses were Diane's. About 9:40 A.M. in that same left branch of the wadi the searchers came upon a second pool of water, and floating in it a white plastic case containing contact lenses. This also was Diane's. It could have been encouraging. It could have meant Jim was still alive. He had found water twice and soon enough to have stopped the dehydration of his body. He had been sufficiently rational to leave several intelligent clues. Beyond the second pool of water two prints of a shoe with heel and plain sole were found. Bedouin wear sandals and the searchers all wore cleated shoes. Whatever dim hopes for Jim's survival may have been aroused by this flurry of discoveries were all too soon dashed to ruin among the mangled boulders of Wadi Mashash.

Not more than a few hundred feet farther into the canyon Scott and his Israeli companions were assaulted by the insufferable odor of a putrefacted body. Ineluctably guided by the stench of it they had little trouble bringing into sight the wretched corpse. They could get nowhere near it because it lay crumpled and festering on an inaccessible outcrop of rock on an otherwise sheer face of cliff. They were too far from it and it was too far gone for a positive identification.

None was needed. The search was over.

Diane was far above and far back in the canyon. Shlomo, an Israeli volunteer, was with her. They had kept in touch with the search party by means of the radio in their jeep. They knew of the clues. They had shared the intense grim suspense which had gripped the searchers deep down in the canyon.

> "Get in the jeep in the shade," Shlomo called to me.
>
> "I can't sit there," I started to protest. Then I remembered my promise and got in and sat down in the shade. It was about 10:30 in the morning.
>
> Soon the radio came alive again. Shlomo listened intently and then began nodding his head. "They have found him," he said.
>
> "Is he dead?" I asked.
>
> "You already knew," he said, looking directly at me.
>
> "He is dead," I said.
>
> "You already knew," he repeated.
>
> "Yes," I said slowly. "I knew."

Scott made his way back up out of the canyon to be with Diane. He tried to persuade her not to wait for the body. He didn't want her to see it.

> "It looked so pathetic," he said, his voice choking. "So unworthy of Jim. When I first saw it I ran forward and shouted, 'Jim, it's Scott and Diane! We've come!' The tears streamed down my face. There was no response at all—no movement.
>
> "Then I borrowed some binoculars and looked more closely, since we were clear across the canyon from where he was. His left arm was completely black, as though charred by the sun. It made

me sick to my stomach to see it, Diane. I don't want you to see
it."

Strange Encounters

During Holy Week, 1966 (Easter was April 10 that year), three
weeks after his second séance with Mrs. Twigg and his return
from sabbatical in England (and two months after Jim Jr.'s
death), Bishop Pike preached at five weekday noon services (as he
had done for many years) in St. Thomas Episcopal Church on
Fifth Avenue, New York City. He used the five half-hour sermons
to wonder aloud with considerable humor about what he had
come to call the *"omni-*affirmations" about God. (His rumina-
tions in that regard would later occupy several pages of *If This Be
Heresy.*) During his years as dean in New York he had collected a
sizable personal following, many of whom annually turned out for
his visitation at St. Thomas. It was a sort of old home week for
them and for the bishop. He made it a point, therefore, to wait at
the door after each service to greet old friends and to banter with
the dispersing congregation. He was at the peak of his form during Holy Week of 1966, and he greatly enjoyed the enthusiastic
comments his sermons were eliciting.

He also met, after one of those services, a man who was to have
a remarkable impact upon his life.

After I had greeted a few people, one of the curates, the Rev. J.
Lawrence ("Larry") Williams, stepped up to speak to me a moment. Pointing to an older man, about my height with a rather
ruddy face, standing near the tract rack, he said, "There is a
minister with whom I am having lunch who would like to speak
to you for a moment."

I told him that I was due at a luncheon with the editorial staff
of *Time* magazine, but that I would be glad to visit with him
briefly, and I smiled over at the clergyman in question. When
finally I had finished the greetings in the narthex I went over to
the gentleman.

"I'm glad to meet you," I said, not having caught his name.

He explained that he had arrived a little early for his engagement with the Rev. Mr. Williams, saw there was a service going
on and slipped into a back pew.

"I wanted to tell you," he continued, "that while you were

talking there were two figures standing behind you. One was a tall
young man—the name 'Jim' was coming through—your son, I
presume; the other was a patriarchal figure, quite a bit shorter—
the name 'Elias' kept coming through, which I believe is the form
in the Greek New Testament and in the Latin Vulgate for the
name of the prophet Elijah."

I was somewhat astounded by this outpouring. Who was this
man? How did he know that my son's maternal grandfather was
named Elias?

Jim Jr.'s maternal grandfather had come by the name Elias neither from the Greek New Testament nor from the Latin Vulgate.
He had been, as a matter of fact, a Russian Jew. Intrigued though
Bishop Pike was by this strange encounter he was more intrigued
by the prospect of luncheon with the editorial staff of *Time* magazine. He decided to resist the blandishments of the ruddy-faced
minister.

> However, not to be abrupt, I said, rather vaguely, I'm afraid:
> "Yes . . . well, thank you. What church do you serve?"
>
> "Well, I'm actually not at a church. I am connected with a
> group called Spiritual Frontiers Fellowship."
>
> That rang a bell, of course. Then, testing what had come
> through Mrs. Twigg, I asked, "Where is that?"
>
> "It's all over," he replied.
>
> That got me nowhere. I tried again. "Does it have anything
> special in New Jersey?"
>
> "Well, our president, a Father Rauscher—of your Church—is
> in New Jersey. Perhaps that's what you're thinking of."
>
> "Yes . . . yes, of course." There it was: the confirmation of the
> information which had come through in the trance séance. This
> was impressive indeed. Things were so busy on my return I
> hadn't even so much as thought about that part of the sitting in
> the intervening weeks.
>
> We parted.
>
> It wasn't until a year and a half later—in Toronto—that I
> learned the name of the man who spoke to me that day in New
> York City. He was the noted American medium, the Rev. Arthur
> Ford, a Disciples of Christ minister.

The imagery is familiar. Four months later, around August 1,
1966, as we have already discussed, Bishop Pike was to have a surprisingly similar encounter with George Daisley of Santa Barbara.

There would be the emissary of the medium (John McConnell), and then the medium. There would be the references to Spiritual Frontiers. There would be the tall young man ("Jim") standing behind and to the left of the bishop. And there would be the maternal grandfather (though we omitted some of the detail of that) standing behind and to the right of the bishop, and the same confusion about the grandfather's name, even including adversion to the Latin Vulgate (though not to the Greek New Testament). What are we to make of all this? Are we confronted merely with some wondrous similitude inherent in the process of spiritual communication? Extratemporal as the spirit world is said to be is it accordingly *natural* that *any* medium tuning in on the same situation will *automatically* pick up the same wave length, the same vibrations? We struggle to comprehend what we do not profess to understand.

What are we to make of this bizarre encounter with Arthur Ford? Was it by happenstance alone that Arthur Ford had a lunch date that day with Larry Williams? (Father Williams, by the way, was no stranger to Father Rauscher's Spiritual Frontiers, nor was he, as is obvious, a stranger to Arthur Ford.) Was it by happenstance alone that Arthur Ford arrived early, found a service in progress, and slipped into a back pew thereby *happening* to notice the two apparitions flanking Bishop Pike while he was discoursing from the pulpit on the *omni*-affirmations about God? We are frankly embarrassed that our obligations to Bishop Pike require us to poke about in this clutter of happenstances. We would, in fact, *settle* for happenstance were there not one further happenstance to go. Was it *really* happenstance alone that the representations of Arthur Ford (as of George Daisley) were in such comfortable harmony with the representations emanating from Bishop Pike's second (March 14) séance with Mrs. Twigg?

We think not. We are up against a persistent dilemma. We may presume that Jim Jr. somehow or another was the *occasion* for all this happenstance, or we may presume that Bishop Pike was being somehow taken advantage of. We pick no quarrel with anybody (least of all with Bishop Pike) who is persuaded on such evidence as there is that Jim Jr. was the solitary author of this bewildering scenario. We wish we could say we were ourselves persuaded that he was.

We are compelled, however, to explore the alternatives. How might Arthur Ford have learned the substance of Bishop Pike's March 14 séance with Mrs. Twigg? That is the nitty-gritty question. Maren Bergrud pops conveniently into mind. Maren certainly could have been Ford's informant. We are nonetheless inclined to think she was not.

Let us pause for a digression. Maren Bergrud took the notes at the March 14 séance. We wonder if that has something to do with the fact that those notes later got lost. It could be that Maren's notes of that séance became incompatible with events as they transpired. Why would Jim Jr. have said on March 14 that he would be with his father "in August"? Why so long a delay? In the circumstances we would have expected a much earlier assignation. Maybe there *was* an earlier assignation which somehow didn't work out. Arthur Ford's importunity of Bishop Pike on that day in Holy Week (for example) failed to elicit an immediate result. Might there not have thereupon been a change of strategy which led to the events of August 1 in Santa Barbara? Maren might then have discovered that her notes from March 14 did not comport with the new strategy. She might have destroyed the notes and somehow persuaded the bishop that "in August" was what they had said. We regret that this may *seem* farfetched because we suspect it probably *is* what happened. It is certainly no more farfetched than the events it attempts to make plausible.

Maren did attend the March 14 séance. She *could* have communicated with Arthur Ford before Bishop Pike went to New York. (She did *not* go to New York.) But why? There had been no reference to Ford in the March 14 séance. Would Maren have been likely to know that the references to Father Rauscher and Spiritual Frontiers pointed logically in Arthur Ford's direction? No. Not unless somebody in England conveyed the information to her. We doubt that the substance of the March 14 séance would have traveled to Arthur Ford by so circuitous and parlous a route.

We are persuaded that Maren Bergrud was largely responsible for the psychic phenomena in the Cambridge flat which led to the first séance with Mrs. Twigg. We think it quite likely she was the source of some of the information that "came through" in that séance. We are persuaded that Maren was in close rapport with

George Daisley. We do not believe, however, that Maren had anything to do with Arthur Ford. She certainly had nothing to do
with either of Bishop Pike's séances with Ford because she was
dead before they took place. It is an outside possibility she contributed something to the strange encounter at St. Thomas Episcopal
Church during Holy Week. But we doubt it. There wasn't really
time, for one thing. Only three weeks elapsed between the March
14 séance and Arthur Ford's lunch date with Larry Williams.

Is there a way Arthur Ford might have gotten his information
more directly? Ena Twigg, of course, comes to mind. She *was* at
the March 14 séance and she *knew* Arthur Ford. She could have
dispatched a letter. That would be the simplest explanation. We
reject it *because* of its simplicity. Nothing that happens in the
psychic world, we have discovered, has a simple explanation. We
do not anyhow fancy Ena Twigg as a correspondent. Palaver is
her idiom as the semblance of integrity is her hallmark. We cannot bring ourselves to believe that Mrs. Twigg would ever know-
ingly do anything that might compromise her reputation for professional integrity as a medium.

In our correspondence with Dr. Ian Stevenson we inquired of
him what he might be able to say about the respective reputations
of Ena Twigg and Arthur Ford.

> Ena Twigg has an excellent reputation as an honest medium. I
> have never heard anything adverse said about her with regard to
> her integrity. I should be very surprised indeed if evidence were
> developed that she had participated in fraudulent activities.
> With Arthur Ford the case is quite different. There seems little
> doubt that on at least some occasions he definitely did cheat. I
> have one report, secondhand to be sure, but I think reliable, of
> his having admitted to fraud when he was alive. And I remember
> that Eileen Garrett once told me that when she and Ford were
> both working together in London (in the 1920s), she found that
> he was cheating by looking at the appointment book for sitters in
> advance of the scheduled sittings. At this organization, all sitters
> were supposed to be anonymous to the mediums!

We had also raised with Dr. Stevenson the curious incident
that occurred when we interviewed Mrs. Twigg and she had suddenly interrupted purporting that one of our mothers was calling
from the spirit world. This had perplexed us since that mother

was, in fact, very much alive. There also, we later noticed, had
been a curious buzz on our tape of the interview at precisely the
moment the mother was reputed to be calling to us. We mentioned that to Dr. Stevenson. We had become more perplexed
about that episode when the very next day in our interview with
Bishop Robinson he reported that he had once had an identical
experience with Mrs. Twigg and his mother was also, in fact, alive.
In responding to these concerns Dr. Stevenson entered upon some
further comments about Ena Twigg and about Arthur Ford.

> Now I will try to answer your question about Ena Twigg's be-
> havior during the meeting you had with her. I have already said
> that, in my opinion, Ena Twigg is thoroughly honest. Unfortu-
> nately, she has become regrettably somewhat vain as a result of all
> the publicity she has obtained, particularly in connection with
> the sittings she had with Jim Pike and her subsequent apparent
> communication from him at the time Diane was searching for
> him in the desert. I think Ena Twigg has become overconfident
> and has possibly damaged a gift she had for extrasensory percep-
> tion. I can imagine that her remark about one of your mothers
> may have been part of an effort to impress you with her powers as
> a medium. You may have noticed that she is inclined to drop
> names, a practice that, in my opinion, indicates a person in need
> of reassurance about himself. The need to impress you may have
> led her to make the incorrect remark about your mother. She did
> something rather similar with me when I last had a sitting with
> her. She claimed to have a communication from my father in
> which he reproached me for not attending his funeral. In fact, I
> *had* attended his funeral and I claim that I would be the best per-
> son to say whether I had or not. For a time, she kept insisting
> that I had not attended my father's funeral, even though I told
> her that I had. Finally, she gave up rather petulantly. This would
> be another example of her overconfidence.
>
> I cannot explain the buzz or hum that occurred on the record-
> ing when Ena Twigg was talking about your mother. Recording
> equipment seems subject to all kinds of capricious behavior which
> is one reason why it will be difficult, I suppose, to *prove* that Pres-
> ident Nixon's tapes have been tampered with. Claims have been
> made that discarnate personalities sometimes give messages by
> making their voices heard on tape recordings and it has been as-
> serted that this happened on fresh, unused tapes under conditions
> where the vocal sounds subsequently heard could not be ac-
> counted for by normal means. However, most parapsychologists

treat these claims with reserve and I know of only one, Professor Bender of Freiburg, Germany, who has so far thought them worth a major research effort.

The foregoing remarks (in the paragraph before the last) are not intended to isolate Ena Twigg from other mediums. Quite a number volunteer information about a person in whose presence they are whether that person asked for it or not. They often seem to start talking spontaneously and giving "readings" to other people who are with them even when they are not having a formal sitting.

I would not count Ena Twigg's error with regard to your mother as an indicator of lack of integrity on her part. It shows a deficiency in her capacity for extrasensory perception obviously and perhaps, if I have offered the correct interpretation, it also indicates the vanity that I have mentioned above. I have already said that she enjoys an excellent reputation for honesty and I am here drawing on remarks made to me by persons in London who know her much better than I do.

Concerning Arthur Ford, I have already said that his reputation was quite gray even during his life. With one exception, he never made himself available for scientific investigation. I tried once or twice to get him to come here to let us study him under better conditions, but he ducked out at the last minute. Nevertheless, a considerable number of persons who had sittings with Arthur Ford were quite impressed by him and I myself once had a most impressive sitting with him. I do not see how he could possibly have obtained the correct information he gave me unless he had been in some kind of collusive correspondence with my secretary which I am sure he was not. I think Arthur Ford had undoubted powers of extrasensory perception, but due to his human failings (with the one exception mentioned) there is nothing on the record of scientific investigations concerning him. It seems likely that he had a talent for extrasensory perception which he sometimes supplemented with information gained normally and used dishonestly. This sort of mix seems to be a hazard of professional mediumship in which the medium is forced, as he sees the matter, to keep getting positive results in order to maintain his clientele and reputation. Sooner or later many of them find ways of insuring against "off days" by obtaining information about their sitters and using it when needed.

Ian Stevenson was also kind enough to bring to our attention a review of Bishop Pike's *The Other Side* by a colleague of his in the Division of Parapsychology, Department of Psychiatry, School of Medicine, University of Virginia, Rex G. Stanford. The review appeared in the *Journal of the American Society for Psychical Research*, Volume 63, Number 4, October 1969, under the title "Religion, Survival, and Psi: Thoughts on Bishop Pike's *The Other Side*." We commend it for technical analysis and general interest. It is by far the best review of that book we have been able to find. Stanford is high in his praise of Bishop Pike's candor and fairness in telling a difficult and controversial story. He is not persuaded that the evidence presented in *The Other Side* necessarily supports the conclusions Bishop Pike reached. (He complains that some important evidence was excluded from the book on account of its personal nature.) He also discloses that—in his professional capacity, at least—he is not so trusting of other people as Bishop Pike was inclined to be.

> Finally, in spite of Pike's reassurance, it is very difficult to rule out the possibility, not really too far-fetched, of collusion between some of the mediums involved.

We are not parapsychologists and our investigation of these matters has not been professional in that sense, but it has been thorough enough to leave us having no difficulty at all sharing Stanford's saturnine observation. We enter on the record, however, in the interest of fairness, Ian Stevenson's qualified dissent.

> I have not made a careful study of the communications Jim Pike received through various mediums and am not in a position to make a valuable judgment about possible collusion among all those concerned. I would be inclined to think, however, that this is quite unlikely.

We find our own opinions to be congruent with Ian Stevenson's estimates of Ena Twigg and Arthur Ford. We agree with him entirely with regard to Ford. We are able to say that we *also* have found nobody who has raised a question with respect to Mrs. Twigg's honesty or with respect to her professional integrity. We have already, on the other hand, raised a question of our own with respect to her judgment (at least) in placing a certain telephone call to Diane Pike in Jerusalem. We share Dr. Stevenson's view that her vanity, especially in relation to the celebrity of her sittings with (and with regard to) Bishop Pike, has led her to excesses of showmanship she probably regrets. Mrs. Twigg's manifest affection for Bishop Pike (and his for her) was too artless to have been feigned. Nor do we believe she would ever by a malicious intent have done him any injury. Ena Twigg has worked hard to establish her reputation for impeccable integrity. Her investment of pride *in* that reputation has convinced us that she would never frivolously compromise it no matter what the stakes.

Ena Twigg did not impart the substance of the March 14 sitting to Arthur Ford. Are we, then, up against a stone wall? Not quite. Must we conclude that Arthur Ford obtained his "evidentiary" information by paranormal means? We think not. Are we driven to a point where we are compelled to presume that Jim Jr. —having provided the information in the first place (through Mrs. Twigg)—had thereupon conveyed it across the Atlantic Ocean several weeks later to an astonished (we would think) Arthur Ford. We fall short of that point.

There remains Canon John Pearce-Higgins, ardent scrivener of séances.

John Pearce-Higgins ("John P-H" to Mrs. Twigg) is an altogether remarkable man. We have many times been told, upon inquiring about him, that he is brilliant, and he is. He is by all odds the most valiant and the most talented champion of spiritualism in all of England. There cannot be a medium with whom he has not sat nor a poltergeist he has not investigated. He is unabashedly reverent about it all. He functions in the colorfully various and wonderfully eccentric world of English psychics as an indefatigably imaginative and querulously avuncular impresario.

Pearce-Higgins's own specialty is chasing ghosts from haunted houses. He accomplishes this (with the help of mediums) by persuading the ghosts ("discarnate personalities," he calls them) that they really are dead. That seems to be the trick of it. Once a ghost understands he is dead he will go away. The trouble with ghosts, according to Pearce-Higgins, is that they are not very bright. He points out that Bishop Pike (who certainly was bright) knew he was dead the moment he turned up in that sitting with Ena Twigg. Ghosts are so dull of wit that they just can't get it through their heads what has happened to them. It is Pearce-Higgins's distinctive vocation to pound ultimate sense into fractious discarnate heads. He is said to have enjoyed considerable success in his dedicated pursuit of this unusual ministry.

The medium Pearce-Higgins favored for communication with

ghosts is (or was) Donald Page, a trance medium, who has a "guide" in the spirit world, and that "guide," we are obliged to report, is (or was) a Chinese doctor who calls himself "Dr. White." We are concerned, however, with a quite different use Pearce-Higgins was to find for the talents of Donald Page (and Dr. White). Pearce-Higgins was dissatisfied with his sitting with Ena Twigg in which Bishop Pike had apparently manifested himself directly after his death, and that dissatisfaction was augmented when, shortly thereafter, Bishops John Robinson and Mervin Stockwood listened to the tape of that sitting and found it wanting. So, Pearce-Higgins turned to Donald Page and through him (with Dr. White's help) got what he considered to be impressive testimony from Bishop Pike and from Jim Jr. (This included the reassuring information that Bishop Pike really had attended the sitting with Mrs. Twigg.) Among other things Bishop Pike told Pearce-Higgins that he had decided to go to sleep for some weeks to rest up from the ordeal in the desert and the misadventure of dying. Thereupon, on October 16, 1969, Pearce-Higgins wrote to Diane Pike in order that she be kept apprised of these encouraging developments.

> I have not as yet told Ena that I have had these communications, and I would prefer her not to know this from anyone except myself. She has her human weaknesses, and she happens to have an extreme dislike for poor Mr. Page and a poor opinion of his work, which admittedly is done quite differently from her own. I fear she will be jealous, alas, and may want to claim the 'Pike' communication as her own private perquisite, and even suggest that what Page has given me is phoney. I could not admit that for a moment. I have used him for three years and he has done yeoman service in dealing with the spirits from haunted houses—indeed I had to get him in to finish off a case which Ena had failed to clear fully—which hasn't made her love him any more! So sad that so many mediums are so bitchy to each other, but there it is. I am very fond of Ena and don't want to upset her, but we have to recognise things as they are.
>
> As soon as this communication is safely en route for USA I will tell Ena what I have had, and have to weather her storms as best I may. She is a much more easy and fluent medium than Page, and no doubt Jim will find it easier to come through her than through Donald Page, but equally I have no doubt that . . . d.v.

I shall get some solid factual evidence from Jim when he awakes, which I will pass on to you of course.

In due course Pearce-Higgins did get further "solid factual evidence from Jim" (and Jim Jr.) which he did pass on to Diane. (He got it, however, exclusively through Page/White. Mrs. Twigg's storms apparently proved more difficult to weather than had been anticipated.) This additional "evidence" (and the means by which it was achieved) is not without its zany fascination, but we have neither room (unfortunately) nor reason (fortunately) to subject it to the sort of penetrating analysis it deserves.

It had been John Pearce-Higgins, as has been mentioned, who introduced Bishop Pike to the demimonde of professional psychics.

How did that come about? In 1959 a laywoman of Bishop Pike's diocese, Mrs. R. W. Hanna of Hillsborough, California, having lost her husband, betook herself to the Alcazar Theatre in San Francisco to seek consolation in a lecture by the Reverend Arthur Ford. She seems to have undergone an instant conversion. One thing led to another, and before long Mrs. Hanna, who was apparently a lady of some means, was traveling about the world as a sort of volunteer courier for the gospel of spiritualism. Early in 1963, in that capacity, Mrs. Hanna sought to make an appointment with Bishop Pike, but he was too busy to see her, and she instead mailed some propaganda to his office. Not long afterward, finding herself in London, Mrs. Hanna got in touch with Mervin Stockwood, Bishop of Southwark, in order to suggest that Bishop Pike be invited to become a sponsor of the Churches' Fellowship for Psychical and Spiritual Studies. Bishop Pike had no real interest in such matters at that time, but he readily accepted the duly forthcoming invitation from a brother bishop on the principle that the *study* of most anything was obviously worthy of his encouragement.

At the time of which we are speaking Mervin Stockwood was Bishop of Southwark and he was also vice-president of the Churches' Fellowship for Psychical and Spiritual Studies. John Pearce-Higgins was at the same time Vice-Provost (as the title implies, largely a sinecure) of Southwark Cathedral and he was vice-chairman of the Churches' Fellowship for Psychical and Spiritual Studies. John Robinson, as it happens, was also on the scene, or part of it, as a Suffragan Bishop of the Diocese of South-wark.

During the summer of 1963 Bishops Pike and Stockwood both attended an Anglican Congress in Toronto. They had several conversations about church renewal which led Stockwood to invite Pike to give some lectures in his diocese on that subject. It came to pass that in May of 1965 Bishop Pike went to England to lecture to some five hundred priests foregathered in Butlin's Holiday Camp at Clacton-on-Sea. And it came to pass that one evening Bishop Stockwood suggested that Bishop Pike join him for dinner with Canon Pearce-Higgins.

> We had a leisurely five-course meal at a good French restaurant and talked of many things—among which, quite memorably, were psychic phenomena. Since I had told the two of them about my forthcoming sabbatical, and of my plans to take this opportunity to rethink reflectively doctrinal questions, using the *facts+faith* method, they suggested that it would be a good idea for me to spend some time in London, where both the Churches' Fellowship and the Society for Psychical Research had extensive files, learning more about verified psychic phenomena as a basis for the affirmation of life after death.
>
> Canon Pearce-Higgins, who spends many of his hours in this field, had offered to guide me in examining available data. As the subject-matter was not of predominant interest to me, however, and as I became so quickly engrossed in my study of Christian origins, I had not gotten around to contacting either the Lord Bishop or the Vice-Provost. I had, from time to time, noted that the press gave news coverage to reports of "hauntings," poltergeists or exorcisms (one by a brother Anglican bishop); and I gained the general impression that people were much more open to the possibility of not only survival but also communication with the dead in England than they were in the United States.

It is not surprising, therefore, that nine months later, after the bewildering epidemic of poltergeist phenomena (David Baar's altered state of consciousness in a pressure cooker), on the morning of February 28, 1966, Bishop Pike placed a telephone call to Canon Pearce-Higgins.

> I then summarized for him the numerous odd events of the past eight days, and expressed to him our reluctantly arrived at

conclusion that all of this somehow related to my son, who had recently taken his life in New York.

"Oh, yes, forgive me for not having expressed my condolences. I do recall a notice in the paper," Canon Pearce-Higgins responded. "Just how long ago was it that your son passed on?"

"It was in the early morning on February 4," I recalled, "so that would be about twenty-four days ago."

"And these phenomena began to occur when?" Pearce-Higgins asked.

"On February 20," I told him.

"Yes, of course . . ." he remarked. "In the case of a violent death—however caused—the spirit is left bewildered and is usually not able to manifest himself until a period of two weeks or so has gone by," was his explanation.

"I see," I replied—though I didn't exactly. "But what would be the point of such things?"

"In such cases there is usually one of two things going on," the Canon answered. "Either the entity is feeling hostility toward someone who is inhabiting the place which recently was his domicile, or the phenomena are attention-getting devices."

"Well, I can't imagine that it would be hostility about my staying on in the flat," I commented, "and if he is trying to get my attention—well, he's got it. What shall we do now? Do you think I should see a medium? I remember your mentioning—who? . . ."

"Mrs. Ena Twigg, yes."

Canon Pearce-Higgins thereupon invoked a device Bishop Pike seems to have been unaware of, but which is, in fact, rather commonplace among mediums and their agents in the cultivation of novice clients. He suggested a resort to the Ouija board. The purpose of such a maneuver seems to be to allay any feeling the potential client might have that the medium or the medium's agent (as is typically the situation) is overeager to solicit business. There is no danger of losing a client by this device. Whatever the merits may be of a Ouija board as parlor entertainment it swiftly disillusions most of those who resort to it as serious practitioners.

That is precisely what happened with Bishop Pike, whose tolerance for parlor games was minimal.

So I called Canon Pearce-Higgins again, reporting what I thought was the ineffectiveness of his suggested procedure, and asked again if he did not perhaps think it would be wise to call Mrs. Twigg.

"Well," Pearce-Higgins remarked somewhat hesitatingly, "I can try to get an appointment with her. She is the best sensitive I know, but I know that she is very busy and has very few appointment hours open. The best I can do is to try. I will call you back as soon as I have some word."

The notion that Mrs. Twigg might have been too busy to see Bishop Pike merits several centuries of uninterrupted laughter.

Pearce-Higgins called back the same afternoon.

Two afternoons later, on March 2, 1966, Bishop Pike had his first sitting with Ena Twigg.

There Is No Immunity in Skepticism

On September 18, 1969, Anthony Towne wrote a letter to Diane Pike. We find we must include that letter here. We are somewhat inclined to disown it, but there is no way we can disavow it. So, we toss it dispassionately upon the waters where it must sink or swim on its own.

> Dear Diane: I have had what may (or may not) be a message ("message") from Jim.
>
> I considered telephoning you but did not trust myself to report the matter accurately that way and decided to write instead.
>
> A brief background is necessary. After the service for Jim in San Francisco I returned at once to NYC for the service there on Saturday in the cathedral and especially for the service Sunday at St. Clement's where Bill spoke. (He will shortly send you a tape of that service together with a transcript of his remarks. He spoke beautifully.) On Monday I went to Philadelphia because I had been invited to participate in a TV talk-show about Jim ("The Strange Life and Death of Dr. James A. Pike" they unhappily chose to call it.) I do not like to appear on television and would normally have declined. But the other guest was to be Arthur Ford whom I had not met and I welcomed even that opportunity to do so. I arranged to have dinner with him before the show. We talked of many things (he casually let me know of his gifts by regretting I had lost my railroad ticket, noting that I had flown to San Francisco via TWA, and at one point by observing

that I very much wanted another drink) including the role of Marvin Halverson in the Toronto séance and the association of Jane Kingman with Halverson and with a later séance. We also discussed my dark suspicions about the role of Maren Bergrud in the early stages of Jim's experiences with psychic phenomena. He wondered of me whether I thought you would be disposed to speak—at what he indicated might be large fees—for Spiritual Frontiers, and implied less explicitly that a similar opportunity might be available to Bill and to me. The program itself was rather sensational despite my prior plea that it not be confined to psychic matters but embrace the whole of Jim's career. For one thing, it began with about six minutes from the tape of the Toronto séance, and for another the questions from the audience were all directed to the psychic domain. So many questions were telephoned in that the 1 hour show was extended to 1½ hours. Arthur Ford was asked if he expected to hear from Jim. He said no that he expected you would hear directly. He was asked if he intended to try to reach Jim. He said only if you asked him. I was asked if you expected to hear from Jim. I said I had not discussed it with you but had read in the papers that you did. I was asked if I expected that you or anyone else would hear from Jim. I said no but I was sure if Jim was heard from what he had to say would be worth hearing. The program exhausted me, I got to bed late, and rose early to return here to Block Island where Bill and I live. The next evening (Tuesday) I had dinner and more drinks than I should have with a friend and went early to bed, thankful, frankly, that the tumult Jim's death had occasioned for me was apparently ended.

Next morning, at the moment just before waking when dreaming still continues, I had the following dream:

I was flying (all my life I have had off and on dreams in which I seem to be flying like a bird, usually happy, even euphoric dreams) among what first seemed to be sand dunes (such as are found at the tip of Cape Cod) but gradually became canyons in very rough terrain. I came upon—flew over—an automobile with nobody in it. Then, in an even deeper canyon I saw several people and went closer to see who they were. As I got nearer—directly above them—only one person remained, a man. I felt I had to reach him, let him know I was there. I brushed against the side of the canyon causing sand to fall down on him. At this point the dream abruptly stopped. I do not know if the man did see me. (It is important that to this point I had no sense that the dream had anything to do with Jim.) Now, still asleep, I had suddenly—I saw nothing, heard nothing—I had an overwhelming *thought:* MUST FINISH BOOK. (This seemed *very* strongly to mean that you must finish the book you and Jim were writing, but less strongly it seemed to mean that Bill and I must finish our book about Jim. It is also pertinent that I am presently behind schedule and under pressure about another book I am writing so the thought "must finish book" would not be an unlikely one for me to have. But that book did not seem to be included in the message of the dream.) Right after that thought I saw—as though on a book jacket (though I saw no book jacket)—three words: DIANE CHING TEXFORD. There was a strong sense that the latter two words were names of persons who would be in touch with you and/or Bill and me *or* with whom we would be in touch and that they would be important for your and/or our books. There was a less strong sense that the three names had to do with a problem you would face when your book is finished about how to put your name on the jacket with an implication that you should use three and not two names. Also there was a strong sense that the three names had to do with a question of remarriage (related to the problem of the names on the jacket). That sense was not that you should remarry, and not that you should not, but just matter-of-factly that you will remarry.

Thereupon, I woke up and it being morning, time to get up, I went to the john and sat where you might suppose I would sit and reflected. My first thought was: my God, have you had a message from Jim? I argued for some time with myself seeking to persuade myself that I had not. It ran all the way from "you just dreamed it" to "that quack Arthur Ford somehow put it all into your mind." (I have had several dreams in the last two weeks in which Jim figured, but with none of them did it even occur to me that any message might be involved.) I finally decided that I could not resolve that question and probably never would be able to. So, I concluded to *assume* it was a message. What then did it mean? The meaning seemed transparently clear up to the last two words. Who were the persons referred to by those two names? I at once had—not by any process of thought but, as it were, out of the blue—two associations with each word, one strongly, the other less strongly: CHING, strongly Ping Ferry, less strongly Jane Kingman; TEXFORD, strongly Arthur Ford, less strongly Rexford Tugwell. (I know or know of all of them. I have met Ping Ferry —Bill knows him better than I do—and once had cocktails with him and his wife (and Bill) at their home in Santa Barbara. I have never met Jane Kingman but have talked with her on the telephone and otherwise communicated in connection with the Foundation she works for and of which I am a member. I also know of her connection with Halverson and one of the séances, and, as I said, Ford and I mentioned her name. I have never met Tugwell but know of him and know that he is at the Center.)

That is about all I can say.

Bill was not here the morning of the dream. He was due that afternoon, so I decided to wait and discuss it with him before writing you. He was delayed and got back only this morning. But I have tried to relay the message, if it is a message, as rapidly as I responsibly could.

At 12 noon on Friday, September 12, 1969, James Albert Pike, D.D., S.J.D., Fifth Episcopal Bishop of California, was solemnly remembered during a Requiem Celebration of the Holy Eucharist in Grace Cathedral, San Francisco. For the last time Bishop Pike would pack the church he had done so much to complete and within which he had served delight to many and scandal to some. The day was raw and on top of Nob Hill the wind was bitter under a menace of clouds hurtling overhead. On the cathedral steps supporters of the Black Panthers passed out broadsides pleading the cause of Bobby Seale, who was then in federal custody in a San Francisco jail. Inside the cathedral a huge, hushed congregation (strangely animated) waited while the paraphernalia of radio and TV clattered into place and a clutter of newspersons fluttered obtrusively down the side aisles: a swarm of mesmerized moths ineluctably drawn to the recollected blaze of an extinguished candle.

To the right and forward of the congregation a large door swung open and Esther Pike, the bishop's surviving children in her wake, briskly entered, the widow-in-exile, her composure defiant as she assumed the pew ordinarily reserved to the immediate spouse, her son on the aisle, her daughters to her right. Moments later, to the left and forward of the congregation another large door swung open and Diane Pike, still unsteady of foot owing to her desert ordeal, burst into a glare of klieg lights, supported to one side by Father Robert Hoggard, her lost husband's friend. Behind Diane, moving slowly, but with her head high, her eyes alertly scanning the congregation, came Pearl Chambers, the bishop's mother, flanked by her sister, his favorite aunt, Ethyl

Larkey. Diane took the aisle seat opposite the bishop's son, Mrs. Chambers to her left, then Mrs. Larkey. Far back in the congregation sat, unnoticed, the former Jane Alvies Pike. The situation was unprecedented. Never before in the history of the Episcopal Church had a Solemn Requiem Mass been offered for a bishop in the presence of three surviving wives.

Thereupon, a long, colorful procession of the clergy made its way down the center aisle, and in it, side by side, Bishop Pike's successor, old friend, and nemesis, Chauncey Kilmer Myers, who would, by Diane's special request, preside as the chief celebrant, and G. Richard Millard, Bishop Pike's conscientious and long-suffering suffragan bishop, who would offer the intercessory prayers. As Bishop Myers drew abreast of Diane Pike she half-rose from her pew and clutched him by one hand as though to give him strength for what cannot have been a happy exercise of his episcopal office. And when at last Bishop Myers settled himself into his cathedral throne far back in the apse (out of sight, it almost seemed) he was so forlorn and shrunken it was as though he might, before the ceremony ended, vanish altogether.

The service opened (following the form of the New Liturgy of the Episcopal Church) with the Bidding, in this case an impassioned eulogy by a particular old friend of Bishop Pike's, Rabbi Alvin Fine. A leading laywoman of the diocese, and Bishop Pike's great and good friend, Mrs. Harold Sorg, read the Epistle (II Corinthians 4.1–12), including a text (". . . we have this treasure in earthen vessels . . .") the bishop had employed almost as the motto of his later theology. It was the Reverend Mrs. Phyllis Edwards, whom Bishop Pike had recognized as the first ordained female deacon in the Episcopal Church, who read the Holy Gospel (". . . for I was hungry and you gave me food . . ."—St. Matthew 25.31–46). Bishop Myers was joined at the Service of the Table by Bishop Pike's two dearest friends in the Episcopal clergy, Darby Betts, rector of St. Paul's, Oakland, and Robert Hoggard, rector of St. Augustine by-the-Sea, Santa Monica, who were concelebrants of the Holy Eucharist.

Occasionally during the long service the sun broke free of clouds long enough to illumine the brilliant stained glass windows in the cathedral clerestory. Depending upon where one was seated in the great congregation he could have looked up to see suddenly emblazed one or another of the "secular saints" and other worthies Bishop Pike had installed there. Albert Einstein. John Glenn. Thurgood Marshall. Paul Tillich. Martin Buber. Karl Rahner, S.J. Pope John XXIII. Geoffrey Fisher, ninety-ninth Archbishop of Canterbury. Arthur Lichtenberger, twenty-first Presiding Bishop of the Episcopal Church. One mourner studied an allegorical window in which were contrasted an image of St. Paul instructing the slave Philemon to return to his master with an image of John Woolman, the Quaker, who had been a leader in the abolition of slavery in the British Empire. It seemed a salutary reminder of Bishop Pike's subtly irreverent wit.

Diane Pike would later recall that the occasional sudden illuminations from the clerestory had given her a comfortable sense that her husband's spirit was present in the cathedral. Throughout the service Diane had provided a sort of running pantomime commentary on the proceedings, nodding her head vigorously to affirm what she liked, shaking it side to side to deplore what she found inappropriate. When the requiem celebration was ended and the bishops and clergy had disappeared up the center aisle the congregation was witness to a remarkable spectacle. The bishop's three children leapt across the aisle into Diane Pike's joyous embrace. They had not seen one another since her return from Israel. Esther Pike stood on the other side of the aisle, arms akimbo, one foot tapping restlessly on the cathedral floor, glaring in undisguised rage at a scene she could not have been expected to relish.

At 12 noon on Saturday, September 13, 1969—one day later—James Albert Pike (1913–69) was the burden of a memorial service in the Cathedral Church of St. John the Divine, New York City, where he had, from 1952 until 1958, flourished as its—"controversial"—dean. The service, which had been choreographed around a setting of Byrd's *Three-Part Mass* by the incumbent subdean (as he chooses to be called), Canon Edward M. West, had the aura of a clandestine medieval pageant. It was sparsely attended. There were not more than several hundred congregants huddled together before a makeshift altar in the midst of the vast cathedral gloom. The sub-dean, resplendent in somber robes, his ample frame surmounted by a glisten of bald pate and a Greek Orthodox beard, was the celebrant of the Holy Eucharist. An eloquent address was intoned by Horace W. B. Donegan, Episcopal

Bishop of New York, under whom Dean Pike had served. "In the name of God, Amen!" he had begun in his wonderfully episcopal baritone, thereby paying subtle respects to Bishop Pike's diminished (or compacted) Holy Trinity. Somewhere nearby in the upper recesses of the cathedral complex the ghost of Bishop Greer may even then have been prowling restlessly in search of his long-lost crucifix. And on the fringes of the motley congregation lurked the ubiquitous Hans Holzer, scientifically trained investigator.

(Anthony Towne, who attended both memorial services, believes he may in the process have become the first person ever to have received Holy Communion one day on the West Coast from the Bishop of California and the next day on the East Coast from the Bishop of New York. He intends to press that distinction with St. Peter when it becomes his turn to make what he trusts will be a non-violent transition to the "Other Side".)

At 12 noon on Sunday, September 14, 1969, in St. Clement's Church, New York City, there was (for the third successive day) another Requiem Celebration for James Albert Pike. The celebrant was the Reverend John Morris, director for many years of the Episcopal Society for Racial and Cultural Unity. This mass was not for *Bishop* Pike. It was not for *Dean* Pike. It was not even for *Dr.* Pike. This mass was for *Jim* Pike. The Associated Press had a reporter on the scene who rendered an account of what he saw. This is how it appeared in the New York *Post* of September 15, 1969.

> The high requiem mass celebrated for James A. Pike was informal and unorthodox, much in the spirit of the man for whom it was said.
> The congregation sat in a semicircle in chairs or on the floor of St. Clement's Episcopal Church at 423 W. 46th St. There were babes in

arms and some of the
women were mini-skirted,
some of the men san-
daled. Children ran in
and out of the austere,
high-ceilinged chamber.
A mother comforted a
crying child and mem-
bers of the congregation
strolled about at will.

Pike's friend and bi-
ographer, William String-
fellow, who wrote "The
Bishop Pike Affair," sat
at a desk on the stage
and spun reminiscences
about the former Epis-
copal bishop of Califor-
nia who died in the Ju-
dean wilderness.

The stagelights on
him, Stringfellow told
the congregation not to
consider his words a eu-
logy. Often he evoked
laughter from his listen-
ers as he described en-
counters between the
controversial former Episcopal Bishop of Califor-
nia and one-time dean
of the Cathedral of St.
John the Divine with
orthodoxy.

Pike, said Stringfellow,
was a man whose passion
for seeking Christ led
him to the desert of the
Holy Land, where he
died. His body was found
last Sunday.

Duke Ellington, who

played his first sacred jazz concert when Pike was bishop of California, came to the stage, sat at a piano and led the congregation in a hymn.

Ellington, who rarely performs alone, then played a melancholy piece from his latest sacred concert.

The call for communion brought most of the congregation to the stage. They formed a circle around the altar under a futuristic chrome-plated cross.

Each communicant took bread from a silver tray, sipped wine from a silver chalice, passed from person to person, then bowed in silent prayer. The chimes of an ice cream truck drifted in from the street with the shouts of children playing.

When the service ended, the church secretary, wearing a red and orange minidress, stood in front of the altar and invited newcomers to join the congregation for coffee.

Several of the men removed the cloth-covered table that had served as an altar. The high requiem mass was ended.

Nobody had asked Duke Ellington to participate in the service at St. Clement's. He had heard about it and had telephoned the church to ask if he might play something from a new composition as his tribute to Bishop Pike. "I loved that man," he explained. Some years earlier, Bishop Pike, having read that Duke Ellington had composed a sacred concert for jazz, got interested, made contact with "the Duke," and the upshot of it was that the first performance of Ellington's first sacred concert took place in Grace Cathedral. The two men got on together famously. They shared an enormous appetite for the business of living and a sophisticated humility about the abundant gifts God had vouchsafed them.

On the following afternoon, Anthony Towne, having had his fill of memorial masses, boarded a train for Philadelphia. When the conductor appeared Anthony was unable to produce his ticket and had to buy another. In Philadelphia he settled into a hotel room reserved for him by his TV hosts and decided to ring Arthur Ford, who was supposed to be in the same hotel. It would make sense, Anthony had thought, for the two of them to have dinner before the late evening talk show.

"Arthur Ford?"
"Yes."
"Anthony Towne."
"Yes, I know you just checked in and was about to call you. I'm sorry you lost your railroad ticket."

Anthony accepted these observations as though the paranormal was his usual domain. It was agreed they would have dinner together in the hotel dining room. Anthony would pick Ford up in his room since Ford was on a lower floor. He was admitted to the room by a ruddy-faced man who seemed to have been drinking although there was no beverage in sight. Indeed, there was nothing in sight save the customary hotel furniture and a large leather bag in the middle of a bed. It was evident that the man had been depositing all his personal property—there was not so much as a toothbrush in the bathroom—in the large leather bag. That seemed odd since the man was going to spend the night in the hotel. It seemed even odder when he proceeded to wrap leather straps around the bag. He secured each strap with a padlock. An-

thony remarked on the humidity. The man was perspiring—
whether from the effects of the whiskey he reeked of or a heart
condition Anthony understood he suffered from or from his exer-
tions with the leather straps.

Several years later, in the course of his research for this book,
Anthony would learn that Arthur Ford had also attended the memorial service for Bishop Pike in the Cathedral of St. John the Divine, and two days later had taken the same train to Philadelphia
that Anthony had taken for their joint appearance on the late evening TV talk show crudely advertised as a discussion of "The
Strange Life and Death of Dr. James A. Pike." Anthony would
later remember little of that talk show except that he had been
uncomfortable, the host had seemed to be a young man on the
make, and Arthur Ford had seemed eager, whenever he could, to
solicit contributions for an organization called Spiritual Frontiers.

What did stick vividly in Anthony's memory was that large
leather bag.

Of "a Goddamned Queer" and the Principle of Parsimony

One woman sent him five hundred dollars in advance for a sitting. I was with him when he did the research for this command
performance. He showed me where to find the information.
Who's Who. School directories.

Before I met Ford I had heard about this kind of thing in other
Spiritualist circles, I'd been told about it. And one day I said to
Arthur, "Are you reading your poems?" And he was frightened
because nobody else was supposed to know what his poems were.
That was the code name for his notes—"poems."

He'd say before a sitting, "I think I'll go back here and read a
little poetry." He kept his poems up to date by reading the papers
constantly and cutting out obituaries from all over the United
States.

He carried these poems of his in a Gladstone suitcase and we'd
hide it under the front seat of my car. Arthur was afraid to die or
have a heart attack in a hotel room because he had the material
hidden.

After his first séance with Bishop Pike which was televised in
Toronto, Canada, Arthur Ford had such an avalanche of mail

that he was forced to hire a correspondence secretary to help him handle it. That secretary (said to be "a middle-aged, effeminate individual" but not identified by name) would later—after Arthur Ford had died—volunteer the above damaging statements to Allen Spraggett, who was engaged in writing a book about Ford (*Arthur Ford: The Man Who Talked with the Dead*. New York: New American Library, 1973). The effeminate secretary and Arthur Ford (who was somewhat effeminate himself) subsequently had parted company on unfriendly terms, according to Spraggett, who wrote his book in collaboration with William V. Rauscher (our friend the priest of Spiritual Frontiers), the heir, by Ford's will, of such of the medium's papers as had not been destroyed, according to Spraggett and Rauscher, "presumably" on Ford's instructions by a former secretary (whom they have not identified by name). Ford's differences with the effeminate correspondence secretary apparently had something to do with the latter's sexual proclivities.

> "He was a goddamned queer," Ford said of his former secretary. "I don't mind queers if they mind their own business, but he was too much."

Spraggett doesn't tell us whom Ford was speaking to when he made those comments, but if we assume them to be accurately reported we might conclude that the damaging information supplied by the ex-secretary was nothing more than malicious invention on the part of a disgruntled ex-employee. As they sifted through the remnants of Ford's literary estate, however, Spraggett and Rauscher were to uncover other damaging information, some of which corroborated the ex-secretary's story. Arthur Ford seems to have been one of the great obit-clippers of all time. He had obits going back many years on prominent decedents and some not so prominent. (Personalities of the churches especially grabbed his attention whether they were cardinals or bishops or merely obscure bureaucrats or bishops' secretaries.) He had files on many of his favorite clients including one on Bishop Pike that went back for years. And Spraggett and Rauscher also found evidence of his "poems"—a notebook with the names of "sittees" and data about them.

At the time of his death on January 4, 1971, a few days short of his seventy-fifth birthday, Arthur Ford, whether he was or was not, in whole or in part, a fraud, could look back with some satisfaction upon an astonishing career (lasting more than five decades) that had made of him certainly the most celebrated and probably the most accomplished American medium of the twentieth century. A virtuoso raconteur, Ford delighted in spinning fanciful yarns out of his fabled past, and many of his tales, told and retold, became inconsistent and conflicting with one another, so that (as he probably intended) by now the facts of his life are pretty much irretrievable from the legend he created out of them. Two variants of that legend were published during his lifetime: his (in collaboration with Marguerite Harmon Bro) *Nothing So Strange*, New York: Harper & Row, 1958; and his (own) *Unknown But Known* (the title neatly sums up the substance), New York: Harper & Row, 1968. Allen Spraggett (with Father Rauscher) has uttered a third posthumous variant which is a rehash pastiche of the earlier two with bits and pieces of this and that and just enough exposure of Ford's fraud on Bishop Pike to make a salable book.

This, then, was the ruddy-faced Disciples of Christ minister who had been insinuated into Bishop Pike's presence in the narthex of St. Thomas Episcopal Church, Fifth Avenue, during Holy Week, 1966.

We return to the question of how Arthur Ford came into possession of certain salient information ("evidentiary" to Bishop Pike) from the bishop's March 14 (1966) séance with Mrs. Twigg: notably the two names imparted (apparently) by Jim Jr. in that séance: "Father Rauscher" and "Spiritual Frontiers."

Spiritual Frontiers had been founded (in 1956) by Arthur Ford. It was his creature. While it had chapters here and there and members and several alleged scientific purposes, it was, while he lived, primarily a quasi-corporate vehicle (serviced in large measure by Father Rauscher) for Arthur Ford's diversities of ministry, a cover, after a fashion, for his vaguely obscured numinous persona. Ford liked to pretend that Spiritual Frontiers (he never held any office in it) was a spontaneous manifestation of grass roots spiritualism. He was content, so he would make out, to be its faithful servant, lending a helping hand as he could. This was a roguishly benign deception on his part. He did, to be sure, serve it, but he was also its principal beneficiary.

William V. Rauscher, president, at the time of the events we are reporting, of Spiritual Frontiers, and a priest of the Episcopal Diocese of New Jersey (Christ Church, Woodbury), has had for many years a sideline preoccupation with the occult. His interest in spiritualism is, we are persuaded, genuine and soberly passionate.* He had a long, close personal association with Arthur Ford. The two men were good friends. He officiated at Ford's burial service. Father Rauscher seems to us to be ingenuous to a fault. He is the sort of fellow who is easily used by disingenuous connivers. We cannot conceive that he would ever wittingly be complicit in fraud or chicanery of any kind. We inquired of Dr. Ian Stevenson his impressions of Father Rauscher and (at the same time) his impressions of journalist Allen Spraggett.

> I should be very surprised if Bill Rauscher was in any way dishonest and I also do not think that Allen Spraggett would be dishonest.
>
> The main deficiency of Allen Spraggett with regard to the investigation of mediumship is that he is not a scientist or scholar but basically a journalist looking for a good story. He talks a lot and it is not at all impossible that he gave out a lot more information than he later realized, or anyone else realized, at the time he was arranging for the various events in which he participated.

How did Arthur Ford learn that Father Rauscher of Spiritual Frontiers had been mentioned in Bishop Pike's March 14, 1966, séance with Mrs. Twigg?

In *The Other Side* Bishop Pike has invoked the principle of parsimony to account for his conclusion that the communications he had received from Jim Jr. through several mediums had probably been authentic. The principle of parsimony holds that we do not accept a complicated explanation for puzzling phenomena if there is a simpler explanation available. We find any possible paranormal explanation of how Ford learned what happened in Mrs. Twigg's parlor far more complex than what seems to us a relatively simple and (given a fallen world) normal one. It is

* See his (in collaboration with Allen Spraggett) *The Spiritual Frontier*, Garden City, New York: Doubleday & Company, Inc., 1975.

among the many vagaries of spiritualism that the more it is taken seriously the more the paranormal comes to seem normal and the normal to seem improbable.

This is what we think probably happened. Just before leaving Cambridge to return to the United States Bishop Pike called Mrs. Twigg to ask if she could recommend a medium in the United States should he have occasion to consult one. She suggested he come for a second séance during which perhaps Jim Jr. would make such a recommendation. He agreed. Mrs. Twigg called Canon Pearce-Higgins to report this development. He advised that Father Rauscher of Spiritual Frontiers might be a good person for Bishop Pike to get in touch with. During the March 14 séance (whether from Jim Jr. or not) Father Rauscher of Spiritual Frontiers *was* mentioned. After that séance Mrs. Twigg called Pearce-Higgins to report what had taken place.

What does this do to Mrs. Twigg's reputation for integrity? Not much, we think. It is the semblance more than the substance of integrity that Mrs. Twigg is fussy about. Pearce-Higgins purports to be engaged in the promotion of scientific investigation of mediumship. Her confidences to him could readily have been offered under that umbrella. Nor do we suppose that Mrs. Twigg solicited information about Bishop Pike from Pearce-Higgins. The man *is* gossipy, however, and how could poor Mrs. Twigg have prevented him from going on about matters that later might or might not prove useful? We strongly suspect, for example, that Pearce-Higgins discovered from Maren Bergrud (or perhaps from Bishop Pike himself) that Bishop Pike had dedicated a new book to Paul Tillich. We further suspect that in a moment of passionate inadvertence he dropped that news in Mrs. Twigg's ear. We do not really think she could have been expected to ignore it.

We asked Dr. Ian Stevenson about Canon Pearce-Higgins especially in relation to the latter's alternate sittings with trance medium Donald Page.

> I have a file on Donald Page. I first heard about him from John Pearce-Higgins. I had a sitting with Donald Page in 1970 when John Pearce-Higgins took me to him. I was not much impressed. The various alleged trance personalities were impressive enough as different personalities. Page could have made a good living on the stage. At one point, a communicator who was supposed to be Bishop Pike manifested and talked for some time with John

Pearce-Higgins. Page naturally knew of John Pearce-Higgins' friendship with Pike, but he did not know of my own friendship with him. I am sure that if a real discarnate Jim Pike had been communicating, he would have acknowledged my presence by saying minimally something like, "Glad to see you here, too, Ian." However, the alleged Jim Pike made absolutely no acknowledgment of my presence in the room.

Subsequently, John Pearce-Higgins withdrew his support from Page because he found him, as he put it to me, making excessive charges in connection with "healings" that he was offering to ill people. It subsequently developed that Page's charges for services were not exclusively monetary. A scandal about him developed and was published in the *News of the World* which is, to be sure, not the most reliable of newspapers. It reported, however, that Page had been persuading young ladies who consulted him to have sexual intercourse with him on the grounds that this would be spiritually beneficial to them. It may be doubted whether Page ever had any paranormal gifts for mediumship, and, on the evidence available, I do not think that he can be taken seriously.

It is much more difficult to write about John Pearce-Higgins whom I count among my friends. I think it almost certain that his courageous espousal of psychical research and his efforts to awaken the interest of clergymen in it held back his advancement in the Church. He has never really represented himself as a scientific researcher. He sees himself rather as a promoter of the study of mediumship and he accepts the evidence of our survival after physical death sufficiently to have become rather well known as an exorcist in cases of haunting and possible possession. The difference between his approach and mine to the phenomena that have interested us both came out vividly on one occasion when I was with him in London. He was describing to me a case in which he had participated as an exorcist. I said something to him about the need for careful recording in notes or otherwise of what happened. He then mildly rebuked me and pointed out that when you are engaged in a religious activity such as exorcism, you cannot at the same time analyze what is going on!

It may be that John Pearce-Higgins did pass on through careless talk information that came to Jim Pike in sessions with Ena Twigg. John Pearce-Higgins is affable and might have given out information without later being aware that he had done so.

To whom might Canon Pearce-Higgins have passed (through "careless talk" or some other inadvertence) information that came to Bishop Pike in sittings with Mrs. Twigg? We don't think

that really matters very much. He might have passed such information to any number of different people. The truth of the matter is that in the special world of spiritualism when a celebrity of
the magnitude of Bishop Pike has a sitting with *any* medium
news of it somehow spreads like wildfire from one end of that
world to the other. It is that simple. That is why we do not find it
necessary (without necessarily excluding it) to postulate any conspiracy or collusion among the several mediums with whom
Bishop Pike had dealings. The psychic world is implicitly conspir-
atorial and it survives primarily by a tacit collusion that has been
built into all its arcane structures and byzantine networks of communication.

We would think it out of the question that Canon Pearce-Higgins might have passed "evidentiary" information directly to
Arthur Ford or George Daisley. That is not the way things happen in the psychic world. There are strict rules which govern that
world but they are rules of indirection. Nor do we think (as we
have explained) that Maren Bergrud was (in this instance) the
vehicle of communication. We would think, in the circumstances,
that information about Bishop Pike's sittings with Mrs. Twigg
would have passed to Ford by way of Father Rauscher of Spiritual
Frontiers. Even here, however, the communication might have
been indirect. (Mrs. R. W. Hanna of Hillsborough, California, as
an example, might have passed through London in those days and
then have passed through New Jersey.) By whatever means such
information might have made its way to Father Rauscher he
would have passed it along to Arthur Ford as so much gossip flut-
tering on the psychic grapevine. He need not have known (and
probably would not have known until long after the fact) that
Ford found a use for it in his first encounter with Bishop Pike.

It is interesting in this connection that Bishop Pike first heard
directly from Father Rauscher in a letter dated August 5, 1966.
Rauscher told him that he had been to France for a psychic con-
clave, had stopped in London on the way back, and had been informed by Canon Pearce-Higgins of Bishop Pike's "interest" in
the psychic domain. He would like to get together with Bishop
Pike, he said, in order to explore that common concern. The letter made no mention of Mrs. Twigg or of the "evidentiary" information (involving Rauscher and Spiritual Frontiers) imparted

by Jim Jr. in the March 14 séance. In *The Other Side*, therefore, Bishop Pike has construed the letter to mean that Rauscher was obviously not involved in any guilty plot against him. He overlooked the fact that the letter established a link between Father Rauscher and Canon Pearce-Higgins. We find it curious that Rauscher's letter happened to arrive within days of various events in Santa Barbara which had precipitated Bishop Pike's first sitting with George Daisley. Had it arrived one week or so earlier than it did Bishop Pike would almost surely have construed it to be one more "evidence" that Jim Jr. was again trying to "reach" him.

One way or another, in any event, the code names "Father Rauscher" and "Spiritual Frontiers" did find a means of conveyance to Arthur Ford, and he, in a seemingly casual way, did flash them at Bishop Pike in the narthex of St. Thomas Episcopal Church. Bishop Pike (probably to Ford's amazement) failed to respond (though he immediately recognized it) to this startling lure. He had an important luncheon date and didn't want to get trapped in protracted discussion with the ruddy-faced minister whose name he hadn't caught. Arthur Ford had nearly missed out on what in the end would prove to be a spectacular last hurrah.

There ensued an interlude of four months (during which Bishop Pike was to suffer no psychic harassment) wherein we may imagine the psychic world and/or the "Other Side" regrouped its forces and settled upon another strategy which culminated in the strange events in Santa Barbara (August 1, 1966) that led Bishop Pike to George Daisley. The arrangements with George Daisley seem to have prospered for nearly a year until the untoward death of Maren Bergrud. Bishop Pike's two sittings with Daisley in July and in August of 1967 (efforts to "reach" Maren Bergrud) were busts and might have terminated his experiences with mediumistic communication had it not been for the timely intervention of an aggressively enterprising professional journalist.

Enter Allen Spraggett. In May of 1967 the Center for the Study of Democratic Institutions sponsored a *Pacem in Terris* conference in Geneva, Switzerland, which Bishop Pike attended. Allen Spraggett was also there on assignment as religion editor of the Toronto *Star*. One night during that conference Bishop Pike and Spraggett stayed up until all hours over cheeseburgers and coffee as the bishop confided in full detail all of his experiences (to that point) with psychic phenomena and in his sittings with Ena Twigg and George Daisley. Spraggett was sworn to secrecy but only Bishop Pike would have expected a journalist to take such an oath seriously. In a little potboiler he wrote Spraggett has described how readily he imparted Bishop Pike's confidences. The potboiler was called *The Bishop Pike Story* ("A Signet Mystic Book from New American Library" published in New York in 1970) and much of it was coarsely cribbed from *The Bishop Pike Affair* (published in New York by Harper & Row in 1967) by William Stringfellow and Anthony Towne.

> Out of those conversations grew the idea for a television séance which triggered the biggest psychic news story since a Colorado housewife, under hypnosis, claimed to have lived before as an Irish woman named Bridey Murphy.
>
> Back in Toronto, after brooding on the idea for a while, I mentioned it to Charles Templeton, then director of news and public affairs for the Canadian Television Network (CTV). Templeton, who had enormous admiration for Pike, but of course knew him only as an arch-rationalist, was excited but wary.
>
> "Will Pike take part in a séance?" he asked.
>
> When I told him about the bishop's psychic experiences, he had only one other question: "Who's the medium?"

There are several versions available as to how it came about that Arthur Ford would be the medium. Two of those versions were offered by Ford and one by Spraggett.

Spraggett's version has it that having talked with Templeton he telephoned Ford, who—after a ritual feint of resistance—readily acceded to the plan. One of Ford's versions had it that he had been reluctant to risk his reputation under such novel circumstances but he had agreed out of admiration for Bishop Pike. In *Nothing So Strange* (the 1968 variant of his legend) he told a different story. According to that version (obviously concocted to minimize the possibility that he might have done prior research) he had arrived in Toronto understanding only that he and Bishop Pike would participate in a televised discussion of a new Spraggett potboiler. (*The Unexplained*, another Signet offering of New American Library published out of New York in 1967: the book is admirably faithful to its title. Bishop Pike unwisely provided a short introduction to it.) The idea of including a séance as part of that discussion—so this version ran—was a sort of last-minute, spur-of-the-moment serendipity.

Now all I needed was Bishop Pike's agreement. My phone call tracked him to the Aspen Institute of Humanistic Studies in Colorado, where he was spending a month as Resident Scholar. His voice when he answered the phone was heavy with sleep, but it was unmistakably his—pleasingly husky, yet supple and fluid. When I told him what I had in mind he was obviously interested.

"Arthur Ford," he said slowly. "Yes, I've wanted to meet him for some time."

Then I told him what Ford had told me—that they had already met, briefly, in St. Thomas Church in New York.

"Really?" said Pike, surprised and intrigued. He remembered the incident vividly of course. "Imagine that. Well, I'd like to renew the acquaintance, then."

By the agency of Allen Spraggett, Arthur Ford had managed to remanifest himself to Bishop Pike in the resplendent narthex of St. Thomas Episcopal Church. And so, on Sunday afternoon, September 3, 1967, Bishop Pike and Arthur Ford foregathered as guests of Allen Spraggett in a CTV studio in Toronto, Canada, for the video-taping of a major document in psychic history. Neither of them was ever to see the product of that taping (though Arthur Ford did see six minutes of it at the outset of the Philadelphia talk show he shared with Anthony Towne) because neither of them was in Toronto when it was aired several weeks later. The video tape itself was drastically edited down to a forty-minute program and in the process the balance of the tape was destroyed.

A full (though rather rough) transcript of the original video tape was made (under Allen Spraggett's supervision) and Bishop Pike and Spraggett and others (including us) have necessarily relied upon that transcript in published discussion of the Toronto séance. The video-taping began with an interview of Ford by Spraggett in which Ford was induced to define, rather clumsily, a medium and to describe how he personally functioned in that capacity. He explained that he blindfolded himself and went into a "yogi trance" and if all went well his connection in the spirit world—Fletcher—would take it from there. Fletcher ("and there was such a person; we've checked him out") he identified as a boyhood chum who had died in World War I. In the course of his fifty-year career Ford had spun so many disparate tales about Fletcher (his "control" from beginning to end) that if indeed there ever really was such a person he has long since been subsumed into a sort of polymorphous specter.

When the interview of Ford began to fray into redundancies Spraggett turned to Bishop Pike, who obliged with a characteristically sprightly dissertation based in the main on chapter 7 of his (then on the verge of publication) *If This Be Heresy*. The essence of it was that whereas he had once affirmed life after death as a matter of faith based upon the traditional teaching of the Church he was by then able to affirm it based upon his study of "the psi factor in human personality" as an exercise of his theological method of *facts+faith*. Despite persistent prodding from Spraggett Bishop Pike refrained from any disclosure of his own experiences with psychic phenomena or of his putative communications from Jim Jr. via Mrs. Twigg and George Daisley.

> Mr. Ford adjusted his posture to a more comfortable position and began breathing very deeply. His head fell to his chest and the deep breathing continued. After several minutes of dead air time, his head jerked and lifted up into a normal waking position and we heard:
>
> "Hello."
>
> "Is it Fletcher?" Allen asked. The response came (excised from the condensed version aired, I understand):
>
> "Yes, my name is Fletcher. I have spoken to you before."
>
> "Yes, that's true," Allen replied.

Allen Spraggett's great-Toronto-séance-TV-spectacular was under way. Fletcher (after some mumbo jumbo about ". . . light, a great massive light, if light can be a mass . . . and suddenly it begins to take form, and it takes the form of people . . .") proceeded to grope and fumble into semicoherence two spectral figures who proved to be Jim Jr. and grandfather Elias. Elias was called "Elijah" but Bishop Pike quickly figured out who he really was. He also found it an indication of authenticity that Ford had got Elias's name right in St. Thomas Episcopal Church whereas Fletcher had scored only a near-miss in Toronto. The fact is that the near-miss is an artful (more or less) ploy mediums use

(and/or their "controls" use) again and again precisely because it
does tend to evoke (in the credulous) an aura of authenticity.

> Ford's voice continued: "That's right, and in their earth life
> they seem to have been quite fond of each other."
> "Right," I affirmed.
> The flow of words continued: "And they are now. I should say
> that the grandfather preceded him here. This boy says that he is
> not, he does not know, he cannot remember, the circumstances of
> his death, it was some tragic way, but he says that he knows now
> that he was falling into the state of mind of, a, I don't know, con-
> dition, and he doesn't remember how or why, except he knows
> that he was not able to think straight, and he wasn't . . . but he
> says 'I will tell you this much, Dad'—he called you Dad—the be-
> ginning was someone whom he calls Halverston. I don't know, is
> the name like Halverston, or Halberston?"
> "In this life or the next?" I asked. I remembered a Marvin Hal-
> verson—I thought, at least—but I had not heard anything about
> him for years, so I had no way of knowing whether he was living
> or dead. The answer came.
> "He's here now, this Halverston. I've seen him here; he seems
> to have come over about the same time the boy did. Do you re-
> member such a person?"

Arthur Ford (or Fletcher) seems to have goofed badly on this
one. Marvin Halverson had not "come over" about the same time
the boy did. He had "come over," in fact, one year and twenty
days after Jim Jr. died. Jim Jr. died on February 4, 1966. Marvin
Halverson died on February 24, 1967. It seems likely to us that
the obituary of Halverson which Ford may have clipped from the
New York *Times* included the month and day but not the year
(as is usual in the *Times*) of Halverson's death. This might have
led Ford into the misapprehension that Halverson had died
"about the same time" Jim Jr. had died. Bishop Pike, of course,
did not know, as we do, that Arthur Ford had the habit of clipping obituaries and filing them away as against a rainy day.

> Ford's voice went on: "Wait a minute, wait, check it out. He
> had, his name was Marvin, and uh, something about some mod-
> ern music, or modern dancing, or art or something, in the church.
> And, uh . . ."

This information about Halverson was included in the *Times*'s obituary about him which was carried on February 27, 1967.

> "There's such a person," I interrupted. I was sure now we were talking about the same one.
>
> My last recollection of Marvin Halverson was that he had been director of the National Council of Churches' department dealing with the relation of the Church to various art forms and architecture. That evening, while waiting to take a plane to Philadelphia to appear on the Mike Douglas Show, I made a telephone call from the Kennedy International Airport to a friend in New York City about another matter, and was given information about Marvin Halverson which began to clear up the mystery of his connection with my son. The very fact that the next "outside" person I talked to after leaving the Toronto group had this information about the most puzzling item in the séance would seem an instance of synchronicity!

The "outside" person Bishop Pike talked to "about another matter" (the impending publication of *The Bishop Pike Affair*) was Anthony Towne. He told Anthony nothing about the Toronto séance. (William Stringfellow and Anthony Towne first learned of Bishop Pike's experiences with psychic phenomena and mediumistic communications when the rest of the world did several weeks later in the burst of publicity which attended the airing of the Toronto séance.) Bishop Pike did ask Anthony whether he had ever known a Marvin Halverson. Anthony had. Marvin Halverson had been his good friend.

(When Bishop Pike says he had no way of knowing whether Halverson was living or dead and "had not heard anything about him for years" he had obviously forgotten another telephone conversation he had had with Anthony Towne. On a day shortly after Halverson's death Anthony himself had told Bishop Pike of the death. Bishop Pike had remembered having known Halverson and said he had liked him and was sorry to learn he was dead.)

In their later telephone conversation Bishop Pike asked Anthony only one question about Marvin Halverson. He wondered whether Marvin might have known Jim Jr. Anthony was able to tell him that Marvin had. Anthony knew this because on the afternoon after Jim Jr.'s death Marvin Halverson had come to the apartment William Stringfellow and Anthony were then sharing (with half the human race, it sometimes seemed) on the Upper West Side of Manhattan. Halverson had been drunk and was carrying a copy of the New York *Daily News* which had a picture and story about Jim Jr. on the front page. "I knew that boy," he had said, over and over again. He did not say in what connection he had known him. His distress seemed out of proportion to the circumstances. William and Anthony were also moderately distressed. They hadn't known Jim Jr. but they did know Bishop Pike. They attributed Marvin's apparent state of shock to his intoxication and thought no more about it until some years later they had occasion to think back on it.

> Then Allen broke in for the first time in several minutes. "Did Halverson know Bishop Pike's son? On earth?" The answer: "Mm, hmm, and he knew Bishop Pike, not intimately, but had done some things in connection with the church, or Cathedral, and he was trying to bring back into the church modern music and the updated . . . so to speak, that's what Jim says."
> For the first time my son's name was used—so casually I almost missed it.

We don't know what whoever transcribed the video tape of the Toronto séance was trying to convey by "Mm, hmm" but we suspect "Ford's voice" at that point in the tape was projecting equivocation. We think "Mm, hmm" means "Maybe he did and maybe he didn't." We think that at this stage Ford may have been probing for a *possible* connection between Jim Jr. and Marvin Halverson. We don't think he knew at that time (as he later may have) that there had been such a connection.

The information that Marvin Halverson had known Bishop Pike ("not intimately") in connection with "the church, or Cathedral" may have been (and Bishop Pike took it to be) a reference to the fact that ten years earlier Halverson had been Dean Pike's guest on his weekly ABC network program originated out of the Cathedral of St. John the Divine. Though there had been mention of that program in various church publications at the time no mention of it was made in the New York *Times* obituary of Halverson.

Arthur Ford would have had to have gone to the public library to read his "poems" to have come up with that particular bit.

A Funereal Interlude

Marvin Halverson was fifty-four years old when he was found one day on a street in Berkeley, California, drunk, destitute, and incoherent. He was taken to a public hospital where he swallowed his tongue and suffocated to death on February 24, 1967. About a week later a congregation of those who had known him in New York City gathered in Judson Memorial Church (then undergoing extensive interior renovations) in Greenwich Village. The Reverend Al Carmines conducted the service, William Stringfellow read the Forty-seventh Psalm, and the late Dr. Truman Douglass gave the benediction. The Reverend George Todd delivered the remarks, which had been prepared (at Todd's request) by Anthony Towne.

> Marvin Halverson was a member of this church, and on occasion he had preached here during the ministry of his good friend the late Robert Spike. It seems fitting that we should meet today in the midst of all this renovation because Marvin never had approved of the decor at Judson and no doubt he will not approve of the result of this renovation but he would have thoroughly enjoyed the interval between what he didn't approve of and what he won't approve of. Marvin himself was always in the midst of renovation. He was never satisfied with what had been done and it was clear he would never be satisfied with what would be done. I think there is something profoundly Christian about that.
>
> Marvin was a restless man. Restlessness was the very condition of his being. All of us here today will remember in this way or in that way how restless he was, how much, therefore, he disturbed us, how much, therefore, he loved us, how much, therefore, he served us, and he served us most, I think, when he most made us uncomfortable. He did that fairly often. He is doing that now. It is almost intolerable—is it not?—to remember Marvin's loneliness and his agony and his concern and his vivacity—to remember his irrevocable restlessness.
>
> It sometimes seemed that nothing Marvin planned to do got done. Marvin did not plan, of course, he dreamed. There were so many dreams. There is no one here today who has dared to dream

so much. I will not list all those dreams because everyone of us knows the list by heart. Marvin did not keep his dreams to himself, as most of us do: he broadcast them, he advocated them, he connived for them, he pleaded for them, he prostituted himself for them, and he destroyed himself for them. There is something heroic about a man who dares believe in his own dreams. How many of us do? And isn't it astonishing, when we stop to think about it, how much of Marvin's dreams *did* get done?

It is not easy to account for Marvin. Who was he? He was a minister, but he occupied only one pulpit—in Wilton, Connecticut—and that for only two years. He was an educator—and served for a time as dean of students at Chicago Theological Seminary—but his students really were those of us here today and many others and his teaching could not have prospered in a classroom. He was a man of vast and peculiar learning who seldom had time to read a book and certainly was not a scholar. He wrote many things and was editor for many more things but he did not write well and was an indifferent editor. He lectured and preached frequently but he was a poor public speaker. He held a number of significant executive positions but the world has seldom known a worse administrator. He was a superb and gifted cook but the cookbook he longed to write—"Cooking for Holy Days and Holidays"—never did get finished. He had a remarkable talent for friendship but he lived alone and was lonely. He came from a farm in South Dakota and spoke feelingly of his roots in the soil but his greatest pleasure in recent years came from his membership in the Century Club here in New York. Marvin was very much a man of the world, and yet he was, I think, an authentic Christian.

Marvin moved in many circles and was at home in none of them, except perhaps this circle gathered here this afternoon for the first and surely the last time. He moved in very high society and in very low society and his limericks delighted both. He was a familiar figure to many of the most exalted artists and intellectuals and churchmen of our time. His ministry in the past fifteen years first at the National Council of Churches, Department of Worship and the Arts, and later with the Foundation for the Arts, Religion and Culture—which he founded—established an opportunity for the Church and the arts which neither of them may deserve. Marvin dared to dream that something like the great confluence of arts and religion of the Middle Ages might be brought about in our own time. It won't be but that won't be because Marvin didn't try. It is somehow worth noting that Marvin had many friends in the Century Club—some of whom are among us now—but one of his closest and dearest friends in his last years tended bar in that same club.

Marvin was a blemished man. More of a man than most of us, there are too many who would say he was not man enough. The hurt that this stigma did to Marvin God alone can say. We, on the other hand, can say, I think, that Marvin's blemish was naked and apparent, and what we did not do to soothe it remains in whatever we have that passes for conscience. Marvin withheld himself too much for his own good—which was a convenience to us—and he gave of himself too much for his own good—with benefits to us that are almost too much to bear. In something Marvin wrote he quoted a wise observation of Truman Douglass: " . . . a Christian is not a good man but a forgiven man." Marvin was a good man, and we are forgiven.

Séance Interruptus or the Sin of Liking Your Own Kind

"This," I muttered to Bill Rauscher, "shoots down the whole Block message."

And how much more?

If, as now seemed ominously possible, Arthur Ford had researched the Pike séance in advance—some critics had alleged this all along—the entire edifice of supposedly evidential messages might crumble.

My mood was somber as I fingered that newspaper clipping.

There was a sense of shock, even outrage; I felt personally affronted. Though long aware of Ford's drinking problem and other foibles, I had believed, and maintained to others, that he kept his mediumship sacrosanct.

"Despite his personal problems," I had said more than once, "Ford never compromised his mediumship."

Now these words seemed hollow.

The outrage was more likely Father Rauscher's. We have a hunch it was *his* shock that caused the fraud to be exposed in *Arthur Ford: The Man Who Talked with the Dead*. It was Rauscher who turned up the calamitous (undated) clipping Spraggett somberly fingered. The clipping (as Rauscher found it among the remnants of Ford's "poems") was identical with an obituary carried by the New York *Times* on September 21, 1958.

Karl Morgan Block, Episcopal Bishop of California, it reported, was dead at seventy-one on the coast.

When we interrupted the Toronto séance (in order to pay our last respects to Marvin Halverson) Arthur Ford (and/or Fletcher and/or Jim Jr.) had begun to introduce what gradually became a dazzling array of personages from the "Other Side," each of whom turned out to have had something or other to do with Bishop Pike. Halverson aside, every bit of information that "came through" was inconsequential trivia, and the more trivial it was the more impressive it was to Bishop Pike. It would serve no purpose to rehearse all of it here. The only purpose it served in the context of the séance (other than perhaps to demonstrate that Arthur Ford had a knack for research) was to bewilder Bishop Pike into failing to notice that Jim Jr. (whom he was presumably there to hear from) couldn't get a word in edgeways. On the tenuous assumption that it is the function of a séance to yield some meaningful word from a departed loved one it may be said that the Toronto séance didn't amount to an impoverished hill of beans.

What it *did* amount to was a brilliant display of Arthur Ford's talents as a medium in the sense of his having been able to litter the video tape with tantalizing "evidentiary" tidbits. Karl Morgan Block was among the "communicators" and every bit of the considerable blather he communicated could have been lifted from his New York *Times* obituary. Much the same could be said of each of the other Toronto "communicators"—what they communicated either *was* in one or another of Ford's "poems" or it *could have been.*

Much is made in discussions of séances (by Bishop Pike and many others) of the possibility that mediums get some (or all) of their information by ESP. Taking that approach some have suggested that Arthur Ford may have gotten some (or all) of his information by extracting it paranormally from Bishop Pike's (or somebody else's) unconscious (or conscious) mind. We profess no competence for estimating anybody's paranormal powers. We think that a matter better left to those who have such powers and to parapsychologists. When Arthur Ford was starting out as a medium extrasensory perception hadn't been invented. It was called mind reading in those innocent days. Arthur Ford is reputed to

have had great skill in that regard. Whether or not his gift for
mind reading (if he ever had one) survived the advent of extrasensory perception we cannot say. We know Ford purloined information from the New York *Times*. We concede he would have
purloined information from Bishop Pike's unconscious (or conscious) mind if he had the means to do it. Purloined information,
however, whether normally or paranormally acquired, is not communication with the dead.

Bishop Pike might have followed up on the Toronto séance
(as Fletcher several times urged him to do) by checking out the
trivia which had been imparted to him. He did not. He was too
busy with other matters to dissipate himself in the pursuit of
trivia. We suspect that is one reason most information conveyed
in séances is inconsequential. Were substantial information to be
imparted it *would* be checked out with unhappy consequences
(we suspect) for the mediums who uttered it. Had Bishop Pike
followed up on the Toronto séance thoroughly we have a feeling
he would not ever have consulted Arthur Ford again. Allen Spraggett did check out one message that "came through" in Toronto,
a charmingly whimsical bit involving two cats and the father of a
lecturer at Corpus Christi College, Cambridge, England. *That*
"communication" went hoist by its own petard when it turned
out the lecturer (Donald MacKinnon, a theologian and an acquaintance of Bishop Pike's) had listed "cats" as one of his recrea-
tions in an English edition of Who's Who.

The net product of the Toronto séance, so far as Bishop Pike
was concerned, was a nagging curiosity about the puzzling intervention of Marvin Halverson.

He did check that out. He found out from Anthony Towne
that Halverson had known Jim Jr. He remembered a big party he
and Jim Jr. had attended in New York on their way to Cambridge. Wondering if Halverson might have been at that party he
checked with the hostess and one of the other guests. Neither
remembered Halverson as having been there but the hostess, Nan
Lanier, whom Jim Jr. had liked (and who was one of the friends
he had told Jim Sr. he would look up on his stop in New York on
the way back from Cambridge) remembered that Jim Jr. had
talked to her *about* Halverson. Diane Kennedy had a friend, Jane
Kingman, who was working at that time, as it happened, for the

Foundation for the Arts, Religion and Culture which Halverson had founded and directed. Jane Kingman knew little about Halverson but was able to report that Halverson had moved to Berkeley when he left the Foundation and had died there in unhappy circumstances.

Bishop Pike was under the misimpression that Halverson might have met Jim Jr. in Berkeley. This could not have happened because Halverson did not move to Berkeley until August 1, 1966, six months after Jim Jr.'s death and six months before his own death. (It is an odd coincidence—but *surely* no more than that— that August 1, 1966, was also the date of the bizarre events in Santa Barbara which precipitated the first séance with George Daisley.)

While they were in Cambridge Jim Jr. had discussed certain sexual conflicts with Bishop Pike on at least one occasion. Bishop Pike also recalled two experiences Jim Jr. had had in Europe that he had suspected at the time were explicit confirmations of those conflicts. Out of these bits and pieces of information (and misimpression) about Marvin Halverson and Jim Jr. Bishop Pike constructed a hypothesis which would have assigned to Halverson (if the hypothesis could be verified) a role in Jim Jr.'s decision to take his own life. How could the hypothesis be verified? Bishop Pike decided to test it (and at the same time to test Arthur Ford) by requesting a second (private) séance to see whether or not Jim Jr. (and/or Arthur Ford) would bear out the hypothesis.

(Bishop Pike also entertained, though it never achieved the dignity of hypothesis, a speculation that Jim Jr.'s death might have occurred by murder and not by suicide. This speculation had several fragile bases—including the fact that two shots were fired— the primary of which was that the medical examiner had concluded Jim Jr. had used his right hand to pull the trigger of the rifle. Jim Jr. was left-handed and the bishop reasoned that in so solemn a moment Jim Jr. would more likely have used his left hand to pull the trigger. We have reflected upon this speculation and think it holds no water [and little reasoning]. Which hand Jim Jr. would have chosen to pull the trigger and which he would have used to steady the rifle would have depended, we think, upon whether pulling the trigger or steadying the rifle seemed more important to him at the moment. There is also the fact that

it was Jim Jr. who purchased the gun. What for? On the rather
wild assumption that somebody else killed Jim Jr. by inserting the
rifle in his mouth we would think it logically follows that Jim Jr.'s
hands would have been quite differently engaged. We have found
nothing that would lead us to question the conclusions of the
medical examiner and the coroner that Jim Jr. died as the result
of a self-inflicted gunshot wound.)

Early in December of 1967 (three months after the Toronto
séance) Bishop Pike was invited to be a panelist for an hour's discussion of psychic phenomena on WHY-TV in Philadelphia. The
panel, which included eight scientists and science writers, also included Arthur Ford. (We think it a moral certainty the program
was engineered by Ford in order to create the very pretext it in
any case came to serve.) Bishop Pike accepted on condition that
there would be no televised séance. (He was told Ford had made
the same stipulation.) The publicity touched off by the airing of
the Toronto séance had generated an avalanche of mail (and
other harassments) unparalleled by any other uproar Bishop Pike
had ever suffered. He was not eager to protract it. The date set for
taping the WHY-TV panel discussion was December 16, 1967.

> Miss Kennedy and I saw this occasion as an opportunity to
> assess more carefully Arthur Ford's gifts. We decided to request a
> private sitting with him following the television taping, and go
> with a list of questions pertaining to mysteries about both my
> son's death and Maren Bergrud's which we were virtually certain
> that Mr. Ford could not research. Moreover, we intended to steer
> the conversation by our questions and comments so that any in-
> formation he might have gathered about other persons would
> figure very little. Also we felt that the degree of directness of the
> responses would give considerable indication as to whether there
> was genuine communication going on or not.
>
> Miss Kennedy and I had made the appointment to sit with Mr.
> Ford following the television taping, and Diane arranged for a
> friend of hers in New York, Miss Jane Kingman, Executive Secre-
> tary of another foundation, to come down from New York and
> accompany us. Miss Kingman was the friend who had been able
> to help us pursue the lead given in the Toronto séance about
> Marvin Halverson, for it turned out she was working for the
> Foundation for the Arts, Religion and Culture, which Mr. Hal-
> verson had served as the first director. Jane knew, then, some-

thing about Mr. Halverson's activities and patterns of life in the
years immediately preceding his death. She knew, for example,
that he had gone out to Berkeley after leaving his job at the
Foundation in New York and had died there on February 24,
1967, more than a year *after* Jim's death. She knew he had been
involved in the use of psychedelic drugs as well as having some
other rather serious problems. She knew he had lived in Greenwich Village. And finally, quite by accident one day she learned
from a Greenwich Village liquor dealer from whom she was buy-
ing a bottle of wine that on the day the news of Jim's death appeared in the New York papers, Marvin Halverson had come into
his store and had commented, "I knew that boy." This all fit with
Nan Lanier's statement in her letter later from London that Jim
had talked to her about Marvin Halverson.

We felt if anything further were to come out about my son's
connection with Halverson it would be well to have Jane there.
Also, we wanted a third witness.

We wish they had chosen somebody else to be a third witness.
The fact that Jane Kingman was employed (for six months at the
time of the Philadelphia séance) by the same foundation Marvin
Halverson had directed has naturally created some suspicion that
she might have been the source of some of Ford's information
about Halverson. We have looked into this matter exhaustively.
Jane Kingman (who was not executive secretary of that foundation but administrative assistant in it) never knew Marvin Halverson personally and knew little about him at that time. She knew
nothing at all about his "activities and patterns of life in the years
immediately preceding his death." She did know he had moved to
Berkeley after he left the Foundation (which was before she
joined it) and that he had died there on February 24, 1967. She
did not know he had been "involved in the use of psychedelic
drugs" or that he had "other rather serious problems." (Marvin
Halverson, to our knowledge, did not use psychedelic drugs; his
problems in that regard were with alcohol and to some extent
with sleeping pills.) Jane Kingman did not know that Halverson
had lived in Greenwich Village.

Jane Kingman does recollect the incident with the Greenwich
Village liquor dealer but she recollects that it happened some
time *after* the Philadelphia séance. Her recollection of what the
liquor dealer told her is entirely consistent with (and Bishop Pike

may have later confused it with) what Anthony Towne told Bishop Pike over the telephone the evening following the Toronto séance. We are satisfied that Jane Kingman knew virtually nothing (at that time) about Marvin Halverson or, for that matter, about Jim Jr. She learned there would be a séance only two days before she arrived in Philadelphia to attend it. She knew nothing of the Toronto séance until it was mentioned in Philadelphia. She did not know Arthur Ford and had never heard of him. She agreed to participate in the Philadelphia séance at the last minute because it sounded like an adventure and because she had normal curiosity as to what went on in séances. We have found no link whatever between Jane Kingman and what "came through" about Marvin Halverson in Philadelphia.

After the taping of the WHY-TV show there was a lunch attended by Bishop Pike, Arthur Ford, Diane Kennedy, Jane Kingman, Walter Houston Clark (one of the panelists), and Father William Rauscher. The conversation during lunch was a continuation of the panel discussion and did not touch on matters likely to arise in the impending séance. In due course the lunch party adjourned (excepting Professor Clark) to Arthur Ford's modest apartment. Father Rauscher (who was meeting Bishop Pike for the first and only time) set up a tape recorder (and we rely on the tape which resulted for our analysis of the Philadelphia séance) as the second (and last) of Bishop Pike's sittings with Arthur Ford got under way.

> After some conversation, we settled down where each of us could be comfortable in the small room which obviously doubled as living room and study. The tape recorder was on the desk, ready to record. Diane was seated by it; Jane was on a sofa; I took a chair directly in front of Mr. Ford, who seated himself in a large red leather chair. He explained that his chair reclined in order to make it easier for him to relax and go into trance.
>
> With no further explanation then, Arthur Ford covered his eyes as he had in Toronto, pushed his chair back into a reclining position, began his deep-breathing exercises and after several minutes seemed to go off into a trance. Father Rauscher addressed Fletcher and, on hearing a brief response, turned on the tape recorder, said, "Fletcher, I'm going to leave you with your guests" and quietly left.

Fletcher wasted little time conjuring up Jim Jr. Grandfather Elias skipped this séance. Instead Jim Jr. volunteered the news that Elias's wife—Alexandra (correctly named)—then a very old lady, would soon be moving to the "Other Side." He correctly suggested that Bishop Pike and Alexandra were not close. Alexandra's name and advanced age Ford could have learned from a number of standard reference books. Given that her daughter—Esther—and Bishop Pike had been divorced (very publicly) only five months earlier Ford would have needed little intuition (and no ESP) to surmise that Alexandra Yanovsky and Bishop Pike were estranged. We think that Alexandra may have been dragged into the Philadelphia séance primarily as warm-up material. The séance was neatly balanced at its other end by a similar wind-down bit which involved another aged lady who, it was said, would shortly die. She did. How Ford might have found out the lady was terminally ill we don't know. Penultimate to that bull's-eye finale there had been an alleged manifestation of Maren Bergrud. Every bit of the (little) information that "came through" in regard to Maren could have been derived from the New York *Times* account of her suicide.

(Actually, the Philadelphia séance did not end with the fatal disposition of the aged lady. Ford hadn't expected Jane Kingman. He couldn't ignore her, however, so after the close of the *formal* séance he tossed a few vaguish prognostications in her general direction. Some years later Jane [by that time] Kingman-Brundage reported to us that none of Ford's "prophecy" about her had been fulfilled.)

The balance (and hard core) of the Philadelphia séance had to do with Jim Jr.'s suicide and Marvin Halverson. This sequence was by all odds the most startling and the most "evidentiary" and the most apparently unresearchable of any "communications" Bishop Pike received from Jim Jr. in any of the twelve sittings he had with four different mediums. The material was so intimate in nature that Bishop Pike excluded most of it from *The Other Side.* We propose to examine that part of the Philadelphia séance closely because it has never been examined (for publication) before. We confess it perplexed us for a very long time. We are not at all surprised that Bishop Pike was so impressed with it that it served as the "clincher" in his argument that the evidence on bal-

ance enabled him to believe—he never said to *know*—the communications from Jim Jr. had been authentic.

We will attempt to paraphrase that portion of the tape of the
Philadelphia séance (as recorded on December 16, 1967, for
Bishop Pike and kept by him until his death when it became the
property of Diane Kennedy Pike). Jim Jr. (it seemed) did most of
the talking with occasional interjections by Fletcher. The voice, of
course, was Ford's—heavy (as though drugged), labored, often
seeming to grope for precisely the right word. There is (at this
point in the tape) an uncanny sense that somebody really might
be speaking "through" Arthur Ford. Bishop Pike and Diane both
respond (after some initial awkwardness) as though they were engaged in serious conversation with Jim Jr. The feeling of reality
about that portion of the tape is quite extraordinary.

Bishop Pike does ask some leading questions. It is he who first
mentions Marvin Halverson. For the most part, however, the conversation is led by Jim Jr. (apparently) and it is very much *as
though* he had turned up at the séance with the intention of
clarifying the mystery about his suicide and Marvin Halverson's
role (if he had one) in it. There is also a decidedly pastoral quality about his apparent manifestation. What he has to say and how
he says it seem carefully designed to reassure Bishop Pike and
Bishop Pike (whether or not the communication was genuine)
definitely *is* reassured. There is something so remarkably authentic
about this emotional interchange that the *feeling* of it becomes
more "evidentiary" than anything that was actually said.

Jim Jr. opened the conversation by saying he was sorry he
insisted on coming back from Cambridge alone. He and his father
had got on so well together while they were in Cambridge. When
he got to New York he had got hold of something which was not
good for him. That was drugs. He ran into some people he had
known from the Coast. He had a friend on the Coast who could
clear things up, if he would. The friend was named Bennett
Tarshish. He had had a problem that had depressed him. That
was homosexuality. Marvin Halverson had something to do with
that. He was an older man who was attracted to younger men. He
was more experienced. He was no more to blame for what happened than Jim Jr. was. Jim Jr. had had experiences in Europe
that had confirmed to him that he was "deviant." He wanted to

be normal. He had tried to write about these things but what he wrote didn't make sense. His fear of his mother had something to do with his problem.

That is the substance of the hard core of the Philadelphia séance.

Jim Jr. and Bennett Tarshish had indeed been close friends for several months in the summer of 1966 up to the time Jim Jr. and Bishop Pike left for Cambridge. Tarshish was about five years older than Jim Jr. In a telephone conversation with Bishop Pike and Diane in March of 1968 (three months after the Philadelphia séance) Tarshish told them his relationship with Jim Jr. "wasn't homo, but it was emotional—more than most relationships with men are." Diane's notes of that conversation also indicate that Tarshish said Jim Jr. had talked with him about his "homosexual urges." He had said these urges stemmed from "fears . . . feelings . . . problems with his mother." His need to "debase himself" and "to scrape bottom," Tarshish said, had had something to do with his homosexual "bias."

Tarshish went on to say that Jim Jr. told him he would not have sex with (male) friends but only with strangers. Asked if Jim Jr. had ever mentioned Marvin Halverson Tarshish paused a long time (according to Diane's later recollection) and said he had never heard that name. Since Halverson didn't move to Berkeley until after Jim Jr.'s death there is no way Jim Jr. could have met him before leaving for Cambridge and so no way he could have mentioned him to Tarshish. (On the tape of the Philadelphia séance Jim Jr. is heard to say he knew Halverson on both coasts. That cannot be correct with respect to the West Coast.) Bennett Tarshish was terminally ill when he talked with Bishop Pike and Diane (though they didn't know it) and he died not long after his last conversation with them.

On their way to Cambridge Bishop Pike and Jim Jr. had stopped in New York for several days. (Bishop Pike took a side trip to Canada, leaving Jim Jr. for part of that time with Nan Lanier.) The night they arrived in New York Nan Lanier gave a rather large party which they attended. Bishop Pike did not later recall that Marvin Halverson was at that party and his later inquiries disclosed no one else who remembered seeing him. Several of the guests, however, knew Halverson and one (a man about Halverson's age) is known to have been homosexual. We believe Jim Jr. may have met Marvin Halverson somehow as a result of contacts he made at that party. After the Toronto séance Bishop Pike wrote to Nan Lanier (who was then in London) to ask about Marvin Halverson and that party. Nan Lanier replied that she did not recall seeing Halverson at the party but she did recall Jim Jr. talking to her about Marvin Halverson. That would seem to mean—however it came about—that Jim Jr. must have met Halverson during that visit to New York.

If Marvin Halverson did meet Jim Jr. at that time there is no doubt in our minds (and we knew him well) that he would have made it his business to get to know the younger man better. (The fact that it was Bishop Pike's son would have added zest to his interest.) Marvin did like younger men and usually they liked him. He used to say he was "queer for architecture students and seminarians," and he was. He was also (at his best anyway) very good with that type of young man. He could be patiently understanding, compassionate, and companionably paternal. There are not a few architects and priests and ministers—no longer so young —who could testify that he helped them enormously at a time in their lives when they were torn by vocational and/or sexual conflicts. Whatever explicitly may have taken place between Halverson and Jim Jr. during that visit to New York we think it quite likely Jim Jr. would have found it affirmative and comforting.

Jim Jr. did talk with his father on at least one occasion in Cambridge about his fears that he might be homosexual. Bishop Pike would later feel he hadn't been much help. He tried to be reassuring. He told his son that our bodies cannot sin and it is only in our minds that we sin. He found the situation awkward. Sex with other men was about as far as you could get from Bishop Pike's "bag" and as with most men who prefer women the subject of homosexuality made him uncomfortable. In our research for this book we encountered a rumor that Bishop Pike had had some homosexual experiences (and had been arrested in that connection). Despite our skepticism we pursued that rumor to its source which did not exist. We did learn, however, from Diane and from an old friend of his (who is homosexual), that Bishop Pike did have one homosexual experience while he was a lonely law student at Yale. He succumbed to the blandishments of another student. He told his friend he hadn't found the experience unpleasant or distasteful. "It was just that nothing seemed to fit together the way it should," he said. Bishop Pike didn't tell Jim Jr. that story, so far as we know. We wish he had.

On two occasions while Jim Jr. and Bishop Pike were abroad together young Jim had had social engagements (both of them with servicemen older than himself) which Bishop Pike suspected at the time (and suspected more strongly in his later retrospect) to have had homosexual implications. On one of the occasions, in England, a marine had invited Jim Jr. out for an evening from which Jim Jr. (seeming depressed) had not returned until the following day. On the other occasion, in Germany (where Jim Jr. had joined his father for a visit to chaplains at a U. S. Air Force installation), the driver assigned to them similarly had invited Jim Jr. out for an evening. Jim Jr. had slept most of the next day. When Bishop Pike asked why Jim Jr. had explained that he had stayed in the driver's apartment (drinking beer) until four-thirty in the morning. Bishop Pike had thought the driver a sort likely to have made advances to Jim Jr. and reasoned that the advances might have been productive since Jim Jr. had stayed so late. These are the episodes (we presume) to which Jim Jr. apparently alluded in the Philadelphia séance as having confirmed to him that he was "deviant."

We would also presume that the two episodes reflected an effort by Jim Jr. (at least in part) to provoke in Bishop Pike more of a response than he seems to have been able to make. The problem Jim Jr. could not live with, then, was his fear that he was condemned to homosexuality. He had contracted the sin that dares not speak its name. He had contracted the sin of liking his own kind. That can be a devastating discovery for a young man raised in a society (and a Church) that counts it manly for a young man to totter off to some battlefield to kill his own kind. Jim Jr. took his own life. There is no question about that. We are nevertheless bold to say that Jim Jr.'s society and his Church were cruelly complicit in his murder. This world and that Church sometimes speak of perversion. There was no perversion in Jim Jr. He needed to make love with his own kind. The pain of that was so unbearable he found it more bearable to kill himself. Where did that pain come from? Answer us that and you will have told us where perversion *really* is.

Jim Jr. did insist on coming back from Cambridge alone. (The fact that he forgot his passport, however, suggests an underlying ambivalence.) He told his father he intended to look up friends (Nan Lanier was one) he had made during their visit to New York the previous fall. He did not look up any of the friends he named. We think he may have looked up a friend he didn't name. We think he may have looked up Marvin Halverson. We think that because of the state Marvin was in ("I knew that boy," he said over and over again) when he came to our apartment the day after Jim Jr.'s death. We think Jim Jr. in his awful extremity may have felt that Marvin Halverson was the only person he knew who might be able to help him. Jim Jr.'s urgent need at that point was for somebody—*any*body—who would affirm his identity by loving it.

If Jim Jr. did look up Marvin Halverson he would have found a man tragically different from the man he may have met five months earlier. During that fall and winter (1965–66) Marvin had plunged into a shattering decline. His drinking (long something of a problem) became incessant. Twice he had been hospitalized. Unable to function he lost his job. (For Marvin that meant he had lost everything.) His friends (other remedies having failed) decided a fresh start somewhere else was the only solution. They were able to find a job for him in Berkeley, California, but it was an academic appointment not to take effect until the fall of 1966. As of early February of 1966 Marvin was drifting about New York drinking whatever he could cadge and making an ass of himself. He still had his apartment in Greenwich Village only because he rented it from friends who didn't have the heart to throw him out. Any encounter that may have taken place in that apartment between Marvin Halverson and Jim Jr. at that time could only have been a disaster for both of them.

Jim Jr. did try to write about these things but by that time he was too far gone on drugs and the notes the police found near his body in that drab hotel room made no sense whatever.

We think it improbable that Jim Jr. ran into some people he

had known from the Coast while he was in New York. Speaking through Ford on the tape of the Philadelphia séance he says that he did, and that Bennett Tarshish could clear that up, if he would. Bishop Pike talked with Tarshish about this. Tarshish was able to say only that there had been a crowd on the Coast that Jim Jr. was part of and that they had been "into" drugs and "into" sex. He said he didn't think the sex was homosexual. He was not able to confirm that anybody in that crowd had been run into by Jim Jr. in New York. We just don't think that happened. The solitary evidence for it is Jim Jr.'s (apparent) statement on the Philadelphia tape.

Everything that "came through" in that astonishing sequence of the Philadelphia séance might seem to have been virtually unresearchable. Some of it, however, could have been learned (or readily inferred) from newspaper accounts of Jim Jr.'s death. There were only three facts that were inaccessible in that way. How could Arthur Ford have found out about Jim Jr.'s relationship to Bennett Tarshish? How could Arthur Ford have found out about Jim Jr.'s relationship (if there was one) to Marvin Halverson? How could Arthur Ford have found out that Jim Jr. had had experiences in Europe that confirmed to him that he was "deviant"? How (stating the matter another way) could Arthur Ford have known that homosexuality was the precipitating cause of Jim Jr.'s death?*

Another Side of the Other Side

Bishop Pike never had another sitting with Arthur Ford. He did have three further sittings in the spring of 1968.

In April of 1968 Hans Holzer inveigled a séance with Ethel Johnson Meyers in New York City. Diane Kennedy also attended.

* A simple solution to this problem has occurred to us. Unfortunately there is no longer any way to verify it. In the wake of the publicity following the airing of the Toronto TV séance Arthur Ford, as has been mentioned, received hundreds of letters which led him to hire the "effeminate" correspondence secretary. Who knows what he may have learned from those letters? Specifically, perhaps one of those letters came from Bennett Tarshish? Tarshish, however, is dead, and (according to Allen Spraggett and Father Rauscher) Ford's correspondence was destroyed not long after *his* death.

(It was "through" Mrs. Meyers that Bishop Pike himself later on "manifested" with news of "Rodamus" and other wonders of the spirit world.) This séance was a disaster. There was a purported intervention by Maren Bergrud, who had nothing whatever to say. Other than that, according to Diane, Mrs. Meyers just sat for the most part mute. Holzer, in his book, attributes the failure of communication to the fact that the telephone kept ringing. We think it must have been Jim Jr. in despair that he would succeed in "coming through" by Mrs. Meyers's paranormal agency.

In May of 1968 Jim and Diane took Bennett Tarshish for a sitting with George Daisley. It yielded nothing.

In June of 1968, on the way back from a trip to Israel, Bishop Pike stopped in London and had his third and last sitting with Ena Twigg. Diane and Scott Kennedy, and the bishop's daughter, Connie, were also present. Everybody who attended found the experience impressive. Much of the time was given over to a lengthy disquisition by Jim Jr. on how things are on the "Other Side." An excerpt of his remarks was included by Bishop Pike at the close of *The Other Side*, as a sort of coda to that book. The remarks have the merit of being intelligible. We do not find anything in them, however, that could not have been invented out of whole cloth (with perhaps a bit of coaching from Canon Pearce-Higgins) by the very gifted and altogether remarkable Mrs. Twigg.

That third séance with Mrs. Twigg (coinciding, as it did, with the completion of *The Other Side*) concluded Bishop Pike's experiences with psychic phenomena and mediumistic communication. Characteristically, he seems to have set the whole matter to one side in order to plunge into other subjects during the little more than one year he had left to live. After his death, however (so many believe), he may have renewed his interest in paranormal communication. He has been turning up ever since in séances all over the world with nearly as great a frequency as the late Edgar Cayce. We think we have not been unduly arbitrary in deciding that a review of such alleged manifestations of Bishop Pike falls outside the scope of this book. Diane Pike has received (especially in the year immediately after Jim's death) many, many, many messages which are purported to have come from Bishop Pike. She has found none of them persuasive. We have sampled a few and have found them shoddy, shabby, and obscenely dull.

(Since his own death, early in 1971, Arthur Ford—like Edgar Cayce and Bishop Pike—has also been reported to have turned up in séances all over the world. It may be that sooner or later he will be moved to vouchsafe us by that means how it was he came by the apparently unresearchable information concerning Jim Jr.'s homosexuality. *That* really would be an "evidentiary" communication.)

It has been our solitary purpose to examine Bishop Pike's experiences with psychic phenomena. We have made no effort to examine the four mediums he sat with in respect of any other sittings they may have had. We offer no opinion about the authenticity of any other paranormal events that may have occurred from the time of the Witch of Endor to this day. We will state for the record that we began this book of the opinion that communication with the dead is impossible precisely because they *are* dead. Nothing we have encountered in the course of researching and writing the book has persuaded us that we should discard that opinion. We are aware that serious study of these matters is taking place by persons competent to do it. We wish them well. It is an important work and a difficult one. We plead the brevity of life and its variety when we let it be known that the period we hope to place at the end of this sentence terminates our active interest in psychic matters.

We had occasion to say (earlier on) that we thought *The Other Side* may have been Bishop Pike's best book. We remain of that opinion. We have obviously come to different conclusions about the meaning of the events he reported. We think we have come to different conclusions (in part at least) because we had facts available to us that were not available to him. We also think we had more time than he ever had for anything to sift through what were, after all, terribly complicated and sometimes almost crazy situations. For all that, if anybody has ever made a better case for the authenticity of communications with the dead than was made by Bishop Pike in *The Other Side* we have not run across it.

Something remains of that book which is imperishable. It is the story it tells of the love of a father and a son. It is the story it tells of two men whose love for one another could not be resolved. It is the story it tells of the struggle of two men to save one another.

Death itself was powerless to end that struggle. In the end that struggle and that love were resolved for both men. Bishop Pike and Jim Jr. have communicated their love for one another across the barrier of death. They have shared the love with us. We have reason to be grateful. *The Other Side* is one more precious gift life has wrenched from the awful gape of death.

PART TWO

A Passion About Jesus

Though if I wish to boast, I shall not be a fool, for I shall be speaking the truth. But I refrain from it, so that no one may think more of me than he sees in me or hears from me. And to keep me from being too elated by the abundance of revelations, a thorn was given me in the flesh, a messenger of Satan, to harass me, to keep me from being too elated. Three times I besought the Lord about this, that it should leave me; but he said to me, "My grace is sufficient for you, for my power is made perfect in weakness." I will all the more gladly boast of my weaknesses, that the power of Christ may rest upon me. For the sake of Christ, then, I am content with weaknesses, insults, hardships, persecutions, and calamities; for when I am weak, then I am strong.

II Corinthians 12.6–10

The remarkable circumstances of Bishop Pike's death, the excitement which attended his public career, the traumas which relentlessly afflicted him in private life, the controversies generated by his opinions, the hostility which his rhetorical manner provoked, the scope and multiplicity of his interests, the velocity and versatility of his intelligence, his indefatigable and catholic curiosity, the undauntedness of his quest for faith obscure the truth that the bishop's piety and his theological convictions actually changed only slightly in the course of his life, from the days of his adolescent earnestness until the week he became lost in the Judean wilderness. His style of thought became more succinct, his rhetorical facility sharpened, his intellectual concerns broadened and diversified profusely, his scholarly pretensions became more realistic and modest while his learnedness increased, his beliefs took better focus, but, nevertheless, his confessional views, for all that he worked and reworked them, altered, in substance, remarkably little through his years. Moreover, his affirmations remained Christian—despite the tumult his witness occasioned—and well within the precincts of biblical faith.

This is not to imply that there was no significant movement in Pike's thought during his life, but, rather, it is to emphasize that the most notable changes concerned not his comprehension of the gospel but his relationship to the Church.

James Pike suffered a terrible love affair with the Church in which he was, simultaneously, wondrously attracted and profoundly repelled, from which he was not divorced until—perhaps—his very last days. It is Pike's love for the Church—not his belief as a Christian—which was at issue in his youthful, self-styled agnosticism, during his brief interlude as a layman, in his successive ecclesiastical roles, in his tireless forensic efforts, in his putative heresies, in those paranormal episodes, in his wistful scholarship, in family and other personal relationships, in the trials and temptations of celebrity, as *pastor pastorum*, in the crisis of his own justification.

The important transformation during Pike's odyssey, in other words, has to do with his piety: his sense of being justified; his understanding of *how* a person is justified; his need for acceptance and his suffering of self-acceptance. The foundation of Pike's piety shifted, discernibly, if reluctantly and slowly, from the problem of the Church to a passion for Jesus. More particularly, there happened over the years, a transliteration in Pike's mind and emotion from the matter of allegiance to inherited churchly institutions and traditions to a compulsion to become well acquainted with the historical Jesus.

In this perspective, the dogmatic content of Pike's beliefs, regardless of inflections or rhetorical nuances, has less prominence than the authority to which he looked, from time to time, in venturing any belief at all. The recurrent question which emerged in Pike's experience, and which he doggedly confronted again and again, concerned religion as distinguished from the gospel; ecclesiological conformity as juxtaposed to the ministry of Jesus. Pike's piety began in anxiety about the "true Church" but ended in the agony of the historical Jesus. The issue which became obsession for Bishop Pike is the Church *vs.* Jesus.

Eventually, Pike chose between the two.

The Erstwhile Agnostic

One of the most familiar stories circulated about Bishop Pike, after he became famous as a cleric, tells of his purported agnosticism as a young man. This phase—some popular magazine versions exaggerated it by calling it atheism—is said to have begun when Pike quit his undergraduate course at the University of Santa Clara and to have lasted until the time he was practicing and teaching law in Washington, D.C., in the early 1940s. The bishop often recited this himself: "I left the college, the Church, and my vocation to the priesthood and was a thoroughgoing humanist agnostic for some years. It was a case of throwing out the baby with the bathwater." Perchance Pike deemed public identification as an "ex-agnostic"—or even as an "ex-atheist"—a credential for obtaining a hearing among the unchurched or the unconverted, or both. He referred to these "intervening years of agnosticism" for evident apol-

ogetic purposes, for example, in A *Time for Christian Candor*.
Sometimes, the agnostic story was embellished with the news that
when he and Esther Yanovsky, being unbaptized and also described as an agnostic, were married, they together prepared their
own marriage service, deliberately omitting reference to deity.
To their consternation, Judge Bolitha Lawes of the District Court
in Washington, D.C., who presided at the event, discarded their
text of this "severely atheistic ceremony," as *The Saturday Evening Post* categorized it, adopting instead the traditional rite of
the Book of Common Prayer, thereby assuring the mention of
God's name at the wedding. That was in 1942; it was Jim's
second marriage. He rarely referred in public to his earlier marriage in 1938 to Jane Alvies, though in confidential correspondence
he once asserted that his first wife was "a lapsed Christian Sci-
entist" and an agnostic. In the same connection, Pike called himself "a lapsed Roman Catholic" and coincidentally during the
same period his mother had ceased to be an active communicant
of the Roman Church.

From this it might seem that not only had Pike become an agnostic, but that he was surrounded, in his closest daily relationships, by other agnostics. If not apocryphal, the much
repeated reports of Pike's agnosticism are, for the most part,
superficial and oversimplified. Though, in 1932, when he transferred from Santa Clara to the University of California at Los Angeles, he dropped out of the Roman Catholic Church, by 1938 he
had become a communicant of the Episcopal Church. The first
marriage was performed by an Episcopal priest and if, at that moment, this was a matter of convenience for two lapsed religionists
of other churches, the involvement of both Jim and his wife Jane
did not remain nominal very long. She undertook instruction for
confirmation. They practiced daily devotions. They attended re-
treats. He read Anglican tracts avidly. He frequented mass, in various Episcopal parishes in and around Washington, on weekdays
as well as Sundays. He induced friends to go to church. He became, in fact, a proselytizer, and prominent among those he so
pursued was his mother. With evident results: he wrote, in early
1939, to "Dearest Mama":

> Think of the many rich, positive things in your life—don't
> deny that the evils exist but emphasize . . . the many nice things

there are. And add to these nice things a renewed interest and devotion to our religion—I'm going to start sending you little things to read—*make* time for them . . . Lord knows Jane and I are busy enough, yet we *make* time for God and let other things find their place—I'm not saying that in a sense of righteousness but rather to show that it *can* be done. And as to being too tired— e.g., I was very tired Tues. after a busy weekend and two hard days + class Tues. night. So I was tempted to rest on Washington's birthday instead of making our annual parish retreat—but we talked it over and decided it was important to us to go. The next morning we got up early so that Jane could get some sandwiches made for the light lunch (she was on a committee to take care of that) and so that I could practice the "Missa Penitentialis"—a mass I hadn't sung before. By 10 a.m., when the retreat started (with ashes and high mass) we were awfully tired—By the end of the day (after Benediction at 4.00) we felt *fine* and have felt fine ever since.

The marriage to Jane Alvies soon faltered; it ended in a divorce for which the interlocutory decree was granted on September 4, 1940, little more than two years from its inception, even though the marital troubles had stirred Jim to try "to help the situation by increased religious devotion, in the form of spiritual reading together and more frequent reception of Holy Communion."

In spite of these evidences of religious zeal and of more than nominal church involvement, the bishop generally asserted that he remained agnostic from the time he left Santa Clara until after the marriage to Esther performed by Judge Lawes, early in 1942. Indeed, in one letter referring to Esther and himself, Pike wrote of "our conversion later that year" (1942) and of the subsequent baptism of Esther and the solemnization of their earlier civil marriage on April 13, 1943, in All Saints Episcopal Church, Frederick, Maryland. No other use by Pike of the term "conversion" concerning his own religious disposition or church affiliation has been found.

The point here is not, however, to quibble over computing the duration of Pike's agnostic episode, but rather to suggest that to label this phase, however it be dated, "agnostic" is hyperbole. What was in issue, during this time in Pike's experience, was not agnosticism, as that is generically defined, but a repudiation of the authority of the Roman Catholic Church. At that time, for Pike, rejection of this Church seems to have had the connotation of renouncing the Christian faith, and thus he called it agnosticism. Later on, he was to regard agnosticism, atheism, all forms of humanism, as essentially religious positions and, belatedly, to appreciate how blatantly religious he himself had remained all through his own "agnosticism." Moreover, that the focus of his so-called agnostic interlude was his repugnance at Roman Catholic authority explains why he expended such efforts shopping for another Church, the authority of which he could accept, and why finding and affirming such a Church was for him virtually the same thing as recovering faith. Still later, of course, this dialectic of Church and faith was reversed, for Pike, when he left the Episcopal Church as a way of verifying his "believing hope" in Jesus Christ.

In any case, leaving Santa Clara, rejecting Rome, abandoning a priestly vocation for a legal career and becoming "agnostic" were all intertwined, as the same event, for young Pike, and, simultaneously, for his mother. Pearl was, some forty years later, past eighty, quite clear and emphatic as to what precipitated it all. "That Jesuit School was not good enough for James," she recalled shortly after Pike's death, "James was much too smart to be at Santa Clara." James had been expansive in his own regard for Santa Clara, often boasting of its eminence as a university in his editorials in *The Owl*, the literary magazine which he had revived in his sophomore year. He devoted, for example, one long article to a book by Dr. Abraham Flexner, *Universities: American, German, English*, which was highly critical "of the faults and even 'foolishness' of our institutions of high learning." Pike noted that Flexner had written "one hopeful paragraph (p. 63): 'It is gratifying to be able to record the fact that there are American colleges which have not succumbed to nonsense . . . Havard, Yale, Princeton, Williams, Amherst . . .' This leads me," Pike continued, "to the thesis of this editorial, namely, that the University of Santa Clara is likewise such an institution."

Courses in scholastic philosophy were required of all students in those days at Santa Clara, and young Pike apparently was an ardent student of the same. In another *Owl* editorial, he expounded upon "The American Doctrine and Scholastic Philosophy":

> Scholasticism is the world's greatest system of philosophy. Americanism is the world's greatest system of government. . . . For truth is *one*—whether found in the ethereal seats of meta-

physics or the tangible constitution of a nation. The greatest
paintings in the world, the most inspiring music, the most beautiful poetry—all are based upon the Christian philosophy of life.
Hence, it would be most probable that the most sound political
system in history should find its sources in scholastic philosophy.

James developed his editorial thesis in quite erudite fashion, but
the nub of his argument was this:

> [T]he origin and object of civil power, the right of resistance to
> unjust laws and the objects of government and laws in them-
> selves, as idealized by the American colonists, were held by St.
> Thomas one hundred years before America was even discovered.

Ironically, the novice scholastic's enthusiasm for the University
of Santa Clara was confounded by his adeptness in the philosophy
into which he had been indoctrinated there. In 1968, Bishop Pike
recalled that precocity, while commenting upon the encyclical
Humanae Vitae, for *The National Catholic Reporter*, just nine
months before he again quit the Church:

> (I)n a course in theology the apologetic for the anti-contracep-
> tion position of Casti Connubii struck me as particularly uncon-
> vincing and, though I had no practical interest in the subject, I
> came to the conclusion that I could not accept it intellectually.
>   In those days it was generally assumed that the papal teaching
> in question was infallible . . . Having learned in the first year of
> scholastic philosophy St. Thomas Aquinas' teachings that a nega-
> tive particular destroys an affirmative universal, it dawned on me
> within a day or two that at the moment I concluded against the
> given principle of moral theology, *eo instanti* and *ipso facto*, I
> had denied the doctrine of papal infallibility.
>   This drove me to reading the history of Vatican Council I and
> then back to the early church fathers and the New Testament
> and I realized . . . that infallibility was not as simplistically sup-
> portable as I had assumed . . . There is such a thing as being too
> logical (but one with a serious interest in scholastic philosophy
> would not have then thought so); and it may have been unsophis-
> ticated of me to deem infallibility so central a doctrine (though
> my mentors then would not have thought so).

So Pike left the college and the Roman Church, as well, but the
action, as solemn as it was to him, was factually no repudiation of
the Christian faith; it was a specific protest against papal infalli-

bility, a rejection of the Roman authority system. At the time, however, so dependent did faith seem to him to be upon ecclesiastical authority that his departure rendered him agnostic in his own eyes.

A Question of Authority

The decision to deny the Roman Catholic Church was a heavy one for James because he conceived it as a crisis of faith. Deprived of the authority of Rome, the youthful scholastic concluded not only that his vocational intentions toward the priesthood were thwarted and his church attendance untenable, but that his faith as a Christian was suspended or curtailed because in conscience he could not submit to this Church. If this was a traumatic matter, it was also premonitive of future crises in Pike's experience in which the dialectic of church and faith was posed.

Perhaps the event has most significance not for its particulars, but for the style which it reveals; not for what it indicates of Pike's beliefs at a specific moment, as to either Church or gospel, but for what it shows about Pike's capability for courage. This was the first episode of which there is detailed knowledge in which Pike ventured his own intelligence against prevalent authority, in which he sought to redeem his conscience against conformity, in which he risked approbation and success for the sake of conviction, in which his independence broke through and his talent to question and probe, challenge and search took clarity as his vocation. As both friends and enemies of James A. Pike concur, this became at once his most admirable and engaging and his most irritating and provocative characteristic.

If Pike was much hurt in his disengagement from the authority of the Roman Church, he did not long indulge his disillusionment, and his precocity was such that, even under the guise of his self-appointed agnosticism, he was soon looking for another Church, catholic in ethos, within the historic succession of Christendom, possessing an authority system more congenial to his intelligence and more acceptable to his conscience than the Pope's Church had proved to be for him. Eventually, he felt that he found these essentials in Anglicanism, but the impact of the decision to quit Rome lingered for a very long time and was evidenced, in multiple ways.

The immediate issue which had outraged him as an undergraduate—the papal proscription against contraception—developed into a lifelong concern about birth control and planned parenthood. While dean of New York and then while Bishop of California, he repeatedly preached and spoke on these topics. Come *Humanae Vitae*, however, he no longer regarded birth control as an issue of sufficient dignity to require those dissenting from the Vatican's teaching to leave the Church. In his 1968 remarks in *The National Catholic Reporter* he counseled Roman Catholic clergy and laity who disputed the papal view to persevere in their opposition from within the Church. "This is a time," he wrote, "for laymen and clergy to show . . . courage . . . to speak one's convictions boldly and to stay in the church."

It was not just a mellowing which accompanies the passage of time that occasioned Bishop Pike's advice in *The National Catholic Reporter* to treat Vatican teaching so differently than he himself had done when he quit the University of Santa Clara and rejected the Roman Catholic Church. Intervening happenings had modified whatever anti-Roman bias he may be said to have formed in the Santa Clara crisis. Most notable had been the impact of the papacy of John XXIII. The ethos of openness and renewal engendered during John's incumbency was such that Pike came to feel that the Anglican Church lagged behind the Church of Rome in its hospitality to reform.

Pike, indeed, had speculated, ruefully, after he had been censured in 1967 by the Episcopal bishops that he would likely not have been placed in such a situation had he remained Roman Catholic. (It did not occur to him, in this speculation, that he might not have been a bishop had he stayed with Rome.) His observation was bolstered by the fact that at an ecumenical service in Wheeling in which he had participated just a few hours prior to the censure he had been loaned a pastoral staff, the ancient symbol of apostolic office, by the Roman Bishop of Wheeling. Moreover, in addition to that unusual ecumenical gesture, the public galleries in the place where the Episcopal bishops met and voted the censure that evening were filled with Roman nuns and Jesuit seminarians from nearby institutions who had come to root for Bishop Pike. In addition, the breach with Santa Clara had been ostensibly healed when he was welcomed there in 1966 as a distinguished alumnus who had become a bishop.

For all of that, the good will which Pike entertained eventually, in various ways and for multiple reasons, toward Roman Catholics and toward the Roman Communion and even toward the papacy did not erase the basic challenge to Rome's authority claims which had precipitated the Santa Clara break and which subsequently featured Pike's public ministry as an Anglican ecclesiastic. And while it would be exaggeration to describe Pike's feelings toward the Roman Church as mere bias or as uncritically hostile, he certainly remained—years and years after the Santa Clara crisis— wary and sensitive about any issues that seemed to him to convey the excessive and untenable authority pretensions against which he had protested as a student and which had provoked him to repudiate the Roman Church then.

That wariness was initially evidenced, in part, in his scrupulous inquiries into the origins, history, and ethos of other churches as he sought to regain his faith by returning to the Church, at length settling within the Anglican Communion. His religious quest went far beyond the comparable interest, one supposes, of most people: he read books and tracts avidly, consulted scores of clergy of all sorts, haunted innumerable congregations, spent long nights studying church history at the Library of Congress. He would not, as it were, make the same mistake again. Later on, long after his return to church membership and the renewal of his priestly vocation, as an Episcopalian, he remained alert to any Roman Catholic contentions that seemed to him to hark back to the extravagant authority which he had first challenged at Santa Clara. When he became prominent, as dean of New York and then as Bishop of California, the matter sometimes became personified in encounters he suffered and enjoyed with ecclesiastical rivals such as Francis Cardinal Spellman, Archbishop of New York, and James Cardinal McIntyre, Archbishop of Los Angeles.

From *Eleanor to* Baby Doll *to Luci Baines*

The press, it must be recognized, exploited these hierarchical confrontations and, perhaps, magnified the element of rivalry.

Still, the Very Reverend Edward West, Canon Sacrist of the Cathedral of St. John the Divine, considers that Spellman and Pike actually hated each other and recalls that during his deanship in New York, Pike felt "compelled" to respond in opposition whenever the Cardinal intervened in public issues.

A notorious illustration of these repetitious Spellman-Pike controversies was one involving Eleanor Roosevelt. Mrs. Roosevelt had become identified with the advocacy of planned parenthood and had been very caustically berated by Cardinal Spellman for sentiments he viewed as "unworthy of an American mother." The Cardinal added, as sanction to his rebuke, that he would not again publicly recognize Mrs. Roosevelt, a pledge which, somewhat later, he retracted. Dean Pike, himself long prominently associated with the planned parenthood movement, rushed to Mrs. Roosevelt's defense, both verbally and physically. He blasted the Cardinal's attack on the former first lady and also found a public occasion in which to appear at her side.

In the course of such altercations with their common foe, Mrs. Roosevelt and Dean Pike became well acquainted and, from time to time, as issues developed, they would consult each other before undertaking public positions. If their collaboration in this manner sometimes caused troubles for Cardinal Spellman, it also occasionally spared him such. In 1957, for example, Mrs. Roosevelt became concerned about whether the pending Lincoln Square development, which provisioned space for Fordham University as well as various facilities for the performing arts, amounted to an unconstitutional benefit for a church-related institution. She sought the advice of Dean Pike, who took the view that it was a financial subsidy—and an extraordinary one—for a particular religious group. At the same time, he explained that the plan had been so devised that there would, theoretically, be open bids received—though the space had been tailored for Fordham and Fordham would be the only bidder—which would make it difficult effectively to attack legally. In the circumstances, both Mrs. Roosevelt and Dean Pike decided to forgo the issue.

Another famous collision between the Cardinal and the Dean was caused by the promotion and premiere in 1956 of a film adaptation of a work of Tennessee Williams entitled *Baby Doll*. The movie had a bold exploitation as a heavy sex show—for those days at least. Times Square was dominated by a huge billboard portraying a lurid *Baby Doll*. The Cardinal sternly cautioned Roman Catholic laity not to patronize the motion picture. He was evidently stirred to his admonition against *Baby Doll* by the way in which it was being advertised and promoted, for his condemnation of the movie was uttered without his having actually viewed it. Walter Kerr, the drama critic of the New York *Herald Tribune*, himself a Roman Catholic, imputed attempted censorship to the Cardinal. Moreover, the Cardinal found a way of connecting *Baby Doll* with communism so that suppression of the film was construed as an issue of patriotism. At this point, Dean Pike intervened in the matter with characteristic forthrightness by entering the theater. Duly accompanied by his wife, Dean Pike went to see the film, "since," as he chided the Cardinal, "I did not feel that I could comment on the important issues which had been raised without seeing it myself." The newspapers published photographs documenting the Pikes going into the forbidden cinema, with poster versions of the *Baby Doll* billboard showing in the background.

On Sunday next, it being the fourth Sunday of Advent, a great throng gathered at the cathedral anticipating Pike's review of the assertedly decadent, semi-pornographic, unpatriotic movie. Anticipation is the appropriate Advent sentiment, of course, but those who flocked to the New York cathedral on December 23, 1956, expecting to be titillated by Dean Pike's comments on *Baby Doll* or by his castigation of Cardinal Spellman were due for disappointment. Pike delivered, that Sunday, an Advent sermon. It was not glib, and not extemporaneous, but a carefully prepared, theologically succinct message:

> This is an Advent sermon, not a Christmas one. Christmas has to do with the right answers, Advent with the questions. The Church is wise in this order of things: the great answers of Christianity mean nothing in this age or any other unless the questions which they are meant to answer are understood realistically. In our day the Church often has been less successful in grasping and protraying the real questions of . . . life than have been the psychiatrists, the poets, playwrights and novelists . . . These great non-ecclesiastical voices of our day serve God (though often they know him not), as they portray with realism and feeling the

wretchedness and bitterness of human life when men seek to live
their days without God, without standards, without meaning,
without a sense of ultimate destiny, without hope.

The dean saw such realism in the film, and, while incidentally
demolishing Spellman's gratuitous references to patriotism in the
controversy about *Baby Doll*, noticed that the director of the
Roman Catholic Film Institute in Great Britain, the Reverend
John A. Burke, had taken a position on this movie similar to his
own in opposition to the Cardinal's view.

> The picture is not a pretty one, but it is a real one: here we see
> human pride, arrogance, greed, deviousness, servility, hate . . .
> Here is uncertainty of purpose, here is real sickness of soul, frus-
> tration and defeat . . . All this is in the context of economic inse-
> curity, racial prejudice, suspicion of foreigners . . . corruption
> . . . of a tawdry community . . .
>
> As I have said, sexual problems figure in *Baby Doll* . . . But
> the movie is not pornographic: sensuality is not portrayed for its
> own sake. And it is portrayed in much less abundance than in
> *The Ten Commandments*, . . . which one Church official said
> every church school child should see . . . in *Baby Doll* . . . evil is
> judged, and the answer is doom: truly, here "the wages of sin is
> death."

So, for Dean Pike, the motion picture dramatized the Advent
task of the Church:

> The Church's job is not to condemn portrayals of real life; its
> job is to provide the answers for the problems which they raise.
> We have the answers all right: Christmas follows Advent. But we
> have not always stated our answers in a way which is existentially
> related to the real problems of human life which stories like this
> underline . . . Until people really face the human situation in all
> its depth and possible degradation . . . its bitterness without re-
> demption, they cannot fully receive the gospel.

Underneath the *Baby Doll* clamor were the central issues of
abuse of authority or displacement of authority with authoritarianism which had caused Pike to turn against the Roman
Church at Santa Clara. In all the years after that break, Pike
missed few opportunities to speak out against such inflated authority claims. Typical was his reaction to the Vatican's condem-

nation of *The Devil's Temptation,* a book about a heaven and hell, by Giovanni Papini. In a cathedral sermon on January 10, 1954, Pike virtually ignored the doctrinal dispute which the book had provoked; his concentration was upon the problem of churchly authority:

> The Vatican's ban on Papini's new book raises . . . questions, not only about the Christian view of the life to come, but also about the proper roles of authority and of freedom in religion.

In his stand against suppression of Papini's book, Pike invoked a New Testament citation which, in the debate leading to his censure by the Episcopal House of Bishops, twelve years later was mentioned in his own behalf:

> In any case, book-burning—or an index of prohibited books—is a futile gesture. If an author's conclusions are untenable, let the strength of sounder truth defeat them, not authoritarian attempts to keep his words from others' eyes. We would do well to ponder in any age Gamaliel's counsel to the Sanhedrin as to the treatment of the early Christians (reported in the Book of Acts) "Let them alone: for if this counsel or this work be of men, it will come to nought; but if it be of God, ye cannot overthrow it, lest haply ye be found even to fight against God." We should not too quickly cry "heretic."

Where the issue of churchly authority cropped up, especially in relation to public matters or social problems, Pike was not only sensitive, perhaps hypersensitive, but also felt that his own experience as a former Roman Catholic rendered him peculiarly competent to be articulate. After he had become himself an ecclesiastic, he seems to have viewed his ready outspokenness against what he saw as false or excessive assertions by the Roman Catholic hierarchy as a definite obligation. The possibility of the election of a Roman Catholic to the presidency—through the candidacy of John F. Kennedy—was thus not a prospect Pike could ignore and, in 1960, he published a short tract entitled *A Roman Catholic in the White House?* questioning whether a Roman Catholic president could be free from undue ecclesiastical sway so as to be able to fulfill his constitutional functions and, especially, to uphold the First Amendment doctrine of separation of church and state. This book was among the pressures which prompted candidate Kennedy to confront the issue head on in a celebrated encounter with the clergy of Houston. Kennedy's forthrightness at the Houston clericus, and his public assurances of the priority of the constitutional responsibilities of the president over any ecclesiastical influences, quieted Bishop Pike's qualms. Perchance, also, Pike by that time had recalled an article which he had written as a schoolboy—when Al Smith ran for president—in which he had argued enthusiastically that no harm would come to the American tradition of church-state separation with the election of a Roman Catholic as president.

Some years later, on July 2, 1965, Lyndon Johnson having succeeded to the presidency, Luci Baines Johnson, who had been an Episcopalian, and had lately been graduated from the National Cathedral School for Girls in Washington, D.C., was received into the Roman Communion and, evidently at her own request, was "rebaptized" by a Roman Catholic priest. The event incensed Bishop Pike, despite his admitted admiration for the independence which the decision of the President's daughter evinced. Recounting his own departure from the Roman Catholic Church and his subsequent reception into the Episcopal Church, the bishop pointedly noted that since he had been once baptized as a Christian in the Roman Church he had not been baptized again when he entered the Anglican Communion. "Rebaptism" he denounced as sacrilege, as a redundant rite, as an empty gesture without sacramental integrity, and, indeed, as an abuse of the sacrament of baptism. The Vatican itself condemned such practices, Pike observed, and Luci's second baptism constituted, he declared, "a deliberate act denigrating another branch of Christendom," and warranting apologies from the President's daughter, from the priest who officiated at the illicit ceremony, and from the Roman hierarchy which had permitted the service. Bishop Pike's protest found support particularly within the Episcopal Church, among Anglo-Catholics, and, in the Vatican itself, from the Reverend Thomas Stransky of the Secretariat for Promoting Christian Unity, who stated that the priest who had "rebaptized" Luci, instead of simply receiving her into the Roman Catholic Church as a person already baptized, had "followed what is a bad practice . . . despite clear rulings to the contrary by the Holy Office."

One of the last pictures
of Jim Jr.

On the day of the Requiem Mass for
James A. Pike, Jr., in February 1966,
with Chris, Cathy, and Esther.

This photo was used for the cover of *If This Be Heresy* (Harper & Row, 1967).

The final sermon from the pulpit of Grace Cathedral before resigning, September 1966.

The resignation.

Press conference to announce the Foundation for Religious Transition at First Unitarian Church in Los Angeles in April 1967, with Ellen and John Downing and Diane Kennedy.

An Antipathy Toward Rome

After leaving the Roman Catholic Church because of his rejection of papal infallibility as dogma, James Pike remained vigilant about pre-emptive attitudes, arbitrary positions, and authoritarian tendencies in the Roman Church. His concern was ecclesiological, as contrasted with confessional, that is, it had to do with the authority of the Church rather than with the doctrine of the faith. He publicly scolded and opposed Rome where it seemed to him there was fault in comprehending the appropriate authority of the Church; but it was not a complaint of his that the Roman Church was apostate. If, in his later years Pike's concern about excesses in Roman ecclesiology diminished, if he finally had more on this score about which to protest in the Episcopal Church than he had ever had concerning the Roman Catholic Church, if, all along, he was carefully prepared and temperate in his public utterances about the authority issue, he was nevertheless, for a while, vehement in his animosity toward Rome. There is little public evidence of this more strident side of Pike's attitude toward the Roman Catholic Church, but it is verified in the confidentiality of letters that he wrote to his mother during the years following the Santa Clara crisis, when Pike's mother had joined her son in renouncing the Roman Church.

The most ardent and distressed letter in that whole correspondence between son and mother was written a few days after Pearl Harbor. Pike was then in Washington, occupied as one of the counsel of the Securities and Exchange Commission and in the midst of defining his commitment as an Episcopalian. The attack upon Pearl Harbor and the American involvement in the war against the Axis powers had so upset Pike that, as he wrote Mama, "it induced a bad case of diarrhea."

> When the rest of Washington was hearing the first terrible
> news, . . . [I was] in an entirely different century—at [Pohick]
> Church, down the river south of Mt. Vernon, built in 1769 and
> designed by George Washington . . . I can assure you that it was
> quite a shock to return to the harshness of present realities and
> hear over the car radio that we'd be [sic] attacked by the Axis—

the enemies of our way of life—the way of life the spirit of which
is so caught in such of our continuing Anglo-American institutions as the English Communion of the Church and as represented
by these beautiful old Va. parish churches which have been centers of the Church's worship uninterruptedly from the first beginnings of Anglo-Saxon civilization on this continent.

. . . being there when all this started was far from anomalous—
it was the most appropriate thing imaginable. The Anglican
Church is definitely the spiritual expression of the way of life
we're defending—its democracy, its frankness, its humility without groveling, its willingness to face facts, to admit weakness, the
lack of authoritarian high mightiness, its freedom from fear and
superstition—all this is the basis of the attitudes that Anglo-
American democracy stands for. The authoritarianism, the fear,
the keeping of people in ignorance and superstition, the heartless
cruelty to the individual—all that the Axis powers stand for has
its spiritual expression in the Roman Church . . .

These strenuous sentiments about Anglicanism as the "spiritual
expression" of democracy, of course, recall paradoxically that
effort, back at Santa Clara, of the undergraduate scholastic who
argued that Thomism was the sponsor of American democracy,
and maybe that explains the bitterness of Pike's conviction, at the
time of America's involvement in the Second World War that
the Roman Church was in league with America's totalitarian enemies:

. . . the actual partnership between the two [the Roman
Church and the Axis powers] was but the fruit of like ideals.
Time will prove that the Axis invasion of Spain was the most important step in this war (and everybody knows now it was the beginning of World War II) and the Papacy directed and financed
it . . . And remember that Vatican-controlled Portugal—in
which the Church and State is one—furnished the Japs with the
island from which most of the attack was made, and Argentina,
more completely under Vatican domination than any South
American country, . . . is actually pro-Nazi. All this is what could
be expected from what is Fascist in organization itself, as it has
been (the R.C. Communion) since the undivided Church. The
Anglican Communion, democratic itself as was the undivided
Church, has given its every support to the effort to preserve our
democratic way of life.

Pike's persuasion that both ideological and practical links existed between papacy and Axis was something which had developed during his work in Washington as one of the bright young lawyers of the New Deal era, though his mention of it in correspondence with his mother, prior to the Pearl Harbor letter, was muted compared to the excited tone of that diatribe. Earlier in 1941, for instance, he had written:

> Particularly distressing these days is the influence brought to bear by the Roman clergy for isolationism and denial of aid to Russia in their . . . defense on the continent of what is our side of this war. Helping Russia and England is helping them to fight *our* war and keep the Axis barbarians from our own doors—and yet 90% of the Roman clergy in a recent poll wanted *no aid* whatsoever to go to Russia in her fight against Hitler. They're more loyal to their own Fascist head than to the interests of our own country and its protection.

Some time later, when America had declared war, his outrage had grown virtually hysterical about the relationship of the Roman Church to the Axis powers:

> Of course, now that the American people are infuriated at the Axis, they'll deny all this in this country now—but their hearts are with the enemy—like to like: Fascist Church, Fascist State—and they can't write off the record (with present unconcern with such "earthly" things as slaughter and bombing of over 1000 Anglo-Catholic churches in England), the fact that they actively aided the Axis from the start of this war in Spain—and the hierarchy in this country were as active as the other prelates in Europe—and they can't write off the record their consistent isolationism, their tolerance and support of Coughlin, their opposition to Irish aid to England. All that is in the record, and when the peace comes let's hope it's not forgotten and that all Fascist forces in the world are unseated for good, even those seated on a golden throne with three crowns.

The stridency of Pike, when he wrote in this same long Pearl Harbor letter about the "Fascist Church," became grandiloquent when he mentioned his Anglicanism:

> My loyalty to the Anglican Communion has grown more and more as the crisis has grown nearer; it is the spiritual expression

of exactly what we're fighting for—and always had been—
Stephen Langton, Archbishop of Canterbury, in 1215 wrested the
Magna Carta from the King, who up to then had been a tool of
the Pope—just one instance in its whole history when the English
Church took its stand against authoritarianism, despotism—and
in its *own* organization and life it *lives* the democratic way and
of course *is for* those ideals down deep . . . As I say, to increased
understanding of the Anglican Communion has been added my
increased loyalty—and appreciation that there is in Christ's Holy
Catholic Church a sanctuary of democracy and openness and honesty and straight-forward dignity where one may express our spiritual aspirations in this terrible struggle.

James pursued his correspondence with his mother avidly
throughout the Second World War, indeed until his death, and
though he returned in his wartime letters to the issues which so
exercised him in the Pearl Harbor letter, the manner in which he
subsequently expressed himself was not so extremely agitated. He
recovered quickly from his hysteria in the immediate aftermath of
the attack on Pearl Harbor, just as he did from the diarrhea occasioned by the same event.

The Proselyte

Pearl's support for her son when James made his stand at Santa
Clara was practical as well as moral. She joined him in repudiating the Roman Church. As James saw it, there was a mutual decision to quit that Church. He construed the severance from
church affiliation and attendance as inherently involving separation from the Christian faith and, even in the midst of his professed agnosticism, the matter of achieving another church connection, unencumbered by the authority problems that had
provoked the break with the Roman Church, was his consuming
interest. And he imputed his own urgency about finding and accepting another Church to his mother. As they had left the
Church together, they must return to the Church together. That
was somehow crucial to the remarkable intimacy of son and
mother. It was the chief subject of the letters exchanged between
them, as well as their direct encounters, from the time that he left

California to pursue law studies in the East until he was ordained. His mother—who in this period had the surname of her second husband, McFadden, eventually did enter the Episcopal Church, though, about the time when James initially became involved in the Episcopal Church, with his marriage to Jane Alvies, his mother had resumed attendance at mass in the Roman Church and was very skeptical about Anglicanism.

It was, on one hand, a tremendous relief to James that both he and his mother had publicly returned to the Church—and been restored to the faith thereby—but, on the other hand, it was a consternation to him that they had not arrived at the same place within the Church since she had rejoined the Roman Communion while he had settled upon Anglicanism. Their correspondence is preoccupied with this issue as James pleaded and argued with his mother to induce her to join him in the Episcopal Church, alternately cajoling and harassing her, seeking, in fact, to proselytize her.

There was little in these letters of James to his mother through all these years concerning the gospel; the focus is upon the Church, upon distinctions among the various churches, upon ecclesiological complaints against the Roman Church, and, often, upon seemingly peripheral or esoteric matters affecting church membership for reasons of sentiment or personal pietism. As to the latter, for example, James frequently reported his delight in the music at a church service he had attended, mindful, in this, that his mother was an accomplished musician, as, in fact, he was himself. Doubtless the musical passages in these letters are premeditated by James as part of his proselytization, for music was an important aspect of the church experience of his mother and himself and he wanted to assure her that this was not diminished but enhanced in the Anglican Church. "A corollary of my changed outlook which will interest you," he wrote to his mother on November 25, 1941, "is the fact that I am no longer so interested in the medieval Gregorian chant—as I've heard more Anglican chant in the places I've been going this fall I've come to like it much better—its lilt and rhythm, its 4 part harmony and in *major* keys. (I still think some Gregorian is nice for contrast, if well done.) 'Anglican chant' is a particularly English Church musical development and . . . I much prefer it . . . I have a book of it now (the official hymnal—in which most of the chants are Anglican rather than Gregorian) and I play them on the organ . . . [T]heir bright cheerfulness accords with the general tone of the churches we've been going to . . ."

In similar vein, Pike's letters attempted to verify that external characteristics of Catholicism have not been lost in Anglicanism, but have been spared corruption or abuse. He frequently mentioned the vestments used at Episcopal services. In 1940, a year in which Mother's Day and Pentecost coincided, he exclaimed: "I'll remember you at Mass tomorrow—It's a great day at St. J.—Pentecost—red vestments and red flowers all over the church." His references of this sort seem never incidental or innocuous, but always carried his intention to persuade Pearl to change churches. In the same letter in which he extolled his preference for Anglican over Gregorian chants, he enclosed a picture of the Pope. "Look at the extravagant (I mean in appearance—not cost) size of the stole . . . Can you picture Christ in that get up? (And this is one of his simpler garbs!) If Christ were to wear a stole at all I'm sure it would be the simple clean-out type of the undivided Church (and used in the Anglican rite today)."

The exuberance of James as an initiate Anglican prompted his mother to reconnoiter the Episcopal Church, as he incessantly urged her to do, but her occasional visits to Episcopal services did not persuade or even much impress her. When she complained to him of the "weakness" and "obscurity" of the Episcopal Church, he responded defensively:

> The Episcopal Church is such a small part of the population out West—(compared with the East where practically every church-goer you meet in our level of society is Episcopalian, and a R.C. or straight Protestant is as rare as hen's teeth) that many of our parishes out there don't function very vigorously—as they do here . . . I would rather have you thinking of these things in one of our vigorous Eastern parishes—or at the service for the opening of the full length of St. John the Divine (see *Time* religion section a week or two ago) which I attended but delayed writing you about until I had time to really tell you all about it, or at the service for the seating of our Primate—or at High Mass at St. Paul's any Sun. . . . Unfortunately we are least numerous and least effective in the West . . . would that you were here to share

with me the glorious witness that we are here for intelligent, unspoiled, open-eyed Catholicism . . .

That was in 1941 and Pike had by then been committed to Anglicanism emotionally and intellectually at least since 1938, but he had yet to establish a regular parish affiliation. He was still looking for that, still church shopping, still attending this parish and that congregation, still frequenting services at two or three different churches on Sundays, as well as seeking out other parishes to go to weekday services. One year, he calculated having visited over twenty-five different congregations of the Episcopal Church in the Washington vicinity alone. To his mother, he styled himself an Anglo-Catholic to underscore his conviction that his Anglicanism represented a return to Catholicism—to Catholicism which remained true and undefiled as compared to the condition he ascribed to the Roman Church. Early in 1939, he discussed in one of his letters to Mama the options in church membership open to Catholics such as his mother and himself:

I think your decision to postpone consideration of Anglo vs. Roman Catholic for a while very sound. The important thing is that you're back in the Catholic Church again. I don't want you to misunderstand my object in talking to you about the Episcopal Church. I thought certain things were barring you from the R.C. Church—and I was showing you a way to have Catholicism without those things—but if you can now have it with them and feel at home in it again that's the important thing. You and I believe the same things (and I hope my returned faith has helped yours), worship the same way and have the benefit of the same Sacraments and both have the ministration of priests ordained by valid successors of the apostles—what branch of the Church each of us may choose is largely a matter of taste and individual inspiration. We have choice among three: the Greek Orthodox, the R.C., and the Anglican—the Greek tho' the first & oldest organization is foreign to our customs and feeling; hence the choice is between the latter two. I believe it (the Anglican) is much freer from man-made refinements and incredible (yes, sometimes superstitious) "doctrines" added in by the Papacy—and our branch is definitely free from the authoritarian attitude that seems to have infected the whole R.C. Church organization from the hierarchy down to nuns and priests. There is a certain humility, a certain man-to-manness about our clergy that make the bearing of Catho-

lic burdens (there are burdens as well as blessings in living the
Catholic life) easier. I believe that the use of the English language contributes to understanding devotion—devotion which
touches intellect as well as emotion, whereas the Latin language,
sonorous as its phrases may be, has an emotional effect only. And
the pure English of the Anglican Mass is sonorous too . . . Likewise I feel there is greater authenticity in the use of *bread and
wine* as Christ commanded. And likwise I believe that our understanding of the sacrament of unction is more in keeping with
Christ's teaching . . . But the *important* thing is that you're back
in the Catholic Church again. Meanwhile read and study and
make up your own mind as to which branch of the Church fulfills
your spiritual needs the best . . . I can conceive of nothing more
important than finding a proper place for the complete
fulfillment of our spiritual needs. As a starter read the enclosed
pamphlet. I'll send you others from time to time.

Pike's anxiety that he and his mother, in being restored to the
Church after the Santa Clara break, jointly have the same church
affiliation and that it be Anglican, Pike's relentless intent to
proselytize his mother, sometimes became impatient. In the Pearl
Harbor letter, previously cited, in which his hostility to the
Roman Church was so excited, he admonished her sharply about
her recalcitrance in the matter: ". . . continue to support them
with your attendance and funds if you will," he wrote, "but remember in your heart of hearts who's been on what side. And remember who's been themselves democratic throughout history
and who's fascist in every marrow."

Apostolic Succession and "the Undivided Church"

He appealed to his mother's love of music, to her aesthetic sen-
sibilities in worship, to her allegiance to the Catholic ethos within
Christendom, to her patriotism, and he attempted to indoctrinate
her in a version of church history which vindicated the Anglican
position. His efforts to propagate Anglicanism with her were heavily supplemented by the tracts and pamphlets and books with
which he bombarded her and implemented in his long and ver-
bose letters, some of which were themselves virtually book-length.

He spent, in research for his letters, much time in the Library of Congress reading church history and then marshaling the data he so gathered to sustain his arguments for embracing the Episcopal Church. Throughout his effort, his central preoccupation remained ecclesiological, as distinct from confessional; his concentration was upon the Church, the authority of the church, and the doctrine of the Church, with little attention to the content of biblical faith or to an understanding of Christ. Such references to Christ as he occasionally made did not concern the historic ministry of Christ or its significance. He took that as settled in the formularies of the traditional creeds of the Church; his attention was fixed upon issues of churchly authority—the regularity of the various church traditions as determined by apostolic succession, the validity of church orders in the episcopacy and the priesthood —upon which, as he then saw it, the possibility of faith was derivative and dependent. In his longest, most belabored epistle to Mama he propounded his views of these matters:

> By the way—as to apostolic succession in the English Church. I haven't time now to trace it all for you and go into the full picture . . . but in the meantime I want to assure you that there is no break in the episcopal succession and no loss of orders. There is no question into which I have gone more thoroughly—(unless you count the Federal Rules)—I have spent many an hour in the Library of Congress reading secondary authorities of all shades of thought R.C., Anglican, Greek, Protestant—also many of the primary source documents—and I was satisfied that without question the apostolic succession has been continuous since the missionaries from the Greek Church planted the Catholic Faith in England in the fifth century. True from about 1100 to 1550 or so the English Church was a good deal of the time under Papal domination—largely by virtue of treaties between particular Kings and Popes; Henry had signed up for a while, then broke; Mary signed up and Elizabeth broke—but all thru it remained the same Church of England with the succession passed on from Bishop to Bishop . . . and it is today the same Church it was in the fifth century when the Orthodox missionaries arrived from Gaul and planted the episcopal succession first at Canterbury then throughout the realm—incidentally, it was an early bishop of the Church of England—St. Patrick—who planted the Catholic Faith in Ireland—the English bishops also consecrated bishops

for Scotland and after the Revolution the first bishop for the American Church was consecrated by three Scottish bishops—he was Samuel Seabury, the first Catholic bishop in the United States. The next three American bishops were consecrated simultaneously in London . . From these original four American bishops the succession has come right down to the present. (Similarly, the episcopate exists unbroken in Canada, Australia, British Africa, India and in other British and English speaking localities)—also the English and American bishops consecrated the bishops for the "Holy Catholic Church in China" and the "Holy Catholic Church in Japan" . . . That, in brief is the story of the apostolic succession in the English Church throughout the world.

The great stress which Pike placed upon apostolic succession was related directly, of course, to his Santa Clara rejection of papal infallibility, which he described, in this same letter, as the "latest (but probably not the last) heresy" of the Roman Church, "the *denial* in 1870 of the basic nature of the Church as resting on the successors of the Apostles (the bishops) acting corporately and the narrowing of the guidance of the Holy Ghost to one man."

For James, papal infallibility was not the only error in doctrine which burdened the Roman Church, there were others, and there was also what he conceived to be surplusage of doctrine (a notion he was later to develop and dwell upon in utterances which came to issue in the censure debate in the Episcopal House of Bishops). Both false dogma and excess doctrine he attributed to intolerable expansion of papal authoritarianism. "Almost without exception," he informed Mama, "every 'doctrine' added by such *human* means is *palpably wrong.*"

> Man's ways are not God's ways; *God's way* was the Council of Bishops—result: every doctrine reasonable—to the sophisticated as well as the simple. *Man's way* in the Western Church after the 11th century was, increasingly more and more dictation by the Bishop of Rome as an oracle—result: "doctrines" and practices revolting to the thinking and a source of superstition to the credulous.

To illustrate, and urge, his argument, he furnished his mother with this chart, by which doctrine as warranted by "God's way" could be handily compared with erroneous teaching, superstitious practice, and surplus dogma as promulgated by "man's way":

Declared by the Councils	*Declared by the Papacy*
The Trinity	The Efficacy of Indulgences
Christ's dual nature as God and man	Compulsory *private* confession
	Compulsory celibate clergy
The Real Presence in the Holy Communion	Transubstantiation (a puerile explanation based on 13th cen-
The Atonement	tury physics now everywhere
The Communion of Saints	discarded)
The Life Everlasting	Half-communion for the laity
The Resurrection	(in direct contravention of
God's help to us through grace	Christ's own *specific* mandate)
Christ the only Mediator	The "Immaculate Concep-
Forgiveness of sins in the mass thru public absolution after confession to God (private confession only in special cases where the penitent is so moved)	tion," of the B.V.M. (no warrant in Scripture or any- where else)
	Mary as the Mediatrix between us and Christ
The growth of the soul "from strength to strength" after death	The Efficacy of Relics (pieces of bone and other material ob- jects connected with Saints— to be venerated)
	A materialistic purgatory run by a vengeful God to be pro- pitiated by bought masses and "vain repetitions" in set prayers
	Strictures against evolution and birth control
	The "Index" telling you what you can & cannot read.

Pike's fixation upon the nature of churchly authority, his passionate repudiation of papal infallibility, his heavy interest in a matter so esoteric and, also, so pedantic as apostolic succession, his preoccupation with ecclesiology as that may be distinguished from theology, his emphasis on Church rather than Jesus, his prodigious, if anxious, effort to persuade his mother to become an Anglican were gradually prompting a definite conception of the

Church to surface in Pike's thought. Stated starkly, his idea was that the doctrine of the Christian faith is defined and declared by the Church through the bishops in council under the guidance of the Holy Spirit. He was insistent about the peculiar relationship of the bishops and the Holy Spirit, referring, for example, to "the voice of the Holy Ghost speaking through the . . . episcopate," or to the bishops as "the seat of the Holy Ghost." So intimate and so exclusive did he conceive this connection to be, that he concluded that with the schism in the Church in the eleventh century, and with all the subsequent divisions in the Church, the Holy Spirit has been inhibited, since the bishops of the whole Church have been unable to convene in council, and thus there has been through nine succeeding centuries a kind of moratorium so far as doctrine is concerned. "The purpose," he said after furnishing his chart of doctrines to Mama, "is to show clearly *which way* has brought the truth to man. The first way—the council of the bishops of the entire Church—has been unavailable to us since the eleventh century, and until with God's help it is made available again—*individual parts* of the Church will err . . . The part of wisdom then is to hold to the original deposit of the undivided Church—which, incidentally, is *enough truth to live by*."

Paradoxically, in the late 1960s during the heresy controversy in the Episcopal Church, while Pike was reviving his objection to surplus doctrine and applying it to ancient formularies, notably the doctrine of the Trinity, some of his opponents in the House of Bishops were essentially upholding his early view of the efficacious inspiration of the Holy Ghost on doctrinal matters through the agency of the episcopacy *in collegium*.

In any case, Pike's idea that there had been a pristine era of the undivided Church, definitive so far as the confession of the faith was concerned, to which nothing could be added so long as the Church remained divided and from which nothing should be subtracted and as to which nothing must be contradicted, had the convenience of really freezing doctrine, in its supposed authentic state, and of then putting it aside and thereby rendering all confessional questions as those of churchly authority. *That* became the only disputed matter upon which everything else turned. Among other things, this notion of Church and its exalted assertion of ecclesiastical authority operative through the episcopacy in council implied, as Pike recognized, a deactivation of the Holy Spirit, but this did not evidently trouble Pike. And, having gone that far, his interest, especially in connection with his mother, was to prove that Anglicanism had been, through the centuries of divided Christendom, faithful to the ancient witness of the un-divided Church, whereas Rome had grievously erred. "Our branch," he informed Mama, "has realized that no part of the Church acting alone can 'count on' the Holy Spirit and that until the entire episcopate can meet again the wisest policy is to refrain from declaring doctrine . . . Since at the Reformation it rejected such of the Roman accretions as had been imposed on it from 1100–1500 and has not since officially added any doctrine, the An-glican Communion doctrinally stands with [the] Eastern Com-munion in adhering to the primitive Catholic Faith and Order of the undivided Church."

An Imperative of Priesthood

The arguments for Anglicanism which James pressed were not readily convincing to Pearl, and she lingered, as has been men-tioned, in the Roman Church until Pike himself was ordained, in all due benefit of apostolic succession; it was that alone which for her practically validated Pike's brief for Anglican affiliation. Mean-while, for years, he pursued his mother, inundating her with his redundant, passionate, urgent letters, augmented by the findings of his studies in the Library of Congress and elsewhere, em-bellished by his excited descriptions of his visits to multifarious churches, supplemented by a quantity of Episcopal Church propa-ganda in tracts and leaflets, sanctioned, and seemingly sanctified, by frequent citations copied from the Book of Common Prayer. His central thrust was consistent and concentrated upon the in-tegrity of apostolic succession in the Anglican Communion and, derivatively, upon the regularity of ecclesiastical orders in the Episcopal Church, the validity and relative purity of Anglican sac-ramental practice, and fidelity of doctrine in Anglicanism to the expression of faith of the erstwhile undivided Church. While he digressed into chauvinistic, aesthetic, ethnic, and other miscel-laneous items, it remained his contention that everything else depended upon the ecclesiological issue—specifically, upon the historic continuity of the episcopate as the peculiar conveyance of the Holy Spirit.

One has to return to Pike's infancy in Oklahoma, and to his school days after the migration of the Pikes to California, to locate the reason for this abstruse obsession of James, in his attempt to rationalize his Anglicanism and Anglicanize his mother. As has been mentioned, their piety was heavily involved, that is, they had jointly determined to quit the Roman Church and were convinced that they must return, somehow, somewhere, sometime to the Church in order to be restored in the faith. And James, as has been said, was radically upset that their return to the Church had not been mutual, but that Mama had again joined Rome while he had discovered Anglicanism. Still, more than piety was involved: there was, as there had been since his early childhood, his vocation to the priesthood.

For all practical purposes James had known no father. The senior Pike was desperately ill continuously after the son's birth and had died when James was barely two years old. The intimacy, the dependency, the intensity of the relationship which grew between husbandless mother and fatherless son substituted for the deceased husband and absent father and this reciprocal compensation was magnified by the hardships of their life in Oklahoma and of their trek west to settle in California. Though later on Pearl married twice more and James had three wives, the primacy of the relationship of mother and son which originated in those first years when they were left bereft of a husband and a father prevailed and survived over each of Pearl's marriages and the first two marriages of James. The pre-emptive connection of mother and son was reflected in some of the letters that passed between them which refer to their respective spouses at a given time as outsiders. James would caution his mother in a letter not to share a certain confidence with her husband; or he would complain that a wife failed to support his vocation diligently. Moreover, Pearl would candidly admit that each of her latter two marriages were entered in order to aid and serve her son's career. It is, it appears, only after all of Pearl's husbands had died, and only after two marriages of James had been dissolved, only by the time of the third marriage of James, to Diane Kennedy, that the relationship of mother and son had muted or matured enough for a wife of James's to be accepted by Mama as a daughter and to be loved by him as an equal.

Pearl was earnestly and devoutly religious, and, from the time that he played with paper dolls—which were priest figures which he arrayed in vestments—James was religiously precocious. In his school days, he studied under a tutelage of priests whom he held in awe. In such circumstances, the priesthood emerged as the vocation for James. It was, perhaps, more a matter of assumption than deliberation; it was, significantly, the vocation most congenial to and least competitive with the love between mother and son. And, let it be suggested, it was much more than even that: the priestly vocation for James was the way in which the intimacy of mother and son could be consummated—a means of assuring that their relationship would retain its pre-eminence and endure indefinitely. St. Paul, in accordance with I Corinthians, would have approved: the priesthood was preferable as a resolution of this relationship to incest.

So the priesthood for James became basic to the covenant between himself and Mama and that fact was a measure of the trauma and outrage of the concurrent Santa Clara decision of mother and son to leave Rome. After that it was much more than a pietistic necessity for both to find their way back into the Church. It became imperative that James recover and resume his vocation to the priesthood. James could not attain that by a return to the Roman Church: he felt he had been too abused by Roman authoritarianism, too much deceived by Roman priests, for that. So he had anxiously and diligently besought alternatives in the Church, and he had become committed to Anglicanism, but to pursue his priestly vocation as an Anglican required the endorsement and the companionship of his mother verified by her joining him in the Episcopal Church.

The prolonged rationalizations of the retention of apostolic integrity within the English Church and its offspring bodies, like the Episcopal Church in America, which preoccupied so much of the correspondence of James with his mother in the years after the Santa Clara break were aimed at proselytizing her by con-

vincing her that the Anglican priestly orders enjoyed historic validity. If James, therefore, became an Episcopal priest, the extraordinary covenant betwixt his mother and himself would be upheld.
His arguments in this regard were sometimes embellished by
other points which commended the Anglican priesthood as exemplary. He implicitly recalled for Mama the Santa Clara episode
and her denunciation of the college as academically unworthy of
her son in this way:

> I also admire the attitude of our Church toward education of
> the clergy. They want our men to go to the best universities (not
> some ingrown institution which seeks to pour the man's life into
> a groove) and then take their theology at a seminary connected
> with, and meeting the standards of, the great universities. Our
> Berkeley Divinity School is connected with Yale; Episcopal The-
> ological School with Harvard; General Theological Seminary with
> Columbia, etc.
>
> (In England our priests are trained chiefly at Oxford and Cam-
> bridge.) They want him to know history, the social sciences, eco-
> nomics, psychology—and be as well-equipped as he can to think
> for himself and help people of all conditions with the best that
> the Catholic faith and modern knowledge can bring to bear.

In the same letter, he associated priestly status with liturgical
practice. "I admire these things and many more. I have felt a *part*
of the Church more than I ever could have under the Roman system of the priestly caste, removed from the obeying, silent laity,"
he wrote. "I think that's why I appreciate so much receiving the
chalice—not only was it Christ's specific command (that should
be enough); but in addition its denial in the Roman Church and
its preservation in ours typifies more than any other single thing
the difference in spirit between the two parts of the Church—in
the whole Church life, *we share the cup*; in the Roman Church it
is kept *for the clergy*." His embitterment, which Mama had
shared, was still evident nine years after Santa Clara when he
compared the clergy of the two churches: "[T]he straightforward
approach of all the Anglican priests and bishops I've met (and
I've met a great many) is quite a different thing than the kind of
domineering, slippery, pompous attitude of the Jesuits . . . I'm of
course excluding individual cases—I'm referring to the *general*
tone and manner."

The Option of Law

Pike's obsession with apostolic succession and with the validity of Anglican orders, and with the general congeniality of the Anglican priesthood, his prodigious effort to be persuasive with Pearl about such matters, happened at the outset of a promising, and, in fact, already flourishing, career in law and in government. He had completed undergraduate studies at the University of California in Los Angeles and at the University of Southern California, and received a law degree from the latter, and then had moved to the East, in 1937, where he was a Sterling Fellow at the Yale Law School—a most distinguished award—under which he earned a doctorate in jurisprudence. He then was engaged as counsel for the Securities and Exchange Commission in Washington, D.C. His sense of isolation from the Church, his temporary loss of his vocation to the priesthood, his separation from Mama, in short, his loneliness during this time, was not assuaged in his marriage to Jane Alvies. If anything, the marriage aggravated his personal situation and, with the complicity of Mama, he rid himself of it. Such relief from loneliness, and, more than that, from his religious consternation, as he may have had in these interim years he found in his work as a lawyer. While simultaneously serving the S.E.C.—when it was yet a vigorous agency wrought by the New Deal under the leadership of William O. Douglas, who had been on the law faculty at Yale while Pike studied there—Pike joined in founding the law firm of Pike and Fischer, conceived and implemented a technical service for lawyers, taught at the law schools at both George Washington and Catholic Universities, and published a casebook on federal civil procedure. With the advent of the Second World War, he was assigned to the Office of Price Administration, where one of his subordinates was Richard Nixon, and subsequently served in the Navy during the war in intelligence operations. Meanwhile, he searched for a new wife—and found one in a student in one of his law classes at George Washington, and, more and more urgently, he concentrated upon the entangled issues of Church and priesthood and the covenant with Mama.

If the law became no more than a provisional concentration, and never became his vocation, never displaced the priesthood as his vocation, it was not for want of ability, diligence, or versatility on Pike's part. As brief as the period of his active work as a lawyer was, and as young as he then was, his contribution to the legal profession was substantial, and widely respected as such by his fellow lawyers. That is most notably the fact with regard to his *Cases and Other Materials on the New Federal and Code Procedure*. The promulgation of new rules of civil procedure in the federal court system in 1939 required not only drastic revisions in the teaching of procedure in law schools but the wholesale indoctrination and continuing education of all attorneys practicing in the federal judiciary. Pike's casebook, together with the subscription service analyzing and annotating cases arising under the new rules which he and his partner Henry Fischer originated, met this need. So definitive was this work that the Pike casebook was still in use as much as twenty years after its first edition. The authoritative mastery of the materials pertinent to the casebook and the service was an achievement of major proportions of Pike as lawyer. Considered together with his status as a Sterling Fellow, with his teaching, and with his government service, this gave every reasonable expectation that James Pike, had he remained exclusively in the law, would have enjoyed increasing influence, recognition, and renown. As it turned out, he never wholly abandoned the law, but retained his right to practice as a member of the bar of the United States Supreme Court and of the bars of the states of New York and California, on occasion contributed articles to law reviews, participated in studies of the relationships of law and theology, lectured often at law schools and bar associations, taught, while Bishop of California and later while on the staff of the Center for the Study of Democratic Institutions, as an adjunct professor at the Law School of the University of California at Berkeley, published a volume on law and ethics, appeared as special counsel in the defense of the Catonsville Nine, and pursued some church-state and related issues of the law while at the Center in Santa Barbara.

When he became a postulant for the Episcopal priesthood, under Angus Dun, the Bishop of Washington, in 1942, Pike renounced the prospects for professional success which then seemed assured had he persevered in the law as both his full-time career and his vocation. His mother pressed him about the matter of leaving such a promising situation as a lawyer for the sake of the Episcopal priesthood; she had, after all, married a lawyer— Claude McFadden—who could aid her son in the legal profession, and, moreover, she was not yet persuaded, for all of James's polemics about the historic validity of Episcopal orders and related virtues of Anglicanism, that the Episcopal Church was a viable option or that the Anglican priesthood was vocationally appropriate for James. His response was critical of the heavy commercial orientation of the legal profession, but idealistic, practically lyrical, about the priesthood:

> As to the law vs. the Christian ministry, *as such:* the law is a noble profession (again, in terms of potential—the actual doesn't quite average up by & large). But if a person is granted the vision to see the realities of life and the only answer to its persistent evil and maladjustment—that answer being the Gospel of Jesus Christ—then he could never rate saving people's property & money—or gaining more for them—as high as bringing their twisted lives into the pattern of Christ, lighting their faces with His gladness and infusing the power of the Holy Spirit into their lives. That is—one cannot, *unless* his standard of judgment is self-interest . . . for one that is a thoroughly convinced Christian and consecrated to Him, that standard of judgment is the essence of sin . . . "original sin"—the thing from which we are to be "saved."

A Fascination for Scholarship

If by the time he was ready in his own being to leave his career in the law and become a candidate for ordination—and hence resume his priestly vocation—Pike can be said to have had a somewhat romantic and pious view of the priesthood, he at the same time harbored an attraction to scholarship which was influential in his vocational decisions. His virtual awe of scholarship had been premonitive in his undergraduate efforts as a fastidious Thomist. His rejection of papal authority arose out of his sense of scholarly responsibility, and from his outrage at what he saw as a corruption of scholarly standards at Santa Clara. When he became a law student and earned his doctorate in jurisprudence, and then entered the legal profession as both teacher and practitioner, he implemented his scholarly interest as thoroughly as he was ever to do, though throughout his ecclesiastical career, this concern for scholarship—his fascination for scholarship—haunted him.

Ironically, Pike's durable scholarly work was, as has been cited, in the law, but he left that as a full-time occupation. Early in his priesthood, his potential in scholarly talent was recognized—in his appointment, for instance, as a tutor at the General Theological Seminary in New York City shortly after he was made a deacon. Characteristically, he fulfilled that post while simultaneously completing a divinity degree at Union Theological Seminary, where he came to regard Paul Tillich as a mentor. He had had, also typically, more grandiose scholarly ambitions for the period he spent at the two seminaries in New York. He had, as a postulant, completed studies necessary for ordination at the Virginia Theological Seminary, near Washington, D.C., and his scheme had been next to go to Oxford for further study and then to return to America for a year's work at the Episcopal Theological School in Cambridge, Massachusetts. His plans were thwarted.

> We moved Heaven & Earth to try to get to Oxford this fall, but the odds all round are against it; the best colleges having no places left; the fact we're "expecting"; the shortage of time; bad living conditions and shortage of food over there. So we've finally decided to go to Union Theological Seminary in New York, which was our first choice in this country. Actually, eliminating the romantic element of a stay abroad, practically everyone I have consulted insists that Union has the strongest theological faculty in the world, with the addition of continental refugee scholars to its already outstanding galaxy; Oxford on the other hand has lost heavily by deaths of notables . . . we still may go over there for the year following. I hope to get in a good deal of work with Reinhold Niebuhr . . . this coming year.

Pike never made it to Oxford for theological study, but the "romantic" idea of it did not leave him and was revived and implemented during the last year of his episcopacy in the Diocese of California when he spent a sabbatical, ostensibly to study theology, at Cambridge.

His tutorship at General and his academic work at Union, where, though he seldom appeared in class, he received a B.D. degree *magna cum laude*, were sufficiently distinguished to attract invitations for both academic appointments and for positions adjacent to the university scene. At one point, for example, John Hines, while Bishop of Texas, who was destined to be Presiding Bishop of the Episcopal Church during the disposition of heresy charges against Pike, strenuously sought Pike's acceptance of a faculty appointment at the Episcopal Theological Seminary of the Southwest. Earlier, while sustaining his own studies at the Virginia Theological Seminary, Pike, who had been made deacon in 1944 by Bishop Dun, had simultaneously undertaken the duties of a curacy at St. John's Church, Lafayette Square, in Washington and launched an ambitious and popular chaplaincy to students at Georgetown University. Then, while still completing degree requirements at Union Theological Seminary in New York, Pike was called to the rectorship of Christ Church, Poughkeepsie, a post which was also charged with a ministry to students and faculty at Vassar College. A little more than two years later, after having once refused the appointment, Pike became chaplain of Columbia University and chairman of Columbia's Department of Religion with a specific mandate to develop the university's religion department, which had previously been nominal, into full academic status.

During his postulancy and his crammed theological studies in the various seminaries, and in the successive chaplaincies he served, Pike's view of scholarship was unduly idealistic and, therefore, superficial. He repeatedly in his correspondence with Mama invoked academic connections to convince her of the worthiness of Anglicanism, for instance, so that when in a letter he would mention an Episcopal seminary he would invariably fortify the reference with notice of its affiliation with some august university. Similarly, when he had occasion to mention to his mother that he was preparing an article he hoped to have published in *The Anglican Theological Review* he identified that journal as "sort of the *Harvard Law Review* in this field." If these were attempts to furnish his case for Anglicanism with snobbery, such items also indicated Pike's sustained concern, in the aftermath of Santa

Clara, for the intellectual respectability and defensibility of the Church and for rational explication of the teachings of the Church.

These were matters much affected by his rejection of Roman ecclesiastical authority claims as intellectually unworthy and unreasonable, but at the same time his repudiation of the Roman way meant that the burden of proof so far as the Church and the teachings of the Church were concerned was something he was himself required to undertake. And so from the time of his so-called agnosticism, Pike was fascinated and often preoccupied with the methodology of faith, by the process of fact-finding, deduction, and reflection that supported any affirmations of faith. It may be that in focusing so intently upon method, Pike tended to overrate academic discipline and fantasize the work of scholarship. Or it may just be that scholarship signified for him a vocational potential which greatly attracted him but which temperamentally he never quite fulfilled. He was to suffer some caustic ridicule of his theological books—A *Time for Christian Candor*, *What Is This Treasure*, and *If This Be Heresy*—as pretentious, derivative, and superficial. Mainly such criticism came from ecclesiastical colleagues, and others who were not themselves scholars, while the professional theologians generally ignored his books. Pike was even faulted by some academics because his *The Other Side* was not a scholarly effort, though Pike had attempted in it no more than a personal statement about his own experiences in parapsychology. It must be mentioned, at the same time, that Pike enjoyed the esteem of his associates at the Center for the Study of Democratic Institutions, though not so much for his contributions related to religion or theology as to those in the field of law. Robert Hutchins was particularly appreciative of Pike's "input" into the *Pacem in Terris* conference in Geneva in 1967. Hutchins regarded the bishop's embroilment in theological dispute during the time that heresy charges were pending, which took much of Pike's time away from the Center, as relevant to the institutional decadence of the churches rather than to the intellectual status of the Christian faith. Meanwhile, all along the way, as college chaplain, as dean, as bishop, as antibishop, Pike's efforts at theologizing, his concern for honesty and lucidity in theology, his emphasis upon communication and credibility in doctrine, if not original or profound or otherwise of scholarly virtue, were nevertheless an emancipating message for multitudes of laypeople within the churches and multitudes more outside the churches.

The Forensic Theologian

In the era of religious revival in the aftermath of the Second World War, then through the phase of social activism in the early sixties, and finally as a period of theological skepticism, churchly decline, and religious cynicism opened in the later sixties, James Pike was distinguished as a forensic theologian. Pike was a masterful apologist—and not a theological scholar, as much as he may have held that work in awe and as much as he may, at times, have felt drawn to the scholar's task. As an apologist, he not only possessed a requisite rhetorical agility, but he had also an extraordinary versatility. In his postulancy he was an apologist for Anglicanism; in his early priesthood he became an apologist for the faith of the Church against the claims of competing faiths represented on the university scene. In the pulpit at the New York cathedral, on nationwide television, and in multifarious ways, Dean Pike thrived as the pre-eminent apologist for the Church and the Church's teachings in the nation. As bishop, Pike continued as apologist to the world at large, but simultaneously he became apologist for the faith within the Church. After that Pike became apologist for Jesus against the Church.

The commonly heard criticism of Pike as forensic theologian—that he was no scholar—was the proverbial complaint that an apple is not an orange. Still, Pike brought to his forensic vocation the training and temperament of a *legal* scholar of demonstrated proficiency. Legal scholarship has traditionally been a narrow discipline in American law and jurisprudence, but it practices some skills apt for the work of apologetics. Thus Pike, by the time he was ordained, had made the empirical method characteristic of legal scholarship his own. That meant a heavy concentration upon the problem of proof. Assertions of authority were not self-validating but had to be verified by precedent. In corollary, there was the necessity to account for all facts that could be ascertained, with the elimination of conclusions rendered either implausible or surplus by the facts. The interpretation of factual data must be as economical as possible, the most simple and straightforward explication must be considered the most likely to be true or at least the most credible. An openness must be always maintained toward the discovery or disclosure of additional or new facts.

Bishop Pike's esteem for scholarship, albeit perhaps exaggerated, coupled with his competence in the specific mode of legal scholarship, occasioned his fascination with the methodology of faith, with the relation of the way a person copes with facts analytically and the possibility of belief. Gradually, his concern for method and his growing conviction that a form of empiricism was appropriate in the theological realm displaced his erstwhile preoccupation with churchly authority. He recognized this change and summed it up succinctly in *A Time for Christian Candor:*

> We cannot establish the Christian Faith by reasoning, but reasoning . . . can help to point toward the most plausible of the alternatives.
>
> Here I can speak from experience. I was raised in a religious tradition which claimed to be able through scholastic philosophy, based primarily on St. Thomas Aquinas (and through him, on Aristotle), to be able to *prove* the existence of God and certain other basic premises of Christianity. In reopening this whole question after some intervening years of agnosticism, while I remained unconvinced that this proof was possible, I did find that a number of the same arguments effectively pointed toward the plausibility of the basic elements of the Christian Faith. All in all, I found Christianity the most plausible perspective on reality and hence acted in faith—by an act of the will—to commit myself to be a Christian again.

Significantly, as the empirical method took the place of the authority issue as his basis of belief, so Pike's theological attention shifted, more and more, from the Church to the gospel, and from the teachings of the Church to the content of the Christian faith. Such distinctions were, later on, when Pike quit the Church a second time to become much sharper, but they began to emerge in his thought and utterance early in his priesthood as he became concretely engaged as a forensic theologian.

Pike's empirical approach repeatedly caused controversies. While it made him open and inquisitive, ready to learn and willing to change, he remained stubbornly naïve toward those who were his opponents in theological disputes and he tended to assume that they operated on presuppositions similar to his own.

In Poughkeepsie, for instance, while rector of Christ Church and Episcopal chaplain to Vassar College, Pike complained publicly about the absence of any courses in the college's religion department on the Christian faith. The prevailing view at Vassar, as elsewhere, had been that no such courses could be instituted and taught without proselytizing, or at least propagandizing, for a specific religon. This was considered incompatible with the asserted religious neutrality of the college. Pike's view was different: he thought religious neutrality to be a fiction, a subtle guise for a faith position being propagated at the college while other faiths, including Christianity, were banished. He saw atheism and agnosticism—any form of secularism—all versions of humanism—as faiths, as equivalents of religion, and, in turn, as competitors of Christianity. It was both false and unfair, therefore, to exclude in the collegiate curriculum a treatment of the Christian faith alongside these alternative faiths which were already being presented. And he argued that the content of the Christian faith could be taught, even by a convinced Christian, without proselytization, so that the inclusion of courses on the Christian faith would not only not threaten the idea of the college's neutrality religiously, but in fact was essential to maintaining it honestly. Pike's challenge to Vassar thus cast doubt upon the basic integrity of the college as an academic and educational enterprise and the ensuing debate, both in the college and in the parish Pike served, which included many Vassar faculty and students, was ferocious.

"The University Question"

The issues Pike raised at Vassar were to be replayed elsewhere in Pike's career, and they also possessed a broader significance in questioning the sentimental relationship that, generally, existed between the American churches and the colleges and universities. In part because of the historic church origins of so many American colleges, they had come to be regarded as offspring or as handmaidens of the churches. That feeling survived long after active affiliation of colleges with the churches had declined or disappeared. At Vassar, Pike was saying that the colleges represented alien, not congenial, terrain, that secularism was not neutral but a form of religion often inculcated academically, and that the Christian faith had a right to be competitively, if not, however, aggressively or pre-emptively, present in the colleges. In all of this, Pike anticipated the concern about the task of the Christian in the university which was to become a prominent theme in the ecumenical movement, articulated by Sir Walter Moberly, Arnold Nash, and John Coleman, and which commonly was referred to as "the university question." It remains contemporaneous in the view, for one example, of Myron Bloy that the university harbors and fosters an "academic ideology" profoundly hostile to biblical faith.

Pike was not long in Poughkeepsie before he was invited to become chaplain of Columbia University. He initially declined the offer, but Columbia pursued him and, upon the second invitation, he accepted and became both chaplain and chairman of the Department of Religion at Columbia in the fall of 1949. There he succeeded, in titles, Stephen F. Bayne, who had lately been elected Bishop of Olympia, and who ultimately became Pike's nemesis, politically, in the censure he suffered in the House of Bishops. During Bayne's Columbia tenure, as in those of Bayne's predecessors, the religion department had been a nominal and casual feature. Bayne had taught a course or two on an informal basis, without regular academic recognition. Pike came to Columbia with a mandate from the university administration, under the presidency of Dwight Eisenhower, to develop a Department of Religion with full and equal academic status. Pike was told that he had *carte blanche*, financially and otherwise, in this effort. In light of the Vassar ruckus, it was a grandiose opportunity to implement his convictions, and Pike lost not a moment in accomplishing just that. Within less than two years, Pike had organized a department offering thirty-seven religion courses, which elicited an immense response in enrollment. The faculty he assembled to staff the department included, in adjunct appointments, such luminaries as Paul Tillich and Reinhold Niebuhr. The swiftness of the transfiguration of Columbia's religion department from innocuous appendage to expansive and prestigious domain provoked resistance from quarters in the university. An attempt was made to curtail funds, which Pike had been committing and spending literally on a *carte blanche* basis, though he was able to meet this threat by showing that ample funds, endowed for the teaching of religion, existed and that if they were not used in connection with his department they could not be lawfully utilized by any other departments. In bulldozing ahead in this manner, while he usually had the sanction of the university administration, he failed politically in his relations with the Columbia faculty and resistance to his efforts hardened sufficiently to cause the Columbia Committee on Instruction to veto several curricular proposals advanced by Pike shortly before the time he left Columbia to become dean of the Cathedral of St. John the Divine. Pike apparently threatened to construe his move to the cathedral as a protest against this faculty action, but was dissuaded from doing so by Grayson Kirk, who had succeeded Eisenhower as president of Columbia University. Meanwhile, the main Vassar issues had all been replayed and the implications of some of them pressed further than they had been at Poughkeepsie. Faced with widespread suspicion that the university chaplain could not be "objective" in the teaching of religion, Pike now argued that commitment was a condition for teaching religion and that, for example, unless one was a Roman Catholic, one could not properly comprehend Roman Catholicism.

In the Columbia episode, Pike was revealing himself as a remarkably obtuse figure politically. He seems to have been quite insensitive to the realities of faculty politics, of competitiveness among university departments for prestige and funds, of an array of vested interests that sudden and sweeping change such as he introduced might threaten. At the same time, his political obtuseness indicated an absence of guile and calculation that endured as one of Pike's attractive characteristics. Moreover, this meant that Pike, in most situations, was not distracted from concentration upon issues for their own sake. It was not the way of the world and, as Pike found out—ruefully—it was not the way of the Episcopal Church, but it was his way and he persevered in it.

The whole constellation of issues pertaining to the relations of the Church and the university, expecially the matter of the teaching of religion, continued to be prominent in Pike's thinking after his *tour de force* at Columbia University. The leading humanist philosopher of the day, Professor Sydney Hook, took it up by opposing religion as an appropriate curricular subject and Pike was ready in his response to Hook's argument to underscore the ideological partisanship which rendered humanism or other secularist views a faith, an alternative to Christianity or other historic religions, despite the asserted "objectivity" or "neutrality" presumed by the Hook position. Early in his deanship, Pike raised these same issues at a general convention of the Episcopal Church, in a much acclaimed address, in which he urged a militant missionary effort by the Episcopal Church on university and college campuses. Later on, he found occasion to reiterate similar concerns when he became Bishop of California by lobbying for elective courses in religion at the University of California at Berkeley.

"Smooth Orthodoxy"

The integration of Pike's legal temperament and competence with the confidence and zeal of his commitment to Anglicanism in his restored vocation in the priesthood made him an exemplary advocate and apologist. It was not long before his unusual gifts in this respect began to be recognized in the Episcopal Church. While still in Poughkeepsie, he was asked to join the authors committee for a projected series, under the editorship of Stephen Bayne, to be published by the Department of Christian Education of the National Council of the Episcopal Church, entitled *The Church's Teaching* and designed for the edification of laity in Anglican history and doctrine. Though each book in the series had designated authors, the manuscripts were subject to review and approval by the committee, which had been constituted to represent broadly various factions and divergent viewpoints within American Anglicanism. No particular attempt was made in the series to reconcile differences; on the contrary, the effort was to find verbal expression which allowed for multifarious, and even conflicting, interpretations. Dr. W. Norman Pittenger, Professor of Apologetics at General Theological Seminary, and Dr. Pike were assigned primary authorship of the volume in the series dealing with doctrine. The result was the book *The Faith of the Church*, published in 1951. It has had an enormous circulation and use within the Episcopal Church and is, still, the closest thing to an official exposition of doctrine that exists.

Pike, when a heresy trial seemed likely, wondered, half-amused but also half-worried, whether *The Faith of the Church* would be invoked to ascertain whether he was heretical. He thought the book too ambiguous and illusive to be used in such a way because he recalled the work of writing the book, which went through ten drafts, as posing the problem of finding a spacious doctrinal rhetoric rather than that of definitively settling doctrine. *The Faith of the Church* was, as Pike later repeatedly spoke of it, an exercise in "smooth orthodoxy." He had once upon a time described apologetics to Mama as "the technique of making conversions." His experience in connection with *The Faith of the Church* as well as his involvements at Vassar and at Columbia had considerably broadened his comprehension of the apologetic task, though his attention was still upon method, succeeding his earlier preoccupation with ecclesiastical authority. He was, as he sometimes remarked, still a lawyer—"who had changed clients." He was, as circumstances required, alternately advocate and defender of the Church and of the teachings of the Church, for all their ambiguity, but it had not yet happened that he questioned the truth of "smooth orthodoxy."

The Cathedral's Vocation

James Pike, hence, became dean of the Cathedral of St. John the Divine in the city of New York. He was, at that point, ascendant in his ecclesiastical career despite his political ineptness; he was a skilled apologist without being a theologian; he was called controversial but this engendered more excitement than hostility; his religious odyssey had already been at once obsessive and laborious yet his faith was probably as naïve as in his adolescence.

If there were critics of Pike who thought his brief stint at Columbia University had been hectic, his regime as dean of New York was breathtaking. Pike filled the cathedral with life. His preaching attracted huge throngs of three to four thousand persons each Sunday, and the congregations would be double or triple that at the great festivals, like Christmas and Easter, or at the times of particular controversies, as when his feud with Cardinal Spellman would periodically erupt, or as when he rebuked the House Un-American Activities Committee or denounced the predatory activities of Senator Joseph McCarthy, or at public ceremonials, as when he was host to the Queen Mother of England or when he honored the work of Jung as that of a "secular saint."

Often it was remarked that Dean Pike restored the cathedral to the venerable vocation of such institutions as intercessor for the total life of the city, and that seems to have been his intention. At the very least he did not allow the cathedral the diminished status of a museum. Promptly upon his appointment by Horace W. B. Donegan, Bishop of New York, Esther and he traveled to England to visit the historic cathedrals there, to sense their ambiance, to recover their purpose, to find precedent. The trip, Pike mentioned later proved disappointing, especially so to him since he had put so much stock in the viability of Anglicanism. He found most of the cathedrals in England—Coventry, which had suffered much in the Nazi bombardments, was an exception—decadent and empty. Yet his disenchantment with the moribund state of the English cathedrals only spurred his determination to make St. John the Divine a lively and relevant place. He restored the cathedral chapter—the staff of clergy under the dean's direction—to a functioning and diversified body, the members of which had specific portfolios reflecting their specialized competence and responsibility within the total ministry of the cathedral. As Canon Pastor, with oversight of an extensive effort in pastoral care and counseling in the neighborhood of the cathedral and accessible to anyone in the city in need, he called the Reverend John Pyle. As Canon Sacrist, directing the cathedral's liturgical practice and sacramental life, there was the Reverend Edward West. As Canon Precentor, Pike named the Reverend John Turnbull, with responsibility for the cathedral's involvement in social and political issues. As Canon Theologian, reviving a function in theological scholarship and workmanship, Pike obtained the scholar who had been his theological instructor, the Reverend Howard Johnson. He signified the renewed status of the chapter as the focus of the cathedral's multifarious and ecumenical outreach by his punctilious insistence that the members of the chapter, along with other cathedral staff, be garbed, according to circumstance or occasion, in vestments or clothing, as the case might be, which his pedantic researches into Anglican tradition had verified as appropriate.

Attentive to the old English style of naming cathedrals for their secular location in a city or similar jurisdiction, Pike promptly secured the designation "The New York Cathedral" as a corporate title for St. John the Divine by so registering it with the Secretary of State of New York. He privately delighted in this official identification, regarding it as a gain in his contest with Cardinal Spellman since the recording of this title for the Episcopal cathedral precluded any public use of the name "The New York Cathedral" to refer to St. Patrick's Cathedral.

At the same time, with Dean Pike's initiative, "The New York Cathedral" developed a program and ministry, as well as an image, which was so rich and diversified, so active and catholic, so concerned for and involved in the destiny of the city that the corporate title was no mere embellishment. In addition to the extensive pastoral work and social action undertaken during his tenure, he revived and implemented the educational function of the cathedral, establishing it as an accessible and free forum, building The Cathedral Library, launching efforts for the continuing education of diocesan clergy, strengthening The Cathedral School, furnishing accommodations for visiting students and artists to pursue independent work. There was a kind of return to the controversies at Vassar and then at Columbia concerning the place of religious studies in the academic realm in his educational reconstruction of the cathedral. In fact, the plethora of study and discussion, inquiry and argument which he instigated there resembled a model of the university as Pike envisioned it.

The Advocate

It was not long before the influence of the cathedral, and of the dean of the cathedral, extended throughout the nation. This was most pointedly the case as Pike's confidence and competence as an apologist and advocate matured. Not only was the cathedral

pulpit his forum as a forensic theologian, but there was much
wider impact as Pike's case for the viability of the Church, and,
increasingly, as the years passed, his comprehension of the Christian faith were transposed from sermons and addresses, from discussions with his colleagues and from his studies, from his pastoral
involvement and social stands into a succession of books. Some of
these were still in the genre Pike called, as he did *The Faith of
the Church*, "smooth orthodoxy" and, like that book in which his
co-author had been Professor Pittenger, several were collaborative
efforts. *The Church, Politics and Society* was based upon dialogue
sermons delivered at the cathedral in association with Canon
John W. Pyle. *Man in the Middle* was similarly done with Canon
Howard A. Johnson, while *Roadblocks to Faith* originated in dia-
logues with Dr. John Krumm, who had succeeded Pike as chaplain of Columbia University. What such books might have lacked
in either scholarship or originality was compensated in spontaneity and freshness, and if these books were not profound, they
were not superficial either. Most of all, perhaps, they were accessible and readable books, for the laity of the Church and for those
outside the Church. Even Pike's own deprecating comment
about "smooth orthodoxy" points to what may be considered one
of the significant contributions of such books. They were published at the height of the so-called "religious revival" of the early
1950s when popular religious books, typified by those of Norman
Vincent Peale, had little virtue in Christian orthodoxy. It was
part of Pike's forensic vocation to achieve a hearing for the
Church and for orthodox doctrine as over against the individ-
ualistic success ethic preached by Peale and as over against the
superficial religiosity which characterized the times. Pike was virtually unique in his apologetic facility, in his gathering fame, in
his splendid forum to confront and expose the challenge which
the "religious revival" constituted for the Church and for Christian orthodoxy.

John Krumm, who was later to become Bishop of Southern
Ohio, has recalled how the book of which he was co-author with
Pike, *Roadblocks to Faith*, came to be published:

> In my opinion, Jim was much more effective as dean of the ca-
> thedral and had a greater influence on the Columbia community
> from that vantage point than he did as chaplain. In a position

where he could be frankly a preacher and in a sense a propagandist, he was at his best. When he pretended to be a reflective scholar, which he certainly was not by temperament, the effort did not succeed. The dialogue series . . . is an example of his imagination and ingenuity. It also illustrates the rapidity with which Jim could lay out plans and put them in operation. The idea of a series of dialogue sermons, representing the conflict between the secularist and the Christian point of view, was first suggested to Jim by me at a reception at Bishop Donegan's house . . . It was suggested that this might be an interesting program on which we could collaborate for the Sunday afternoon services at the cathedral during the summer session of Columbia University. By a few quick questions Jim clarified the idea in his mind and was off to talk with other people at the party. Following that he was asked to stay for dinner with the bishop, but somehow he managed to make some telephone calls, and he telephoned me about ten o'clock at night to say that he had accomplished the following: he had outlined the topics for six evensong services, he had arranged to have them published in book form by Morehouse-Barlow, he had secured an agreement from the American Broadcasting Company to have them broadcasted on a coast-to-coast radio network, and the whole project was thus launched in a matter of a few hours during which he also keep up usual brisk conversation with guests both at the reception and at the dinner party later.

The momentum of Dean Pike enabled him during his cathedral years to expand his audience far beyond the precincts of St. John the Divine and further than the readership of his apologetic books unto a national television constituency. "The Dean Pike Show" ran, altogether, for six years on ABC-TV, every Sunday afternoon. It treated every and any topic, relating the same to the Christian faith, with a candor and spontaneity which attracted millions upon millions of viewers. Frequently, the format would include Esther Pike, though not as a foil for her husband but rather as an emphatic and independent person with her own convictions and her own style. Occasionally, too, the Pike children would be present in a telecast, and often guests would also appear. The program was done live, which made its extemporaneous quality the more impressive. It was a venture which aptly utilized, and was simultaneously sustained by, Pike's remarkable intellectual agility and the extraordinary catholicity of his interests.

Meanwhile, there were more books—basically of a pastoral nature—produced with apparent facility. A friend of Pike's remembers keeping an appointment with him at the cathedral one afternoon. The dean emerged from his office at the scheduled time to ask his visitor if he would mind waiting a half hour while he finished an urgent project. Later, Pike explained the necessary delay. He had realized, the day previous, that he had to meet a deadline for a manuscript for a publisher and, since no manuscript existed, he had stayed awake most of the night dictating the book into a machine to be transcribed. Pike had been working on this task when his guest arrived for their appointment and needed just a half hour more to complete his dictation. The book, subsequently published under the title *The Next Day*, had literally been composed in less than twenty-four hours!

Besides this volume, Pike published, while dean, several other pastoral books, utilizing in them an adaptation of the case method familiar to him from his legal studies, including *If You Marry Outside Your Faith* and *Beyond Anxiety*, in which the apologetic task and pastoral care are related to each other.

A *Vicarious Relationship*

If—in both his apologetic and pastoral books—Pike was still engaged in forensic theology, still occupied with explicating doctrine, but not yet questioning the doctrine *per se*, still seeking fresh expression of ancient confessions of the faith, it may be because of the restraint upon his theological position exercised by Howard Johnson, whom he had called to the cathedral to take residence as Canon Theologian. In Dean Pike's initial enthusiasm to restore St. John the Divine to the historic vocation of cathedrals, redeeming it from museum status, and distinguishing it from just another very large church, he had found precedent for such a post within a cathedral chapter, although in practice designation of canon theologians had long since been discontinued in the English cathedrals and was not then known to have ever before been implemented in a cathedral in the United States. To institute such a position at the New York cathedral required interpretation of the need and appropriateness of it to the bishop and to the ca-

thedral trustees, as well as amendment to the statutes of the cathedral. To persuade these authorities to act affirmatively on the
matter, Pike relied heavily upon a provision of the cathedral's
charter which made a purpose of the cathedral that it be "a center
of intellectual light and leading in the spirit of Jesus Christ." He
felt keenly about this aspect of the cathedral's life and, shortly
after Johnson's appointment as Canon Theologian was confirmed,
he wrote to him at some length about his effort to achieve recognition of this:

> [O]ne of the aims of my administration has been to emphasize
> that we are an educational institution . . . a policy of which your
> coming is an important part. You perhaps would not appreciate
> the problem the way I have known it as a priest in the Diocese
> for some years: The Cathedral Chapter was not held in particu-
> larly high repute, and no one thought of us as an educational
> institution, which is one of our primary raisons d'etre. By a con-
> sistent emphasis on our educational function, and upon the qualifi-
> cations in their respective fields of those we've been adding to the
> Chapter . . . we have effected a remarkable change in the atti-
> tude toward the function and reputation of the body known as
> "the Dean and Chapter"—and this in a rather short time.

Pike's concern to resuscitate the educational dimension of the
cathedral's ministry was certainly genuine and, doubtless, it was
significantly motivated by his experiences at Vassar College and at
Columbia University, but it was not the only reason that he
besought Howard Johnson as his Canon Theologian. Johnson and
Pike had met in 1942, when Johnson was a curate at St. John's
Church, Lafayette Square, in Washington, and while Pike, still in
the Navy, still engaged with his law firm, was so preoccupied
about whether to become an Anglican and whether to return to
his vocation to the priesthood. In that period of crisis for Pike,
Johnson became both his companion and mentor. By that time,
Johnson already possessed impressive academic credentials and
had begun a career in the Church as a scholar. Simultaneously
with his curacy at St. John's, at the time he met Pike he was an
adjunct member of the faculty at Virginia Theological Seminary.
In the circumstances, Johnson became Pike's tutor, furnishing instruction and guidance during Pike's postulancy, as well as entering a deep friendship with both Jim and Esther which endured for

many years and which embraced, among many other things, his relationship as godparent to Jim Jr., the first son of their marriage. Johnson's influence personally upon Pike and specifically upon his return to the Church was so significant that it became common knowledge and, as Pike emerged as a celebrity, it became mythologized. Thus, it was frequently remarked by acquaintances of both men, and, on occasion, by Johnson, that Johnson had "converted" Pike to the Christian faith. In retrospect that seems hyperbole, particularly in view of the evidence in Pike's correspondence with his mother of the scope of Pike's independent effort to reclaim a church connection and thereby verify his Christian faith during the years in aftermath of the Santa Clara episode. It would appear more accurate to affirm that Johnson furnished an intellectual sustenance that Pike very much needed in order to rationalize his commitment to Anglicanism and his return to a priestly vocation.

However it be styled, there is no underestimating the influence of the relationship of Howard Johnson and James Pike upon both of them. When Pike was named dean of New York, Johnson was a visiting fellow at St. Augustine's College at Canterbury, in England, and joined Jim and his wife on their visits to English cathedrals in search of precedents which could be implemented at St. John the Divine. It was then that consideration was initially given to establishing a Canon Theologian within the New York cathedral's chapter to which Johnson would be appointed.

Whatever its more public aspects in relation to the cathedral's educational mission, as between the dean and the Canon Theologian, Johnson's work was to study and to think, to guide and to critique, in short, to continue the role which he had earlier had during Pike's postulancy of furnishing theological undergirding for the multifarious, versatile, and hectic efforts and utterances of the dean. Johnson resumed his tutelage of Pike at the cathedral, and Pike, whatever pretentions at independent scholarship he may otherwise have entertained, was mindful of this status in their relationship. Shortly after the New York *Herald Tribune* reported Johnson's advent as Canon Theologian, Pike wrote Johnson that he was "obviously . . . embarrassed about the phrase in the Trib that your theological scholarship will be under my direction! As a matter of fact one of the principal reasons we want you here is so that theological scholarship of the rest of us will have better direction." To that, Johnson replied:

> How absurd of you—even in jest—to be "embarrassed" about the phrase in the Trib! To be "under *your* direction" in theological scholarship would not be a bad position. "Roadblocks to Faith," which I read in toto going to and from London this week in the train, convinces me that I'm going to be in good hands! However, your Canon-Theologian-elect begs leave to render his first service (certainly a small one) by calling attention to the fact that the heresy of Marcion appeared, not in the third century (as you affirm) but in the *second* century. M. was condemned in 144. You can expect more of this sort of thing in future!

A good many opinions survive assessing the relationship of Johnson and Pike. One colleague of both of them at the cathedral during Pike's regime there has spoken of Johnson as Pike's "sustainer—he could make Jim face up to the absurd lines he was taking . . . These were . . . expressed in the 'fine print' aspect of what Jim wrote or said." Certainly, Johnson filled an essential need for Pike, and much more than a merely pedantic one. He furnished content and correction and context for Pike's intuitive and impulsive and brilliant advocacy. But Johnson also restrained and refuted and scolded and, perhaps, suppressed Pike's own theological quest. Johnson kept Pike's utterances within the style and substance permissible in Anglican orthodoxy. Potentially, it could have been a stifling relationship for Pike, but it seems instead to have been one in which, hyperactive as he was, the vicarious implementation of Pike's intellectual interests and capacities in theology through Johnson were, for a time being, sufficiently fulfilling for Pike. Not much mention has ever been made of what this intense and curious relationship meant for Johnson. He died, remaining silent about it. Yet there was genuine reciprocity in their friendship, and such correspondence as still exists which, over the years, passed between them evidences a vicarious need on Johnson's side to have a public impact and recognition which in some sense Pike met. Johnson's letters to Pike contain repeated references to his self-consciousness about matters involving his own publicity, stated, characteristically, with both minute detail and mock humility. Moreover, Johnson's role as a virtual conspirator in the precipitation of the Sewanee controversy, mentioned

hereafter, which was the event which firmly established Pike's reputation as a social radical, lends emphasis to a conclusion that
while Pike may have found substitute expression of his aspirations
toward theological scholarship in Johnson, Johnson discovered in
Pike a celebrity with whom he could identify.

In any case, the relationship had deep mutuality and it was, indeed, productive, in terms of the viability of the cathedral's vocation, in many of the public stands which Pike undertook while
dean, in the quality and appeal of Pike's preaching, and, notably,
in the writing of what probably is the most durable book Dean
Pike published, *Doing the Truth*, a volume of social ethics which
enjoyed wide usage in seminaries and colleges as well as elsewhere,
and which reflects the intimate and intricate collaboration which
Pike and Johnson achieved for a while.

When Pike was elected Bishop of California, Howard Johnson
remained on at the New York cathedral, but they continued to
correspond and, for a time, Pike would seek Johnson's counsel.
Some inquiries were, as they had been earlier, footnotes. "Could
you send me the source of two quotations from Soren
Kierkegaard: 1. 'Purity of heart is to will one thing.' 2. 'True religion . . . is the profound humiliation of man, the boundless love
of God, and and endless striving born of gratitude.' Thank you."
So Bishop Pike wrote Canon Johnson in 1962. Other contacts
would be more substantial: Pike sought Johnson's criticism of the
first draft of *A Time for Christian Candor*, a book which did
much to provoke heresy charges against the bishop. There were,
after Pike's move to California, other communications, too. Pike
supplied some assistance for a tour of the Anglican Communion
that Johnson had been commissioned to undertake; they corresponded about the so-called Blake-Pike church union proposals;
Johnson changed executors in his will, dropping Pike; and a variety of disparate matters. But the relationship diminished with the
absence of the direct and daily access in which each had thrived
at St. John the Divine, and by the time of Pike's travail about the
heresy charges and the attendant events—the suicide of Pike's son
and Johnson's godson; Pike's resignation as bishop; the divorce
from Esther; the marriage to Diane Kennedy; quitting the
Church a second time—the voice of Johnson in Pike's life had become silent. When James Pike died in the wilderness in Judea,

Howard Johnson was living as a virtual recluse on an island in the Caribbean.

Occasionally, speculation is now heard within the Church, among clergy who had known both Pike and Johnson, as to how the lives of each might have been different had Pike remained as dean of New York and disavowed the episcopacy or had Pike, upon becoming bishop, brought Johnson to California with him. That mainly proves how unique, and how intriguing, the relationship was. Certainly it had some Frankenstein dimension to it. As one close witness suggests: "In many ways James was HJ's creation, then the creation got out of hand . . . and started behaving like its own being . . . In an academic and theological way it was the cutting of the umbilical cord." If that be so, it represents a certain irony, since it had been the tutelage of Howard Johnson in James Pike's decisions favoring Anglicanism and ordination to the Episcopal priesthood that had previously severed a similar cord with Mama.

The Problem in I Timothy

On the evening of February 4, 1958, a party which Esther and Jim Pike were hosting at the deanery of the New York cathedral was interrupted by a telephone call from San Francisco for Jim. He promptly shared the news it brought with the guests, clergy, and faculty who had been at a meeting of The Church Society for College Work that day at the cathedral. James Albert Pike had been elected Bishop Coadjutor of California! A coadjutor, in Anglican orders, has the right of succession to a diocesan bishop, and the incumbent in California, the Right Reverend Karl Morgan Block, had been ailing for some time and was due soon to retire. The ecclesiastical formalities for the election of Episcopal bishops are such that a majority vote must be won respectively from laity and clergy delegated from parishes to a convention of the diocese. In this election, Pike had been chosen on the sixth ballot by 221 lay votes (193 required) and 57 clerical votes (56 required).

A general elation which the guests gathered at the deanery momentarily enjoyed in this news subdued as the realization quickened that Pike's acceptance of the California see, presuming that his election would have necessary concurrence from the other dioceses of the Church, would mean the loss of his ministry in New York. "If Jim had been defeated, it would obviously have been for the wrong reason and therefore . . . we must rejoice in the election." Chaplain Krumm of Columbia summarized the sentiment at the party, "But what will become of us on Morningside Heights?"

Krumm supplied an answer to this question in a letter he wrote to Bishop Pike more than four years later: "A superb Whitsunday sermon by Howard last Sunday made the Cathedral seem like old times . . . by which I mean, *alive!!* I am dismayed at it . . . It is a conspiracy to make it a museum."

A similar view prevails since Pike's death, especially among those of his friends given to tragic interpretations of his last years, when they constantly preface recollections of Pike with remarks like "If only Jim had remained in New York as dean." In fact, at the party that February night in 1958, some friends present pressed Pike very hard not to accept his election, their chief arguments being the extraordinary congeniality of his talents with the deanship and the need, in the Church and in the nation, for his virtually unique ministry as Dean Pike. To such appeals, Pike entered no refutations, but simply repeated—enigmatically, as it seemed at the time—"It's California. I wouldn't accept anywhere else, but it's California. I went to school at Santa Clara. It's returning home."

A month or so earlier, Pike had considered refusing to allow his nomination in California. He was aware that there was heavy opposition within that diocese, and elsewhere in the Episcopal Church, to his becoming bishop, and he had confided in a letter to Mama that he had "considerable doubt about the election itself . . . Yet I have not yet been able to come to a decision clear enough to withdraw." His uncertainty was justified, given the narrowness of the vote which finally did elect him, and further documented by the extremely close poll of the dioceses in confirming his election. Moreover, his qualms about permitting his name to go before the California convention were raised by his belief that he was being openly opposed because of his reputation for controversial social convictions, but this was a cover for a more personal attack, a challenge to the legitimacy of his marital status.

The most vehement of those against Pike's elevation to the episcopacy had sought to disqualify him before the electoral convention on grounds that the dissolution of his marriage to Jane Alvies lacked ecclesiastical sanction and that this tainted his marriage, or purported marriage, to Esther Yanovsky as far as the canons of the Church were concerned so as to bar Pike from episcopal office. This position, if the facts supported it, acquired a certain dignity from the passage in the First Letter to Timothy, authorized in the Book of Common Prayer for recital in the service of consecration of a bishop:

> *This is a true saying, If a man desire the office of a bishop, he desireth a good work. A bishop then must be blameless, the husband of one wife, vigilant, sober, of good behavior, given to hospitality, apt to teach.*

The effort to deny Pike nomination failed, the anti-Pike vote at the convention proved insufficient to prevent his election, but opposition to his confirmation persisted and, though the exact tally remains secret, it is known that the concurrence of the bishops to his election was by a slim margin. One bishop who subsequently admitted his refusal to concur was Eric Irving Bloy, Bishop of Los Angeles. Cued by I Timothy, Bloy had concluded that Pike's second marriage was ecclesiastically invalid and that since Pike's first wife then resided in San Francisco, if Pike became Bishop of California he would be living in scandal with two wives in the same city. Oddly, as strenuous as Bloy's stated conviction in the matter was, it did not hinder his participation, along with fifteen other bishops, led by Henry Knox Sherrill, then Presiding Bishop of the Episcopal Church, in the consecration of James Albert Pike to the episcopacy on Ascension Day—May 15—1958.

The quarrel attending his becoming Bishop of California was one controversy which Pike did not relish. For one thing, it was a very ambiguous affair, not only because of well-founded suspicion that his enemies were exploiting a personal tragedy in his past to conceal their hostility to his social witness, but also because of the anguish the challenge to his marital status caused Esther. Moreover, it meant that he was forced to recall the turmoil of the first marriage and to relive its failure, and at a moment when his career was ascendant and, indeed, when his vocation to the priesthood was widely affirmed. He mentioned all this to Esther, in a note scribbled to her sometime prior to election, when a possibility still existed that he might be disqualified as an episcopal candidate.

> Needless to say this has all been a bit tedious for me to relive; but I remain grateful for 15½ years of a genuine marriage, our four children, and 13 years in holy orders with what has appeared to be a useful ministry; and if I am removed from consideration for the bishopric of Calif. because of this long-dead aspect of the past I can take comfort in the fact that St. Aug. would, by the same attitude, have [been] barred . . . from the See of Hippo, and that I have as Dean of N.Y. a job I'm enthusiastic about, and which would be difficult to leave in any case. And as to all this I adopt St. Augustine's words: "O felix culpa, O happy guilt that brought me so great a redemption."

Pike was surprised, as well as hurt, when the disposition of his first marriage became so stubborn an issue in his election and confirmation as bishop. He had thought the matter settled, but it kept haunting his life. It was a factor in the dispute he suffered with his successor as Bishop of California, Kilmer Myers, in connection with his third marriage to Diane Kennedy. It was one of the things which motivated some who sought his trial as a heretic, and some who were glad when he was censured by the House of Bishops. It came to the attention of the authorities of General Theological Seminary in 1946, when Pike's appointment as a tutor there was pending, because of derogatory reports uttered by an anonymous informant. It was investigated by Bishop Angus Dun at the time Pike applied to become a postulant for holy orders under Dun's jurisdiction. So the issue plagued Pike throughout his life, never quite being laid to rest.

When the Very Reverend Hughell Fosbroke, dean of General Theological Seminary, asked him about the ecclesiastical status of his first marriage, Pike responded, testily: "Two successors of the Apostles having reviewed the facts, I have since regarded the matter as 'res adjudicata'—as closed." The two "successors of the Apostles" to whom Pike referred were Bishop Dun, who had been informed, Pike told Fosbroke, "fully of the facts connected with my annulled marriage," and the Right Reverend Bertrand Stevens, Bishop of Los Angeles, who, as Fosbroke heard from Pike, "readmitted me to communicant status . . . and, on a basis of certified application and supporting affidavits, ruled the first marriage invalid." When the matter was reasserted because of Pike's nomination for the "bishopric of Calif." he expressed astonishment to Esther that the inquiries made by General Theological Seminary had not disposed of the issue. "I received my tutorship and G.T.S. (on whose board I now serve) has generally not been regarded as lax on ecclesiastical questions!"

Pike had stated flatly, in writing, on February 27, 1946, to Dean Fosbroke that there had been an ecclesiastical annulment of the marriage to Jane Alvies:

> You need not have been reluctant to ask me about the matter and I am happy to be able to relieve your mind. Doubtless your informant did not know the one essential fact: what in civil law was my first marriage was annulled upon my application by the Rt. Rev. W. Bertrand Stevens, Bishop of Los Angeles, on March 23, 1943, and Esther and I were married in the Church on April 13, 1943.

Pike offered, at the same time, further information to Fosbroke, should he be interested "in the details behind Bishop Stevens' ruling." He also consulted Bishop Dun, requesting that Dun write to Dean Fosbroke about the matter.

The version supplied to the dean of General Theological Seminary has, through the subsequent years of Pike's life and since his death, endured in general circulation, namely, that the first marriage was annulled. Occasionally such references would be made in the media, it was the version accepted by friends of Esther and Jim, and no less an authority than *The Bishop Pike Affair* gave credence to it, in a footnote: "It is interesting to note that a judgment of ecclesiastical annulment had been entered with respect to Bishop Pike's first marriage."

O felix culpa! After Pike's death, a document was found which furnishes a different version of the asserted annulment. It is a letter written by Dean Pike to Philip Adams, an attorney in San Francisco and a prominent Episcopal layman there, who served under Bishop Pike as chancellor of the Diocese of California. The correspondence does not bear a date, but the contents indicate that it was received by Adams during the time, prior to Pike's election as bishop, when reports were circulating about the disposition of the first marriage which might eventuate in removing Pike from consideration for the office. The letter set forth, in scrupulous detail, the facts of the first marriage, the civil divorce dissolving the marriage on ground of "extreme cruelty," and the various communications between Pike and Bishop Stevens as to the ecclesiastical consequences of these facts.

The Pike-Adams correspondence establishes these items:

(1) A few days *before* the civil divorce action with respect to Pike's marriage to Jane Alvies was initiated, Pike met with Bishop Stevens, at his diocesan offices, to ascertain the ecclesiastical effect of the contemplated secular divorce. As Pike wrote Adams: "Here was the lawyer's mind at work on my part: having been married in the Episcopal Church, I wanted to know what the status of things was." Pike reported to Adams that Bishop Stevens, at this conference, "On hearing the facts, . . . declared that the first marriage was void under the canons . . . He agreed with the decision my counsel and I had made not to seek a civil annulment or a divorce on the ground of adultery, due to the inevitable publicity and harm to people and the ease of a divorce in California on the ground of 'extreme cruelty.' "

(2) Pike filed a divorce complaint on July 23, 1940. Jane Alvies made a cross complaint, and Pike consented to a default judgment. On September 4, 1940, an interlocutory decree granting the divorce, to take final effect within a year, was entered in the Superior Court of Los Angeles County. The final decree was uttered in due course, a year later.

(3) Meanwhile, on August 5, 1940, Pike wrote to Bishop Stevens, setting forth in detail his version of the marriage and of the failure of the marriage and referring to the pending civil divorce, to apply for an ecclesiastical annulment of the marriage. "I believe," Pike stated, "that my case falls within 'lack of free consent,' a ground of annulment specified in the marriage canon. Her consent to share her life and love was not given at all; my consent to share my life and love was given, but it was not 'free,' because induced by fraud. Or, to put it in another way, there was never a real marriage between us."

(4) No action was taken upon this application nor, apparently,

was any written acknowledgment of it made. "My recollection is," Pike explained to Adams, "that Bishop Stevens told me on the *phone* that the application was in order, but that it was premature, in that the civil action was not complete, and that I should re-apply, with supporting affidavits, after the entry of the final decree." The relevant canons then applicable provided that such applications be made one year after a final decree in a civil action had been entered. By that tabulation, Pike was not entitled to petition for a church annulment of the first marriage until on or after September 4, 1942.

(5) Pike and Esther Yanovsky were married by Judge Lawes on January 29, 1942. Several months later, during a summertime visit to Los Angeles, Esther and he talked with the priest who had presided at the wedding of Pike and Alvies in 1938, and then saw Bishop Stevens, who urged him to "clear the matter up." In his correspondence with Adams, Pike indicated that he thereupon filed an application for annulment.

(6) On November 27, 1942, Bishop Stevens wrote in a letter to Pike:

> My dear Mr. Pike:
> On November 5th I sent you a notice that I had restored you to communicant status. Apparently your bad mail arrangements have prevented your receiving it. Anyway you may consider yourself in good standing.

The bishop had also written, on November 6, to the priest who had married Pike and Alvies about the matter, and Pike furnished Adams an excerpt from that letter.

> My dear Father Dodd:
> Mr. James A. Pike, who has been married contrary to the canons of the Church, has petitioned for restoration to communicant status. He had previously discussed with me the possibility of an ecclesiastical annulment of his previous marriage. At that time (which was before his marriage) I gave him encouragement to present his claims. He did not do so, however, and remarried. Now in his petition he restates the facts previously related to me and after careful consideration I believe (and so decide) that he is entitled to restoration of his status as a communicant of the Church in good standing.

(7) Pike declared to Adams that Bishop Stevens's restoration of communicant status, evidenced in the above cited letters to Pike and Dodd, constituted an annulment of the first marriage even though, as Pike put it to Adams, Stevens was "using as his ground his opinion as to the nullity of the first marriage." "I realize now," Pike added, "since the application came after a civil marriage, that this was the appropriate canonical form, since a decree of annulment has its appropriateness in order to permit remarriage in the Church, and of course he used the nullity ground as a basis for his decision of restoration. However, at the time, I wanted it cast the other way and wrote him to that effect."

Adams was thus furnished this excerpt from a *handwritten* letter from the Bishop of Los Angeles to Pike, dated March 23, 1943.

> Dear Mr. Pike:
>
> I am sorry that I have been so rushed during the past few days that I have not been able to answer your kind letter. I am quite sure that under the conditions you may assume that your previous marriage was invalid from the Church point of view. I can say that if you were now petitioning for the right to re-marry I would (with the necessary legal approval) give my consent. It is my opinion that upon the baptism of your wife and a blessing from any priest of the Church that your present marriage is a Christian marriage from every point of view and that you and your wife are entitled to all sacramental and other privileges of the Church.

(8) By this time—the spring of 1943—the ecclesiastical status of the first marriage was not just a matter of legal tidiness for Pike, but of great practical significance, since he had decided to resume his vocation to the priesthood and had pending, in the Diocese of Washington, his admission as a postulant for holy orders in the Episcopal Church. The standing committee of that diocese, acting as the ecclesiastical authority in the absence of a sitting bishop, did approve Pike's postulancy, and, when he assumed office in 1944, Bishop Dun concurred. Pike interpreted these actions to Adams as acceptance by the standing committee and Bishop of Washington of the cited letters of Bishop Stevens to Dodd and to Pike as "a firm determination of the nullity of the first marriage."

Meanwhile, implementing the March 23 letter, the marriage of Esther and James was solemnized at a service at All Saints

Church, Frederick, Maryland, on April 13, 1943, by the Reverend
Samuel S. Johnston. Their first child, Catherine, born to them
the previous November, witnessed the ceremony.

The information which Adams received manifestly stands at
variance with the tenor of Pike's much more succinct recapitulation of events concerning the ecclesiastical status of the first marriage supplied to Dean Fosbroke at General Theological Seminary.
Pike's letter to Fosbroke had a categorical sound: "Bishop Stevens
readmitted me to communicant status on November 6, 1942, and,
on a basis of a verified application and supporting affidavits, ruled
the first marriage invalid on March 23, 1943." (The canonical
ground of annulment was the impediment to marriage specified in
❡ 3 (2) of Cannon 17.) Pike's statement to Adams, on the significance of the same communications of Bishop Stevens, was more
careful, and, one might say, more lawyer-like:

> On going all over this after many years this letter (March 23,
> 1943), rather than being strictly speaking, a Decree of Annul-
> ment, is (by analogy to the Civil Law) a Declaratory Judgment
> or Advisory Opinion, but equally based on sworn facts and with
> the same conclusion.

This construction seems to have satisfied qualms about whether
the ecclesiastical status of the first marriage constituted a barrier
to Pike's standing for election to the episcopacy. It does not resolve the discrepancy between the position Pike took in the General Theological Seminary matter and that in his correspondence
with Adams twelve years later. And, perhaps, the discrepancy cannot be resolved; perhaps it was just the case that Pike deceived
Dean Fosbroke by misstating that there had been an annulment
when, in fact, there had been none. On the other hand, Pike indicated in his letter to Adams that he had made an effort to
locate the pertinent papers and refresh his recollection quite
specifically, and that in itself could account for the more factually
exact information which Adams received. It is relevant, too, that
the marriage to Jane Alvies had been a deeply disturbing experience for Pike and that by the time it was dissolved, he had come
to feel that he had been importuned in entering it in the first
place. In his mind, the marriage was not merely a mistake, but a

nullity in the inception. His communications with Bishop Stevens give weight to that view. Thus, it can be suggested that with his restoration to communicant standing, then the solemnization of the marriage to Esther and his admission to postulancy, Pike came to think of the marriage as having been annulled, or the equivalent thereof, even though in a precise, procedural sense, under the existing canons, there had been no decree of annulment. This view would, of course, also allow for innumerable instances, in conversations with friends or in interviews with the press, when Pike did not challenge the generally circulated story that the first marriage was annulled. For him that was the truth, *de facto* if not *de jure*, and it was a greater effort than circumstances required to clarify what had actually happened in the disposition of the first marriage. Had he—and Esther—not suffered the matter enough, without incurring obligation to recite about it fastidiously when more or less casual reference was made to it?

Nevertheless, it should be noticed that those—particularly Bishop Stevens's successor in the Los Angeles see, Bishop Bloy—who opposed Pike's elevation to the episcopacy because of the first marriage had, whatever other motivations might have informed them, basis in the facts for their position. Bloy had access to the records of Bishop Stevens's dealings with Pike, but those records showed only that Stevens had restored Pike as a communicant and that no official action was taken on any application for annulment. Moreover, two items, upon which Pike heavily relied in making his case to Adams that Stevens had—in effect—uttered a "declaratory judgment," could not have been among the information to which Bloy had official access, one being a telephone call, the other a handwritten note sent to Pike. The canons are very specific about requiring annulment decrees to be recorded in writing and preserved in diocesan archives, and Bloy must have known, when he voted not to concur in Pike's election, that no such instrument existed.

There lingers a conundrum about why Pike, lawyer that he was, did not pursue timely application for an annulment, especially since he had made premature inquiries which had found encouraging response. He married Esther in civil ceremony before the time appointed for such application, but why not wait a few more months—a year perhaps—and have the issue settled, and then marry Esther? Answers, now, are speculative to such questions; what is known—confirmed in letters to his mother at the time—is that Pike was very eager to marry (or to marry again) and had not yet determined to be priested. Query, too, whether Pike was entirely confident that he had conclusive ground for annulment. The civil divorce had been arranged on cross complaints alleging cruelty because, as Pike told Stevens, that was the quietest, most decent, easiest way to do it. Yet the fact is that Pike, with Mama's aid and urging, had engaged detectives to keep Jane Alvies under surveillance and that they had failed to secure admissible evidence to support a divorce action on the ground of adultery. Whether these circumstances would satisfy the canonical requirements for nullification of the marriage was never decided. In any event, Pike did not seek annulment before marrying Esther and it was only some time later, when he recommitted himself to the priesthood, that "clearing up" the status of the first marriage in the eyes of the Church became an anxiety for him.

An Apostolic Succession

The candor of Dean Pike's correspondence with Philip Adams about the Alvies marriage quieted the qualms and questions that had been circulated in California about whether, in church practice, his marital history should be construed as a barrier to Pike taking office as bishop. His name was offered at the diocesan convention charged with choosing a successor to Bishop Block, and Pike was elected, though by small margins in each rank of the dual voting system and only after several inconclusive ballots. If in New York City there was widespread public regret, both within and outside the Church, at the prospect of Pike's departure from the cathedral and the loss of him to the city, along with much personal concern among his friends about the consequences of this move for Jim vocationally, in San Francisco the gossip and dispute attending his election subsided, and was quickly surpassed by anticipation of his advent. Suspense was added to expectation by the slowness with which the concurrence in his election of the bishops was received; the requisite affirmative votes were recorded only a few weeks before the consecration was scheduled. The excitement was engendered by Pike's celebrity—unlike most bishops, it was not his election that brought him prominence, he brought fame to the office—and people assumed that the focus of national attention for which the New York cathedral had became reputed would shift to the see of San Francisco when Dean Pike became Bishop Pike.

On Ascension Day, 1958, the date being May 15, the consecration took place. The cathedral on Nob Hill was jammed to capacity with upward of two thousand persons, including a diverse and ecumenical host of ecclesiastics and a full array of academic and civic dignitaries, while tens of thousands more witnessed the ancient rites on live television. The service began, to the triumphant sound of "All Hail the Power of Jesus' Name!", with three long processions, one moving down each of the aisles of Grace Cathedral. Sixteen bishops of the Episcopal Church participated as co-consecrators of the new bishop with Henry Knox Sherrill, the Presiding Bishop. Edward Lambe Parsons, retired third Bishop of California, by then become venerable, but still remembered as a social radical of the Depression era, was one of the sixteen, and appropriately so, since the apprehension had currency in California that Pike would emulate Parsons. The Bishop of New York, Horace W. B. Donegan, who had called Pike to the deanship of New York and had been the patron of his ministry as dean, was in attendance, as were some bishops destined to become Pike's detractors—notably Stephen Fielding Bayne, then Bishop of Olympia, and J. Brooke Mosley, Bishop of Delaware—as well as some who became staunch defenders, like John Craine, Bishop of Indianapolis. The most anomalous presence among the bishops was that of Eric Irving Bloy of Los Angeles.

Assuming places in the chancel and the nave were hierarchy and clergy of other churches, from the Armenian Apostolic across Christendom's spectrum to the Southern Baptists. Apart from Pike himself, the most famous clergyman to witness the consecration was the Reverend Billy Graham. The presbyters attending the bishop-elect were Dr. Charles W. F. Smith, under whom Pike had studied at the Virginia Theological Seminary, and Pike's erstwhile tutor, Canon Howard Johnson.

With everyone in place, amid a profusion of color and symbol and glare, Bishop Sherrill began the celebration of the Holy Communion, in the context of which bishops traditionally are ordained. The solemn moments came shortly following the sermon preached by the dean of Episcopal Theological School, John Coburn, when Pike was presented before the Presiding Bishop, seated in his chair near the high altar, with the words:

> Reverend Father in God, we present unto you this godly and well-learned man, to be Ordained and Consecrated Bishop.

Thereupon Bishop Sherrill demanded that testimonials of Pike's election and confirmation be read aloud and, after that, required of Pike this oath:

> In the Name of God, Amen. I, James Albert Pike, chosen Bishop of the Protestant Episcopal Church in California, do promise conformity and obedience to the Doctrine, Discipline, and Worship of the Protestant Episcopal Church in the United States of America. So help me God, through Jesus Christ.

Then followed certain prayers in litany, after which the Presiding Bishop addressed the bishop-elect:

> Brother, forasmuch as the Holy Scripture and the ancient Canons command, that we should not be hasty in laying on hands, and admitting any person to Government in the Church of Christ, which he hath purchased with no less price than the effusion of his own blood; before we admit you to this Administration, we will examine you in certain Articles, to the end that the Congregation present may have a trial, and bear witness, how you are minded to behave yourself in the Church of God.

Next Pike was publicly examined, according to the form set forth in the Book of Common Prayer:

Sherrill: Are you persuaded that you are truly called to this Ministration, according to the will of our Lord Jesus Christ, and the order of this Church?

Pike: I am so persuaded.

Sherrill: Are you persuaded that the Holy Scriptures contain all Doctrine required as necessary for eternal salvation through faith in Jesus Christ? And are you determined out of the same Holy Scriptures to instruct the people committed to your charge; and to teach and maintain nothing, as necessary to eternal salvation, but that which you shall be persuaded may be concluded and proved by the same?

Pike: I am so persuaded, and determined, by God's grace.

Sherrill: Will you then faithfully exercise yourself in the Holy

Scriptures, and call upon God by prayer for the true understanding of the same; so that you may be able by them to
teach and exhort with wholesome Doctrine, and to withstand
and convince the gainsayers?

Pike: I will so do, by the help of God.

Sherrill: Are you ready, with all faithful diligence, to banish and
drive away from the Church all erroneous and strange doctrine contrary to God's Word; and both privately and openly
to call upon and encourage others to the same?

Pike: I am ready, the Lord being my helper.

Sherrill: Will you deny all ungodliness and worldly lusts, and live
soberly, righteously, and godly in this present world; that you
may show yourself in all things an example of good works
unto others, that the adversary may be ashamed, having
nothing to say against you?

Pike: I will so do, the Lord being my helper.

Sherrill: Will you maintain and set forward, as much as shall lie
in you, quietness, love, and peace among all men; and
diligently exercise such discipline as by the authority of
God's Word, and by the order of this Church, is committed
to you?

Pike: I will so do, by the help of God.

Sherrill: Will you be faithful in Ordaining, sending, or laying
hands upon others?

Pike: I will so be, by the help of God.

Sherrill: Will you show yourself gentle, and be merciful for
Christ's sake to poor and needy people, and to all strangers
destitute of help?

Pike: I will so show myself, by God's help.

Bishop Sherrill finished the public examination with a prayer
for the bishop-elect and then, as the great congregation sang the
Veni, Creator Spiritus, invoking the action of the Holy Spirit,
Pike, who had until now been clothed in a simple white garment,
a rochet, was vested in the episcopal habit. The consecrating bishops came forward to form a circle, Pike kneeling in their midst,
and, following another prayer, the bishops, severally and jointly,
laid their hands upon his head. The Presiding Bishop spoke:

Receive the Holy Ghost for the Office and Work of a Bishop
in the Church of God, now committed unto thee by the Imposition of our hands; In the Name of the Father, and of the Son,

and of the Holy Ghost. Amen. And remember that thou stir up the grace of God, which is given thee by this Imposition of our hands; for God hath not given us the spirit of fear, but of power, and love, and soberness.

Thus, following ancient precedent and solemn practice, James Albert Pike was made bishop. As a coadjutor, he would presently succeed to the chair of the Bishop of California. In the enumeration kept in the Episcopal Church in the United States, he became the 555th person in historic succession to the apostolic office.

To Bishop Pike, Henry Knox Sherrill then promptly delivered a copy of the Bible, repeating this admonition:

> Give heed unto reading, exhortation, and doctrine. Think upon the things contained in this Book. Be diligent in them, that the increase coming thereby may be manifest unto all men; for by so doing thou shalt both save thyself and them that hear thee. Be to the flock of Christ a shepherd, not a wolf; feed them, devour them not. Hold up the weak, heal the sick, bind up the broken, bring again the outcasts, seek the lost. Be so merciful, that you be not remiss; so minister discipline, that you forget not mercy; that when the Chief Shepherd shall appear, you may receive the never-fading crown of glory; through Jesus Christ our Lord. *Amen.*

The consecration done, the celebration of the Holy Communion proceeded and the service ended, to the herald of trumpets and the pealing of the cathedral's bells, as the new bishop rendered his blessing to the congregation, to the city, and to the world.

Pastor Pastorum

Pike's tenure as coadjutor was more brief than had been expected; within a little over four months of his consecration Bishop Block had died (on September 29, 1958), and he had become the diocesan bishop or the ordinary, as bishops in jurisdiction have traditionally been called.

In the consecration rite, Bishop Pike had not only received those admonitions prescribed by rubric for those vested with epis-

copal office, but also he had suffered the further, personal ad-
monishments addressed to him in the sermon of Dean Coburn.
Coburn had cautioned "Brother Jim," as he called Pike, to direct
his "contagious enthusiasm" to "those things which are above,
where Christ sitteth on the right hand of God." That meant, according to Coburn, among other things, engagement in controversy "as a last resort and not as a first resort." And Coburn urged
Pike, as the bishop now of a particular diocese, to refrain from
calls that would come to him from elsewhere. "You are now
bound in a common life with the clergy and people of this
Diocese. In their service you will at last be given that freedom
which is the perfect freedom of all the servants of the people of
Christ."

Whether it occurred to Pike, at the outset of his episcopacy,
that there were any discrepancies between the prudence counseled
by his old friend John Coburn and the admonitory words from
the order of consecration in the Book of Common Prayer is not
known, but the fact is that he bore the yoke with his diocese
cheerfully, dutifully, and energetically. If assessed by the usual criteria, Pike's eight-year incumbency must be accounted an extraordinary success. In that time, the number of parishes and missions
increased from 112 to 124, communicant strength grew from
about 67,000 persons to nearly 84,000, active clergy rose from 175
to 188. There were more baptisms, more confirmations, more ordinations, more marriages solemnized than ever before in the diocese; the only significant statistical decline was, curiously, registered in burials, which fell from 1,701 to 1,583. The income of the
diocese much more than doubled—from $390,000 in 1958 to
$892,000 in 1964—despite a change in the system of collecting
money from parishes from a compulsory or assessment method to
one of voluntary contributions.

The most visible evidence of Pike's diligence and effectiveness,
as measured by conventional standards, was, and is, the completion of Grace Cathedral. Located in a dominant site on Nob Hill,
overseeing the whole city of San Francisco, Grace Cathedral is the
first major Anglican cathedral in the United States to be finished.
In making this task a priority of his episcopacy, he saw the cathedral as a necessary and significant symbol of the Church's care

and hospitality for the whole life of the city and not merely as some denominational monument. "San Francisco's stature and personality are notably international," Pike remarked about the effort to complete the building. "How right, then, that its citizens of many faiths should be completing on its heights an internationally renowned cathedral as 'a home of prayer for all people.'" Pike implemented this theme in raising the three million dollars required for the project, securing gifts from the full spectrum of San Francisco's business and community leadership. On the very day, for example, that he first convened the committee for funding the cathedral, Pike recessed the meeting briefly, went across to the Fairmont Hotel on Nob Hill, and returned to his committee with a one-hundred-thousand-dollar pledge from the Fairmont's owner. The whole enterprise became a civic event. At the service of Thanksgiving which celebrated the start of the construction which would finish the edifice, the mayor of San Francisco, George Christopher, citing the charter of Grace Cathedral, declared that the cathedral "stands in the community as a symbol of the supremacy of God in human life. We desire that it may minister to all the people of the community." When the construction was done and the cathedral was consecrated at ceremonies which, the press reported, attracted ". . . representatives of all faiths, Federal, State, and City officials and civic leaders, commanders of the armed services, heads of the consular corps, representatives of the cities and towns of the diocese, and leading citizens of California," an editorial about the event was entitled "Grace Cathedral—a 'Grace' for All."

The accomplishment of the cathedral—the public applause accorded the event and the pride engendered among California Episcopalians—temporarily muted, if it did not entirely mollify, the factions of clergy and laity which had been so vigorously opposed to Pike's election and which remained after his consecration anxious because of Pike's reputed social radicalism. It is doubtful that Pike had even considered the political ramifications of completing the cathedral or of making the task his first priority; certainly there was no intent or attempt on his part to appease opponents by finishing the cathedral. His motivation was an extension of the concern he had shown as dean of New York to restore the cathedral's vocation and that was greatly enhanced by his view of his elementary duty as a catholic bishop, possessing a pastoral authority and ministry extending to the whole of society.

Anyway, applause subsided and vanity was soon dissipated, and the bishop's intent to implement his theological understanding of the apostolic witness to society became obvious to all when the clerestory windows in the nave and certain bay windows were installed in the cathedral. Earlier windows had featured the usual saints, but these represented themes of reform and prophecy and honored modern persons, including Bishop Parsons, Pike's most politically controversial predecessor. Furthermore one series of windows portrayed pioneers in secular endeavors—from Albert Einstein to Thurgood Marshall to John Glenn—to affirm the versatility of the Holy Spirit in the world. To be the more emphatic, the style of the new windows was contemporary, rather than medieval, and very free in design, in use of form and color. Some of Pike's opponents loudly denounced these adornments as sacrilegious, and others found them to be political. For Pike, the windows signified his commitment to an open episcopacy exemplifying the outreach of the gospel, rather than one dwelling on the glorification of the Church or of a denomination, and this concern took focus in the fabric of the cathedral itself, as well as in the hospitable style the bishop brought to it.

A notable instance of this hospitality was the appearance, in 1960, of Dr. Eugene Carson Blake, Stated Clerk or chief executive officer of the United Presbyterian Church in the United States, to preach in the pulpit of Grace Cathedral as a guest of Bishop Pike. The occasion coincided with a general assembly of the National Council of Churches convened in San Francisco. Dr. Blake, a former president of the National Council, and a restless leader in the ecumenical movement, had conceived a proposal for church union embracing bodies both "truly catholic and truly reformed" and, desiring a maximum hearing for his audacious idea, he had sought an invitation from Pike. "I knew," Blake has commented, "that being where Pike was bishop, the sermon would be heard." And so it was, by a huge congregation and through widespread news reports. In the media, the church union plan came to be labeled "the Blake-Pike proposal," but, in fact, it was wholly Dr. Blake's conception, which Pike welcomed and obliged with a forum. Once launched so auspiciously, the proposal issued in the organization of the Consultation on Church Union, though the consultation has yet to come to ecumenical maturity.

In the same spirit of his episcopacy, Pike embraced Dr. Martin Luther King, Jr. The bishop supported an invitation for King's appearance at the 1964 general convention of the Episcopal Church against vehement opposition from many delegates and some of the other bishops; Pike addressed the Southern Christian Leadership Conference; along with many of his clergy, Pike had been in Selma. In 1965, the bishop welcomed Dr. King to Grace Cathedral, where he preached. That incited much cursing from critics and antagonists. One of the letters published in the *Pacific Churchman*, the newspaper of the Diocese of California, after King's visit typified the opposition sentiment within the Church:

> As a 20 year member of the Episcopal Diocese of California I am being rapidly driven to the exit . . . Our bleeding heart Bishop Pike continues his assault on status quo based on an attitude of love of fellow man. He declares that no set of rules can "be absolute for man" . . . An extension of this thought is revealed by the presence of Dr. King in the Grace Cathedral some weeks ago. For the sake of love and freedom does Bishop Pike intend to support economic boycotts as advocated by Dr. King?
>
> As a dismayed and disgusted churchmember I wish to point out that Dr. Martin Luther King . . . has been cited by the Louisiana State Legislature as having been affiliated with more Communist front activities than many Communist Party members. I am proud to believe in God, American principles, and the worth and dignity of man—be he any color or heritage.

If an outburst such as this be stereotypical of much of the anti-Pike sentiment which surfaced during Pike's incumbency that does not justify the inference that *he* could be stereotyped, as a "bleeding heart" or in any other way. His witness was too versatile, eclectic, ecumenical to be simplistically classified. He sponsored a night ministry on the streets of San Francisco to care for derelicts, drug-users, hippies, homosexuals, runaways, prostitutes, potential suicides, but he at the same time launched a mission to bankers, brokers, traders, and corporate personnel in the city's financial district—an effort later imitated in New York City by Trinity Church on Wall Street; he served on the California adjunct of the United States Commission on Human Rights; he supported the unionization of migrant farm workers; he joined other Episcopalians in condemning implicit racism in the Goldwater presidential campaign; he often addressed forums of the establishment including The Commonwealth Club, the bar associations, the California Republican Convention; he revived the red mass to intercede for the administration of the courts and the practice of the law; practically every convention which gathered in San Francisco sought his presence; he fought against Proposition 14, which would have had the effect of repealing California's open housing policy; he pressed his concern for planned parenthood; he urged equal status for women in church and society; he initiated community action programs in racially troubled Oakland and proposed bringing Saul Alinsky to the scene; he initially opposed the Supreme Court's school prayer decision—along with Everett McKinley Dirksen and other worthies—but later changed his mind; he revived the infrequent practice of "dual ordination," rendering episcopal orders to a Methodist minister; he advocated the curricular recognition of religious courses in state colleges and universities; he was skeptical about a Roman Catholic in the White House; he supported the Vietnam war to the end of his tenure as diocesan bishop, though later he joined the resistance to the "illegitimate authority" which prosecuted the war.

If the range of his concerns and involvements was manifold and diverse, it is also the truth that Bishop Pike's public positions on church matters or on social and political issues were never easily predicted, and, moreover, he retained throughout his public career a faculty of openness, a readiness to learn, a gift for listening, a freedom to change his views that was exceptional. Pike was no ideologue and never acquired a vested interest in the stands that he took. If anything, while Bishop of California, his approach to both political and theological subjects was cautious in the sense that he cared deeply for the office of bishop and for restoring the historic pastoral vocation of bishops. An example of his essential attitude is found in his letter to his clergy on "freedom of prophecy and limitations thereon" circulated in 1965. By that time, opposition to Pike's episcopacy and to the increased involvement of clergy of the diocese in public issues was quite vocal. "One of the corollaries of this increased activity of the clergy," Pike wrote, "has been an increasing burden upon your Bishop (gladly borne) of defending the right of clergy so to involve themselves beyond the borders of ecclesiastical housekeeping, pastoral care, sacramental acts, and morals as limited to one-to-one relationships." The letter states Pike's premises for clergy involvement in this way:

> Each of us by our ordination vows are to be constrained from public positions which are contrary to the Catholic Faith or canon law. Fortunately we are part of a generous tradition and these limits are broad ones. For example, we do not regard councils and conventions of the Church as infallible. (As to the General Councils, see Article XXI: ". . . And when they be gathered together, (forasmuch as they be an assembly of men, whereof all be not governed with the Spirit and Word of God,) they may err, and sometimes have erred, even in things pertaining unto God.") . . . On the other hand, when after considerable consideration, an official deliberative body has taken a position, a clergyman is particularly supportable in his proclaiming of it or acting it out.
>
> Our freedom of prophecy can result in divergent voices within the Church. There are those who think this is bad, some pointing out that this causes "confusion among the laity." I think it is good, and the solution is not to quell the divergence but rather to educate our laity in the nature of the Anglican heritage, which has always been like this—even prior to the Reformation, and I hope will always remain such.

As in his efforts to restore the vocation of cathedrals, first in New York and then in San Francisco, Pike as bishop was concerned—before anything else—with renewing the episcopal office, with relating his own conduct as a bishop to the apostolic tradition, with precedent. And this was a concern made all the more emphatic by his training and disposition as a lawyer. In this sense, Pike was not only not a stereotype liberal or ideologue, he was, in fact, not radical, but orthodox, not innovator, but renovator.

The Ordination of Women

One of the loudest uproars occasioned by Bishop Pike's role as restorer or renewer of the church tradition happened when he recognized the holy orders of Deaconess Phyllis Edwards. Mrs. Edwards, a former schoolteacher and widowed mother of four children, had attended theological school and become a deaconess in the Episcopal Church, serving initially in the Diocese of Olympia. After she entered Pike's jurisdiction in the Diocese of California she worked in the so-called Mission District of San Francisco's inner city, where she particularly distinguished her ministry by her active dedication to justice for the black poor.

Until 1964, women in the Episcopal Church could be "set apart" and "appointed" as deaconesses, but they could not be ordained to the three offices of ministry—deacon, priest, bishop— because custom (though not canon law) reserved these to males. Elsewhere in the worldwide Anglican Communion this custom was beginning to be questioned and, in turn, the nature of the ministry of deaconesses was being appraised. The subject had been breached at the Lambeth Conferences in 1920, 1930, 1948, and 1958. Then at the general convention of 1964, in St. Louis, the Episcopal House of Bishops voted to alter canon law affecting deaconesses by substituting the word "ordered" in place of "appointed." Without dissent, the House of Deputies, which, by the way, had voted at the same convention not to seat women as deputies to future conventions, concurred. In consequence of this canonical change, Bishop Pike announced his intention of ordaining Deaconess Edwards to the perpetual diaconate, one of the orders of ministry customarily limited to men. He proposed thus to implement the decision of the general convention since, as he saw it, the term "ordered" could refer to nothing other than ordination to the full ministry, just as it does for male ordinands.

His announcement incited fright at the prospect of women becoming not only ordained ministers in the diaconate, but in the priesthood and the episcopacy, and a furor ensued which was the forerunner by a full decade of the controversy in the seventies about the ordination of women in the Episcopal Church. Though Pike, somewhat naïvely, had supposed he was engaged in no more than compliance with the change in the canons, his intention was received so provocatively that he determined to seek clarification of the issue at the next meeting of the House of Bishops, in the fall of 1965, and temporarily deferred any action as to Deaconess Edwards. The underlying issue, which the St. Louis vote had apparently only succeeded in confusing, was whether deaconesses are merely specialized laywomen or in holy orders, and, if in holy orders, whether in the diaconate, the so-called third order of ministry, with the same status as male deacons with access to the other two orders of priest and bishop, or in a fourth order reserved to deaconesses or female deacons excluded from succession through the other orders. In effect—although the debate on these matters was by no means coherent—the bishops opted for the view that deaconesses constituted a fourth order. A week later, Bishop Pike held a service of "investiture" at Grace Cathedral to give recognition to the clerical status of Deaconess Edwards. He caused her to be listed with the other clergy of the diocese, counting her seniority from the time that she had first been "set apart" as a deaconess. At the cathedral service, Deaconess Edwards took the oath of conformity to the doctrine and discipline of the Episcopal Church, which is required of all ordinands, and he bestowed a stole upon her as a symbol of office, placing it over her right shoulder in the same manner that male deacons are vested. The discrimination which the bishops had endorsed, however, remained, for Deaconess Edwards, though now "ordered" and now no longer anywhere to be regarded as a layperson, was nevertheless still not eligible to perform the most elementary service of a deacon—the distribution of the elements of the Eucharist. The investiture was, as Bishop Pike commented at the time, "but a little step forward" in the recognition of women "as persons" in the Episcopal Church.

Whether Pike as bishop heeded for very long the prudence counseled by Dean Coburn in the sermon at Pike's consecration to eschew controversy is subject to different opinions. What seems clear is that Pike did heed the admonitions of the Book of Common Prayer for a bishop's consecration, and that it was exactly his earnestness in this—specifically the enjoinders to be attentive to Scripture and to practice the apostolic office as pastor and teacher—that repeatedly excited opposition and agitated controversy. Perhaps Pike's forensic agility accentuated this, perchance a person of different temperament could achieve both Coburn's prudence and fidelity to apostolic precedent, but it is the sincerity of Pike's regard for the episcopal office and authority, and the seriousness of his effort to restore these, rather than radical theological or political opinions as such, that proved so threatening to others, including most of his brother bishops, and that kept him in tumult and dispute. More often than not, in terms of the biblical witness and early church tradition, his views could only be classified as cautious and conscientious. This is specifically verified in Pike's pastoral letters, which repeatedly appeal to biblical citations and ancient practice, and which shun the religious banalities and sentimental triteness all too characteristic, nowadays, of such utterances. One of the bishop's exemplary pastorals addressed the phenomenon of glossolalia, which had a wide occurrence in the churches under Pike's care. The letter, which was required to be read in all churches of the diocese on the third Sunday after Easter, 1963, opens in this way:

> To the Faithful in Christ Jesus in the Diocese of California:
> Grace be unto you, and peace, from God our Father, and from the Lord Jesus Christ.
> With regard to new movements of thought, devotional life and action in the Holy Catholic Church from apostolic times to the present, the Bishops of the Church have always been confronted with special responsibilities of a two-fold character: (1) They are called upon as consecrated by the Holy Spirit operating through the consent and action of the visible Church, to be open to manifestations of His revelation and power in an incalculable and unpredictable variety of ways; and (2) to safeguard the peace and unity of the Church, and to maintain its doctrine, discipline and worship against the threats of party spirit, sectarianism, and a distorted focus upon any particular type of phenomenon attributed to the Holy Spirit by movements within the Church . . . [We] are now confronted with the necessity of exercising this dual responsibility.

The letter, which Pike wrote after receiving a report he had commissioned on the subject to which, among others, a theologian, a New Testament scholar, two psychiatrists, parish priests, an anthropologist, and a parapsychologist had contributed, and after his own study, relied, as might be expected from Pike, heavily upon the pastoral concern expressed in the epistles of St. Paul about "speaking in tongues." Pike, adhering to Paul's example, sought to "keep it in perspective, namely, as only one possible aspect of a 'variety of gifts and diversity of administrations,' involving some

people, but in no wise essential—and in any case subordinate to
the gift of love and to the unity of Christ's Body, the Church."

The pastoral letter on glossolalia evoked controversy, too; this
time Pike was denounced as too conservative just as elsewhere he
suffered denunciation as too radical. Neither accusation was
worthy of the truth of Pike's solemn intent to be diligent in "the
Office and Work of a Bishop of the Church of God."

Pastoral Crises

During the interregnum of Pike's self-defined agnosticism, the
young man had become virtually obsessed with the matter of ecclesiastical authority. He conceived faith to be contingent upon
church membership and upon affirmation of or acquiescence to
the authority of the Church as arbiter and instructor in the faith.
He viewed the authority of the Roman Church as impaired and
corrupted by an extraneous claim of papal infallibility and he concluded that Rome's authority had degenerated into authoritarianism. Pike sought, with evident zeal and with some anxiety, a
Church which had been spared such excesses and abuses but
which could confidently trace its authority in doctrine and polity
to the apostolic era. He had eventually settled upon Anglicanism,
with the permission if not enthusiasm of his mother, and this
renewed allegiance to the Church enabled him quickly to resume
the vocation to the priesthood that he had wanted since childhood, though thereby putting aside his solid and brilliant work in
law and in legal scholarship.

His preoccupation with the authority issue, as might have been
predicted, diminished much once he became a priest, and practically vanished in the course of his episcopacy. As bishop, Pike no
longer felt need for an elaborate justification of ecclesiastical authority. Once himself in authority, he was free of this compulsion
to rationalize it. To be sure, there were moments when he could
not refrain from baiting his peers in the Roman Church about the
difference between their asserted authority and his understanding
of the episcopal office. In his letter to his clergy on "Freedom of
prophecy and the limitations thereon," he wrote: "The positions
individual clergy have taken either by words or participation in

group action have not always matched my own views, but this is not requisite (or entirely desirable, since I have not patterned my administration after that of the Cardinal Archbishop of Los Angeles, and it can hardly be said that we have a monolithic Diocese!)." Yet, essentially, as bishop, Pike lost interest in the question of authority. He was a bishop of the Holy Catholic Church; as such, he exemplified apostolic authority appropriate in the Church; that settled the problem for him. In this, as has been mentioned, he showed historic sense, a comprehension, a conscientiousness so remarkable that it proved to be an embarrassment to many of his fellow Episcopal bishops. Remembering the hostilities and hesitations attending ratification of his election, it might have been supposed that other bishops would welcome the eagerness and solemnity with which he applied himself to being a true bishop. Instead, many of them found his demeanor threatening, an exposé of their own banality and compromise, a violation of the fraternal etiquette of the House of Bishops. To add injury to insult, he became insistent that bishops should be theologically informed and competent and articulate. And what was most aggravating of all was the fact that, meanwhile, he had become the most successful of all the bishops according to worldly criteria of material, financial, and numerical growth.

Ultimately, James A. Pike became so emancipated from his own anxiety about authority that he utterly relinquished his authority, and reached the point where belief was no longer critically dependent upon ecclesiastical authority. He had moved— through a lifetime—from church dogmatics to confession of the gospel, from "smooth orthodoxy" to personal faith, from—in his own words—the "ontological" to the "existential."

This shift is connected to the fact of Pike's quick boredom. In New York, at St. John the Divine, Canon West had noticed that after a very short time, Dean Pike had become bored, despite the vigor and excitement his ministry there engendered and despite the widespread acclaim evoked by his witness there. Even more did he grow restless in the administration of his diocese.

One significant factor feeding his boredom while bishop was the recurring necessity to respond theologically in his role as *pastor pastorum*. In this, for the first time, he was on his own, without surrogates or tutors, such as Howard Johnson had been. Thus his inclinations for study and thought, for reflection and expression returned to prominence. He entertained again the dream of his seminary days of studying in England with a great theological faculty, his old friend Robert Hutchins tempted him with an invitation to join the Center for the Study of Democratic Institutions as a theologian-in-residence, he was tantalized by a summer's stint in New York City devoted to reading and writing and to preaching at Trinity Church, he found both stimulation and nourishment, intellectually, in his ever-increasing travels to colleges and universities across the nation. As early in his episcopate as 1960, he began to delegate assignments to his suffragan bishop, George Richard Millard, and to canons-to-the-ordinary on the replenished cathedral staff, and to assorted other aides, including, notably, Esther Pike. His wife acquired such prominence, indeed, in the administration of his office that she came to be called, among seminarians and younger clergy, "Mrs. Bishop."

The upshot of Pike's efforts to find room for his versatile and mobile interests, to secure respite from administrative tasks, and to relieve his boredom was no lessening of pressures but their multiplication. And this acceleration mounted geometrically as internal opposition to Pike developed and became outspoken within the Diocese of California and within the House of Bishops. Throughout, personal and private crises accrued until they could no longer be contained or repressed or neglected. Not very long before his death, Pike wrote:

> All my life—or as far back as I can remember (psychoanalysis has helped some here)—my pattern of response to disappointment, deprivation or failure—or to what threatened to be such—had been the extension of areas of activity with attendant multiple and diversified preoccupation. In the case of a person fairly capable at various types of things he gets involved in, this pattern inevitably opens up increasing numbers of opportunities in the respective facets, leading eventually to *hyperactivity*. When by such means all of one's time, energy and thought-spaces are occupied the result is the increasingly effective suppression of awareness and concern about unfulfilled areas of the personal scene.

"To illustrate this fully," he added, "would require that I here and now write my autobiography (which I would regard as premature)."

Pike was accurate about his *"hyperactivity"* serving as both compensation and escape in relation to personal problems. Yet, astonishingly, in the midst of his hectic, sometimes frenetic circumstances, he stopped drinking. He acknowledged his alcoholism, confessed it, sought help, joined Alcoholics Anonymous, went dry. He renounced alcohol on June 30, 1964. Thereafter, save a single reported lapse of a day or so, he remained totally dry.

Jim Pike had been an enthusiastic drinker for a long time. It was not uncommon, for instance, for his preparation for extempore appearances on "The Dean Pike Show" on network television to be not much more than several extra dry martinis. He accounted, after he became a member of AA, that he had been an alcoholic since 1952, about the time he became dean of New York and entered his celebrity, a period, coincidentally, in which he frequently suffered insomnia. For many years he supposed that booze sustained his hyperactivity, but his incipient alcoholism grew in those years when he was dean and then bishop to such proportions that it ceased to be any sort of sustenance and was debilitation, radically affecting his marriage and family, accentuating his fatigue and harming his health, risking his safety and courting public exposure and scandal to his episcopacy. There were several close calls, so far as the latter is concerned, some of them terrifying incidents. Three times he was intercepted by police of the San Francisco Bay area, found drunk, confused, wandering on the streets late in the night. Once he made an uproarious appearance at an official event in Washington, D.C., amid haughty and prestigious company. On a more ridiculous occasion, he complained on a transcontinental flight to an airline stewardess that the martini she had served him was unsatisfactorily mixed. He volunteered to demonstrate for her edification, and for the benefit of the other passengers, a better recipe for the cocktail. Standing in the aisle of the plane, he merrily performed this rite. A companion traveling with him had tried to dissuade him, suggesting that he would surely be recognized, but he discounted the possibility and persisted. The stewardess later showed the bishop's associate an issue of *Time* magazine, available to passengers on that flight, which featured a story, with photographs, of Bishop James A. Pike, making his identification certain for those who had not otherwise recognized their exuberant volunteer bartender.

When he became abstinent, it did not remain a private matter either. He was unabashed in his admission of alcoholism, enthusiastic in his esteem for Alcoholics Anonymous, caustic in critique of the falsely judgmental view of alcoholics prevalent in the churches. Speaking in New York City, in 1966, to the National Council on Alcoholism, Pike argued that "non-church people are less judgmental than church people" toward alcoholics and that "pillars of the Church" had thus "made it difficult for the alcoholic to face his problem . . . We've made it necessary for him to tell lies, first to his wife and then to himself. We can never judge another person." From the day he went dry, for the rest of his days, he had innumerable opportunities to exemplify the pastoral concern toward alcoholics he urged upon the Church. His open recognition of his own drinking problem rendered him accessible to other alcoholics, especially clergy, and, even while he constantly remained, wherever he went, in contact with AA, receiving counsel and support, so simultaneously he took time to meet and help many, many other alcoholics.

A poignant instance of his sense of ministry in this regard concerns the Bishop of South Florida, Henry I. Louttit, whose charges of heresy against Pike eventuated in the censure of Pike by the House of Bishops in 1966. Bishop Louttit, whatever their theological differences or whatever their public disputes, shared with Bishop Pike the condition of alcoholism. It was a fact widely known in Louttit's own diocese, particularly among his clergy, since he on occasion appeared drunk in public and also on other occasions failed to make appearances because he was drunk. His problem with alcohol was common knowledge, as well, among his colleagues in the House of Bishops. But in both *his* diocese and in the House, the matter was treated with a certain kind of discretion, that is, it was overlooked or neglected. Instead of helping Bishop Louttit, most everyone privy to the issue humored him. It was, indeed, just that attitude—of humoring Henry—that caused Louttit's heresy charges to be uttered against Pike. One evening in September of 1966, Bishop Louttit, heavily intoxicated, decided to "do something" about Bishop Pike, who had first offended Louttit in the Sewanee incident years before and who had lately upset Louttit by a speech he had given at the Florida Presbyterian College in St. Petersburg. Louttit spent some hours that night telephoning other bishops, complaining to them against

Pike, and asking their concurrence in his complaints. Most did concur, if some only by way of humoring Henry because he was drunken. Many were aghast in the days that followed when Bishop Louttit published his charges with the names of those that he telephoned subscribed, without there having been any intervening formality. Henry had, certainly, been humored; he took the responses to his phone calls as authorizations for a heresy presentment. That done, the etiquette which prevailed among the bishops was that it was better—or easier—to prosecute Pike than to expose or embarrass Louttit. It is, of course, this episode that explains the incoherence of the first version of the Louttit presentment against Pike and why that was, as the controversy developed, withdrawn and a more carefully drafted set of charges substituted.

Pike soon learned of the heavily ambiguous origin of the charges against him. He was not angry. He was sorry—and, at some moments, he was amused. And he acceded to the concealment of the truth, for Louttit's sake, if not for those bishops who had carelessly or unwittingly become Louttit's cohorts. A nationally syndicated newspaper columnist found out about it, too, and was persuaded by Bishop Pike not to write an exposé. Early in 1967, when *The Bishop Pike Affair* was being researched and written, commissioned, as the book had been, to document the whole story of the heresy controversy, the authors encountered editorial interference from Pike at only one point: he was insistent that the relevance of Louttit's alcoholism to the instigation of charges be omitted. By the time the heresy issue was spent, at the Church's general convention in Seattle, practically all of the bishops knew the truth, but nobody told.

Pike was not being a gratuitous victim in this, so much as he was offering help, as a fellow alcoholic, to Louttit. Indeed, the two bishops—though in public vehement antagonists—maintained friendship and communication through it all, and found a deepened affinity, enabling them to meet and talk privately about their alcoholism with Pike trying to encourage his brother bishop to join him in AA. Louttit was Pike's chief accuser while, on another level of their relationship, Pike was Louttit's chief pastor.

Nor is the instance of Bishop Louttit the only citation of Jim Pike's outreach as a recovered alcoholic. This ministry of his continued until his death, embracing, as has been said, scores of clergy and churchpeople, as well as others, including another bishop whose alcoholism provoked such public scandal that he was removed from his jurisdiction. The fact that it was a bishop who had voted to censure Pike did not inhibit Pike's sympathy and help at a time when—as this bishop's wife wrote to Pike—"It is a sad but sorry truth that there are no people in the House of Bishops who care enough about one of their brothers."

The Acceptance of Suffering

One element which can be seen in James Pike's career is the movement in his life from the "ontological" to the "existential," a change gradual at first but which gained momentum as his interest in ecclesiastical authority waned. But also disclosed is a basic understanding of the meaning of human suffering which he once articulated in a sermon at St. John the Divine, on Palm Sunday, 1955:

> Suffering does not mean tragedy. Suffering is tragic when it is without meaning and without fruit. Suffering embitters and hurts . . . when one . . . cannot evoke from it new fulfillment . . . Jesus' Passion . . . is unique, not in the degree of suffering, but in the . . . power and meaning which came forth from that suffering.
>
> Especially is this so when one voluntarily enters suffering, as Jesus did . . . But even when the suffering comes upon us in a way we cannot avoid it, our acceptance of it can have a similar voluntary character, and thus lose its degradation, when we accept it as a means of grace and seek positively to use it in the service of God and our neighbor.

The transfiguration of suffering so abundantly verified in Pike's experience as an alcoholic and in his utilization of that to reach and care for other alcoholics did not spare his marriage to Esther, or their relationships with their children, from conflict and pain. The regeneration which was to issue finally from the hurt and humiliation of these relationships would await a different outcome, one which, in a sense, required the death of the marriage. There is no way to decipher, much less evaluate, cause or symptom in the history of the marriage and family life of Esther and Jim, though Pike, after he stopped drinking and as he said regained "clarity" was ready enough to accept principal responsibility for the end of their marriage and he candidly admitted the distress his alcoholism had occasioned. With his drunkenness, there had come redundant stormy confrontations, an agenda of recriminations harking back over nearly a quarter century, and a human impasse which the mere surrender of alcohol on his part could not affect. By the date Jim went dry, in 1964, Esther was committed to divorce. She had taken initiative to obtain one in 1962, consulting an attorney and announcing her intent to her husband. That prompted Jim to submit to psychoanalysis—and intensively, twice a week for nearly four years—and also to attempt to involve Esther with him in some mutual counseling with a clergyman-psychologist well acquainted with both of them. Esther was unmoved in her desire for divorce and though for a period in 1963 they together undertook marriage counseling with another clergyman, the outcome had become inevitable. Late in 1964, Esther, having retained legal counsel, required that the bishop no longer live in the Bishop's House. As sanction, she threatened to move out, with the children, an event, she recognized, which would likely receive scandalous publicity. It was agreed that the Bishop's House would continue to be used for official meetings and entertaining, with the understanding that Pike's access to the residence would be limited to such occasions and that he would arrive shortly before and depart immediately after each one. From that time, until he established quarters in Santa Barbara as a member of the Center for the Study of Democratic Institutions, Pike lived from a suitcase, stopping in hotels while traveling and when in San Francisco staying with, as he put it, "discreet friends." Esther did grant an exemption to this arrangment in the extenuating circumstances due to the death of their son Jim Jr., which coincided with Pike's return from his Cambridge sabbatical for the 1966 convention of the diocese. He was then assigned a remote room in the Bishop's House locked from access to Esther's quarters in the master bedroom.

A formal separation agreement, with financial arrangements which Pike found very burdensome and felt were somewhat vindictive, had been executed in May of 1965. Within the next year

or so, Pike relinquished his office as diocesan bishop, accepted appointment to the Center in Santa Barbara, and moved there,
where he received one visit from Esther prior to the divorce
decree, which was entered on July 25, 1967. Speaking of hyperactivity, it was in this same time—between the separation and
divorce—that the internal political opposition to Pike's episcopacy
galvanized within the diocese, that the heresy controversy reached
crescendo, that Pike virtually barnstormed the nation, that he
published three books, that he returned to some law work by
teaching at the University of California Law School at Berkeley,
that he confronted his son's suicide, that he became beguiled with
parapsychology, that he endured the death of Maren Bergrud,
that he plunged into affairs of the Center at Santa Barbara, that
his intense relationship with Mama was reasserted, that he met
and fell in love with Diane Kennedy, that he became disenchanted with the Episcopal Church, that he entered his obsession
with the origins of Christian faith and fixed his sight upon the
person of Jesus.

In any case, the marriage with Esther was dead: long since. In
addition to the dilatory implications of his alcoholism for the fate
of the marriage, there were earlier omens of its death, there were
even some adverse portents predating their marriage. Among the
latter was the terrible loneliness Jim felt in his separation from his
mother when he went to Yale Law School, compounded as that
was by their joint renunciation of the Roman Church and their
mutual sense of loss of a church relationship. He was vulnerable
at Yale and a single, casual homosexual episode there dramatized
that and partly prompted his eagerness to marry, as if marriage, by
definition, would assuage his loneliness and protect his person. In
his anxious situation the first marriage happened and practically
from the inception its fragile and immature basis made certain its
failure. When that marriage was dissolved, the same awful loneliness resumed, though by this time Pike was auspiciously launched
in a legal career in the nation's capital. In his long letters to
Mama he confided his loneliness by protesting it: "I've started
getting around a little—which is very good for the ol' morale," he
told his mother not long after the divorce from Jane Alvies. "Find
that once I get thinking along those lines I have more friends and
possible social connections than you would first realize when you

first find yourself single." He reported dutifully and in elaborate
detail to his mother about each girl he encountered and considered as a prospect for a new marriage, including his notice of
Esther Yanovsky, in a class he taught at George Washington University Law School: "Tomorrow evening we're having a nice little
dinner party—I'm having over that student I spoke to you about
—I finally decided to 'break the ice'—this is the first date but
we've talked at length on the phone a number of times. She's *very*
nice."

Once married to Esther, the earlier marriage haunted the new
marriage. There was the recurring hassle about the ecclesiastical
status of the first marriage when Pike became a postulant, when
he was appointed tutor at General Theological Seminary, and
when he was nominated as bishop. In the midst of those inquiries
there lurked a heavy temptation to idealize the second marriage
by contrast to the asserted nullity of the first, creating a continuing burden upon the marriage of Esther and Jim whenever their
marriage failed to fulfill its inflated image.

Yet in certain crucial respects the marital relationship was not
so different between Pike and his first and second wives. Within
the intense, exclusory relationship between Mama and Jim, both
wives were regarded as outsiders, as were, also, the successive husbands of Pearl. The letters between mother and son repeatedly
refer to their respective spouses as if the marriages are auxiliary to
the primary relationship. Pike was not always sensitive to this and,
early in his marriage to Esther, after Esther had taken on the correspondence with Pearl to which Jim appended footnotes and
postscripts, he expressed surprise that his mother complained of
neglect:

> I'm glad you wrote me. You know I wouldn't want you to feel
> neglected or that we were out of touch. I didn't know that you
> didn't feel that our joint letters were from me; I felt that they
> said just the same things and brought the same news and that it
> was fine for both of us to write to both of you and that that was
> the ideal . . . Yet . . . I'll try to find time to write in between
> times.

Through the years in Poughkeepsie and in New York City, the
intimacy of mother and son remained somewhat muted, if only

Two bishops, C. Edward Crawther
and James A. Pike, at the Center for the
Study of Democratic Institutions,
Santa Barbara, California, in 1967.

Wearing
the "Resistance button"
in spring 1968.

Above,
with Mrs. Diane Kennedy Pike

Below,
at the Qumran Caves
in the Holy Land, May 1968.

Wife and mother at grave site,
January 1970.

JAMES A. PIKE
BISHOP
(P.E.C.U.S.A.)

✠

BORN 1913
OKLAHOMA CITY, OKLA.
DIED 1969
JUDEAN WILDERNESS

WE HAVE THIS
TREASURE IN EARTHEN
VESSELS, TO SHOW THAT
THE TRANSCENDENT POWER
BELONGS TO GOD
AND NOT TO US
II COR. 4:7

"AND LIFE IS VICTORIOUS!"
MANDAEAN BOOK OF PRAYER

R. Scott Kennedy.

because of geographical distance, but when Pike became Bishop of California, Pearl moved to San Francisco, to be near him. By the time of the suicide of Jim Jr., with the marriage to Esther in profound distress and, what with other developments, his episcopacy in crisis, it was to Mama that Jim turned to express himself. Arriving back in Cambridge to finish his sabbatical, he wrote her:

> I have been busy as a bird dog from the minute of my return; but it's good "work therapy." Returning to Jim's and my flat was not depressing, as I feared; somehow the place evokes principally happy memories of our close companionship . . . [though]I do have rough moments; but . . . there haven't been many "blanks" for depressed thoughts.

A few days later, he sent Mama a redundant letter—"The days are passing quickly . . . it has left very little room in the mind for grief—which is just as well; of course, pleasant memories of things done and places been with Jim come to mind—and of course I am quite conscious of his being alive." Subsequently, when Pike moved to Santa Barbara, Pearl accompanied him and, for a while there, they shared the same apartment. That proved to be, perchance, a little too intense or—on account of Maren Bergrud— impracticable, and for the rest of the time he lived in Santa Barbara, Pearl was quartered elsewhere.

Related both to the special intimacy of mother and son and to the way in which the issues of the first marriage haunted the second was Pike's eagerness to find a wife who also served as working colleague. Both Jane and Esther were law students. He had found Jane, however, inadequate to assignments that he gave her in connection with his legal work. Esther, however, was more than satisfactory in this role, and, while Jim was in the Navy and pursuing seminary studies, she looked after his interest in the law firm, specifically the highly demanding technical work necessary for the services on civil procedure and OPA regulations which the firm published. Esther was different from the stereotype helpmate and something other than the well-known, self-effacing woman standing behind every successful man; theirs was closer to a professional relationship. This feature of their marriage gradually changed over the years. While Pike was dean, Esther was his partner in the network television show, the ideas for those productions often were hers not his; they planned at various times joint writing projects though none got implemented; in California she was active enough in his administration to become tagged, sometimes in ridicule, as "Mrs. Bishop Pike," as has been noticed. Eventually, this peculiar aspect of their relationship turned inside out and Esther's role became more competitor than colleague, she was more threat to him than help, she was an obstruction rather than an embellishment to his vocation. "A pattern developed," Pike once confided, "of my virtually procuring Esther's consent for any policy or administrative decision." He was humiliated by the arrangement: "If the decision emerged out of a group, before letting it be settled, I would excuse myself, go to a phone in another room, and 'clear' with her; I later learned that this routine had been surmised by my colleagues." Yet, for a long time, he acquiesced in order to "save conflict." Related, in Jim's recollection, was Esther's "long-standing habit of impugning my motives, particularly distressing in regard to my involvements with causes which were very much engaging my energies and feelings and as to which there was hostile opposition from people inside and/or outside the Church." In the last two years of his incumbency which were otherwise so tempestuous, the bishop found Esther's attitude secretive and subversive. She had sided with his enemies and detractors. If at the outset of the marriage she had been a partner, at the end of it she was his emasculator. "Involved," he remembered, "was . . . the real or imagined basis of a power over me or, to put it more neutrally, way of relating to me . . . and a real dislike." Esther's sanction was the threat of publicity about the death of the marriage and the scandal likely to be imputed to it, but, as Pike learned, the maintenance of pretense was more intolerable.

Scandal did not have to be fantasized. There had been infidelities in the marriage, going back to when Pike was dean of New York, though on Jim's part not before that, despite Esther's vehement accusations. If Esther's suspicions were magnified as to time and place, opportunity and number, they were nonetheless justified in principle. Withal who can say that marital infidelity is greater if there be a single episode or if there be many misadventures? Pike did take some elaborate precautions in the situation, for instance in having a private telephone line installed the number of which he made available only to women he encountered from time to time. On the other hand, after Esther had evicted him from the Bishop's House, he did not always stay, contrary to his own words, with "discreet friends." Sometimes he lived with Maren Bergrud and sometimes she traveled with him on speaking tours. In public circumstances he would naïvely identify Maren as his staff associate. Maren was largely incompetent as an assistant in any of Pike's interests, in part because she was frequently in a state of emotional tumult or disoriented by her use of assorted pills and potions. And rather than showing discretion she openly campaigned for the divorce from Esther and her marriage to Jim. She intervened most heavily in the aftermath of the suicide of Jim Jr., sharing the apartment in Cambridge, and importuning the man she professed to love with her occult and spiritualist nonsense. Her sanction, as she sought to possess Pike, was the threat of her own suicide, repeatedly, ritually invoked and, finally, enacted in desperate confrontation in which Pike's alternatives seemed to be his own destruction or her self-destruction.

Meanwhile, the marriage was rendered the more melancholy by Pike having become impotent with Esther. This bothered him much and he sought professional counseling about it and apparently received advice to indulge in extramarital sexual relationships. The problem of his impotence had been foreshadowed earlier in the marriage. Pike recalled, before he died, that the marriage had originated not only in his eagerness for an "abiding relationship" but in Esther's "rebound" from breaking off a relationship with a "man she loved." They decided to marry on New Year's day after Pearl Harbor and, under the uncertainties of the war affecting how long they might be able to be together in the same place, determined to be married right away, within the month of January 1942. As the appointed date approached, however, "Esther cooled off" and proposed to postpone the wedding. Pike resisted this and the marriage happened on January 29, 1942. "Anyway," Pike has written, "the day we married was a very unhappy one for her. The General Counsel for the O.P.A. had given me a week for a honeymoon and we took the train late that afternoon for Miami, whence we were to fly to Havana. That evening in our compartment on the train she did not want intimacy because she didn't 'feel well.' " After the putative honeymoon,

Esther informed Jim that she would continue full time in legal editorial work and carry a schedule in night law school so that having children was precluded. Nevertheless, a daughter—Catherine—was born only to be followed by a miscarriage, in what the doctor had told them was a double pregnancy, in September of 1944. Both attached guilt to the miscarriage. "We felt and feel very sad about it—and what is worse—we feel that we are not blameless," Esther confessed to Pearl, while Jim, in a separate letter to Mama, echoed, "It was a rather chastening experience; we feel that in a measure it is a judgment on our trying to do so much."

Jim had been anxious to have children, the more so because of Esther's reluctance; he thought that this would be a bond in the marriage, settling its ambiguous beginnings and strengthening it where it was fragile. Four children—Catherine, James Jr., Constance, Christopher—were born to the Pikes. There were good times when the children were young, especially when the whole family was together in summers, in the fifties, at Wellfleet on Cape Cod. Yet, even as their father had had slight opportunity to know his father, who had died when Jim was a baby, these children had too few chances to relate to their father. Pike's increasing celebrity, his successive obsessions, his hyperactivity, his incipient alcoholism, his frequent absenteeism, the unhappiness and, later, the unconcealed hostility between mother and father, the peculiar confusion of roles between parents—all these—and more —hurt the children. If it be concluded that they knew Pike too little as a father, it might as much be said that in reality they had *two* fathers: Jim and, as surrogate father, Esther. More than anything else, the crisis which enveloped Jim Jr. in his late adolescence—his involvement in the "hippie" scene in San Francisco, his use of drugs, his apprehension about homosexuality, his fantasy about his mother as a masculine image, his incredulity about the love of others for him, his self-rejection—exposed the poignant circumstances of each of the Pike offspring. At last, the eldest son's cry became the father's urgent concern. Pike made a prodigious effort to listen to Jim Jr., to understand him, to achieve communication, especially in the interlude they shared in England. It was, somehow, not enough to obviate the boy's suicide.

Nor was Pike spared retribution of the surviving children. Shortly after the divorce from Esther, there was Connie's apparently feigned attempt at suicide. Perhaps more emphatic, as a sign of the depth of estrangement the children felt, was the fact that, following Pike's death in Judea, Christopher lent himself to a sect of the Jesus movement, wherein he was exhibited as a convert—the son of the notorious renegade bishop propitiant for the sins and omissions of his father.

The marriage died. The children began lives elsewhere. Esther re-entered San Francisco society and would eventually marry again. In the aftermath of the divorce, Pike's anguish did not fester. Suffering did not dehumanize Pike. He did not waste himself in self-recrimination. Nor did he become angry with God. He offered his suffering to others as pastoral care, particularly to fellow clergy in marital troubles or to those alienated from the Church, to those, as he put it, "in religious transition."

He met and loved and married Diane Kennedy. Jim was rejuvenated. A third wife: he came to regard Diane as his first wife. The new life they shared had its inception in the generosity of forgiveness and self-acceptance. That Palm Sunday sermon in 1955 was premonitive, when Dean Pike had declared:

> What we should attribute to God is the grace and illumination which turns what for some people would be a source of tragedy and cynicism into an avenue of witness to God and of healing to men. Thus, glory and joy have often enough shown through pain and suffering that men have even thanked God for suffering.

The Burden of Celebrity

These crises, personal and pastoral, affecting Pike's marriage to Esther and his relations with his children, were much compounded by the phenomenon of his celebrity. The subject is at once mysterious and complicated, too entangled with personality and with talent to distinguish cause and consequence readily. Yet some aspects of Pike's celebrity seem clear: certainly the incessant demands upon his attention and time as a public person competed with his ability and opportunity to relate to his own children. His own description of his sabbatical is ironic as he reports a withering array of interests and activities as a respite:

> The relative quiet of Cambridge was obviously welcome. My older son, Jim, who is with me, started right away in the Cambridgeshire College of Arts and Technology . . . We were fortunate to find a small but modern third floor "walk-up flat" . . . In addition to the business of living . . . my time is divided between study, attendance at lectures, dialogue and some selected opportunities at communicating developing thoughts . . . I pretty much limited acceptance of speaking invitations . . . e.g., the theological societies of Oxford University and Trinity College, Dublin, "Agnostics Anonymous" of London University . . . some TV and radio dialogues, the Wells and Lincoln Theological Colleges, and addresses at chapel at the colleges of the University . . . I have been invited into "Soundings," the Divinity Faculty group which began the current "theological revolution" . . . and the "D" Society, concerned with the relationship of current cosmological theories and theology, and I am participating in a debate at Emmanuel College . . .
>
> As to lectures, there is an abundance of riches. It took real discipline to limit myself to the courses most relevant . . . *The Logic of Theological Statements . . . Judaism at the Time of Christ, Christology—A Study of Method,* and *The History of Christian Doctrine in the 2nd and 3rd Centuries* . . . [A]s to study, I am reading avidly, not only in these specific areas, but also contemporary theological thought with special reference to Christology and comparative western and Oriental religious thought . . .

In the same letter from Cambridge, he also reported that he did many of the household chores in the flat he shared with Jim Jr. (and Maren Bergrud), including washing the dishes.

There is an apocryphal story, still occasionally recited within the precincts of the New York cathedral, which expresses the issue of Pike's celebrity in connection with his family. When Pike was dean, it was not unusual for tourists and visitors at the cathedral to loiter around in hope of a glimpse of and greeting from the famous cleric. Pike was aware of this and when he passed through public places of the cathedral he was alert to notice such folk. One day, the story goes, he arrived, in the accustomed hustle, by taxicab, at the cathedral gate, where a cluster of people were gathered. Taking them to be celebrity seekers, as he passed them he paused momentarily to shake hands. The cluster was his own family, Esther and the four children.

The burden of Pike's celebrity was central in his confrontations with opponents within his diocese and also in coping with his detractors in the House of Bishops. The anti-Pike factions in California were incensed by the very idea of the Church embroiled in controversy: publicity about finishing the cathedral construction might be acceptable, but publicity linking the Church with issues like legalized abortion or the campaign against Proposition 14, or associating the Church with Martin Luther King, Jr., or Saul Alinsky, was much more than they could either comprehend or tolerate. They became determined to put a stop to it. This opposition to Pike's leadership remained undercover and frustrated for some time, but finally, in 1965, a delegation of wealthy and influential laypeople, including three corporation executives, uttered an ultimatum to the bishop that he "would remain silent on public questions and stay out of social action involvements—with specific reference to race, housing, braceros [Mexican day laborers] and community organization . . . or else . . . be cut off at the pockets." Meanwhile, in the House of Bishops, a comparable climax came when the maneuver developed to censure Pike instead of submitting him to trial. The heavy wording of the censure resolution likewise aimed to quiet him. It is the notoriety attached to Pike's utterances, the "tone and manner of much of what Bishop Pike has said"—rather than the content of his views—that so greatly agitated the censuring bishops. It was this connotation of the censure which prompted Bishop Daniel Corrigan during the debate to protest the intent of the censure resolution to condemn Bishop Pike "in some deep sense to death." Paradoxically, the reason for the scheme to substitute the censure of Pike for a heresy trial—later openly acknowledged by the principal architect of this strategy, Bishop Bayne—was the fear of adverse publicity in which the Episcopal Church would suffer a medieval image.

Throughout the tumult of his episcopacy, both at home in his diocese and at large on the national scene, Pike was slow to recognize how provocative his celebrity had become to others. He made, as has been mentioned, a sustained effort to be consci-

entious in his office, relying with notable consistency upon Scripture and ancient churchly tradition in both the conception and
execution of his administration, and he sometimes fretted that he
was too cautious. Furthermore, by the time he had become
bishop, he was enough accustomed to celebrity that he took it
more or less for granted; he was not particularly self-conscious
about it; it represented a talent or gift which he accepted and
which he regarded as an asset in his forensic vocation in the
Church. That was demonstrated in his tenure as dean of New
York, and it startled and mystified Pike when he finally realized,
during the censure session at Wheeling, that the acclaim and
pride engendered by his celebrity while Dean Pike had somehow
been transposed into envy and animosity for him as Bishop Pike.

If Pike himself was unsophisticated about his own fame, it was
never a mystery for Mama. Pearl was not troubled by it from the
time of the Oklahoma State Fair "best baby" honors. She
regarded her son's celebrity as virtually his birthright. On the
other hand, this same phenomenon was an enormous burden in
the marriage to Esther, and, during the prolonged anguish which
eventuated in divorce, Esther repeatedly used Pike's notoriety as a
sanction against him by threatening to void the privacy of the
dying marriage altogether.

The extreme example of the burden of celebrity for Pike was
the murderous ridicule to which he was subjected by one Frank
M. Brunton, an elderly retired Episcopal priest, resident in
Phoenix, Arizona. Fr. Brunton had his active ministry in South
Florida—under Bishop Louttit—prior to his retirement in Arizona.
For years, Brunton composed rhymed verse, scurrilous and defamatory, which he dispatched to Bishop Pike every week and which,
at times, he circulated elsewhere in the Church. Though the out-
put of Brunton's doggerel was vast, a single excerpt documents
the pathological antipathy this aged man bore toward Pike:

> An evil man is bishop pike—
> The Anti-Christ as many say—
> He preaches what the devils like—
> On each and every passing day—
> God's angel chorus sighs and weeps—
> And how our Lord must suffer too—
> This pike may soon be gone for keeps—
> Praise God!—If only it is true!

In a note accompanying the above item, Fr. Brunton confided to Bishop Pike that he had been saying "for years" a prayer for "news of your expulsion,—or your death."

Any public person must endure a quantity of criticism, including some unfair or malicious, and Pike received these regular communications from Brunton without complaint to Brunton or to his ecclesiastical superiors until Brunton began to implement his hostility in other ways. In the summer of 1965, while the matter of ordaining Mrs. Edwards was pending, Brunton drafted a petition to the House of Bishops charging Bishop Pike with heresy, gathered signatures from fourteen clergy in the Phoenix vicinity, and forwarded it to the Bishop of Arizona, Joseph Harte, for transmission to the House. The charges, uttered without evidence, accused Pike of repudiating the Virgin Birth, denying the Trinity, "the empty tomb," the bodily Resurrection and Ascension, of failing to celebrate the Feast of the Annunciation, and of intending to ordain a deaconess. Bishop Harte, whom Brunton later reported had praised him as a "valiant warrior for the Church Faith," forwarded the Arizona charges to the House, and they subsequently became a basis for an inquest into Pike's views on doctrine conducted at the meeting of the bishops at Glacier Park, Montana, in the fall of 1965.

Subsequently, in the same year, Bishop Pike undertook a visit, during his sabbatical in England, to the Diocese of Matabeleland in Rhodesia, that jurisdiction being the so-called companion of the Diocese of California under that program of the Anglican Communion, conceived largely by Bishop Bayne, by which dioceses in different parts of the world were yoked for "mutual responsibility and interdependence." Bishop Kenneth J. F. Skelton of Matabeleland had paid an official visit to San Francisco in 1964, and Pike took advantage of his being overseas the next year to reciprocate. The mission was aborted, however, by the intervention of the rebel apartheid regime of Rhodesian Premier Ian Smith. Bishop Pike was held incommunicado for several hours and then expelled from Rhodesia. It was later discovered that Bishop Pike's visit to Rhodesia had been preceded by communications from Fr. Brunton to Prime Minister Smith which, among other charges, labeled Pike "a notorious racial agitator." It was apparently on the basis of this intervention by Brunton that Pike was detained and then required to leave Rhodesia. Shortly after this episode, Bishop Pike returned to San Francisco to report directly to his diocesan convention about his attempt to visit the companion diocese in Africa and it was coincident with that same trip that his son's suicide occurred. Fr. Brunton, upon hearing news of the boy's death, it will be recalled, dispatched the message: "Thank God for one less pike."

That condolence from Brunton, plus his Rhodesian intervention which had both obstructed Pike's official duties and endangered Bishop Skelton as well as Bishop Pike, added to Brunton's boast of instigation of the Arizona "heresy" charges, broke Pike's tolerance of the abusive poetaster, and he complained to Bishop Harte, within whose jurisdiction Brunton lived, and to Bishop Louttit, under whose canonical authority Brunton retained his clerical status, about the importunities and aggressions in which Brunton persisted. Harte ignored the matter; Louttit said that he had sometimes admonished Brunton to refrain from circulating his defamatory material and, though Brunton had not heeded him, Louttit thought no further action appropriate against this "good and elderly priest."

Despite continued, manifold outrageous provocations of Fr. Brunton, and though evidence was uncovered linking Brunton to the John Birch Society, Pike did not press the question of ecclesiastical discipline and did not pursue the appropriate civil remedies. He bore Brunton's assaults as a cost of his convictions and his celebrity and that acceptance of the matter points to the generally straightforward attitude Pike took toward his fame and publicity. At best he received his celebrity as a gift or talent to be utilized, not for his own glory or aggrandizement, but to gain a hearing for his apologetic, initially for the Church, then, as time passed, for the gospel. He saw no reason to hide light under a bushel. He understood how inextricably communication in modern American circumstances had become implicated in the means of publicity and how his own notoriety furnished access to multitudes that might otherwise never hear a voice expressing the concerns of Church and faith. So he used his celebrity to publish his message—there was throughout his career astonishingly little publicity that magnified Pike as a personality or indulged his image—and he lent his access to publicity to others—as when Dr. Blake sought the patronage of Bishop Pike's hospitality to announce his church union proposal, or as when Dean Francis Sayre of the Washington cathedral exchanged pulpits with Dean Pike of the New York cathedral and each then preached in the other's pulpit to rebuke McCarthyism, or as when Pike served Bishop Donegan as a kind of foil on social issues throughout his tenure as dean by furnishing public stands in the name of the Church but sparing the bishop the flak.

The most memorable episode in which Pike allowed his celebrity to be used by others to dramatize the Christian social witness is the Sewanee controversy. The University of the South at Sewanee, Tennessee, is owned by the Episcopal dioceses of ten Southern states. The trustees of the university had in 1952 refused admission of black students to the School of Theology and that had precipitated the resignations of the dean and eight faculty. Early the next year the trustees, resisting pressures for an urgent review of their racist policy, appointed a new dean and replaced some of the resigned faculty, creating an impasse, meeting boycott with lockout. Meanwhile, however, the university had decided to confer an honorary degree upon Dean Pike and to invite him to be the baccalaureate preacher at commencement in June of 1953. In February of 1953, Dean Pike announced publicly that he declined the "degree in white divinity." The day following his refusal, Pike received a telegram from the graduating class of the School of Theology which read: "Congratulations on your defense of Christ's Church. Faith can move 'mountains.'" An Indian word for "mountains" is Sewanee. And so the mountain was moved. The deadlock was broken, and the trustees at their next meeting reversed their policy and, in 1954, a black student was admitted. The shadow of the Sewanee incident was a long one. Bishop Louttit, for example, was a trustee of the University of the South at the time and he was incensed about Pike's public exposure of the scandal. He had assured Pike that eventually the institution would be integrated and had been eager that Pike accept the honorary degree as a way of embellishing Sewanee's image. Other bishops, mainly from the Southern dioceses, admitted that their votes in opposition to Pike's election as bishop had been influenced by his refusal of the Sewanee invitation. Those who have supposed that the episode shows Pike to have been precipitous or a publicity seeker willing to embarrass the Church to gain a headline are mistaken, however. From the time of the faculty resignations, Pike had been in communication with those seeking to integrate the University of the South through his former tutor, Howard Johnson, who had become a faculty member at Sewanee. It is out of that connection that the idea of Pike's declination as a strategy to break the impasse that had developed emerged. But the situation was more one which illustrates Pike's willingness to have his celebrity used than one which betrays self-serving inclinations on his part. As Johnson wrote, in the midst of the controversy, to Pike: "We lay many burdens on you. You are good never to complain. The energy and time many people put into complaining about burdens, you put into carrying them."

Bishop Pike's generosity with his name and with his access to publicity meant that he was frequently sought after by those with causes and concerns which might benefit, as did the deposed Sewanee faculty, from the public exposure which identification with Pike could furnish. But, at the same time, this rendered him vulnerable to exploitation by those with motivations more ambiguous than his own. He was cruelly deceived by the purported mediumship of Arthur Ford, and he was set up for that abuse in the famous televised séance in Toronto where communication with his dead son was reported by an overeager journalist. And, for another example, the relationship which he allowed with the Reverend Fred Morris, erstwhile rector of St. Thomas Episcopal Church on Fifth Avenue, New York City, was parasitical. For many successive years, Bishop Pike came to that church to preach at noontime weekday services during Lent. His visits are remembered as among the rare modern occasions upon which St. Thomas's nave would be packed with people; his remarks would always receive coverage in the New York City press. Morris delighted in the notoriety of these events, and pointedly boasted about the attention Pike's presence brought, until, that is, the censure happened. At that, Morris wrote and paid for the publication of a booklet entitled "Bishop Pike: Ham, Heretic, or Hero" which was widely distributed at the 1967 general convention of the Church in Seattle, where the heresy controversy reached a denouement. This effort of Morris, who had so long gloried in the free prominence which Pike brought to him, to disassociate himself from the bishop, now censured, was later implemented further

after news of the Toronto séance by Morris' public withdrawal of
the customary invitation for Pike to preach at St. Thomas the
next season. This time Morris garnered as much publicity in repudiating Pike as he formerly received from association with him.

Still, if Arthur Ford gravely importuned Pike, or if the Reverend
Morris was crudely opportunistic toward Pike, it must be acknowledged that Pike himself was almost incredibly naïve for a person
of his experience and longevity in the public eye. One might have
expected him to be wary or cynical, but in truth he was neither. A
young priest who accompanied Pike to Selma observed: "I was
right there with him. He's childlike! And I was delighted with
him. When we first got there he was clapping his hands with the
crowd, saying 'Amen' with them . . . and then later singing 'We
Shall Overcome' with them."

Furthermore, Pike constantly attributed high motives to his enemies and detractors, minimizing or overlooking evidence to the
contrary. Throughout the heresy hassle, he supposed that his opponents were concerned with substantive theological issues, even
though, by the time of the Wheeling censure, it was clear that
factors of envy of personality, and of church politics were far more
influential than matters of belief. Thus there is a special poignancy in the characterization in the censure resolution of Pike as a
"publicity seeker" when it is taken into account that Bishop Louttit had made elaborate arrangements with the Associated Press for
publicity for his heresy allegations *before* the charges were made
known to Bishop Pike, or that Bishop Bayne, who became the
chief strategist in the handling of the whole affair at the Church's
national headquarters, had engaged a professional poll to ascertain
that a heresy trial would have a negative impact on the image of
the Episcopal Church and later had retained new public relations
counsel to handle publicity for the church establishment in the
controversy—a step which resulted in the exclusion of views favor-
able to Bishop Pike from the "Today" show on network television. That same poignancy is the more emphatic when it is
recalled that the known instances of Pike calculatedly acting to
influence publicity involved his attempts to stop it, as his attempt
to suppress news of Louttit's alcoholism in its relevance to the utterance of the heresy charges, or his effort to exclude any imputa-
tion of homosexuality in relation to his son's suicide, or his re-

quest to various media correspondents to publish nothing about the Toronto séance—an appeal which itself shows Pike's naïveté and which was in fact dishonored.

If anything, Pike's lack of cynicism or self-indulgence in connection with his public notoriety was modified by caution. He gradually became more and more concerned to have precedent in Scripture and ancient church tradition for his conduct of his office as bishop and for his confessional views. His yearning to study was part of that. His assignment of an aide to safeguard against overexposure in the media was pertinent, too. This meant that, as United Press International once put it, "The maverick bishop sometimes shocks his audiences by being less radical than they expected him to be." While at the outset of his public career his outspokenness, especially on social issues, brought him attention and fame, as time passed this was reversed and his celebrity was sufficient to bring controversy to the issues he bespoke, until at last it was the fact of his celebrity itself which was controversial.

Matters of Conscience

Whatever their medieval purpose, whatever their status in Puritan America, heresy trials in this century, in this country, have had little dogmatic substance or doctrinal significance. A reason for this is that the American denominational ethos has facilitated schism and the formation of new sects, spun off from the established churches, in circumstances where confessional disputes otherwise might have issued in heresy proceedings. The theologically deviant have had an option of quitting a denomination and organizing as another church. Schismatical sectarianism has been more expedient than resort to ecclesiastical sanctions against the heretical. At the same time this fact has tended to moderate the historic churches, making them somewhat more hospitable to a diversity of interpretation and conviction than otherwise might have been the case.

Those heresy trials which have taken place in modern American church history have, generally, only ostensibly involved theological quarrels. For the most part, they have been covers for mul-

tifarious issues but tenuously connected to church doctrine *per se*.
Heresy proceedings have had, instead, much to do with mere ecclesiastical discipline, with church politics and power struggles
among factions or personality conflicts among dignitaries, with
the maintenance of incumbent authority against threats of dis-
sidence or non-compliance, with transgressions of ecclesiastical etiquette, with attempts to repress or discourage premature or otherwise unacceptable social and political views. The trial in 1924 of
the retired Episcopal Bishop of Arkansas—William Montgomery
Brown—is virtually the classic case. It was instigated because of
widespread opinion that Brown was a Marxist, though he was
charged with not adhering literally to the Apostles' Creed. There
is a similar background to the celebrated trial, in 1906, of the Reverend Algernon Crapsey, who quaintly styled himself "the last of
the heretics."

This was also true of the heresy charges thrice leveled against
Bishop Pike, in 1961 by a group of clergy from Georgia, in 1965
by Father Brunton and his Arizona cohorts, in 1966 by Bishop
Louttit and the bishops he had solicited (See Appendix). These
recurring allegations of Pike's doctrinal heterodoxy furnished a
façade for a congestion of other items—political, psychological,
personal—which had roused antipathies and animosities against
Pike. Among them were the long-lingering objections to his second marriage, the aggravated memories of the Sewanee episode,
resentment that he had been elected bishop and envy of his
successes as bishop, concern over his hyperactivity, jealousies provoked by his celebrity, doubts about his loyalty to the fraternity of
bishops. The question of heresy, in a generic or definitive sense,
had little to do with the charges against Pike or with any
demands for his trial or with the ways in which these charges and
demands were dealt with in the Episcopal Church, even though
the word "heresy" captured headlines, distracted church leaders
and diverted the laity, and pre-empted public attention for several
hectic years. Just how remote theology tends to be in modern
heresy proceedings was verified in the Bishop Pike affair by the
fact that when the controversy reached a climax, during the deliberation in the House of Bishops in which Pike was censured—not
for his confessional views but for his rhetoric in expressing his convictions—it was ruled that substantive theological discussion or

evidentiary material as to the scope and content of Anglican belief could not be heard.

Yet if the heresy tumult was not about theology for most of his peers, it was squarely about that for Bishop Pike. Among all the characters on the scene, Pike was steadfast, and practically solitary, in seeking to address issues of doctrine and belief, as his profuse, redundant writings and his frenetic sermonizing and speaking while the heresy charges were pending show. He barnstormed the nation, agitating tens of thousands of people, both inside and outside the Church, about rudimentary theological questions. He capitalized the heresy accusations as an opportunity to teach and preach, edify and confront, discuss and debate. "I know that people come to hear 'the heretic' partly out of curiosity," he told a reporter. "But I look upon this as a golden opportunity to communicate with a lot more people than I might reach otherwise." This was vintage Pike speaking. Whether as spokesman for "smooth orthodoxy" or putative heretic, he was vocationally consistent; he was Pike the apologist, the advocate, the forensic theologian.

The theological task was integral to the vocation of a bishop, as Pike saw it, and as, indeed, the rite of consecration in the Book of Common Prayer affirmed, and so it was a matter of conscience for Pike. To perform that duty and function of a bishop to nurture the belief of the people of the Church, and to defend the faith in the world, required, as an elementary necessity, that a bishop be informed theologically and able to communicate meaningfully. The mere recital of venerable or familiar creeds, the words of which were void of comprehension or credibility, was not enough. A bishop could not countenance or encourage superstition or ignorance in the place of intelligent faith. From the outset of his episcopacy he had urged more serious and studious attention to theology upon his fellow bishops and many of them had been irked by his proddings. In 1960, when the House of Bishops convened in Dallas, for instance, a pedantic and ponderous pastoral letter had been uttered declaring the Episcopal Church "irrevocably committed to the historic creeds . . . as an indispensible norm for the Christian Faith." The rigidity and quaintness of the Dallas pastoral disturbed a number of other bishops in addition to Pike, but they were denied opportunity to debate it and Pike mentioned—premonitively—to the House that if the letter were adopted he could be found heretical. That was the first occasion in which the thought that Pike might be a heretic was publicly uttered.

One irony in the heresy controversy that subsequently engulfed Bishop Pike and the Episcopal Church was that if Pike had not been a bishop, and a celebrity, and so energetic an apologist, but, instead, had been a theological scholar or a seminary professor, upholding the same confessional views, there is scant likelihood that he would have suffered accusation as a heretic. There were, after all, academic theologians publishing, coincident with the heresy scandal, far more novel or radical propositions than Pike ever contemplated. In fact, Bishop Pike endured the condescension of some of the so-called "death of God" theologians because, in their view, he was so conventional and orthodox. Whether this challenge from the theological left influenced Pike to move in the direction of scholarship in his sabbatical venture and, then, by resigning his jurisdiction and joining the Center for the Study of Democratic Institutions at Santa Barbara as "theologian in residence" or "worker priest in the purple," as he styled it, and, in turn, to pursue with increasing zeal and concentration the study of Christian origins and of the figure of the historical Jesus is not certain. But it is clear that he was so prompted, in part, by the fierce reluctance of his episcopal colleagues to take theology seriously and to deal with theology contemporaneously.

To some extent, therefore, Pike welcomed the heresy charges as furnishing a forum in which the Church's confessional stance could be examined and renewed and through which many people might be theologically edified. Whatever his personal fate, that would be a gain.

The theological encounter which Pike anticipated as an opportunity in the heresy controversy never happened in the House of Bishops. Once the Louttit charges were publicized, the effort of the Episcopal Church establishment was to obviate a trial by settling upon a political solution. The Presiding Bishop, John Hines, appealed to Bishop Louttit and the other presenters to wait until the bishops met at Wheeling, West Virginia, before insisting upon "final action against Jim Pike." "I hope," Hines wrote Louttit on September 26, 1966, "some other means can be worked out by which what you wish to achieve can be achieved and without the spat of emotions which is bound to be forthcoming." Shortly thereafter, Bishop Hines appointed an Ad Hoc Committee to report to the House at Wheeling, Bishop Louttit having agreed to hold back his presentment until that time. The committee was chaired by Angus Dun, retired Bishop of Washington, a patriarchal figure in the Episcopal Church, the bishop who had ordained Pike in 1946 and who, in 1960, had presided over the committee which wrote the Dallas pastoral letter. Dun was, by then, both venerable and partially infirm by reason of deafness, and served as figurehead of the Ad Hoc Committee. Its real presence was Bishop Stephen F. Bayne, Jr., then second-ranking Episcopal Church prelate, who emerged as chief advocate and architect of a political disposition of the Pike case. The price exacted for holding the presentment in abeyance was membership on the Dun committee of three bishops (including Bishop Louttit) who had subscribed to the charges against Pike. Pike, at the same time, was not only not named to the committee, no bishop representing him was included upon it. Moreover, despite his repeated requests, Pike was not allowed to appear before the committee to state his side of the dispute precipitated by the Louttit charges which the committee was convened to examine. Thus, as the Wheeling session of the House of Bishops gathered, on October 27, 1966, it finally dawned on Bishop Pike that the heresy hassle was not diversifying or enlightening theological discourse within the Church, at least among the Episcopal Church hierarchy. Wheeling was a political event in which, according to the scenario which had been projected by Bishop Bayne, Pike's accusers and detractors were to be appeased by the spectacle of Pike's demeanment and a heresy trial was to be, for the sake of the Church's image, avoided. Bishop Pike was censured at Wheeling. The resolution read, in part:

> [W]e feel bound to reject the tone and manner of much that Bishop Pike has said as being offensive and highly disturbing . . . And we disassociate ourselves from many of his utterances as being irresponsible on the part of one holding the office and trust that he shares with us.
>
> His writing and speaking on profound realities with which Christian faith and worship are concerned are too often marred by caricatures of treasured symbols and at the worst, by cheap vulgarizations of great expressions of the faith.

If Pike was shocked and dismayed by the personal harshness of the censure, he was bewildered and appalled that the whole process by which it had been engineered could happen without his being afforded elementary due process, that is, without his having occasion to confront his accusers and to make his own response to them. And, hence, while the vote was being tabulated at Wheeling, the focus of the heresy squabble shifted in Pike's mind from theological forensics to due process of law, from confessional disputations or doctrinal rhetoric to whether or not an accused person could obtain a fair hearing in the Church. For Pike, the issue of due process was as much one of vocation and conscience as that of the theological task of bishops.

Bishop Pike should not have been shocked or surprised at the humiliation at Wheeling of being excoriated without ever having had opportunity to face his accusers and speak for himself before the Dun committee. Wheeling was an escalation of the similar treatment he had received at the time the Arizona charges were pending, in 1965, and of his experience at the infamous secret meeting at O'Hare Airport in 1966, which turned out to be a prelude to the Louttit heresy charges. The Presiding Bishop, in execution of a resolution at the St. Louis general convention, had appointed a Theological Committee prior to the 1965 meeting of the House of Bishops held at Glacier Park, Montana. The committee was chaired by Bishop Richard Emrich of Michigan, and as members had Bishops Angus Dun, Stephen Bayne, Jonathan Sherman, John Klein, and James Pike. It was to this committee that the Arizona heresy charges were referred by the House. Thereupon, Bishop Pike was "excused" from its deliberations. Bishop Emrich rejected several requests of Pike that he be allowed to answer the charges and it was only after the committee had prepared a report that he was summoned. When he appeared, he was directed by Emrich to read the report, which has never been made public, but which Pike recalled contained a general affirmation of the value of theological inquiry, set aside the Arizona charges, distinguished between official church teaching and the views of any one person, and accused Pike of "self-aggrandizement," "publicity seeking," and "unilateral teaching." That session was terminated without Bishop Pike having a hearing. Ultimately, at Montana, a compromise happened which struck the censorious paragraph from the report on the condition that Pike reaffirm to the House of Bishops his "loyalty to the Doctrine, Discipline, and Worship of the Episcopal Church." Afterward, Bishop Pike deeply regretted consenting to this action, feeling that it was a denigration of himself and an evasion of the issues of theology and of due process which had surfaced with the Arizona charges.

When early the next year an article appeared in *Look* magazine by Christopher Wren, entitled "Search for a Space-Age God," which discussed various "new" theologians but focused particularly on Bishop Pike, then in the midst of his Cambridge sabbatical, there was an uproar among the bishops. Many of them apparently had construed the Montana "loyalty oath" as a promise of silence on Pike's part and interpreted the Wren article as a betrayal by Pike. Their agitation was such that the Presiding Bishop summoned a secret session on March 5, 1966, of the metropolitans of the Church, that is, the bishops designated as presidents of the nine provinces into which the several dioceses are regionally grouped. Bishop Pike was also asked to appear, necessitating, for him, a twenty-four-hour-round-trip London to Chicago to London journey. The meeting, at a motel adjacent to O'Hare International Airport, initially convened without Bishop Pike, he having been instructed to await the summons of the metropolitans. After about two hours, the call came and Pike was admitted to their presence. The burden of the confrontation, as Pike remembered it, consisted in the main of nit-picking criticisms of the journalism of *Look* magazine, rather than any inquest into Bishop Pike's beliefs. The implication was very heavy, however, that Pike had somehow, through the publication of the *Look* article, failed to honor the Montana oath. Pike, in the circumstances, agreed to write a letter to the editors of *Look* in clarification of *his* convictions upon the agreement that the same letter would be circulated to all members of the House of Bishops. Upon arriving back in England, the bishop wrote a six-page single-spaced letter which he dispatched on March 8. He had expressed skepticism to the metropolitans that any such letter would be published, and his letter was not published by *Look*. More significantly, his letter was not circulated to his agitated peers of the House. He had again been effectually denied a hearing.

The denial of due process to Bishop Pike was underscored by the heavily judgmental tone of the censure resolution. It was, Pike

felt, "far more serious than any charges contained in the presentment brought by Bishop Louttit," affecting as the censure did
"my work, my ministry, my professional standing and my per-
sonhood." When, at last, at the end of the debate at Wheeling,
Pike was allotted ten minutes to make a statement—he in fact
spent eighteen minutes—the cruelty of the whole process by
which he was being denigrated was poignantly dramatized. Pike
had chosen to make no statement of his own in response to the
impending censure, but to read to the House comments he felt
pertinent from other worthies—St. Augustine, and Hans Küng,
the Jesuit theologian who had been so prominent in the Second
Vatican Council, and Angus Dun, who had, by the politics of the
occasion, been cast in the role of sponsoring the censure. Bishop
Pike recalled a paper which Dun had written, in 1924, while on
the faculty of the Episcopal Theological School in Cambridge,
Massachusetts. "What are needed" from the theologian, Dun had
said, "are honesty and integrity, fearlessness and steadfastness, in-
trepidity and determination. Freedom in theology is a necessary
condition for multiplicity in theology . . . If there were in the
Church only one united theology in the sense of one united party
line this would be a sign not of catholic freedom but of un-
catholic compulsion. One Lord, one faith, one baptism, but
different theologies!"

If heresy trials in the past have often been a screen for persecutions or reprisals, Pike, at Wheeling, in the moments after the
censure was done, threatened to reverse that historic association.
He invoked a canonical right to demand a trial as the only way
then available to him to secure a semblance of due process. It was
a startling and sudden reversal of the situation: at once confound-
ing the stratagem of appeasing Pike's accusers by censuring him,
restoring the theological issues to prominence, transferring political initiative from the managers of the Church and from his opponents in the House of Bishops to Bishop Pike himself.

Vindication at Seattle

Three issues had come to the forefront with Pike's trial demand
—the scope of theological inquiry in the Episcopal Church, the
question of ecclesiastical due process, and, entangled with both of

these, the personal denigration of Pike by the censure vote. A curious aspect of the prolonged controversy over the alleged heresies of Bishop Pike is that relatively few persons, including many of those privy to the events, realized then or since that at least on the twin issues of theology and due process, the bishop was vindicated, and impressively so. The subjective issue remained ambiguous or, simply, subjective. At the Church's general convention at Seattle—the former see of Bayne as Bishop of Olympia—in September of 1967 a commitment to openness in theological inquiry and social witness was endorsed and canonical reforms were enacted safeguarding due process in ecclesiastical proceedings which, together, virtually obviate a repetition of heresy charges such as those to which Pike had been subjected. Whether remembered much as vindication for Pike, they did in fact constitute, as he later put it, "a happy outcome" of the great heresy controversy.

The vagueness of the recall of Pike's victory at Seattle can be, in part, accounted for by the general circumstance that derogatory or defamatory charges are inherently more interesting and evoke more attention than any subsequent disposition of such allegations. Dismissal or acquittal or similar relief for an accused never quite erases the original infamy associated with charges and seldom receives as conspicuous attention in the media. It is not surprising, therefore, that Pike is more remembered as putative heretic than as vindicated bishop. Also, the form of Pike's Seattle vindication was legislative rather than judicial, and adoption of a policy or amendment of canon law is less dramatic than a trial. Moreover, the Seattle actions which constituted Pike's vindication are of general scope, pertaining to his situation but applicable beyond that, and while it may be suggested that this enhances their long-range significance, at the same time this diminishes the excitement of the immediate outcome.

Most of all, however, though Pike was vindicated at Seattle, it is not at all clear that he was exonerated. The legislative changes there enacted may assure an ample theological freedom in the Church and may guarantee ecclesiastical due process, but they did not expunge the censure of Bishop Pike. In any case, Pike was content with what was accomplished at Seattle and withdrew his demand for a trial, and thus terminated the heresy controversy.

This may be interpreted as his magnanimity, or as evidence of his typical political naïveté, or as an indication that he had become bored with the whole thing and that his interests had been excited elsewhere.

A Disturbing Intrusion

However any of these factors affect the recollection of Bishop Pike's fate at the Seattle convention, there was, on the very day of his vindication in the heresy controversy, another happening which eclipsed the news of his triumph. A headline in the Seattle *Post-Intelligencer* broke that other news this way: PIKE CLAIMS 'TALK' WITH DEAD SON. There followed a report of a meeting and a purported séance in which Pike had participated with the famed medium Arthur Ford in Toronto, a few weeks prior to the general convention. That encounter, parts of which had been placed on video tape, to which Pike had almost casually consented and to which Ford was said to have only reluctantly agreed, had been the brainchild of the unusually enterprising Canadian journalist Allen Spraggett. An edited version of the tape had been shown on television in Canada without arousing any unusual response and that tape was later routinely destroyed by the television station in Toronto. This event had not gained particular attention in the United States, though details of it were known to several American newspeople. Bishop Pike, in fact, had requested those who knew of it to publish nothing about it. Meanwhile, the publicity about the heresy hassle was reaching a huge volume as the Episcopal general convention convened in Seattle, despite the efforts of Bishop Bayne and the Church's specially engaged public relations staff to minimize it. Frustrated, perhaps, because the encounter that he had framed between Bishop Pike and Arthur Ford had received so little attention, or perhaps unable to bypass opportunity, Spraggett appeared on the NBC "Today" show the morning of the day that the Seattle convention was to resolve the heresy issue by enacting the canonical reforms which would virtually obviate future heresy proceedings in the Church. Ostensibly, Spraggett was to be interviewed in promotion of a book he had written about parapsychology. Though his book made no reference to Bishop Pike, or to the recent Toronto séance, Spraggett managed to attach to the news about Pike originating from Seattle by discussing the story of the supposed communication through Ford's mediumship of Pike's dead son. A torrent of publicity ensued—most of it, at least from Pike's viewpoint, inflated, misleading, or inaccurate. In that deluge, the word that Bishop Pike had prevailed in the heresy controversy was practically overwhelmed.

These circumstances caused Pike surprise and consternation. He had not attributed "hard news" value to the Toronto session. He had participated in it without much forethought. He had had no inkling that the episode would be exploited. But the bizarre potential of the Toronto séance had now been capitalized, and Pike was forced to respond to the *Post-Intelligencer* headline defensively. He was besieged that day at Seattle, as in the next days and weeks, by reporters from media of all sorts seeking angles and embellishments of the séance story. No one seemed interested in heresy any more, much less in stolid ecclesiastical legislation precluding the notion of heresy in the Episcopal Church.

What a boon for Pike's detractors! Their defeat in the heresy confrontation would now be scarcely noticed, while they were furnished with fresh ammunition to prosecute Pike's defamation. The Toronto incident, especially as rendered so sensationally by Spraggett, was all Pike's enemies needed to show his incorrigibility, to prove his appetite for attention, to insinuate his instability, or to verify his unorthodoxy. At the same time, those who had been his friends and allies throughout the turbulence over heresy, those who had looked to the disposition of the Bishop Pike affair as decisive for broader concerns of church renewal and reform, heard the séance publicity with astonishment and dismay. Some, knowing no more than what the press published, felt compromised by Pike. Few who had been associated with Pike in the struggles over theological freedom and ecclesiastical due process were ready to be in his company in extemporaneously explaining whatever it was that had happened in Toronto. Many expressed condescension of the sort often reserved for the ill. In the very hour of vindication at Seattle, Bishop Pike found himself virtually alone.

Post-Wheeling Dealings

The censure was not erased by the Seattle general convention, and though on the substantive questions of theology and due process Pike felt, with ample justification, vindicated, the enterprise of Spraggett in exploiting the séance in Toronto had accomplished the aim of the censure strategy—the isolation of Bishop Pike from the Episcopal Church. "We do not think," the Wheeling document declared, Pike's ". . . obscure and contradictory utterances warrant the time and the work and the wounds of a trial. The Church has more important things to get on with." It seemed at Seattle that fortuity had implemented this paragraph of the censure resolution.

Bishop Pike had not been alone at Wheeling. The galleries there had been jammed with sympathizers and supporters, including a number of nuns and some Jesuit priests from Roman Catholic institutions nearby. Among the bishops a significant minority stood with him. The final tally on the censure was 103 ayes to 36 nays, and there was indication during the debate that some of those who voted for the resolution did so with enormous reluctance. Bishop Horace W. B. Donegan of New York, for example, addressed the House, mentioning that Pike had been "my very able and loyal dean for six years":

> I shall vote for the statement, but I profoundly regret the charge of irresponsibility. This is an attack on a man's integrity. We have refrained from putting Bishop Pike on trial for his theology. But, brethren, according to my judgment, by this statement we are condemning him without trial at a deeper level of his personal integrity, and I hope the document will be amended at this point.

It was not amended, despite attempts of several bishops to alter the text so as to mitigate it. Nor did the cogent question raised by Paul Moore, then Suffragan Bishop of Washington, who subsequently succeeded Donegan to the see of New York, deter the majority:

> Why is it that the House has not censured any of the rest of us who have spoken, acted out or allowed to occur within our dio-

ceses greater blasphemies than the treatment of items of doctrine less than solemnly? I speak of church doors closed against members of another race, clergy denied backing of their bishop because of their Christian social views, public impugning of the motives of fellow bishops.

Those who might have felt shame or similar qualm in publicly supporting the condemnation of Pike were spared immediate exposure by the refusal of the Presiding Bishop to allow a roll call vote, though subsequent diligence enabled a reconstruction of the vote identifying those for and against by name, and that was published, prior to Seattle, in *The Bishop Pike Affair*. A minority statement, subscribed to by twenty-two bishops, which commended Bishop Pike for attempting to face "the demands, intellectual and theological, of our time in history" was received by the House after the censure had been done.

On the next morning, the immediate political aim of the censure having been nullified by Bishop Pike's demand for a trial, the House of Bishops unanimously adopted a resolution introduced by the Bishop of Massachusetts, Anson Phelps Stokes, Jr., calling for the establishment of a council to "rethink, restructure and renew the Church for life in the world today." It was, to Bishop Pike at least, a poignant and ironic action, as if, the censure having furnished a catharsis for assorted hostilities which they had harbored against him, the other bishops were now ready to act in the way which he had urged upon them over and over again.

The Stokes resolution was to provide inspiration for the eventual political disposition of the heresy controversy after Wheeling. If that political outcome at Seattle did not expunge the censure of Pike, it did meet not only Bishop Pike's substantive concerns about theological freedom and due process but also these same interests of other bishops who constituted the minority at Wheeling, and meant that the humiliation to which Pike had been subjected would become unique in Episcopal Church annals.

An Ombudsman

The canonical requirement for the Presiding Bishop, upon receipt of a demand for trial, is to proceed with promptness—that being an essential element of due process—to appoint a board of inquiry to investigate the matter to determine whether grounds exist to warrant a trial. The board functions similarly to a grand jury, and in this instance would have to determine whether the censure passed by the House of Bishops constituted a derogation of the character of Bishop Pike. There would seem to have been little doubt what the board must conclude if it convened.

The insistence of Pike upon his canonical rights created an excruciating political dilemma for the Presiding Bishop, and for Bishop Bayne—whose censure strategy had failed—but it also highlighted an extraordinary legal situation affecting whether a timely or competent trial could be had at all. The 1964 general convention had neglected in the rush of other business to fill three existing vacancies on the Court for the Trial of a Bishop and, since that time, a fourth vacancy had occurred by reason of the death of a sitting member of the court. This meant that, despite the canonical necessity for a speedy disposition, until this defect could be cured at the 1967 general convention, there was no trial court with a quorum to hear any matter. At the same time, to fill the court vacancies from among any bishops who had voted, either way, on the censure at Wheeling would raise the problem of prior prejudice on the principal issue to be adjudicated on the part of any such appointee. Part of the absurdity of this situation was the fact that the bishop in charge of the dispatch of business at the 1964 convention, and hence the person responsible for ensuring that the judicial appointments were placed on the agenda, was none other than the Bishop of South Florida, Henry I. Louttit, the chief accuser of Bishop Pike, who knew, when he uttered his presentment of charges against Pike, that his own inattention had caused the Church to be without a court competent to conduct the trial he sought. For those, like Bishop Bayne, worried about the image of the Church, the prospect was horrendous, for not only was there now the risk of a mandated trial for which there was no ecclesiastical court, but that fact might well furnish Pike with standing to resort to the civil court for remedy.

If this judicial snarl provided some pretext for delay on the part of the Presiding Bishop, none was needed. His inclination was, anyway, to put off the canonical procedure as long as possible and to persevere, in spite of the political debacle at Wheeling, in seeking a political modus out of the controversy. The morning after the censure vote and Pike's surprise demand for trial, Bishop Hines pleaded for a "cooling-off" period for all concerned, though he pledged also to appoint the board of inquiry "with all deliberate speed"—a phrase newsmen quickly noticed had become euphemistic for procrastination. Bishop Pike therefore sought, immediately after Wheeling, a more definite commitment on the board's appointment and he did receive from Hines a verbal assurance that the board would be constituted before the end of 1966.

That year expired without that having happened. Hines's malingering, however, on legal process concealed his prompt political initiatives. Secret contact was established with Bishop Pike to explore how a trial might be obviated. This delicate mission was undertaken by the Very Reverend John Coburn, dean of the Episcopal Theological School in Cambridge, Massachusetts, and prospective president of the House of Deputies of the general convention. Coburn was an appropriate "ombudsman," as Pike named him, not only because of his long-standing friendship with Pike, including his role in preaching that prescient sermon at Pike's consecration, but also because Coburn occupied a unique prestige among bishops, having himself previously declined election to the episcopacy on more than one occasion. Furthermore, Coburn was in a position to assess the question of theological freedom in the Episcopal Church from the perspective of the seminaries and of the stake for theological education and ecumenical relations involved in the whole heresy hassle. If that implicated some vested interest on Coburn's part in the ultimate outcome, it at least represented a wider view of the matter than the bishops had evinced at Wheeling.

Dean Coburn wrote Bishop Pike, on November 23, 1966, a letter which opened the door to mediation:

> I want to express my concern about where the Church now stands in this matter. There is an opportunity arising out of your request to the Presiding Bishop for a very creative and significant step forward to be taken in the Church's understanding of itself and its mission to the contemporary world. If the Church does not use this opportunity creatively now, it will be nothing short of a tragedy. If the issue is smothered or if it is related simply to you as a person who is a bishop of the Church, a unique opportunity will be lost.

Pike encouraged Coburn and, in late December, the dean traveled discreetly to California for direct conversations with Pike. An agreement emerged from their talks whereby, if he wished to do so, the Presiding Bishop would name a commission on theological inquiry, with diverse points of view represented and heard, including that of Bishop Pike, which would seek reforms in the manner in which the Church dealt with doctrinal diversity, deviance, or novelty. For a reasonable time, while the commission was at work, Pike would forbear pressing his right to immediate convening of the board of inquiry.

The Coburn arrangement was an implementation of the principle of the Stokes resolution and, further than that, to Pike it was the charter for the kind of theological effort that he had in various ways persistently urged upon his fellow bishops ever since he had registered objection to the *pro forma* pastoral letter issued from Dallas in 1960. Pike was appreciative of Coburn's role on another count, too, the due process issue. Coburn was sensitive to Pike's hurt at being denied a fair hearing throughout the events preliminary to the censure, and so Coburn's mediation resulted in a commission in which Pike would have a hearing, but meanwhile Pike had been privy to the construction of the commission proposal, even to the extent of drafting suggestions for the public announcement which the Presiding Bishop would make about it.

Bishop Hines, on January 12, 1967, appointed a committee of bishops, priests, laymen, and a theologian not an Episcopalian to advise him in relation to the theological situation with which the Episcopal Church was faced. "This situation," his statement read, "includes some of the perplexing questions implicit but not resolved in the session in which the House of Bishops in Wheeling, W. Va., sought to deal with the issues raised . . . by the possibility of a presentment against the resigned bishop of California." The committee, for which Bishop Bayne was named chairman, was authorized to examine "the nature of 'heresy' . . . today," and to give "an appraisal of . . . procedures with reference to a trial for heresy," as well as to comment on the "scope of freedom in the Church" on theological issues and of "legitimate openness in our Church for theological reformation." Among Hines's appointees were the distinguished New Testament scholar Paul

Minear of Yale Divinity School, he being the non-Anglican; Dr. John MacQuarrie of Scotland, then currently teaching at Union Theological Seminary in New York City; Professor Albert Mollegan of Virginia Theological Seminary; Louis Cassels, then religion columnist for United Press International; and Theodore Ferris, rector of Trinity Church, Boston. By prearrangement, Bishop Pike, the same day, issued a statement welcoming Hines's "creative—indeed historic—step which gives a comprehensive opportunity" to confront "the nature of the current theological revolution," and commending "the Presiding Bishop's statesmanship and sensitivity to the needs and prospects of our Church in our day."

Perhaps Pike's remarks were somewhat gratuitous, since he had had so much to do with the design and mandate of the new Bayne committee, but that did not diminish his genuine gladness for the potential it offered. Nor did his satisfaction at this development cause him any illusion that the outcome of the Bayne committee, in itself, could alter his status as a censured bishop. The committee, though august, was no more than an ad hoc body, responsible only to the Presiding Bishop, with no capability of repudiating or otherwise undoing the censure of the House of Bishops. Two days after the announcement of the Advisory Committee on Theological Freedom and Social Responsibility, Bishop Hines acknowledged this limitation of the Bayne committee. He appeared at a press conference in San Francisco, where he participated, along with Bishop Pike, in the installation of Pike's successor, the Right Reverend C. Kilmer Myers, as Bishop of California. A transcription of that news conference includes this exchange:

> *Hines:* I think there is considerable dissatisfaction in the Church with what happened to Bishop Pike . . . the whole process brought up questions in some people's minds as to whether he was dealt fairly with. I have been dilly dallying . . . because the Church did not and does not want a process which might issue in a heresy trial. The Church does want clarification. . . . it might be the good part of judgment to create a committee of competent people who will take a look squarely at these problems . . .
>
> *Reporter:* Would you personally favor a reconsideration of the censure . . . ?
>
> *Hines:* I can't answer that question.

Nonetheless, Bishop Pike had decided he would cooperate with the Bayne committee and declared, at the same press conference in San Francisco, that while he was not surrendering his legal options, he was "content that the Presiding Bishop delay further . . . the appointment of the first of the bodies involved in canonical due process" pending the outcome of the Bayne committee effort.

Theological Freedom and Social Responsibilities

The Bayne committee convened on three occasions during the ensuing months and received papers responsive to its agenda from several "advisors" which it had chosen. They represented the Anglican spectrum, including, on one hand, the Bishop of Georgia, Albert Stuart, who had received the charges against Pike from some of his clergy in 1961 and who had later subscribed to the Louttit presentment and then had voted to censure Pike, and, on the other, Paul Moore, the Suffragan Bishop of Washington, noted for his active social witness, who had made an eloquent defense of Pike during the Wheeling debate. From the University of London, there was Dr. Eric Mascall, Professor of Historical Theology, and, also from England, the Bishop of Woolwich, John A. T. Robinson, who had become, if anything, more celebrated than Pike on the contemporary theological scene for his book *Honest to God*. The distinguished Jesuit scholar John Courtney Murray, was among the advisors, as was Dr. John Knox, the New Testament theologian, plus Mrs. Harold Sorg, a layperson from the Diocese of California long active in the national Church; J. V. Langmead Casserley, Professor of Philosophy at Seabury-Western Seminary; Dr. Arthur Vogel, Professor of Dogmatic Theology at Nashotah House Seminary; and Bishop Pike himself.

By mid-August 1967 the Bayne committee rendered a report to the Presiding Bishop, who promptly circulated the same to delegates to the impending general convention scheduled to convene in Seattle about a month later. Chief attention, as might be expected, focused upon the report's view of heresy as "anachronistic" and its suggestions for canonical revisions which would make the occurrence of any future heresy proceedings very unlikely by

requiring that ten bishops subscribe to any presentment of charges
—instead of only three—and by adding a condition that no trial
could go forward without a two-thirds vote of the House of
Bishops.

The need, the report urged, of the Church today was not to
hunt heretics but to "encourage free and vigorous theological
debate, application of the Gospel to social wrongs, restatement of
Christian doctrines to make them more intelligible to contemporary minds, and experimentation with new forms of worship
and service." It continued:

> Any risks the Church may run for fostering a climate of genuine
> freedom are minor compared to the dangers it surely will en-
> counter from any attempts at suppression, censorship or thought
> control . . .
> God makes men free. It does not behoove His Church to
> hobble their minds or inhibit their search for new insights into
> truth.

To implement this commitment to theological inquiry, the Bayne
committee proposed programs for the preparation and involvement of laity and clergy in theological dialogue, greatly developed continuing theological education for clergy, establishment of
a standing commission on the Church's teaching, and a restructur-
ing of the corporate activities of the bishops of the Church to enable more theological study and discourse.

The Bayne report dealt obliquely, though not subtly, with the
Wheeling censure, by suggesting that if theological views are expressed which are deemed subversive, the Church should be able
to disassociate from those positions without attack upon the character or motives of the person dissenting. The document, as if
seeking to soften the Wheeling action, went on to comment:

> "Censure" . . . is not now in the Church's official vocabulary
> and we do not argue for it. But we are agreed that if "censure"
> (as the word is commonly used) were to enter into the Church's
> procedures in dealing with recalcitrant problems, two things must
> be unequivocally clear. First, a judgment of "censure" ought never
> be applied to statements of theological or moral *opinion* or teach-
> ing, but only to *acts*—perhaps specifically only to acts which
> openly and notoriously violate essential elements of order and
> decency, or subvert the essential processes of the community.

Second, no such judgment should ever be made except after every safeguard of due process has been provided.

Bishop Pike greeted the issuance of the Bayne committee report as a "breath of fresh air," and indicated that he would go to the Seattle convention in a conciliatory mood. Withdrawal of his demand for a trial would depend, he mentioned, upon the disposition of the report's recommendations by the convention. Religious News Service quoted Pike as saying that if the report were "endorsed" by the general convention it would mean implicitly that the "censure would be erased," making it possible for him to "honorably withdraw" his trial demand.

Opposition to the Bayne document was heard quickly from some factions within the Episcopal Church which had sought a heresy trial and had not been successfully appeased by the censure. The American Church Union, which has historically been identified with militant Anglo-Catholicism, denounced the report as "a disservice to all Bible-believing Christians." Its ratification by the general convention, the A.C.U. argued, "would be the most radical and destructive action," because of its "rejection" of the "concept of heresy." The report, the A.C.U. statement declared, "would seem to indicate that the committee has considered these charges and finds Bishop Pike 'not guilty.' This would seem to bypass the official judicial processes set up by the Church." The New York *Times*, however, noted that the Bayne committee had "stopped short of recommending a total ban on heresy trials for tactical reasons. It was thought that a total ban could not be maneuvered through the general convention but that the current report stood a good chance."

Politics at Seattle

The political situation attending the Seattle convention was more Byzantine than Anglican. Pike's most vehement accusers and his most ardent admirers both felt that only a trial would suffice to resolve the controversy. The substitution of the censure for a trial had satisfied most of Pike's detractors in the House of Bishops, but only barely so, and any apparent dilution of the censure or any action which expunged the censure would wreck this delicate majority. At the same time—if a trial were still to be avoided—the censure had somehow to be ameliorated in the view of Bishop Pike and the significant minority of bishops who had stood with him.

Meanwhile, in the months between Wheeling and Seattle, the Bishop Pike matter inevitably became entangled with other issues plaguing the Church which were to claim attention at the 1967 general convention and thereafter. Black Episcopalians had organized a caucus to press for a serious commitment of church funding in aid of community organizations in the nation's black ghettos. Students and young people planned to turn the convention into a giant teach-in, for the edification of their elders, about the genocide in Vietnam, resistance to the draft, representation of the young within church structures, the "new morality," the culpability of church investments, the imminence of world hunger. The Episcopal Society for Cultural and Racial Unity, which had pioneered in the struggles for racial justice and civil rights in the earlier years of the decade, scheduled Saul Alinsky for an address to its meeting adjacent to the convention. Some of the younger bishops were apprehensive about how the disposition of the Pike case would affect their future influence on social issues and church renewal. The right-wing ideologues in the Episcopal Church— some of whom had participated in instigating heresy charges against Pike—openly sought to increase their political clout in the government of the Church and had campaigned, with appreciable successes, for the control of budgets in some dioceses as well as of delegations to the convention. They aimed at restricting the Church's emphasis upon the concerns of blacks and youth and upon matters of church renewal by gaining at least an effectual veto over church finances, and their activities in the period immediately prior to Seattle, involving as they did some churchpeople who were also members of the John Birch Society, were enough to occasion the fear that there would be a *coup d'église*. That development was forestalled at Seattle and did not mature in a sudden take-over, but by infiltration and by attrition and because of the abandonment of the Episcopal Church in subsequent years by droves of youth and blacks and others, it was accomplished by the time of the general convention in Louisville in 1973, where the leadership of John Hines as Presiding Bishop, especially as he had sought to revive and sustain the Church's social mission, was repu-

diated. That Hines's leadership suffered that fate, at the hands of
the very factions within the Church which were determined to
discredit or expel Bishop Pike, underscores the political reality at
Seattle. What happened there to Pike would be immensely
influential in how a plethora of *other* issues, which Pike inimita-
bly symbolized, would be sooner or later decided.

Be that as it may, for Bishop Bayne and his colleagues in the incumbent management of the Church, the overriding consideration was public relations, not theology, and not politics, except
as politics may be derivative of public relations. The worry was
still the so-called image of the Episcopal Church. A trial *had* to
be avoided. High-powered public relations staff had been retained.
The line was developed and propagated that the Bayne report had
all but settled the Pike controversy before the convention had
even met. There was, as legal counsel cautioned Bishop Pike, a
peril that he would become victim of a "snow job." Bishop Bayne's
PR people were successful in persuading a network television
news show to cancel interviews which the network had solicited
and scheduled about the Pike dispute on the grounds that it had
been virtually rendered moot, prior to Seattle, by the Bayne report. Bayne himself replaced that program, using the opportunity
to pronounce the reasonableness of the Bayne report. "Does this
mean that the whole Pike affair will just die down if your report is
accepted . . . ?" he was asked; "In the sense that it would be a
juridical cause, I would hope that it would die . . . Yes, I think
Jim, Jim would like it and I think everybody else would," Bayne
responded. In the same "Today" show television appearance,
Bishop Bayne seemed to attempt a softening of the censure's attack upon Bishop Pike's so-called vulgarity. "Bishop Pike says
[things] in particularly challenging ways," Bayne remarked, "and
I think has won a response from people." Since one of Pike's
most repeated sayings, to which crudeness had been attributed—it
being the single specific example of Pike's rhetoric cited in the
censure as proof of the irresponsibility of his utterances—was that
a conceptualized doctrine of the Trinity is a "heavy piece of luggage," another exchange in the same interview was poignant.
Bishop Bayne had been asked by Hugh Downs, "Today" host, his
thoughts about "the future of Christianity" in the contemporary
world and whether the Church possessed the "flexibility" to survive in it. To that, he replied: "I think we've got to learn to travel

light . . . The heart of the gospel is not all that big, and I think we've *got* to learn in this world to travel very light."

In line with the public relations effort to minimize the Pike controversy and to insinuate that it had been practically settled by the Bayne report, the item was located late on the convention agenda—two days before adjournment—when the most routine matters are usually considered. A resolution was presented to the House of Bishops, introduced by some preliminary comments by Bishop Bayne, which called for the *affirmation* of the report of the Advisory Committee on Theological Freedom and Social Responsibility. The House was not called upon to adopt or endorse the report or any of its recommendations for either the furtherance of theological inquiry and dialogue or the insurance of due process. "Affirmation" of the report was spelled out in the resolution as expressing a "hope that [the report] will serve to create a new climate of free, responsible thought and action within the Church," as commending study by agencies of the Church of "plans and programs needed to implement the suggestions of the Committee," and as requesting the appointment of another "ad hoc committee to prepare appropriate canonical amendments" for future consideration. Bishop Hines stated that, though he regretted it, "we cannot consider specific canons at this time." The hard-core anti-Pike forces, while persistent in their desire for a good old-fashioned heresy trial and hence still discreetly hopeful that Pike would be unsatisfied with the resolution and keep his demand for trial, found little objection to so vague and indefinite a memorial. A majority, weary of both the underlying controversy and the protracted convention, were prepared to vote the resolution. Bishop Pike, and those whom he consulted, were very wary about it. Pike's public commitment had been to withdraw his trial demand if there was at the general convention an endorsement or adoption of the Bayne proposals which would implicitly "erase" the censure. At the same time, however, the public relations campaign engineered by Bayne had spread an impression Pike's withdrawal was assured, as a practical matter, before the convention by the release of the Bayne report and that any generally affirmative action on the report would suffice to dispense with a trial. If the prospective resolution was in fact worthless, without effect upon the censure, without assurance for any reform, and Pike therefore persevered, would his justification for doing so be recognized, or would he be thought to have betrayed the commitment to relinquish his right to trial?

Such was Pike's dilemma, as the vote passing the resolution was counted. During a recess for lunch, Pike met with a few friends in a dank bar across from the Seattle spaceneedle to weigh the question. Diane Kennedy was present, as were Anthony Towne and William Stringfellow. The upshot of that caucus was a decision to seek formal clarification when the House of Bishops reconvened of the implication of the "affirmation" of the Bayne report for the Wheeling censure. The record, it was felt, had to be unambiguous about that. An approach was made to Stuart Wetmore, Suffragan Bishop of New York, a colleague of Pike's from his days as dean of St. John the Divine, who somewhat reluctantly consented to put a question to the Presiding Bishop. Meanwhile, Pike drafted a letter reiterating his demand for trial "forthwith" to hold in readiness should the reply to the Wetmore query require its use.

The House gathered after lunch, under the impression that at last the Pike affair was done. Bishop Wetmore obtained recognition from the Presiding Bishop. He put *the* question:

> Is it correct to understand that the action of the House in affirming and commending the committee report has the impact of removing the statement of censure against Bishop Pike adopted at Wheeling?

Bishop Hines answered: "It does not."

There was consternation, if not panic, in the House of Bishops. A motion was made to appeal the ruling of the chair and there ensued a parliamentary snarl about that motion. It failed to obtain the two-thirds vote required. Some bishops complained they had been misled as to the significance of the resolution affirming the Bayne report. Amid the general pandemonium, Bishop Pike arose to read the letter he had ready:

> When the Bayne committee report was released, I indicated that should it be ratified by the House of Bishops I could honorably and responsibly . . . withdraw the demand for judicial proceedings . . .
>
> But it was decided not to present the Bayne committee report: the purport of what was adopted this morning was not clear to me

and I was weighing, with advice of counsel, whether . . . to with-draw the demand. Now in response to Bishop Wetmore's raising a point of information, you have stated without qualification that this morning's action does not erase the impact of the Wheeling censure . . . I simply call to your attention the mandatory char-acter of the provisions of the canon I had no choice but to invoke in October and ask that the proceedings be initiated forth-with . . .

Thereupon, the Bishop of Missouri, George Leslie Cadigan, made a motion to erase the censure, but it was usurped by a motion of adjournment which prevailed by the assenting shouts of the bishops.

In the disarray of the occasion, it was overlooked that the care-ful phraseology of the Wetmore query contained a way to obviate a trial even at that late moment. Bishop Wetmore had not asked whether the censure had been erased, but whether the *impact* of the censure had been. "The word 'impact' was the key word," Bishop Wetmore later recalled. "I drafted the question and passed it to Jim. He chuckled." Few other bishops caught the nuance; Bishop Wetmore had suffered throat surgery which weakened his voice and his projection when he asked his question was low. "I apparently was not able to say it so the Presiding Bishop could hear," Wetmore has said. Bishop Hines has indicated that he did not notice the crucial term—"impact"—and that if he had his rul-ing might well have been different. On such fragile circumstances weighty matters are determined.

That night was crowded with frantic caucuses. If some bishops were distressed at what seemed an attempt by Bayne, in offering the report, to finesse the Pike case by seeking only "affirmation" rather than adoption of the document and the recommendations it contained, others by now were so weary of the controversy— and of Pike as a personality—that they were ready to quit the scene altogether. Bishop Pike himself was ambivalent—on one hand, he had become bored with the heresy dispute and his mind was more active on other fronts, but at the same time the un-fairness of the whole manner in which the heresy crisis had been handled aroused him and he was deeply suspicious that the mere affirmation of the Bayne report would issue in any substantive re-newal or reform respecting either theological freedom or due process within the Episcopal Church. Whatever motivated Bayne to treat the report so innocuously, the fact stood out that the condition precedent for Bishop Pike's withdrawal of the trial demand—so delicately wrought by Dean Coburn—had not been fulfilled. Perhaps the only happy faction at the convention that night was the one which, all along, had wanted to put Pike on trial, which at that moment seemed a certainty. Their satisfaction in the turn of events had been embellished by the perfunctory receipt of the Bayne report which had removed or indefinitely postponed the threat of significant change in the Church. In hindsight, the fact is relevant that in the years since the Seattle convention, which coincide with an expanding influence of theologically dogmatic and politically reactionary Episcopalians within the government of the Church, nothing has happened to implement the Bayne report recommendations.

Except for what did occur at Seattle. The Right Reverend Leland Stark, Bishop of Newark, having accomplished some homework, introduced on the morning after the uproar amendments to the canons altering how presentments of charges against bishops could be uttered. The Stark amendments essentially embodied the canonical reforms recommended in the Bayne report. Though it had been maintained by both Bayne and Hines the previous day that the pressure of time at the convention precluded consideration of changes in the canons, the Stark amendments were adopted, and, moreover, the unusual provision was made that they become effective forthwith.

Some substantive change did happen. The Bayne recommendations would not merely be "affirmed" and then allowed to evaporate entirely. The Stark canons meant that the process by which Pike had been vilified could not be repeated against another bishop in the future.

For Bishop Pike, this was enough. He addressed the House:

> In the light of the passage of principal canonical changes protecting this House and the members thereof from proceedings on the part of a relatively small number of its members, and requiring due process of law . . . I feel sufficiently content about the righting of things. Thus when the Deputies have concurred, I will, with the consent of my co-presenters, Bishops Myers and Craine, withdraw my canonical demand for proceedings.

The House of Deputies promptly concurred. The canons had been reformed. Theological freedom had been affirmed—and Bishop Pike assumed, somewhat naïvely, that there would be an effort to activate the various Bayne report proposals about that. He felt vindicated, though the censure remained and he might not be said to have been exonerated.

It is perchance a measure of Pike's "victory" at Seattle that his most vehement enemies and opponents within the Episcopal Church soon found other targets for their wrath, notably John Eldridge Hines, the Presiding Bishop. In the years that followed the Seattle convention, Hines strove increasingly and mightily to be responsive to the outcrys and the disaffections of the young and of the dispossessed. If Hines could not fairly be designated radical in his leadership, with Pike absent as a target, he was treated as if he was radical. And, by 1973, Bishop Hines had been driven from office.

Was Bishop Pike a Heretic?

The question left unresolved at Seattle—the one apt to linger as long as any memory of James Albert Pike—was whether Bishop Pike was verily a heretic. Did he, to use the language of the canons under which he was accused, hold and teach "publicly or privately and advisedly, any doctrine contrary to that held" by the Episcopal Church?

An answer to that requires that Anglican doctrine be ascertainable with a degree of clarity and definiteness sufficient to render a charge of heresy coherent. A standard or measure of orthodoxy is necessary. It is not obvious that there is such. The Anglican Communion has nothing in its inheritance comparable to the Westminster Confession in the tradition of the Reformed churches or to the Lutheran Augsburg Confession. There are the formularies of the Articles of Religion published in the Book of Common Prayer, as ratified in the United States in 1801 by the general convention of the Episcopal Church. They were promulgated in America then because of the exigencies occasioned by the American Revolution and the formation of the new nation and the consequent change in Anglicanism in America from a mission of the Church of England to an autonomous national church. The Articles are a virtually verbatim copy of the earlier Articles of the mother church adopted in the sixteenth century. In the circumstances they represent a heavily acculturated composition and this fact is generally acknowledged in the Episcopal Church. The Articles are regarded as quaint—of historical interest, but hardly as definitive of doctrine. Even the most enthusiastic of Bishop Pike's accusers never thought to invoke the Articles against him. The Articles do uphold the ancient Creeds, in this manner: "The Nicene Creed, and that which is commonly called the Apostles' Creed, ought thoroughly to be received and believed: for they may be proved by most certain warrants of Holy Scripture." It had been urged repeatedly while various charges were pending against Pike that he denied the Creeds, or parts thereof, though he thought of his effort as explicating them and never repudiated their recital or other use within the Church. Thus, how the Creeds are interpreted becomes crucial to an appeal to the Creeds as assessor of heresy. Are the Creeds to be understood as reporting historical fact or as expressing theological truth? Shall they be read with simplistic literalism, as some of Pike's accusers argued, or stylistically and symbolically? Do the Creeds represent reportage or metaphor? Or must such questions be answered one way or the other? Can there not be within the Church room for a diversity of interpretations of the Creeds in conjunction with their common use?

These questions plagued the Episcopal Church, as well as other churches, long before the Pike heresy controversy. It became one of the sad footnotes to the censure of Pike under the nominal auspices of Bishop Angus Dun that Bishop Pike could cite in his own behalf a proposal Dun had offered in 1924, while he was a seminary professor, that the historic Creeds be deemed optional in liturgical practice until they could be studied by scholars with the purpose of revising creedal language so as to be more comprehensible. Professor Dun had put the problem:

> The practical question is not whether the great classical formulations of faith in Christ . . . within our creeds enshrine permanent truths and values, but whether they serve . . . to . . . share or sift faith in Christ in our day . . . For increasing numbers there are clauses where the mind goes blank as the words are

repeated, where many honest but non-reflective minds feel a vague uneasiness, where the more youthful and more ambitious minds revolt, where the more middle-aged and indolent minds surrender the effort to think their situations through, and where the more docile minds recognize sacred mystery working where they cannot understand.

Under these circumstances it cannot be said that it is the creeds which unite us . . . There are at least certain public indications that it is the creeds that divide us . . . [T]he basis of our unity and our continuity lies deeper than creeds.

It had been, of course, the latitude and generosity of belief and interpretation traditional, if not consistent, within Anglicanism's existential unity and historic continuity that had so persuasively appealed to young Jim Pike in the days when he was so intensely searching for a church connection that he could enter in conscience. Through the years, he had retained that admiration for the breadth of Anglicanism. On the eve of his departure from the cathedral in New York he declared that he considered the fullest expression of the biblical message "is found in the Anglican heritage . . . I believe that this is the most Catholic, most Protestant, and most liberal tradition in Christianity."

This same conviction about the Anglican genius was artfully embodied in the book on doctrine, The Faith of the Church, which Pike had co-authored with Norman Pittenger. Bishop Pike recalled this often, if sometimes somewhat ruefully, during the heresy tumult because that book had as much stature in defining doctrine as anything currently in official use in the Episcopal Church and he could envision himself in an absurd trial in which that book was cited as doctrinal authority.

Others in the Episcopal Church sensed the same element of the absurd in the heresy effort against Pike and in his censure. The Witness, a church magazine of liberal stance, in October 1966, editorialized:

In the days preceding the meeting at Wheeling the press reported the death of the "Red Dean" of Canterbury, and we were led to reflect on the maturity of the mother Church of England in dealing with the eccentric and the innovators among her clergy. Bishop Barnes of Birmingham, Bishop Robinson of Woolwich, the "Red Dean" were never subjected to the humiliation which Bishop Pike was subjected to at Wheeling.

The open spirit of the mother church had been affirmed in the words of Archbishop William Temple, in 1938, when a report commissioned by the Archbishops of Canterbury and York, *Doctrine in the Church of England*, was published. It was the product of fifteen years of work by twenty-five scholars and ecclesiastics on the nature and ground of Christian doctrine as perceived in the Anglican Communion; it has been a book widely studied in Anglican seminaries, and was a principal source for the Pike-Pittenger volume. In introducing *Doctrine*, Temple emphasized that it was not intended as a *summa theologiae*—such would be, said Temple, a *monstrum horrendum*. "The Church of England has no official Philosophy and it certainly was not our desire to provide one for it."

Heresy trials and, indeed, the idea of heresy were anomalies in Anglicanism quite some time before the Bayne report reached that conclusion. It was, perhaps, in the last (and only) trial of an Episcopal bishop for heresy—that of Bishop Brown in 1924—that this was exposed most cogently. There, after refusing to admit evidence on the latitude of doctrine in Anglicanism, the ecclesiastical court stated that the doctrine of the Church was a matter of judicial notice and it took judicial notice that what the Episcopal Church held was contained in the Book of Common Prayer. After the verdict, which condemned him as a heretic, Bishop Brown remarked:

> We have utterly failed to draw from the court a statement of any standard of orthodoxy. But this failure is our greatest triumph, because it was our contention, from the outset, that it could not be done.
>
> We are told only that the doctrine is contained, but not formulated, in the Prayer Book, in the Collects, in the Scriptures. So doubtless it is contained in the Dictionary . . .
>
> [I]t will have become obvious to everyone whose mind lives in this scientific age, that a charge of heresy can not be sustained. More than that, it will become obvious to everyone that such a charge can not even be stated. And what is obvious to everyone sooner or later must become obvious to theologians.

It took forty-three years for Brown's prediction to be fulfilled by the recognition, in the Bayne report, by theologians and ecclesiastics of what had long been obvious to everyone else.

Probably Bishop Pike himself was to blame for the notion that he was a heretic. When he first mentioned the term, while expressing his qualms about the narrow creedal views contained in the 1960 Dallas pastoral letter, he gratuitously furnished his enemies with a suggestion of how they might discredit or destroy him. Once the association of Pike with heresy gained notoriety, every word or phrase he uttered became subject to distortion, to excerption out of context, to misrepresentation, a process sometimes abetted by his verbal skill in shorthand, and his jaunty, flippant talk. Furthermore, the media, through the years in which various heresy accusations were circulating, tended to characterize Pike's views in more emphatic style than the texts of his writings and speakings justified. A *Time* magazine cover story on the bishop dated November 11, 1966, just after the censure, for an example, declared: "There is hardly a dogma in the creed that Pike has not at one time or another denied."

The hyperbole of the press in reporting on the heresy controversy points to the prominence of rhetoric, as distinguished from theology, in the whole contretemps. Both the Arizona charges and the Louttit presentment cite press clippings, in hodgepodge fashion, in support of their allegations, while, of course, the censure document objects mainly to the tone and style of Pike's utterances, but not the content. The censure did not challenge Bishop Pike's orthodoxy, it condemned his rhetoric as vulgar, irresponsible, contradictory.

"Vulgarization" is, perhaps, best left aside, because it seems a determination pertaining as much to a hearer as to a speaker, there being no objectively vulgar words. Yet, in one respect, it was an odd claim since Pike had expressed himself in pithy terms for a long time without provoking ire, and, indeed, elicited widespread admiration for his gift of communicating to supposedly cynical and unbelieving modern generations. In 1953, in a sermon at St. John the Divine, for instance, he had styled the Holy Spirit as "the esprit de corps of the Christian fellowship," and had continued by remarking that the Trinity was "a concept which seems to say that we have three gods rather than one," without inciting hostile response.

Placing the issue of "irresponsibility" in abeyance for the time being, the censure's allegation concerning Pike's "often obscure and contradictory utterances" was particularly curious, too, at least to anyone who had, in fact, been attentive to his utterances, oral and published, during his public prominence. The inference, at the censure, was very compelling that few of his peers who endorsed this rebuke were relying upon direct knowledge of what he had said rather than an impression they had somehow acquired other than by reading his articles and books or listening to him speak. What emerges from the latter effort is neither obscure nor contradictory, for the most part, but remarkably redundant. What is noticeable is not how novel his views were, but how often reiterated in similar language. What is shown is not so much how his mind changed, but that his mind changed little.

Pike's theological redundancy can be verified, in relation to the multifarious charges of heresy—the Georgia clericus complaint, the Arizona allegations, the Louttit presentment, and the echoes of these which he had to confront from some clergy and laity in his own diocese—by comparing some of his sayings before he became a bishop with those later utterances found to be so provocative.

(1) On the charge Pike "denied the doctrine of the Blessed Trinity" (as the Arizona statement put it):

In a sermon on May 4, 1953, Dean Pike said:

> In regard to the formulation of the doctrine of the Trinity, we must distinguish what was being communicated from the way the Church has normatively communicated it . . . [W]hat was being expressed is the living experience of the active power of God in three distinct relationships, and the conviction that in each of these experiences the Christian is in touch with God himself, a God who is one, not three.

In a statement in the *Pacific Churchman*, in September 1965, Bishop Pike wrote:

> As is clear from "A Time for Christian Candor" I regard as unintelligible and misleading to men of our day the classical formulation of the doctrine of the Trinity, as couched in the late Greek philosophical concepts of the fourth and fifth centuries. I affirm of God all that has been affirmed of the "three Persons."

(2) On the uniqueness of Christ and the doctrine of the Incarnation, which Pike was charged with denying:

In a sermon preached at St. John the Divine, Christmas Day, 1954:

> The uniqueness of Christ lies not in a claim that He is the only revelation of God or the only power of good in the world, but in the fact that by Jesus Christ . . . we measure and evaluate all other revelations and actions . . . We make Him the final measure because not only was God revealing Himself through Christ, but God was in Christ, having translated Himself into the language of human life, revealing His very self and acting directly to save us and bring us in fellowship with Himself.

In A *Time for Christian Candor* (1964), at page 112 *et seq.*:

> So in the revelation in Jesus Christ the uniqueness lies not in the *fact* of revelation or in the Source of what is revealed, but rather in the Avenue of that Source's revelation—at the right time the right man related aright to Him who is ever there and ready to be revealed . . .
>
> Hence, Christians are those who see in this man in history, this particular man in a particular time and place, the all-out acting out of the being of God . . .
>
> And in and through this we know, as much as we can know, what God expects our life to be like, and what He is like toward us. Thus we can assert honestly, in the words of the Nicene Creed, that Jesus Christ is "God of God, Light of Light, Very God of Very God," He is the One against whom we would measure any other reported experience—through all the centuries . . .

(3) On the allegation that Pike denied the Virgin Birth:
In *The Faith of the Church* (1951), pages 86ff.:

> There have been Christians, down the ages, who in their proper desire to emphasize the deity of Jesus have tended to slight the balancing fact of His manhood . . . The Nicene Creed has always stood as the guarantee of the fact . . . that God *was made man*.
>
> It is this double truth that the phrases *conceived by the Holy Ghost, born of the Virgin Mary* were intended to affirm. . . . The Church has always insisted on the theological meaning of the creedal statement about the birth of Jesus—namely, that He is a new creation . . . [A footnote to this passage states: There is no disagreement within the Church on the theological meaning of the Virgin Birth. We recognize that some have difficulty as to the historical account.]

At page 139 *et seq.*, in A *Time for Christian Candor* (1964):

> For generations, many intelligent people have been put off
> from Christianity by the Church's apparently absolute proclama-
> tion of the Virgin Birth narratives as both history and dogma. On
> the other hand, many others have felt seriously threatened when-
> ever the historical truth of the narratives has been questioned
> . . . Further, in any era, with any conceptual or semantic equip-
> ment, it is difficult to devise propositions or images which ade-
> quately carry the paradox of Who Jesus Christ is; that is, a
> particular man in Whom the fullness of God dwelt and acted . . .
>
> What is needed, then, is candor about the difficulties in hold-
> ing these narratives to be historical, which arise from the text of
> the New Testament books themselves, and boldness in making
> clear that their historical truth could hardly be regarded as an
> essential of the Faith, and at the same time affirmative use of
> the image liturgically and in the folk activities which surround
> the Christmas season.

Whether or not any of the aforementioned views of Pike, either
the earlier Pike of the fifties or the later Pike of the sixties, could
be said to be heretical, so far as Anglicanism is concerned, they
were manifestly neither obscure nor contradictory, as the censure
stated. Mainly they show consistency, perchance redundancy in
Pike's thought, over a long period, and thus they reiterate the
question of why his positions on these items should have provoked heresy charges in the sixties, when the same did not cause
such controversy a decade or more previous.

One reason that can be assigned for this situation is the relative
popularity of the Church during the so-called religious revival of
the fifties compared with its more defensive posture in the sixties
when "new theology" became a vogue. Bishop Pike became
quickly identified with the latter not so much because of the radical tenor of his theology but because of his attitude of openness
and willingness to listen and learn. In 1952—in commenting upon
an incident in which a fundamentalist minister had publicly
burned a page from the Revised Standard Version of the Bible—
Dean Pike had said: "We do not believe in Christ's Incarnation
because of the passage in Isaiah: we see meaning in the passage in
Isaiah because of our belief in Christ's Incarnation. Thus we need
not fear to face honestly the results of honest scholarship, and we
should do so because the God of the Church is also the God of

truth." He emphasized his approach further: "If we hold 'the faith once for all delivered to the Saints' we need not fear new information which scholars provide us as to the text, the translation or the historical setting for various parts of Holy Scripture." The same attitude informed his comprehension of the ancient Creeds. In another sermon at the New York cathedral, on May 11, 1958, shortly after he had been elected bishop, he summarized:

> All this has been stated and restated: in the Bible, in the writings of the Fathers, in the Creeds . . . Attempts have been made to formulate it in various "confessions of Faith" of various religious traditions . . . the theological task, the task of formulation and expression, is important and right. But none of these formulations are final. What is final is the Gospel, the Word behind the words.

True to his own word, two of the theological (as distinguished from pastoral, apologetic, or ethical) books which Pike wrote, both of which became fodder in the heresy inferno—A Time for Christian Candor and What Is This Treasure—took as their principal motif the II Corinthians passage, at chapter 4, verse 7: "But we have this treasure in earthen vessels, that the excellency of the power may be of God, and not of us."

It was this elementary openness to new information or insight, this readiness to face the facts, insofar as the facts could at a given moment be ascertained, that was the basis for Pike's theologizing and, more significant, his faith as a person. He bespoke this, too, early in his ecclesiastical career. On November 7, 1954, he told a congregation at St. John the Divine that the "first act need not be blind faith, or a lead in the dark. It is a choice for what is the most plausible, most coherent view of things." By the time his book entitled If This Be Heresy was published (four days before the 1967 Seattle convention convened), Bishop Pike was still making the same point, if more elaborately:

> A man can believe what is shown to emerge from . . .
> a. Examination of relevant data,
> b. The drawing of a plausible inference from the data,
> c. Affirmation of the consequent hypothesis by faith, and
> d. Action based on this faith-affirmation.

Having overlooked the earlier sermon, the New York Times's religion editor, Edward B. Fiske, referred to the publication of that book and, specifically, this part of its contents, as "throwing" down another gauntlet of nonorthodoxy."

Perhaps it *was* a gauntlet, if only because in the midst of the "theological revolution" of the sixties many supposed it inappropriate for a bishop of the Church to be attentive to skeptical questions or "new" data. Clifford Morehouse, sometime president of the Episcopal House of Deputies, an impeccable conservative in all respects, had written, in 1964, that it "is sad when a bishop or priest of the Church confuses its members by expressing his own doubts and denials. The layman has a right . . . to expect them to teach the faith of the church rather than their own private opinions . . . When . . . a bishop, with the best will in the world, tries to restate the Faith in terms of contemporary knowledge, he may . . . sow the tares of confusion . . ." It is this sentiment, voiced by Morehouse, which was shared by enough bishops to censure Bishop Pike for "irresponsibility." The issue of confusing the laity had been an undercurrent in the heresy controversy all along. Pike had noted that in *If This Be Heresy* by including a dedication to "The Little People" and by commenting in the book: "Earlier a leading American bishop, having heard I was doing another book . . . had sent me a blunt letter urging me not to write it. He said in effect: we know these things, Jim, but don't let 'the little people' know . . . I did not accede to this gnostic and condescending distinction . . ."

One reason Pike did not share this condescension for the laity was that he was far better informed about their concerns and their capabilities than his peers seem to have been. His preaching and speechmaking, his articles and books, the great publicity which attended him meant that he was inundated, while the heresy case was pending, with thousands upon thousands of letters (as well as direct contacts with congregations and audiences) which document the crisis of belief which multitudes of "little people" were then suffering and which nominate Pike as both spokesman and pastor. The sentiment was not unanimous, of course. Bishop Louttit, for example, heard from an anti-Pike rector in San Francisco that "many devout, loyal, and generous Churchmen have had their confidence in the Church sorely shaken." But it was an impressive response, one that Pike could not ignore, typified by this statement, from the letter of a church-woman in the Midwest: "This is a very long over-due thank-you note . . . I have not always agreed with your position. Even so, your statements and positions have at least enabled me to gain firmer convictions of my own . . . To me, your openness to movement and change has spread . . . hope."

Ironically, many of the most distinguished theological scholars of the day shared the appreciation so evident among laypeople for Bishop Pike's efforts. Hugh Montefiore, of Cambridge University, admired him for "putting aside the intricacies of dogmatic theology to concentrate on the big issues for the ordinary man." His colleague at Cambridge, theologian Donald MacKinnon, who saw much of Pike during his sabbatical, named him "a man of integrity and humility, with a remarkable honesty and openness of mind." Henry Pitney Van Dusen, president of Union Theological Seminary in New York, wrote: "Within the spate of current books seeking to speak to the 'de-Christianized' man, of which *Honest to God* is the most talked-about and presumably the most read, Bishop Pike's *A Time for Christian Candor* is, within my knowledge, far and away the ablest." The same book, reviewed by the respected journal *Theology Today*, won praise, as did its author: "His is a courageous and daring voice in our midst, ready to probe and criticize sanctified traditions so that the Gospel may be allowed to break through as light and life." Even Bishop Bayne, after Wheeling, had a good word for Pike as one who "has awakened a lot of people to the fact that a lot of theology is word-mongering—and that there is nothing behind the words." That admission of Bayne, though it might have more fittingly been made before Wheeling, was received by Bishop Pike with bitter-sweet satisfaction, since it had been Bayne who had the assignment of responding, from the pulpit of Trinity Church in New York City, to the series of sermons that Pike had delivered during the summer of 1964, when he had been the Select Preacher, in the same pulpit. Those sermons, which provoked an uproar which fed into the heresy controversy, were the raw material of *A Time for Christian Candor*. They dwelt upon exactly the problem of "wordmongering" that Bishop Bayne belatedly acknowledged.

In connection with the conundrum—was Pike a heretic?—mention is required of some material in the book *If This Be Heresy*. The reference is to chapter 7, the section entitled "Life After Death." If, consistent with the Bayne report, and recalling the liberality of Archbishop Temple, the chapter does not qualify as heretical, it does raise questions because it is such a strange potpourri of topics—immortality, the extension of the psyche, extrasensory perception, glossolalia, psychedelic phenomena, synchronicity, psychokinesis and telekinesis, mysticism, various psychic phenomena, "ongoing life." Curiosity about this material is whetted further because it was published at a time when, on one hand, the bishop was being harassed as a "reductionist" who had oversimplified belief, while, on the other hand, this book itself insists upon Pike's empirical method, which he sometimes put in shorthand as "facts+faith=belief." Pike was, at this juncture, complaining about the problem of "overbelief" but the chapter cited seems, on the face of it, to be a prime instance of "overbelief." The material is confused, but insofar as it may have been offered as an elaboration of the meaning of resurrection it appears very vulnerable theologically.

Chapter 7 has an explanation, however, furnished by Maren Bergrud, who was associated with Pike in the hectic interim in which this book was composed. She claimed primary authorship of this part of *If This Be Heresy*. One other instance in which Pike used a ghost writer is known: that involved an article for a law journal. And it was acknowledged by Pike that *The Other Side* was a work of co-authorship with Diane Kennedy. Evidently, in the press of events after Wheeling—his obligations in Santa Barbara, his campaigning the country, his marriage with Esther reaching crisis, his grief for his son still active—he allowed Maren Bergrud to ghostwrite some of this book. That was probably the closest Pike ever came to heresy.

On the whole, however, the theological work of Bishop Pike was, as the English journal *New Christian* described it, ". . . commonplace. This is intended as a term neither of abuse nor condescension, but of praise." That assessment is further explicated in the *New Christian* by Anthony Dyson, chaplain of Ripon Hall, Oxford, in this way:

> The appeal to any magisterium (whether Pope or Bible or Confession) becomes problematic, moreover, precisely because the institutional Church cannot be unaware of, though it may try to turn a blind eye to, the pluralism of academic theology. With

the increasing *haute vulgarisation* of this theology, the problem
can only become more acute. Helmut Gollwitzer, in his review
of *Honest to God*, found it remarkable that Robinson's remarks
about the language of faith and the proper agnosticism of our
God-talk should have so sensational an effect. It has obviously
not got around, he continues, that in evangelical theology since
the Enlightenment "statements of this kind are partly accepted
as self-evident while the rest of them, even if they are in dispute,
are at all events certainly commonplace." But people are astonished to hear these things and thus ascribe to them an *"avante
garde* character." But now that these ideas are penetrating the
Church and forming the minds of many younger clergy, who
among the Babel of theological voices is to receive the accolade
of orthodoxy, and who is to decide?

An Interlude on Olympus

The six months Bishop Pike had spent at Cambridge on sabbatical from his episcopal duties had enormously excited his interest
in theological studies and simultaneously that had accentuated his
boredom with administration. He found himself resenting the
daily burdens of office as an interference with his intellectual life,
and that frustration had been compounded by the gathering personal crises connected with the suicide of his eldest son and the
death of his marriage. For all his hyperactivity, he had reached a
point where, as he explained, "I had to make a decision—I'm not
twins. I have been aware of an overextension of two roles: that of
administrator and leader as bishop, and that of teacher-scholar."
Pike resigned his jurisdiction effective September 15, 1966. Canon
law requires that such a resignation be accepted not only by the
standing committee of the diocese, but that it receive consent
from the other bishops. Though astounded by this development,
the standing committee in the Diocese of California assented to
the bishop's resignation "with deep regret," while the concurrence
of Pike's fellow bishops came much more readily than had the
similar action necessary to confirm his election eight years before.
In his letter explaining his decision, addressed to the Presiding
Bishop, Pike summarized his reasons:

A six months sabbatical . . . is obviously inadequate . . .
Back on the job, I am all the more aware of how difficult it will

be for me to continue a dual role of scholar-teacher and admin-
istrator-leader. I am not growing any younger and this conflict
has in fact been characteristic of me all my adult life in two
professions, always keeping me much too busy in terms of legitimate allotment of time for family life, rest and reflection.

Pike had been moving toward this decision for some time. It
was resolved by the sabbatical experience during which, he said, "I
experienced the sheer joy of staying with something for more than
one disconnected hour." He had considered other options. In
1965, the year before the sabbatical, he had established a so-called
Strategy Committee, composed of clergy and laity from the diocese, to advise him on an elaborate plan he was considering to de-
centralize the diocese in the hope of increasing the involvement
of churchpeople in the government of the Church and of reduc-
ing the work load—though not the authority—of the office of diocesan bishop. By this scheme, the diocese would have been
divided into three regions each of which would have a suffragan
bishop, resident in the region, styled by the name of the region—
as the Bishop of San Jose, *et al.*—and sharing such episcopal
duties as confirmations, ordinations, institutions and dedications
and supervising missions, college work, social relations, stew-
ardship, and the like. Mindful of the troubles Pike was then having in the House of Bishops, a wag remarked, on hearing of his
plan, that Pike would thereby have his own "house of bishops."
The Strategy Committee's deliberations were inconclusive or, anyway, overtaken by other events, including Pike's decision to resign,
but it may have had a certain influence on the resignation because
it digressed from its terms of reference and became an *ad hoc*
evaluation of Pike as a bishop. A memorandum about its deliberations during the spring of 1965—about a year before Pike's decision to resign—noted, for instance, that "the Committee has become . . . stuck on the matter of the person, behavior and
qualifications of our bishop." Instead of a critical examination of
the inherited centralized diocese structure familiar in the Episcopal Church, which Pike's reorganization into regions or sub-
dioceses would have radically altered, the committee focused on
"our present bishop" who "has serious deficiencies which make
that kind of structure to a considerable degree inoperable." Thus,
within this group "the key to 'strategy' is either to correct or elim-
inate our present bishop." On the other hand, the sentiment was

expressed in the committee that "what we may be witnessing before our eyes in our Diocese is God's proof that, even with a brilliant and inexhaustible person for a bishop, the inherited episcopal system—unimaginatively accepted as is—simply will not work in our day . . . In other words, if such be at all true, our Committee may have been missing a chance to help the whole Church think through its new tasks and begin to work with new methods, while we dutifully defended old axioms of Establishment and helped kill a gifted bishop."

Coincident with the discussions in the Strategy Committee, the internal anti-Pike factions in the Diocese of California were growing very bold and vocal, filling columns in the diocesan newspaper with diatribes against Pike, speaking out in vestries and in parish meetings, threatening to cripple the diocese financially unless the bishop desisted from social and political involvement. Bishop Pike was determined not to surrender to this latter ultimatum, but he did ponder whether, if he resigned, the social mission of the diocese might be enhanced by the removal of himself as so conspicuous a target. In that connection, Pike took comfort, after his resignation announcement, that the diocesan convention which met on September 15, 1966, to elect his successor, after nine ballots and twelve hours of frantic politics, named C. Kilmer Myers, famed for his pioneering inner city ministry on New York's Lower East Side, as the Sixth Bishop of California. In announcing Myers's election to the convention, Bishop Pike had commented: "It will be nice to be remembered as one of California's conservative bishops!" Myers and Pike had been friends since 1946, when both were tutors at General Theological Seminary in New York City, and Bishop Pike greatly admired the boldness and determination of Myers's social witness. Doctrinally, as the San Francisco *Chronicle* was prompt to note, the two bishops differed, though that might mean more freedom for Bishop Myers to speak out on politics and social issues. As the *Chronicle* observed:

> Arch-conservatives, for example, will no longer be able to use "He doubts the Virgin Birth!" as a cover for their seething resentment of the bishop's sociological or economic views. Myers believes in a literal Virgin Birth—although he denies that this is required belief for an Episcopalian.

On another front, if Pike entertained the thought that his resignation as a bishop in jurisdiction might mitigate or quell the apprehension and animosity that had entered into his relationships in
the House of Bishops, he was promptly and emphatically dis-
abused of the notion. Barely a week after his resignation took
effect, the Louttit presentment was published.

Some months before deciding to resign, Pike consulted his old
friend Robert Hutchins, who made a suggestion to him that he
join Hutchins's think tank in Santa Barbara—the Center for the
Study of Democratic Institutions—as a "theologian in residence."
It was arranged that Pike would become a member of the Center's staff, concentrating, as a "worker-bishop," on the role of the
Church and its relation to other institutions in American society
and pursuing his concern, aroused during his sabbatical, for the
theological significance of the Dead Sea Scrolls and related recent
"finds" and the effort to reconstruct the historical origins of Christianity.

After settling in his new quarters in Santa Barbara—the only
member of his family who accompanied him was his mother—the
bishop returned to San Francisco to preside at the convention
which would elect Bishop Myers (and which would pass a resolution that, henceforward, Pike would be styled an "Auxiliary
Bishop of California") and to make his valedictory. His farewell to
San Francisco was nearly as great a civic event as his consecration
had been eight years earlier. A splendid testimonial dinner with
eight hundred guests was held at the Fairmont Hotel. The appropriate dignitaries of politics, education, labor, business and indus-
try, the professions were present, as well as religious and ecclesiastical leaders of all sorts. Rabbi Alvin Fine of the city's Temple
Emanu-El was the principal speaker. His tribute was to Bishop
Pike's concern for human beings as the measure of his ministry
and, it was reported, these remarks "brought tears to the eyes of
many" present. A special television program, documenting Pike's
tumultuous tenure, was done by station KRON-TV in San
Francisco. A huge congregation jammed Grace Cathedral to hear
his farewell sermon. Though their divorce had become a moral
certainty, Esther, for one last time, cooperated in all necessary

public appearances. On September 5, the San Francisco *Chronicle* covered the cathedral service:

> Bishop James A. Pike said farewell as rector of Grace Cathedral to an overflow throng yesterday, and the great gothic pile reverberated with laughter and at the close many an eye glistened . . .
>
> This was the sort of thing . . . a readiness to stick his neck out, whether it be on a trampled-on civil liberty or an outmoded dogma—that made Bishop Pike's appeal far more than Episcopalian. Hundreds there yesterday to say farewell to the bishop . . . were of other faiths.

The bishop's sermon acknowledged the opposition pressures and threats of economic reprisal against his social and political involvement. As the *Chronicle* stated:

> [I]n his ranging [Pike] hit upon last week's union-election victory of the Delano farm workers. He commended the part his diocese took in the struggle, despite "threats from Mr. Bigs to cut off financial support." His roving glance set up his next remark nicely: "Maybe we'll make up today what we sent to Delano."

Bishop Pike's new venture at the Center in Santa Barbara was not seen by himself as any diminishment of his involvement. "I am not going into pure scholarship as if in a monastery," he told United Press International. John Cogley, long associated with the Center himself, observed in the New York *Times*, when the resignation announcement was made public, that the bishop "has removed himself from many of the protections afforded by a high ecclesiastical post." He would be vulnerable at Santa Barbara in different ways than as a bishop. Cogley continued:

> He will become one more member in a group of intellectuals, some of whom accept a form of the traditional faiths, some of whom are entirely indifferent to religious questions, and some of whom are opposed to the theological presuppositions as unworthy of serious attention. He will be given no special deference, nor will he seek any.

Cogley thought the rubric appropriate for Pike's decision to join the Center's staff was found in one of Dietrich Bonhoeffer's letters written from the Nazi prison where he awaited execution for his part in the plot to kill Hitler: "We are proceeding toward a time of no religion at all . . . How do we speak of God without religion? . . . How do we speak in a secular fashion of God?"

If nothing else, the Louttit charges, then the Wheeling censure, then the pre-Seattle politics, not to mention the finalization of the divorce from Esther or other personal issues, spared Pike a monastic existence at the Center. On the whole, his new colleagues there understood his situation in terms of conflict between a dissenter or reformer and an institutional status quo—that Pike was a cleric and that the Church was the institution was happenstance. And they sympathized with him on the due process issue —on the recurrent denials of a fair hearing—and were supportive of his "taking his case to the people" by barnstorming the nation speaking and preaching. In any case, his relationships in the Center staff were neither perfunctory nor superficial, and, in spite of distraction or interruption, he made some impressive contributions both in response to the work of others and in his own work. That was evident when he was present for the daily no-holds-barred discussions of the staff, sometimes with distinguished visiting persons in dialogue. He accompanied Harry Ashmore and several more from the Center to the *Pacem in Terris* conference in Geneva in 1967, and he researched and wrote and presented several substantial monographs, including papers on "Fair Taxation for the Churches," "Ad Hoc Conscientious Objection and the First Amendment," the viability of first-century Christianity in the twentieth century, "The Church and Women," the apparent conflict in biblical texts on obedience to governing authorities, "The Conflict of Archaism and Idealism in Institutions." Retaining his flair for popularizing, he utilized material assembled in learned and lawyerlike fashion for the Church taxation paper, in which he advocated ending of preferential tax treatment of the churches, with certain adjustments to allow for community uses of church premises, to publish an article on the same subject, though not in the same style, in *Playboy*. In that, as well as in others of his Center monographs, notably his analysis of archaism in churchly institutions and the theological scholarship grounding his advocacy of the ordination of women, Pike disclosed, again, that remarkable prescience or anticipation of issues that so often caused him to be named prophetic. Whatever *that* faculty of intellect be properly called, Pike was abundantly so endowed, and that fact was more excellently evidenced in his papers prepared for the Center than, say, in his extemporaneous preaching when he was dean or when he was bishop, or than in most of his books, which were admittedly, for the most part, hurriedly prepared. To that extent, Pike's term at the Center afforded him something of the opportunity for concentration that he so desired. His time at the Center was one of solid accomplishment, but it was destined to be short. In 1969, the Center was drastically renovated. Fifteen of the staff, including Bishop Pike, left; four so-called Senior Fellows remained and subsequently the staff was further augmented. By that juncture, however, the focus of Pike's concentration was becoming very definite, and his sense of expectation was growing keen indeed.

A Change of Heart

Diane Kennedy and Jim Pike became deeply in love. They had first met, as has been mentioned, when she enrolled as a student in a summer session course at the Pacific School of Religion which Pike taught in the interim between the announcement of his resignation as bishop and his move to Santa Barbara. "I was both surprised and pleased," she had occasion to write to Bishop Myers, "to find a famous and obviously very intelligent man to be a very sensitive, responsive person who listened attentively to his students' questions or comments and gave each one full consideration . . . Moreover, he was able to accept criticism—indeed welcome it—and to receive and incorporate ideas offered by others into his own frame of reference."

Pike had formed a small foundation to integrate his continuing extracurricular activities to his duties on the Center staff—his literary and speaking commitments and his ministry as a *pastor pastorum* at large—which Maren Bergrud had nominally directed; after her death in the summer of 1967, the board of the New Focus Foundation invited Diane to become director. She moved to Santa Barbara toward the end of August and soon brought an order to the operation that was a marvel to those, including Jim, who had suffered the extraordinary disarray over which Maren had presided. Diane accompanied Jim to the Seattle convention and in the months immediately following that event collaborated intensely with him in writing the manuscript of *The Other Side*, in addition to her coping with the deluge of queries and requests that inundated Pike after the publicity of the Toronto séance story. In this experience, as Diane has vividly recalled, they found "complete mutuality"—"we rejoiced in our unique compatibility in every regard." The decree of divorce from Esther had been granted before Diane came to Santa Barbara and hence Diane and Jim felt free to "date." Though the two had met initially in the juxtaposition of student and teacher—even as had Esther and Jim—the relationship of Diane and Jim matured into one of peers. "We work as a team and personally we also relate on a par," Diane has written. "I needed a man of Jim's strength of character, intellect, imagination and will—and forcefulness of personality . . . and I think Jim needed a person as free of emotional deprivation as I to respond with fullness and joy to him. His resilience," she told Bishop Myers, "has been remarkable in that regard. In spite of the hurt and sense of guilt he brought from his relationship with Esther—not to mention his wounds from the loss of his eldest son and from the various ecclesiastical battles with the Church—Jim is not crippled or handicapped emotionally . . . Jim is not a person who bears grudges or who carries resentments. He is loving and forgiving . . . He has given freely of his love to me and has responded with joy and health."

These tributes to the love that grew between Diane and Jim were commended to Bishop Myers in connection with their decision to marry, and to seek the blessing of the bishop upon their marriage. A host of persons who witnessed the happening of their love attested to its good effect. For one very important thing, Diane was secure enough in herself and in her affection for Jim to be able to like and affirm Pearl in a way in which Mama was not threatened, as had been the circumstance in Jim's two previous marriages. Julian Bartlett, the dean of Grace Cathedral, observed shortly before Diane and Jim were married: "I have known Jim well for some fifteen years. He seems to me to be freer in a healthy way than I have ever known him to be . . . He has a characteristic enthusiasm, but there is more than that . . . Jim seems . . . happier than I have ever known him to be." Another clergyman, "equally fond of Esther and Jim," said: "I have noted . . .

the real change which has overtaken him . . . [and] have sense⌐
beneath the old enthusiasms and ebullience, which are still there,
a far deeper sense of security and settledness."

There had been some relaxation of the previously stern view of
the canons of the Episcopal Church with regard to marriages in
the Church of previously married persons since the time that Pike
had confronted that problem as to the ecclesiastical status of his
first divorce in relation to his second marriage. The requirement
that had now to be met was a finding by a bishop in jurisdiction
that a previous marriage was "spiritually dead." Such an episcopal
judgment allowed that "Any person in whose favor a judgment
has been granted . . . may be married by a Minister of this
Church." A year's waiting period after a divorce conditions such a
judgment, and in the case of the second Pike divorce, the civil
decree, granted on July 25, 1967, anyway required a one-year wait
to become final.

On September 8, 1968, Jim and Diane met with Bishop Myers
and told him of their intention to be married and of their desire
that he marry them. They soon thereafter filed a formal application detailing, as the canons require, facts to support a judgment
as to the "spiritual death" of the previous marriage and setting
forth reasons why the applicants believe that their marriage would
succeed. They sought, at the same time, permission for Diane to
be confirmed by Jim in the Episcopal Church, she having been a
lifelong Methodist, and reiterated their wish that Bishop Myers
preside at the marriage, assisted by other clergy, including Bishop
R. Marvin Stuart of the Denver Methodist Church jurisdiction,
an old friend of Diane's, Rabbi Alvin Fine, who had addressed
the testimonial dinner at Pike's farewell as diocesan bishop, and
Edward Crowther, the Anglican bishop whom Pike had aided
when Crowther was expelled from South Africa for opposing
apartheid and who had become a member of the Center staff in
Santa Barbara.

Bishop Myers had indicated, when the subject was first raised
on September 8, that he would act upon the application with the
advice of two members of the Diocesan Marriage Committee. On
October 14, the day following Diane's confirmation, the couple
met again with the bishop, at which time a date was set—
November 14—for the prospective ceremony and the bishop con-

sented to officiate and approved of the proposed assisting clergy. Diane and Jim were told they could send out invitations to the marriage. Jim wrote then promptly to Esther and, after receiving a call from Esther, telephoned their children. He asked his son Chris to be best man. They contacted Dean Bartlett to reserve the chapel of Grace Cathedral, and the dean wrote them: "The Chapel of Grace is reserved for 8:00 P.M. on November 14th . . . God bless—and I am very happy for you." Some precaution was taken against premature publicity, and Bartlett's note reported that "The 'front name' is: 'Smith wedding.' "

The House of Bishops convened the next week for its annual session in Augusta, Georgia, and both Myers and Pike were in attendance. The amiability of the communication between the two bishops was disturbed there. Myers became irritated because Pike had told some other bishops about the marital plans and, in what Pike later described as "strongly prelatical" tone, warned that his ruling on the pending application was subject to the recommendation of the Marriage Committee advisors.

The following Monday, October 28, Bishop Myers dispatched a telegram to Santa Barbara stating that, on the recommendation of the advisors, he must deny the application. Jim and Diane were flabbergasted. They phoned Myers—both of them on the line—and asked if further information were needed to support the petition, but Bishop Myers said that this was not necessary, that the former marriage was clearly dead spiritually but that the difficulty was in approving the contemplated marriage. A letter followed the telegram in which Myers said that he lacked a "devout conviction" that the union of Diane and Jim would succeed. After another telephone conversation, Myers agreed to receive letters from persons who had direct knowledge of the relationship between the two and who thereby had a basis to assess their marriage prospects. A veritable deluge of correspondence—overwhelmingly affirmative—reached the bishop and presumably his Marriage Committee advisors within the next few weeks, the writers including an array of psychiatrists, clergy, psychologists, lawyers, and counselors. Two days before the date originally chosen for the nuptial Eucharist, a time which had been initially selected more to suit the bishop than the couple, another telegram was received in Santa Barbara which said that the Marriage Committee advisors had recommended and the bishop regretfully concurred that approval not be given the marriage of Jim and Diane, but that application might be renewed after eighteen months.

Bishop Pike was saddened, baffled, indignant, dismayed. There were no reasonable grounds of which he was aware for the position Bishop Myers had taken, and no explanation as to why, after the encouragement which he and Diane had enjoyed that the marriage would happen on November 14, Myers had seemed to change. There were some clues about which to speculate. In a very frank letter to Esther, written November 21, Jim surmised that Bishop Myers had been "pressured" while at the Augusta meeting. And he wondered aloud whether comments of Esther figured in the matter. "Kim mentioned your name . . . and I learned since . . . that just before he left for Augusta you and Myers had been together socially and that you were expressing yourself negatively about *The Other Side*." Pike's impression that *that* book was somehow being cited to impute instability to him was, in part, supported by the first long telephone conversation which occurred after news of the denial of the application had been received. A transcript of that discussion includes the following exchange:

> *Pike:* Now, if it's on the ground that the proposed marriage is not well grounded then I would want to know naturally what you have to say about that . . .
> *Myers:* It is. I just don't feel in my conscience that I could bless the marriage in this instance, at this time. On the basis of what seems to me to be you—the way you are put together—and I certainly would feel that I would need a much longer time to have it shown to me that there was sufficient reason for me to think that this would be a Christian marriage, and at this point I am not convinced that it could be, and, therefore, because I am not convinced I can't give my blessing to this marriage any more than I would any marriage where I had that doubt.
> *Pike:* So the doubt is that Diane's and my marriage would be a Christian marriage. Well, the thing is because of the way I am put together?
> *Myers:* That's right.

The confidence of others who had written to Bishop Myers on the prospects of the marriage of Jim and Diane did not alter the view that Myers had taken and on December 10 he wrote to Pike reiterating that he would "be glad to review the matter of your proposed marriage after the lapse of eighteen months," and expressing his "hope that you will not consider remarriage outside the Church." This same letter stated formally the bishop's ruling on the status of the marriage to Esther:

> With regard to your marriage to Esther, it is the recommendation of the members of The Marriage Committee to me that it be declared spiritually dead. That is my judgment.

Jim and Diane decided to be married on December 20. After consulting the chancellor for canon law of the California diocese, Pike realized that the bishop's judgment as to the past marriage cleared the way for the new marriage, the evaluation of a proposed marriage being within the competence of *any* minister of the Church once a judgment pertaining to the "spiritual death" of a past marriage had been rendered by a bishop. As much as Jim and Diane had desired the blessing of Bishop Myers and, indeed, that he officiate at their wedding, his approval of their marriage was not canonically required for them to be married in the Church. They thereupon asked the Reverend Robert E. Hoggard, rector of St. Augustine's Church in Santa Monica, a minister well acquainted with both of them, and he gladly agreed to marry then. Though not strictly obliged to do so, Fr. Hoggard consulted his bishop, the Right Reverend Eric Bloy, of the Diocese of Los Angeles, the same bishop, paradoxically, who had so strenuously opposed Pike's confirmation as a bishop because of his previous marital status, and Bloy declared that Hoggard was free to make his own decision in the matter in light of the judgment of Bishop Myers regarding the marriage to Esther. The wedding took place, then, on the rescheduled date of the twentieth of December, 1968.

That was, unhappily, not the end of the issue. The honeymoon of the newlyweds was disturbed by a letter which Bishop Myers circulated to all the clergy under his jurisdiction and, further, to all the bishops of the Church, on the Monday following the ceremony. This is the full text of that communication, which was also released to the press:

Brethren:
As you know, it is not my custom to discuss the marital matters of persons under my pastoral care as Bishop of the Diocese. I

regard these as personal and private in character. However, the wide publicity accorded the marriage of Bishop Pike on Friday, December 20, 1968, and his own statements to the press, prompt this brief, preliminary message to you so that all of you may understand my role in the matter.

Originally, Bishop Pike made application for permission to remarry, and asked me to give my blessing to the marriage. I declined to grant the application, and advised him of my reasons. He then asked for a declaration of his marital status, and I wrote a letter, dated December 10, 1968, which he interpreted as a "judgment" which left him free to marry. However, this letter had *no* relation to his proposed marriage (to Diane Kennedy) and was not intended to be an approval or blessing of that marriage in any way.

I feel it important that the clergy of the diocese fully understand, beyond any possibility of doubt, that it was and is my conviction that I could not bless Bishop Pike's marriage and that I could not officiate at it. This is my position still, whatever the technical basis on which he proceeded.

In light of the problems brought about by the entire situation, I want to take this occasion to personally request that no Rector, Vestry, Vicar or Bishop's Committee invite Bishop Pike to perform any sacerdotal function by preaching, ministering the sacraments or holding any public service in this diocese until further notice from me to the contrary.

> Faithfully,
> ✠C. Kilmer Myers

The utterance of this letter only deepened Pike's mystification concerning Myers's attitude toward the new marriage, the more so because Pike was thoroughly confident that Myers's own judgment about the previous marriage had made this one canonically permissible. If Myers could not furnish his blessing nor officiate, while a great disappointment, that alone seemed to Bishop Pike no grounds to denounce the marriage publicly and to make an extraordinary request that Pike be barred from sacerdotal functions. Moreover, Pike soon found that Myers's action had the effect of a sanction. A long-standing invitation for Pike to preach during the upcoming Lenten season in another diocese was withdrawn "for reasons of episcopal reciprocity." The issue became further complicated as a divisive factor in the Diocese of California, tending to rally clergy into anti-Myers/pro-Pike and pro-Myers/anti-Pike factions. Some friends of both bishops made various attempts at mediation, and Pike, after seeking conversation with Myers without avail, issued a lengthy *Kalendar* of the controversy which he circulated to all those who had received Myers's letter. Pike pondered whether he should once again invoke his canonical rights to demand a trial since the incident had cast a cloud upon both his marriage and his ministry, and he had had no hearing and no opportunity to respond to any allegations that might have formed the basis of Myers's action. These circumstances provoked Pike because it seemed to him to obviate the very due process reforms in the canons achieved at Seattle. Knowing that another trial demand might be in the offing, the Presiding Bishop, John Hines, asked three bishops to visit with both Bishop Myers and Bishop Pike, "to learn all that they can from you concerning the background and fact of Jim's recent marriage, to learn whether or not there are grounds for the resolution of the problems involved . . . and to counsel me concerning this."

Events were moving toward a confrontation that would be a curious, inverted, ironical replay of the earlier controversies in which the question of the ecclesiastical status of Pike's first marriage threatened his entrance and his advancement in Episcopal orders. Then, abruptly, Pike dropped the matter entirely. He had, throughout his life, as Bishop Wetmore once observed, constantly "reached for issues," yet here, with an issue ready, Pike, uncharacteristically simply withdrew. He confided his reasons in a letter to Wilburn Campbell, Bishop of West Virginia, written on St. Patrick's Day, 1969:

> I had planned to file a demand for judicial proceedings as I did after the "Wheeling dealing" (resulting in the good outcome on the matter at Seattle) . . . However, I waited hoping for some less burdensome solution as, on their own initiative, one group after another (including the Standing Committee of the Diocese) approached Kim . . . [B]ut nothing eventuated . . . [I]n the course of all this time going by Diane and I have reached the point that it doesn't really matter any more. You can only hurt so long about something. All anger has gone too and a considerably higher priority than would be involved in pursuing what is the ecclesiastical equivalent of a libel action to its victorious finish,

namely our bringing to fruition the work I began on my sabbatical at Cambridge in 1965, Jesus in the context of his times, as
shown by all the new finds, Qumran and the others. We go to Israel . . . [T]he vast jigsaw puzzle is now almost complete . . .

The Church Alumnus

It soon appeared that the Pikes had reached a more momentous
decision than the abandonment of the dispute with Bishop
Myers: they quit the Episcopal Church. For Jim, of course, this
was the second time he had come to the conclusion that he could
not in conscience uphold a church affiliation. It was also for him a
decision which completed the dialectical relationship between his
marital status and his church membership. As he had fought
earlier to defend the integrity of his second marriage against assertions that it affected his standing as a communicant and his vocation as a priest and then as a prospective bishop, so now he was
convinced that the significance of his third marriage necessitated
his renunciation of the Episcopal Church and of his ministry
within the Episcopal Church.

The public became aware of the departure of the Pikes from
the organized Church through an article in the issue of *Look* magazine dated April 29, 1969. In that piece, Bishop Pike reviewed his
arguments that the institutional churches in America suffered from
"a rapidly growing *credibility gap*," a "*relevance gap*, which is
even more devastating," and an "increasingly grave *performance
gap*," points which he had previously developed in *If This Be Heresy*. He noted in *Look* the increasing exodus of clergy and laity
from the "standard-brand churches," and cited a current book of
Hans Küng, the Roman Catholic theologian so influential in the
work of the Vatican Council under Pope John XXIII, *Truth-
fulness: The Future of the Church*, in which Fr. Küng suggested
that what distinguishes those "just inside" the Church from those
"just outside" the Church is "believing hope." "*Believing hope*
for the Church is precisely what I no longer possess. In fact, I
now know that I really have not had such hope for quite a long
time," Pike wrote. Freely acknowledging the impact of the marriage controversy upon the decision to leave the Church, Pike

insisted that this conflict was a final straw: "It was not that the personal event magnified the malaise of the Church. Rather, it served to neutralize the long-standing emotional tie to a sick—even dying—institution."

The *Look* article, for all its sharp critique of the Church, was not cast in a merely negative tone; indeed, in it Pike spoke of leaving the Church in order better to implement the ministry that he and Diane shared, particularly the study of Christian origins and the practice of a "nomad" life-style which they had become convinced was more in accord with primitive Christianity.

> The origins of Christianity were infused with the spirit of the desert, the nomadic life of the wilderness: God on the move with his people, no finality other than God, no "temples made with hands" . . . As the ancient Qumrân *Manual* says, "This is the time of clearing the way to go to the wilderness."

In that spirit, the Pikes became "church alumni" and announced, in *Look*, that they had formed a foundation to extend research and study in the origins of Christianity and to be a center for reorientation of persons, like themselves, in the midst of "religious transition."

Bishop Pike indicated, in conjunction with this public disclosure of his departure from the organized Church, that he would formalize the break by notifying the ecclesiastical authorities in the Episcopal Church that he had, as the canons put it, abandoned the communion. This would set in motion a procedure by which he would be temporarily suspended from exercising his episcopal office and, after a six-month period, could be officially declared to have "abandoned" the communion by the House of Bishops. Technically, such abandonment would not revoke Pike's status as a bishop, since the orders of a bishop are deemed indelible, that for the sake of preserving the continuity of apostolic succession.

Bishop Hines represented the diversity of reaction to this decision. "Some will rejoice," he predicted. "Some will be sad." "The Church," he continued, "will miss the constructive use of the talents God bestowed upon Bishop Pike, but on such a pilgrimage, one can only wish the pilgrim well." In the latter comment, Hines ignored or missed the most cogent point that Pike had tried to make: that for the sake of "the constructive use" of his talents for the Church Pike was leaving the Church. In that intent, Pike had been much influenced by other notorious recent departures, including those of Bishop James Shannon and Father James Kavanaugh from the Roman Church. Pike admired the courage and integrity of these pilgrims, and others, less well known, like them. The regard was mutual. James Kavanaugh, for instance, had written to Bishop Myers when the instability of Jim had been insinuated as a factor in the marriage dispute:

> Jim Pike has not given me answers, he has only filled my mind with important questions. It does not become a simple question of: "Do I believe him?" It is rather a matter of his helping me to open my mind to a new reality . . . It is only that he, in a unique and special way, has given me greater insight and greater hope . . . Jim Pike has once again helped, humbly, courageously, with his childlike determination to know. I thank him.

In the weeks immediately following the announcement in *Look*, Jim and Diane were deluged with inquiries from persons in, as they styled it, "religious transition" who needed help, wanted counsel, offered support, affirmed the Pikes' decision. They were soon engaged in establishing, through the foundation they had started, programs for "retooling" those leaving the conventional churches, especially clergy dropouts from various denominations and communions. For Jim and Diane, the scope of this response to their quitting the Church was much more than a confirmation of their analysis of the contemporary state of the Church, it was also an authentication of the conviction they shared that Jim's vocation as *pastor pastorum* now required freedom from the burden of making an apologetic for the ecclesiastical institutions and from the attrition of time and talent which embroilment in redundant, quaint, collateral controversies in the Church entailed. They plunged ahead, initiating an intensive pilot program for clergy in transition and their families for the summer of 1969, as well as planning their next visit to the Holy Land to pursue the Christian origins issue in the fall of that year.

If some were joyous, while others were sad about Pike leaving the Episcopal Church, others were dismayed, as Bishop Hines had also anticipated. Through all the storms that had attended Bishop Pike's ecclesiastical career, there were many Episcopalians who re-

tained "believing hope" for the Church because Pike remained
within the fold. The decision to quit shocked them. John Krumm,
who had succeeded Pike as chaplain of Columbia University and
had been his close friend and frequent ally, and soon to become a
bishop himself, protested the course that Jim took. In response,
Jim wrote to reassure Krumm that "I believe the same things as I
believed before," but "when every avenue had been cut off from
serving from within, while respecting those who are permitted so
to do and choose to do so, we felt generally called to serve from
'outside the camp.'" Pike emphasized the same view that the viability of the Church had changed rather than Pike's convictions—
that, virtually, the Church had excluded him rather than he having abandoned the Church—in a postscript to the Krumm letter:
"In other words, I am about the same as I was when you and I
were outraged at what was done to our Sewanee friends and their
colleagues." And in the same reply to Krumm, Pike reveals how
personal aspects are entangled with theological concerns:

> I didn't file the demand for trial, because one does get tired of
> fighting . . . and would rather use the same energies con-
> structively in getting abroad a more adequate and alive image of
> Jesus, of man's whole transcendent potential and unidolatrous
> style of life—one in which the *personal* comes first rather than
> being brushed aside as not important to discuss. My counseling
> for some years, and our mail more and more shows that it is this
> latter which has been the straw that broke the camel's back in
> case after case, the cold diffidence within the Church to the end
> of just hurting persons by the Church.

There had been many signals along the way forecasting Pike's
move from "just inside" to "just outside" the Church. For one
thing, he was constantly confronted with the issue. A letter from a
Connecticut resident, in 1967, is representative of hundreds of
others. "Your continuing adherence to a formalized church puz-
zles me," the letter stated. "I can hardly believe that security is
your motivation." Right after the Seattle convention that year,
Pike wrote this correspondent, "I have reason to believe that by
staying within the Episcopal Church I have been able to bring
about at least some modest changes," to which he added, somewhat wistfully, "I feel any advance we make toward this end is at
least another small reason to stay . . . until we know—as I am

sure we will within two years at the least—what the fate of the institutional Church is in our day."

Some months later, in the *National Catholic Reporter* for August 14, 1968, Bishop Pike was urging dissenting clergy and laity "to speak one's convictions boldly and to stay in the Church," but there was ambivalence in him. Indeed, at the convention in Seattle, on the day the canonical changes were enacted that he deemed vindication enough to justify withdrawal of the demand for trial, in the presence of the few persons gathered with him for what he dubbed, in the circumstances, a "victory lunch," Bishop Pike had broached the idea of a "church alumni association." Reference was made to the discussion, in *The Christian Century* for November 8, 1967, by one of the luncheon guests:

> Brood upon it. If we do indeed live in a post-Christian world, as some have claimed, or if we thirst for a religionless Christianity, as others have claimed, or if God is in some curious sense dead, must we not dispose ourselves responsibly to our vast lost past? Those of us inclined to recollect with gratitude what the churches have done for us will not wish outright to abandon remnants of beloved institutions. Rather might we not give support to them, trusting they will serve well also those who follow after us into the deepening gloom? We do no less for the Metropolitan Museum of Art, or latterly the Museum of Modern Art . . . Meanwhile, permit me to suggest that . . . Bishop Pike be unanimously installed as first president of the Church Alumni Association, subject, of course, to ratification by COCU . . .

If the notion of a "church alumni association" was treated that day in Seattle somewhat facetiously, it nevertheless lingered in Pike's mind and became an increasingly serious option in the months thereafter. With the heresy controversy quieted at last, Bishop Pike found himself more pastorally vulnerable than ever before in his role as a "worker-priest in the purple," especially sought out for counsel by clergy, including several other bishops, who had grown disenchanted or who had dropped out of the active church ministry or who were contemplating such a decision. Moreover, his involvement at the Center for the Study of Democratic Institutions became more concentrated and this enabled him to make a more disciplined and documented analysis of the American churches as archaic and failing institutions. In such a context, the painful dispute regarding his marriage to Diane was enough to nudge him from "just inside" to "just outside" the Church.

After the public disclosure of the decision to quit the Church, the bishop was duly suspended from episcopal functions awaiting the formal action canonically required to certify his abandonment of the communion. Some dickering took place between the Presiding Bishop and Bishop Pike as to whether the requisite six-month period before such certification could be waived; if it could, then the action could be taken at a special general convention which was due to be convened at the University of Notre Dame in September of 1969, thus sparing the House of Bishops an extraordinary meeting to act upon the Pike issue. Diane and Jim had already completed arrangements for another journey to Israel in furtherance of their researches into Christian origins— Jim wanted particularly to explore the wilderness region where Jesus is said to have remained for forty days and to have suffered the temptations of the devil himself—and they were not to be at the Notre Dame convention. Pike withheld the waiver Hines sought.

The prospect as September approached was thus for a church convention in South Bend that would be unusual, perhaps historic, in two respects. For one thing, it would be the first convention in a very long time in which Pike would be absent and there would be no Bishop Pike pre-empting attention or dominating the agenda. In the second place, the Notre Dame meeting was to be a "special" convention, structured to be more open and representative, notably for blacks, women, and youth and others previously generally excluded from such deliberations; hence, ironically, the issues urged there would be the very concerns Bishop Pike had so often pioneered. The prospect for Notre Dame was that Pike would be there in spirit but not in person.

The prospect was fulfilled. The Notre Dame convention was, as *Time* described it, "radicalized . . . making the issues of racism and Viet Nam its dominant themes." At it, the Episcopal Church "became the first major denomination to recognize . . . the 'reparation' demands enunciated in . . . [the] Black Manifesto." Hindsight might consider Notre Dame a last hurrah of "radicalism" in the Episcopal Church, albeit, as well, a first hurrah, since the commitment to social change uttered there was to be systematically repudiated both in action and in neglect. The theologically and socially reactionary factions in the Church, deprived at Notre Dame of the lightning rod which Pike had been for them, found other targets and, despite the rhetoric of social witness in South Bend, effected a *coup d'église* manifested in the years following the special convention in the hounding of Bishop Hines into his premature resignation as the Presiding Bishop, in an extensive purge of national staff personnel, in constriction of the Church's budget, and in the placement of persons of conservative persuasion in key policy-making positions in the church structures.

Even more extraordinarily, the prospect was fulfilled in the fact that the search for Bishop Pike, lost in the Judean desert, coincided with the Notre Dame convention and virtually overwhelmed the news of it; "even in disappearance," *Time*, along with many others, remarked, Pike "once again upstaged." The House of Bishops sensed both poignancy and paradox in the coincidence—perchance providence—of these events in the resolution unanimously adopted when news that the bishop's corpse had been found reached Notre Dame:

> *Whereas*, Many in the Church were and are hurt and bewildered at the seeming inability of our normally inclusive community to accept and understand James Pike in his pilgrimage, so that at the end he felt forced to renounce our brotherhood; now, therefore, be it
> *Resolved*, That the House of Bishops give thanks to God for the life and prophetic ministry of James Albert Pike and recognize the depth of our loss in the dying of this creative and compassionate man.

Thereafter no formal action was ever undertaken to certify Pike's "abandonment of the communion." His disclaimer notwithstanding, when Bishop Pike died he was still a member and a bishop of the Episcopal Church.

A Consummate Obsession

The death of James A. Pike in Judea stopped his second departure from the Church. The ecclesiastical procedures for certify-

ing his abandonment of the Episcopal Church had not been
formalized in time for his death. In a curious way, this situation
emphasized the elementary issue of Pike's lifelong agitated relationship with the Church—the conflict, as it emerged, inexorably,
reluctantly, between Church and faith. On the last occasion when
Bishop Pike ventured the wilderness, his attention was fixed upon
Jesus; his quest sought the origins of the gospel, and he comprehended, with utter lucidity, that the Church, for himself anyway,
had become an inhibition to such a commitment. With a characteristic candor, therefore, Pike had renounced his church connection. There was no repudiation of the gospel implied. It was not a
matter of loss of faith, as he had supposed when he had left the
Church once before as a young man. Quite the contrary, this time
his quitting the Church meant his emancipation as a human
being. It signified his believing hope. It represented a penultimate
act of faith for him.

Years earlier, in comparably solitary circumstances, Dietrich
Bonhoeffer bespoke a similar tension inherent in the historic dialectic of Church and faith, as John Cogley had remembered when
he heard the news of Pike's resignation as Bishop of California.
This was the issue of religion vs. the gospel, ecclesiology vs. theology, doctrinal recitals vs. confession, authority vs. conscience, the
Church vs. Jesus, idolatry vs. faith.

Because he himself was an ecclesiastic, Bishop Pike felt this
conflict most acutely in terms of idolatry or "ecclesiolatry," as he
sometimes called it. In his writing and speaking, coincidental with
the heresy controversy, he kept returning to St. Paul's admonition
concerning the frailty of the Church and the transience and rela-
tivity of churchly institutions and traditions as "earthen vessels"
to which no ultimate dignity could be imputed and to which no
justifying efficacy must ever be attributed. And, consistent with
that, his growing awareness of Christian origins rendered the servant image of Jesus compellingly attractive to Pike. As James A.
Pike became less and less religious, it can be said that he became
more and more Christian.

Poignantly, it was a Jew who, perchance, most clearly recognized the extraordinary metamorphosis Bishop Pike had suffered,
and most readily affirmed it. On the day after Pike's body was
buried in Jaffa, the Jerusalem *Post* published an article by the re-

nowned New Testament scholar at Hebrew University in Israel
Professor David Flusser—a person so marvelously immersed in the
biblical saga that, in meeting him, one imagines him to be a first-
century personality. Dr. Flusser wrote: "Pike's . . . attitude was
surely deeply Christian. We will eagerly look forward to . . . his
book about Jesus. It will be . . . a stimulating book, in which
there will be no difference between the 'historical Jesus' and the
'kerygmatic Christ.' "

The dialectic of Church and faith became so intense for Pike, of
course, because he had once himself been eagerly idolatrous about
the Church. Once upon a time—just after he moved to Santa Barbara—Bishop Pike commented to a newsman that his resignation
as bishop did not indicate his disenchantment with the Church
"because I was never enchanted." The remark was hindsight. Verily Pike had been enchanted with the Church. During his professed agnosticism, he remained so literally enraptured with the
Church that he construed his separation from the Church as
depriving him of faith; so completely enamored was he then that
he was desperate and became obsessive about returning to the
Church. In the intimacy of his correspondence with Mama he
posited a pristine era of "the undivided Church" and he romanticized Anglicanism as the residue of that era within Christendom. Later on, he sought to transpose his idealization of the
Church in the congregation that he, in association with John
Coburn, established and guided and nurtured at Wellfleet for the
Cape Cod summer colony. That effort, launched while Pike was
dean of New York, was never publicized, but the Chapel of St.
James the Fisherman had very high priority for Pike as a detailed
model—in design, in liturgy, in teaching, in lay participation, in
social concern, in pastoral care—of Pike's idyllic Church. Meanwhile, in similar vein, but with a fanfare befitting the premises, he
implemented his grandiose view of the Church at the Cathedral
of St. John the Divine. During this period in his life, whether
building St. James the Fisherman or upbuilding St. John the Divine, there was still a primacy of the Church over faith in Pike's
thought which, if less anxious than earlier in his experience, was
no less emphatic. He summed it up in an Easter sermon in 1953:
"The existence of the Christian Church is the best argument for
the Resurrection."

Had James Pike been of more pedestrian and less catholic intelligence, the event of his episcopacy might have occasioned the atrophy of his mind and of his witness. He might, as bishop, have become religiose and mundane. He might, foolishly, have confused the station of bishop with the verification of faith. He might have succumbed to ecclesiastical success or regarded his office as a vested interest in the preservation of the ecclesiastical status quo. His episcopacy did not conform or stultify Pike. Albeit he completed Grace Cathedral and otherwise much embellished the life of the Church in San Francisco and in the nation, Pike continued to grow, to ask, to search and stretch, to listen and challenge, and that, perhaps, the more so because he was no longer under theological tutelage. When, in 1960, Bishop Pike wrote an article for *The Christian Century* series "How My Mind Has Changed," though he still styled the issue of faith in churchly categories, he made public mention of the freedom of the gospel from the Church:

> (1) I am more broad church, that is, I know less than I used to think I knew . . . (2) I am more low church, in that I cannot view divided and particular denominations as paramount in terms of the end-view of Christ's church, and I do regard the gospel as the all-important and as the *only final* thing. And (3) I am more high church, in that I more value the forms of the continuous life of the Holy Catholic Church . . . These forms include liturgical expression and the episcopate.

The tenor of the *Century* piece sharply differed from the Dallas pastoral letter, with its rigid ecclesiology, which the House of Bishops had promulgated shortly before Pike's article was published. And the contrast between the two utterances was dramatically underscored when the Georgia clericus used the latter to charge Bishop Pike with heresy.

In his changing understanding of the relationship of the Church and the gospel and in the dynamics of Church and faith, there was, for Pike, more involved than an open and active mind or the spirit of either a pioneer or a pilgrim. There was the matter of authenticity, of the recovery of origins, or, in the parlance of lawyers, the significance of precedent. James Pike was not an iconoclast. It remains a measure of the degeneration of the Church that he was ever so regarded. One of the books which Pike read in

his avid pursuit of Christian sources in his last years was Marcel
Simon's *St. Stephen and the Hellenists*. Pike marked the book
with marginal notes and exclamations, many of which indicate his
sense of identification with the text. One passage with which he
could readily empathize was this:

> Rather than revolutionary preachers of an entirely new mes-
> sage, Stephen himself, and Jesus as Stephen sees him, are, in the
> most precise meaning of the term, religious reformers. Stephen's
> position vis-a-vis post-Mosaic Israelite religion and official Judaism
> seems to me to be very much like that of the sixteenth-century
> Reformers vis-a-vis medieval Catholicism. None of them intends
> to make innovations. Their eyes are turned to the past . . .
> [Stephen] is against . . . his Jerusalemite . . . contemporaries
> because, and insofar as, they practise a debased and corrupted
> form of religion . . .

Bishop Pike's concern for authenticity, for a recall of the past that
would renew the present, did not assume that knowledge of the
origins of the gospel was fixed and foreclosed. The radical potential of his interest was already evident in 1955, when news of the
scrolls which had been found in caves near the Dead Sea raised
apprehension that the discoveries would distress Christianity.
"Christians have nothing to fear from whatever facts may be discovered," Pike told a cathedral congregation. "The more we can
know about the historical orientation of the life and thought of
Jesus the better."

Some weeks before, in March of 1955, in another sermon, he
had foreseen how his eagerness to know all that could be learned
of Christian origins risked being at odds with the ecclesiastical
and religious status quo. "Independence of spirit means a cross,"
he observed. "Simple conformity to the prevailing mood . . .
spares one the cross." His foresight was fulfilled in his excoriation
at Wheeling, but there, in the moments he was allowed for response, he made no personal defense but pressed his appeal to
precedent. He cited the past views of Angus Dun on the ambiguity of the Creeds to expose the sham of the use of Bishop
Dun as sponsor of the censure. Then he invoked St. Augustine on
the fitting conduct of theological inquiry and discourse:

> If what I have written is not according to the truth, then let
> him only hold fast to his opinion and refute mine, if that is possi-

ble, and let me know of it, too, and impart his knowledge to everyone else whom he can reach. The method I sum up in this sentence is brotherly discussion.

More than anything else, certainly more than any issue of doctrine or any item of rhetoric, it was Bishop Pike's obsession for authenticity—as that came to supersede and transcend his regard for authority—that threatened and enervated his peers in the Church. It was this which made his being obnoxious. He had become more concerned with the Jesus of history than with prospering the church establishment; he actually raised questions which posed the gospel against the Church. The Church would somehow have to be rid of his presence.

A blunt way to put the issue that arose between Pike and the Episcopal Church is that Pike was too diligent, too conscientious, too resolute in his vocation as a bishop. If that caused bafflement and provoked hostility among many fellow bishops, it nonetheless was recognized as Pike's virtue elsewhere. John Cogley's memoir, at Pike's death in Judea, recalled his pastoral outreach to colleagues at the Center in Santa Barbara. "James Pike was happiest, and at his very best," Cogley noted, "when he was fulfilling some office proper to a priest or bishop." Malcolm Muggeridge affirmed the same, in the *New Statesman:* "Poor Bishop James Pike lost and found dead in the Desert of the Temptations. More fearful symmetry . . . A true bishop of our time . . ." The orders of the episcopacy in apostolic succession are said to be indelible. Whatever the theological status of such a view, it is empirically the truth for James A. Pike.

Thus, despite the redundancy in much of his theologizing, an extraordinary shift occurred during Bishop Pike's life in which he was freed from idolatry of the Church by his passion about Jesus. There were detours and vagaries and temptations and distractions, triumphs and calamities and humiliations and obstacles along the way, but by the time he reached Judea, his hyperactivity had become reconciled with his obsessiveness, and he knew but a consummate obsession, concentrated upon Jesus, which engaged and transfigured the profusion of his talents and interests and energies.

There were, and are, those unable to comprehend Pike's situation toward the end of his life as other than madness. In the Bayne committee report, rendered at the Seattle general convention, however, the paper of Arthur A. Vogel, an academic theologian subsequently made Bishop of West Missouri, contained a clue to a different exegesis. Vogel wrote: "We might add that life in Christ, since it embraces the crucifixion and Christ's death to self, should enable the Christian inquirer to be completely open to the truth. If the Christian has died to himself to the degree necessitated by the cross of Christ, he is by that fact completely open to the truth of God's love . . ." One might imagine that, somehow, Vogel had seen the notes of a sermon Pike had preached on February 10, 1952, which said: "In the Cross of Jesus Christ we see . . . [that] God accepts me though I am unacceptable, thus enabling me to accept myself."

The death to self in Christ was neither doctrinal abstraction nor theological jargon for James Pike. He died in such a way before his death in Judea. He died to authority, celebrity, the opinions of others, publicity, status, dependence upon Mama, indulgences in alcohol and tobacco, family and children, marriage and marriages, promiscuity, scholarly ambition, the lawyer's profession, political opportunity, Olympian discourses, forensic agility, controversy, denigration, injustice, religion, the need to justify himself.

By the time Bishop Pike reached the wilderness in Judea, he had died in Christ. What, then, happened there was not so much a death as a birth.

The Death Papers of Bishop Pike

The body of James Pike was removed from the place it had been found in the desert, on September 7, 1969, to the appropriate facilities at the Institute of Forensic Medicine in Jaffa, where an autopsy was done and this report made:

STATE OF ISRAEL—THE HEBREW UNIVERSITY
THE LEOPOLD GREENBERG INSTITUTE OF
FORENSIC MEDICINE
JAFFA, ABU KABIR   TELEPHONE 822764

REF. No. 775/69   JAFFA 16 September 1969

English Translation from Hebrew Protocol No. 775/69

On the 7.9.69 a post mortem examination was performed by the undersigned on the remains of JAMES PIKE, aged 55. The body was brought by ambulance no. 501180 on the request of the Bethlehem police. Identity was established by personal belongings. The post mortem was performed on the same day.

The protocol was written at the time of the examination.

1) Body of an adult male, which appeared to be middle-aged, clothed in the following clothes:

    a) Checked shirt

    b) Long trousers with a leather belt

    c) Sox

    d) Black shoes

In the trouser pockets a wallet containing 190 £ and various papers. In another pocket 72 £ 65 agarot, and a key from the Intercontinental Hotel.

On the left hand a watch with a metal band.

The body in a state of advanced putrefaction with the skin peeling easily away from the deeper layers. A considerable amount of maggots in various stages of development all over the body. Here and there mainly in the exposed areas of the body the skin much darker, probably due to the effect of the sun.

2) No post mortem lividity or rigor mortis because of the putrefaction.

3) Very severe putrefactive changes on the head and the soft tissues of the eyes destroyed by the maggots.

4) The skeleton of the nose intact. In nostrils putrefactive fluid.

5) The mouth open, in oral cavity fluid of putrefaction.

6) The neck without signs except those of putrefaction.

7) In the right inguinal region an old operation scar. Otherwise no external signs over the rest of the body, besides those described of putrefaction.

8) The bones of the skull intact. The brain in a state of putrefaction. No signs of haemorrhage.

9) On opening the trachea in situ presence of fluid of putrefaction. The skeleton of the throat intact.

10) On opening the pleural cavity fluid of putrefaction present.

11) Fractures of the right ribs 6, 7, 8 in the anterior axillary line. The fractures simple and do not protrude into the pleural cavity.

12) The lungs in a state of putrefaction.

13) The heart in a state of putrefaction, but here and there are found small foci of calcification in the coronary arteries and in the aorta.

14) On opening the abdominal cavity fluid of putrefaction present. All the abdominal organs in a state of putrefaction.

15) Besides the fractures in the ribs, the skeleton intact.

At the time of the post mortem it was known from the investigation that the deceased disappeared in the desert seven days previously.

On the basis of the post mortem examination and taking into account the police statement the undersigned gives his opinion as follows:—

In the body that was in a marked state of putrefaction no anatomical cause of death was found. (The fractured ribs do not explain the appearance of death.)

The degree of putrefaction is compatible with death from 5–7 days before the performance of the post mortem.

7.9.69   Dr. J. Meyersohn

All of the Mediums Say He's Dying

The widow of Dr. James Pike said yesterday in Jerusalem that she had a vision of her husband dying in the Judean Desert the night before his body was found there last September.

Mrs. Diane Pike, who arrived back in Israel last week at the head of a tour group, said the vision had come to her in her room at the Intercontinental Hotel when she was wakened from sleep. A few hours later, a search party found his body on a crag. The former bishop had been dead several days.

Since her return to the

U.S., Mrs. Pike said, she had received dozens of letters from mediums in the U.S. and abroad passing on purported messages to her from her late husband. But the messages, she said, either used words or expressed thoughts that were plainly not her husband's or they were so general as to be meaningless.

Although she and her husband had gone to mediums—particularly to communicate with Dr. Pike's dead son, James Jr.—Mrs. Pike said that she had not gone to one after her husband's death. "I didn't have any feeling that he wanted to communicate with me through a medium," she said.

Mrs. Pike, who lives in Santa Barbara, Calif., has completed a book on the events of last September entitled "Search." It will be published next month. She has also begun writing the book on "the historical Jesus" which she and her husband came here to research. It will be in the form of an historical novel except for the final third, which will consist of textual notes.

The two-week "study-tour" she is leading was planned with her husband but after his death she decided to continue with it alone, she said. The 31 persons on the tour—all from the U.S.—are being taken to places associated with the birth of Christianity and then participate in discussions led by Mrs. Pike and her brother Scott on what they had seen.

Mrs. Pike said she will return with a similar tour in August.

Yesterday, she attended the dedication of a park in Katamon named after her late husband.

In describing the vision she saw last September, Mrs. Pike said she was wakened by two sharp knocks on her door but opened it to find no one there. Returning to her bed, she closed her eyes and saw the figure of a woman approaching, she said. "When I opened my eyes, I could still see her. She was walking towards me. There was an extremely kind smile on her face and I thought that this was death. I said out loud 'No, please. Go away.' And she disappeared."

Two hours later, at
3:30 a.m. Diane Pike
continued, she was wak-
ened by voices saying
"All of the mediums say
he's dying." Sitting up in
bed, she began praying
"Oh please don't let him
die now, just a few hours
before we find him."

Then she saw her sec-
ond vision. It was of her
husband lying still on a
cliff ledge similar—but
not exactly like—the
place he was to be found
that day. Mrs. Pike said
she went next door to
her brother's room to de-
scribe what she had seen
and in the course of talking to him, the vision returned.

This time, however,
she could see her hus-
band's spirit wrenching
loose from his body. She
described it as white and
cloud-like, human-shaped
but with no discernible
limbs. "Even though it
had no mouth, I saw
that he was smiling."
The spirit drifted up to
the canyon top where a
large group of similar
spirits were gathered.
Among them, Mrs. Pike
said, she recognized Jim
Jr.

The vision ended with
the spirits drifting up-
wards.

Mrs. Pike said she had
never had a vision before
or since.

This story, by Abraham Rabinovich, appeared in the Jerusalem *Post* on January 22, 1970. Diane Pike's vision had occurred a little more than four months earlier, the night before Bishop Pike's body was found in the desert. The vision is described in greater detail in Diane's book, *Search*. We think it far and away the most authentic of any of the psychic phenomena we have been called upon to examine. We don't know how to account for it nor do we think it needs to be accounted for. It is what it is and it means what it means. Nobody had to clip obituaries or dabble in the paranormal to concoct it. It obviously was created out of the concrete anguish Diane Pike had undergone. It is genuine. It would make no more sense to subject the vision to analysis than it would make sense to exhume Bishop Pike's body in order to see whether or not his spirit has actually departed from it.

And Life Is Victorious

Bishop Pike favored cremation of a body, and that is what Diane would have directed had not the law in Israel forbidden it. (Not even the law can forbid the sun, however, and Bishop Pike's body had by grace of the sun suffered a near cremation by natural process.) On the evening of September 7, 1969, Diane had (by her own insistence) identified her husband's body at army headquarters in Bethlehem.

> The body was covered with a light blue sheet and had been placed in a coffin-shaped tin box. As A Ben Schmauel led me to the box, he lifted the sheet and began to pull it down, exposing the head. The stench was terrible and I looked to see Jim's head completely black and very enlarged. His head was turned to the left side so that I saw clearly only the right side of it, but I could see that his eyes were completely gone—there were only sockets surrounded by swollen flesh. His mouth was open, but his nose and ear were hardly distinguishable. His neck was so swollen that from the back of his head down to his back there was only straight black flesh—puffy. I could make out no hair on the head.

His shirt was pulled open in front, exposing a bare and very swollen chest. His right arm lay exposed, the sleeve pulling tight around the upper arm, the skin black and puffy. I pulled the sheet back to expose the remainder of his body.

The right leg was bent and caught up above the left leg, which was underneath. His pants were torn in the seat, exposing torn, raw flesh—red and white through black pants and flesh. He still had his shoes and socks on, but his legs were also puffed, filling the stockings and bulging out of the shoes. His pants were pulled up, exposing more of the black skin.

As I looked Chief Schmauel said, "Is it your husband's body?"

I said, "Yes, it is my husband's body. It is his head, it is his shirt, those are his pants, his shoes and socks. Yes, it is my husband's body."

The body was taken to the Institute of Forensic Medicine in Tel Aviv (Jaffa) for autopsy. Diane had no interest in flying the body back to California. The cost of "preparing" it (a pretty hopeless undertaking anyhow) and "air-freighting" it would have been huge. Bishop Pike had long complained about the high cost of American burials. It seemed to Diane that the body should remain in Israel where death had come to it and where Bishop Pike had so often felt at home. She was sure he would have wanted to be buried in Israel in the circumstances. Mrs. Chambers and the bishop's surviving children readily assented to her decision.

Where to bury the body in Israel presented a problem. There were only three Protestant cemeteries in all of Israel. One was in Jaffa. (There is another in Galilee, and one near Bethlehem.) Since Jaffa was adjacent to Tel Aviv and since that cemetery was in the charge of an Anglican priest (Henry Knight) Diane and Scott agreed that early the next morning (after receiving the autopsy report) they would drive to Jaffa and check out the cemetery. They found a small, cloistered park, tree-shaded and quiet within its high walls and bolted gate. In the New York *Times* on September 9, 1969, James Feron concluded his excellent report on the burial of Bishop Pike with a description of the scene.

> A quiet sea lapped at
> the shore, a dramatic
> contrast to the parched

environment in which Dr. Pike had died. His wife said he had hoped to experience the area in which Jesus, according to the Gospels, had gone to pray and meditate.

Dr. Pike's burial place, St. Peter's Protestant Cemetery, is surrounded by slums at the southern end of what was once an Arab port. To the north are Greek Orthodox and Moslem cemeteries, similarly small.

The Protestant cemetery contains a few dozen graves, some of them with broken headstones. Four graves near Dr. Pike's contain the same inscription: Here Lies an Unknown Seaman, 27 Nov. 1942.

Dr. Pike's grave is marked by a cross. It is under a large fig tree and of all the graves in the cemetery, it is the closest to the sea.

The shore of the Mediterranean Sea by Jaffa resembles the shore of the Pacific Ocean near Santa Barbara. Diane and Scott fell in love with St. Peter's Protestant Cemetery. The Arab caretaker said he could have the grave dug (despite the heat of the day) by late that same afternoon. It was decided to have a burial service at 5 P.M. that day (September 8, 1969). Diane inquired of the people in the Institute of Forensic Medicine whether she might be allowed to bury the body in the same aluminum container it had been in since it reached Bethlehem. (Health laws prohibited leaving the body to decay naturally into the earth as

Diane would have liked for it to do.) Permission to use the aluminum casket was granted. Scott purchased a golden rug to cover it with and that was that. Diane had offered to pay for the casket but was told that would not be necessary.

The night before the burial John and Ellen Downing, friends of Bishop Pike and of Diane, had arrived in Israel. They were too late to join the search but they were not too late to help bury their friend. James Feron had been on hand throughout the week of the search and he was on hand for the burial.

JAFFA, Israel, Sept. 8 —Dr. James A. Pike, whose body was found yesterday on a ledge in the Judean wilderness, was buried here today in a tiny cemetery by the Mediterranean.

Mrs. Pike was at the grave as the Rev. John Downing, an Episcopalian priest and a friend of the Pikes, conducted the service.

Mr. Downing and his wife, who are members of Dr. Pike's Foundation for Religious Transition, came to help search for Dr. Pike but arrived only in time to bury him. Dr. Pike and his wife became lost in the desert last Monday after they took a wrong turn in their car. Mrs. Pike reached safety at the Dead Sea Tuesday morning after a 10-hour trek over rocky ledges and through the desert.

The cemetery, softly shaded and less than 100

yards from the sea, was selected by Mrs. Pike this morning. Only a handful of mourners and some newsmen were present.

Mrs. Pike, her lacerated legs and arms reminders of her ordeal, placed a "peace cross" on the coffin before it was lowered.

A medallion that combines a cross with the symbol of the drive for nuclear disarmament, it was similar to one worn by her husband for years, Mrs. Pike said. The one buried with him actually belonged to Mrs. Downing.

"The peace cross is a symbol of his concern for peace in the world," Mrs. Pike said. "He thought that was what Jesus stood for. Therefore the cross and the peace symbol together are very appropriate."

Mrs. Pike said she would be leaving Israel tomorrow for her home at Santa Barbara, Calif., with her 20-year-old brother, Scott Kennedy, who arrived last week. Both were with the search party when the body of the 56-year-old churchman was found yesterday.

Israeli officials have determined that Dr. Pike,
a former Episcopal
Bishop of California,
died in a fall within 24
hours after his wife left
him to seek help. He had
apparently sought to fol-
low her.

Mrs. Pike, 31, nodded
occasionally as Mr.
Downing conducted the
service, reading from the
Psalms and from Paul's
letter to the Corinthians
and the Romans.

Mrs. Pike, her brother
and Mrs. Downing stood
together, arms linked, occasionally smiling at each
other. Only the drone of
an airliner circling to
Lydda Airport and the
whir of cameras broke
the silence.

To the very end the whir of cameras and at the end a handful
of mourners and some newsmen.

Four months later, early in January of 1970, the bishop's
mother, Pearl Chambers, and his aunt, Ethyl Larkey, and a
"study-tour" group led by Diane Pike and Scott Kennedy began
their two-week visit in the Holy Land with a solemn pilgrimage to
the grave in Jaffa. They arrived by bus very early one morning. It
was a bright, sunny, breezy day and the small sequestered enclave
of St. Peter's Protestant Cemetery seemed an oasis of peace. The
Arab caretaker and his brood of youngsters mingled with the
group. Mrs. Chambers and her sister placed flowers on Bishop
Pike's grave which was still marked only with a simple cross. It
was winter and the fig tree was bare of leaves. As the group made
its tearful way back up out of the cemetery through a grove of
pine Mrs. Chambers, resplendent in a bright blue coat she wore

like a cloak, settled wearily onto a stone bench. Too old for tears she sat motionless for some time rapt in octogenarian prayer.

In November of 1970 a stone was erected over Bishop Pike's grave. The stone (called "Jerusalem stone") was limestone quarried near Jerusalem. Diane asked that it be left rough on the sides and back to symbolize the rocks in the Judean desert.

The upright slab of the stone reads:

JAMES A. PIKE

BISHOP

(P.E.C.U.S.A.)

Born 1913
Oklahoma City, Okla.

Died 1969
Judean Wilderness

The horizontal slab of the stone reads:

"WE HAVE THIS
TREASURE IN EARTHEN
VESSELS TO SHOW THAT
THE TRANSCENDENT POWER
BELONGS TO GOD
AND NOT TO US."
II COR. 4:7

"AND LIFE IS VICTORIOUS!"
Mandaean Book of Prayer

We wrote to Diane Pike a few years later to ask why she had selected for Bishop Pike's gravestone a quotation from the "Mandean" Book of Prayer.

> I chose the quote from the *Mandaean* (please note spelling) Book of Prayer because Jim had loved it. During the last year or so, he often used to quote that phrase "And life is victorious" as one of the finest statements of religious affirmation he had ever heard. And moreover, I had the sense of its being in keeping with Jim's whole life, in the sense that I could just imagine archeologists 1,000 years from now digging up that stone and trying to piece it all together. I put "P.E.C.U.S.A." on the stone for

the same reason: partly to identify what kind of bishop Jim was, but also because I thought it would be a challenge to archeologists to figure out what the heck *that* was, and how the Mandaean Book of Prayer is related to a Protestant Episcopal Bishop. Since Jim's whole life was an enigma to most people, those touches of enigma on his gravestone just seemed to fit for me.

On a drear, rainy day early in February of 1971 Diane and Scott and a few friends gathered to dedicate the enigmatic gravestone. John Downing uttered the dedicatory prayer.

O God, You have led Your people in times past to choose the Rock for markers and guideposts; for walls and temples; as places of strength, succour and sacrifice. Be with us today as we use this Rock to mark the final resting place of the earthly vessel of your servant James Albert Pike, Bishop.

We dedicate this stone in memory of a modern pilgrim, priest and prophet, whose search for the truth led him many times through the valley of the shadow of death. But Life is victorious. And our search for Truth and victorious life has been greatly aided by the life and witness of James Albert Pike.

May this Rock symbolize his life to us and to those who will follow in his steps. Let it be a marker, a guidepost, a stone in the wall of our inner temple, a source of strength as well as a memorial of his life, as we continue our search for truth in Peace and Joy.

Amen.

Like Father Like Son

In a family conversation Jim Jr. had once said that if he should die he wanted to be buried off the Golden Gate Bridge so he could watch the city of San Francisco. He got his wish all too soon. John Riley, an Episcopal priest and good friend of Bishop Pike, made the arrangements for that burial. In a taped conversation with Scott Kennedy on November 21, 1972, John Riley told the story of Jim Jr.'s burial in the bay.

It was a terrible day. There was one of the biggest storms ever to hit San Francisco County. Jim and Esther drove over early that

morning with the ashes to my house. We had some tea and orange juice. I had contacted a member of my parish who had a
huge yacht. It had once been a rum-runner which really pleased
Jim. My friend hired a mechanic to spend two days to get the
boat out of mothballs. It was winter and the boat was out of the
water. It took two days to get it seaworthy. We drove from my
house to the yacht harbor and met my friend and his family on
board the yacht. He got his clearance to leave the dock and go on
out. It was the roughest trip I have ever been on. We were way in
the back of the boat with the ashes trying to have sandwiches and
coffee but spilling everything all over the place. Finally, Jim said,
"How far do we have to go?" I had already checked with Phil
Adams who told me there was no rule about it. We could scatter
the ashes anywhere on the water. We got about three hundred
yards inside the Golden Gate. My friend said he just didn't want
to take the boat outside the bridge. Jim was very humorous about
the situation. His humor was very relieving. He made jokes about
not wanting to empty the ashes into the wind and have Jim Jr.
back in the boat all over the sandwiches. We figured a way to
turn so the ashes could be tossed out towards the sea and with
the wind. I opened the container and poured the ashes over the
side. Jim read the committal service. He cried like a baby all
through it. Esther was crying too. It was very moving. Then we
turned back into the harbor. We were very silent all the way
back.

Include the Bishop's Bones

When he isn't writing about Bishop Pike Anthony Towne is a
poet. For some time he had wanted to write in a poem about
Bishop Pike. He also wanted to write a poem about the Holy
Land, which he got to know because of Bishop Pike. Events kept
getting in his way. Daniel Berrigan and the FBI, for example. But
one day there came a letter from the *Anglican Theological Review*. The letter said that W. Taylor Stevenson, Editor-in-Chief,
was looking for poems for the *Review*. He wanted verse of high
quality. This was part of an effort the *Review* had undertaken to
foment the recovery of tradition. That seemed a tall order to Anthony. He decided the time had come to write a poem about the

Holy Land and that he would write the poem for Bishop Pike. He did write a poem. It was printed in the *Review* in its issue of January 1974.

Capernaum

A poem for "the recovery of tradition which we seek"
W. Taylor Stevenson

Introit THE monarch butterflies and the meadowlarks
it must be fall, time to recover
with little Latin, no Greek
the *agenbite of inwit*
"verse of high quality"
Lord, so many men, so few fishers

I

Mount Tabor. We ascended in a reckless taxi.
Bishop Pike's mother weeping, widow, old aunt,
A jolly Franciscan, sepulchral grin, played
Ave Maria on a cobwebbed organ;
Over there, he giggled matter-of-factly,
Armageddon will be fought.
Transfigured
Moses, our Lord, Elijah
Did not seem to notice the gothic wretchedness.
Home on the Range from the bell tower,
a scratched recording.
Descending, I closed my eyes tight, wanting
desperately to see where I was.

Refrain *Timor mortis conturbat me!*

II

"On Friday we rested our case,
rejecting the traditional opportunity for defense."
bitten again by inwit pang
Behold He comes: the Prince of Peace
turn tart face, say 'Yes' or 'No'
Once in a month of Fridays there is good.

III

Masada. We scrambled up like refugees in drag.
    sunlight fierce as zealots' daggers
    the Dead Sea cirrus-mirrored blue
    Bedouin stealth, the mountains of Moab
    and the Judean desert, dry as Dracula
Water. Those who find it are few.
    two palaces, summer and winter, Herod's
    cavernous cisterns, the swimming pool
      a mosaic steam bath
Who hauled the water through that needle's eye?
    Cleopatra comes to mind, craving
    the kingdom of Judea, Herod's
      (include the bishop's bones)
    and Eleazar who said 'No' to Silva
    "nor anyone else but only God"
Conculcated, some bones, plaits, sandals, a stove
    fragments of a scroll of *Ecclesiasticus*
    "our freedom as a glorious winding-sheet."
    on the lower terrace of the winter palace
      I am dizzy.
We descend. The Israelis will build a cable car.

Refrain   *Timor mortis conturbat me!*

IV

Her love is orderly like rage
    the poor, drunks, the homeless, offcasts
      (again and again, the nitpick of inwit)
    companied, companioned
"I am not wandering; in writing this way.
      I am meditating."

V

Capernaum. We meditate among the ruins like cows.
    the saucer sea of Galilee
      holds its breath
The very spot where Jesus preached the word.
    so green, it is cool under the trees

a lark on a basalt flour mill, ancient
 butterflies
Tell a story. Tell the long tale of great delight.
 cured the man with palsy, bed and all
 the centurion's servant, so great faith
 Peter's mother-in-law, she served dinner
 the swine of Gadarene perished in that sea
 remember Levi's banquet, publicans and sinners
Called Peter, Andrew, James, John. Called Matthew.
  uttered
 the terrible anathema
 these ruins testify
So. This is the sundered city where it all began.
  the ministry of Jesus
 the word that thunders
  gently
 in the screech of time
We get back in the bus. It is time to depart.

EPILOGUE

Expectans expectavi: *A Homily Commending James A. Pike**

> But we have this treasure in earthen vessels, to show that the transcendent power belongs to God and not to us. We are afflicted in every way, but not crushed; perplexed, but not driven to despair; persecuted, but not forsaken; struck down, but not destroyed; always carrying in the body the death of Jesus, . . . so that the life of Jesus may be manifested in our mortal flesh. So death is at work in us, but life in you.
>
> II Corinthians 4.7–12

* Given at a requiem mass celebrated at St. Clement's Church, New York City, September 14, 1969, by William Stringfellow.

Three days before James Pike was found dead in Judea, the vicar of St. Clement's told me that this congregation desired that the service this morning be a thanksgiving for the life and for the witness of Bishop Pike. The intention, he said, was that this Eucharist happen whatever the outcome of the search in the desert: whether by this morning Pike remained missing or if discovered he be dead or living.

The subsequent events make this a requiem: Jim Pike is buried in the ground and we pray for his repose. Yet the original intent for this service was different from a dirge, and that intent—which is the only thing which persuaded me to participate—remains sound. Whatever the particulars of his fate, there is good reason in the church today, as there was ten years ago and as there was a year ago and, for that matter, as there will be ten years from now, to pause in gratitude to God for Bishop Pike.

Events make this a requiem, but it is not merely a requiem; if my homily, on the fortieth Psalm, is also a eulogy, it is incidentally so.

> I waited patiently for the Lord, and he inclined unto me, and heard my calling,
> He brought me also out of the horrible pit, out of the mire and clay, and set my feet upon the rock, and ordered my goings.
> And he hath put a new song in my mouth, even a thanksgiving unto our God.
> Many shall see it, and fear, and shall put their trust in the Lord.
> (Psalm 40.1–4, Book of Common Prayer)

None of us here can overlook the fact of Bishop Pike's death, or the way he died or where he died.

We can say nothing of his private death, save to affirm God's mercy, though there are many who knew him or who knew of him who have spent a week titillating themselves with gruesome guesses and cruel speculation about that.

Yet beyond his solitary crisis, there has been the public death of Bishop Pike, which the whole world, more or less, has beheld and by which, it cannot be gainsaid, many have been fearfully edified.

Discontent with the fables and fairy tales about Jesus which churchly tradition has hallowed, and unsatisfied, if nonetheless respectful, about mere scholarship, Pike wanted to know the truth about Jesus—or, at the least, he had to have all of the truth that *he* could know of Jesus. He had, in the last years, become excited by glimpses of the splendid humanity of Jesus, and he had to see more. How unusual—how threatening to some of his peers; how efficacious for other folk—to have a bishop with such a passion for Jesus that he forsook ecclesiology!

That passion would require return to the historic sources of the gospel. So Pike would go, again and again, to the habitat of Jesus, to the places where Jesus prayed and preached and healed and walked and even to where He had been tempted by the power of death in the wilderness. Most of us stay satisfied with Sunday school hearsay about Jesus and, thus, we fancy that His forty days in the desert were an ascetic exercise—contemplation, uplift, fasting, perhaps a turn at yoga. The biblical version is contrary. The wilderness episode for Jesus means suffering transcendently the versatility of death's aggression against human life. Perhaps it is this reality of the wilderness experience that explains why the biblical accounts speak of Jesus being "directed" or "driven by the Spirit" or "led" into the desert. Sooner or later, for every man, there is a confrontation with death in desolate circumstances. We have recently heard that this very thing has happened to James A. Pike, in a remarkable way. It is the ministry of Jesus—"driven by the Spirit," as the book says—to be there, in the wilderness, before any man enters it.

That Bishop Pike's wilderness experience should be so literal is not, I think, to be taken as a macabre coincidence but with matter-of-factness. Though *Time* magazine regarded Pike as impetuous and erratic, in truth the man was possessed by an extraordinary patience. All of his life, and, then, for some time, as he died in the desert, Pike was waiting patiently for the Lord.

> *Blessed is the man that hath set his hope in the Lord, and turned not unto the proud, and to such as go about with lies.*
> *O Lord my God, great are the wondrous works which thou hast done, like as be also thy thoughts, which are to us-ward; and yet there is no man that ordereth them unto thee.*
> *If I should declare them, and speak of them, they should be more*

than I am able to express. (Psalm 40.5–7, Book of Common Prayer)

The conflict between the churches and Jim Pike, since the period of his collegiate agnosticism, was elemental and redundant. The issue was not heresy on the part of Pike, but blasphemy on the part of the Church as such. It was the very curse of Israel: the Church insinuating herself in the place of God; the Church boasting God's prerogatives; the Church depriving and exploiting human beings by playing God.

One of the other translations of this Psalm reads: *Blessed is the man who makes the Lord his trust, who does not turn to the proud, to those who go astray after false gods!* Well, that expresses what was the matter between the Church, as all of us know her, and Bishop Pike. Even when controversy between the two became ensnared in the mechanics of the Trinity, what was at stake was the Church as a false god. Sometimes it became narrowed to "the tradition of the Church," or "the good name of the Church," or "the prosperity of the Church," or sometimes it was defined as just the Episcopal denomination or as the fraternity of bishops, and when it did become so limited, in ways like these, the vanity of the proud would become vindictive. Still, the issue contested remained consistent: the Church, in one sense or another, as idol.

Remembering the admonition of St. Paul—that the infidelity of the Church does not dilute or vitiate God's witness to Himself in history—I argued mildly against Bishop Pike quitting the organized Church on the ground that the gesture lent too much dignity to the Church's apostasy. Bishop Pike must have loved the Church, but terribly, to hope for so long that within his lifetime she would become and be again merely herself, a servant of humanity in Christ's name instead of a preposterous phony deity importuning humanity.

Pike had the grace, while exposing the Church as false god, not to be proud of his own thinking, and speaking, and writing. "If I could create a perfect image of God," he said repeatedly, "it would be blasphemous . . . another idolatry." That did not impress pedantic theologians and was unappealing to ecclesiastical pride, but it *is* the spirit of the psalmist: *O Lord my God, great*

are the wondrous works which thou hast done . . . If I should de-
clare them . . . they should be more than I am able to express.

> *Sacrifice and offering thou wouldest not, but mine ears hast thou*
> *opened.*
> *Burnt-offering and sacrifice for sin hast thou not required: then*
> *said I, Lo, I come;*
> *In the volume of the book it is written of me, that I should fulfil*
> *thy will, O my God: I am content to do it; yea, thy law is within*
> *my heart.* (Psalm 40.8–10, Book of Common Prayer)

All religion is based upon a false presupposition that an acceptable sacrifice can be offered to God which at once proves and
guarantees the moral worthiness of the supplicant. Both biblical
faiths differ from the religions in this respect, and this represents
such an elementary distinction that neither Judaism nor Christianity can properly be called religions. In fact it is when the biblical faiths become religious with this foolish notion about sacrifice
and justification that they are exposed as corrupt.

The biblical insight is that God has no need of our offerings
and is disinterested in our attempts to please or to appease Him.
In other words, God's love for human beings is unconditional.
Analogically, anybody who has ever suffered the love of another
knows that: love is undeserved: love cannot be purchased: love
cannot be earned: love is a gift. It is curious that something
which is such common knowledge—the unconditional character
of love—should incite so much resistance and disbelief on the
part of the beloved, particularly when the one who loves is God.
Yet in some fashion all of us have this struggle because wrapped
up in it is the tender, terrible mystery of what it means to be a
human being. The event of becoming a Christian—I am not
discussing the sacrament of baptism or joining some church or
taking a trip down Billy Graham's aisle—concerns the very same
thing. To become a Christian means to abandon opposition to
God's affirmation of one's humanity. St. Paul, echoing the psalmist,
testifies that to be a Christian involves this death to self and this
rising as a new man in Christ every day.

James Pike struggled incessantly, fiercely, often beautifully, sometimes elegantly, openly and honestly with this issue of burnt offerings and justification. As such things are measured, he had much

to sacrifice. That was verified when he was ordained a priest, leaving a brilliant start as a New Deal attorney that would surely have led him to appointment to the federal bench or into elective politics or could have brought him certain wealth. It was demonstrated again in the fifties at the height of the religious revival when Sheen and Peale and Graham and Pike became national celebrities, Pike as the apologist for what later—when he had outgrown it—he called "smooth orthodoxy." Pike even survived as a man his astonishing success—judged by ecclesiastical, which is to say, worldly, ethics—as Bishop of California. In his incumbency, despite a plethora of other endeavors, he attracted more converts, performed more baptisms, confirmed more communicants, deployed more clergy, raised more pledges, started more missions, oversaw more church construction than any other Episcopal bishop, and, as a bonus, he finished building Grace Cathedral. As resigned bishop he joined Robert Hutchins on Olympus, but he was not spoiled there. He possessed, at one time or another, all those things with which men, vainly, make self-justifying claims: professional achievement, wealth within grasp, the envy of his peers, applause, influence, fame, status. He lost them all, discovering over and over that God requires no such things, and thereby the gift of his life was constantly renewed. In that, he was content.

> *I have declared thy righteousness in the great congregation: lo, I will not refrain my lips, O Lord, and that thou knowest.*
> *I have not hid thy righteousness within my heart; my talk hath been of thy truth, and of thy salvation.*
> *I have not kept back thy loving mercy and truth from the great congregation.* (Psalm 40.11–13, Book of Common Prayer)

When Pike was dean of New York, this city became a great congregation. The cathedral where he presided and preached was, for those years, a living place, not a museum, not just a stop for the tourist buses. His administration as dean was regarded at the time, and is so remembered, as radical and novel. Actually, the truth is the other way around: Dean Pike restored St. John the Divine to the original vocation of cathedrals, and its consignment, both before his office there and ever since, to the rank of museum is a novelty. People, not especially churchpeople, but the people of the city, sense their loss when the cathedral is silent and aloof. A Harlem friend, who telephoned me the day news arrived of Pike's death, said: "When he was dean, we all had a voice."

It was as Dean Pike that Jim Pike became notorious and that detractors began their complaints that he was a publicity seeker. The answer to that, of course, is that he was. If the calling of the cathedral is as a voice for humanity in the city, then the cathedral's dean is called to be vocal. The sheer volume of publicity which attended Pike while dean and then as bishop causes some to overlook the fact that very little of that news had to do with Pike as a personality; most of it that he generated, in contrast to the publicity his enemies instigated, was about issues and not about personality. Indeed, as Anthony Towne and I were to discover in writing *The Bishop Pike Affair* in the midst of the heresy tempest, Pike was incredibly naïve so far as personal publicity was concerned. He persisted in dealing with issues, while others were trying to discredit him as a person. But if that be so, be consoled because it is a prophet's lot to be opposed and abused as a man while publicizing the Word of God. It is no virtue for a prophet to be quiet in the great congregation.

> *Withdraw not thou thy mercy from me, O Lord; let thy loving-kindness and thy truth alway preserve me.*
> *For innumerable troubles are come about me; my sins have taken such hold upon me, that I am not able to look up; yea, they are more in number than the hairs of my head, and my heart hath failed me.*
> *O Lord, let it be thy pleasure to deliver me; make haste, O Lord, to help me.* (Psalm 40.14–16, Book of Common Prayer)

One of the incidental indignities which the dead must suffer is the condescension of their survivors. Especially at wakes and burials and requiems, the living assume a superiority toward the dead. It is not just that they pontificate; the survivors tend to talk as if they are immortal and have *that* eminent perspective upon life which, obviously, the dead never attained, as is proved by their very deadness. Everett Dirksen endured, ruefully, no doubt, just such indignity the other day during Mr. Nixon's eulogy. It is an odd circumstance, since the dead manifestly have the certain wisdom that there is no immortality.

In this condescending vein, many who survive Bishop Pike remark how marred by tragedy his life was. One marriage ended in annulment, another in divorce, a third was criticized ecclesiastically as a scandal. A son committed suicide. A close working associate died in a bizarre incident. He was an alcoholic and even joined AA. You know as well as I do how this conversation goes.

I refute none of these facts, but I deny that Jim Pike's life was a chronicle of tragedy. I see it as triumphant.

There is, as the dead know, no immortality, but there is resurrection. These are different things, though they be carelessly confused, especially in church. Immortality postulates an idyllic afterlife in another world; resurrection concerns the expectancy of a final and consummate transcendence of death for this world because humans have seen and experienced the imminent transcendence of death here, in this world, and now, in this history, and, already, as it were.

The gospel of Christ bespeaks resurrection. The ministry of Jesus verifies resurrection, not only upon Easter, but in all the days earlier—in His victory over death in the wilderness, in His power over death in healing, in His authority over death when confronting Caesar's claims, in His intercession that humans be delivered from death in the Lord's Prayer. The credibility of the resurrection as an ultimate promise for humanity rests upon specific triumphs over the power of death which occur in common life. Death, in many guises, pursued Bishop Pike relentlessly, and in many instances did Pike live in the resurrection, transcending death's power. The most obvious example is Pike's witness against racism, symbolized early in his public career by his refusal of the Sewanee honorary doctorate in "white divinity." Racism is a work of death in this world and the effectual undoing of racism is an instance of resurrection.

This is how I think of Bishop Pike's concern in situations, like his son's suicide, which others call tragedies. I see them as among death's assaults, not to be borne as devastation or defeat, but to be transcended in the power of the resurrection to which human beings have access now. That Bishop Pike took an interest in parapsychology does not carry the connotation of playing games at Ouija boards or indicate hallucination. In the context of his life it refers to the possibility of transcendence of death in yet another guise, quite consistent with, for example, that earlier encounter with death in the Sewanee episode.

> *Let them be ashamed, and confounded together, that seek after my soul to destroy it; let them be driven backward, and put to rebuke, that wish me evil.*
> *Let them be desolate, and rewarded with shame, that say unto me, Fie upon thee! fie upon thee!* (Psalm 40.17–18, Book of Common Prayer)

After Bishop Pike was censured in 1966 by the Episcopal House of Bishops, he received a letter from an elderly woman, who wrote: "This is about the way I prayed for you—'Now look, Jesus and Moses, you have to help Bishop Pike. The wolves are after him.'" It was an apt intercession for Bishop Pike, not only at the time of the censure and the subsequent heresy ruckus, but at most any juncture in his life, including during those last days in the desert, that one was moved to pray for him.

The wolves seemed always to be after him. Death pursued him relentlessly, as has been said. Most poignant, perhaps, was the lust of that pursuit of him within the Church. The plain truth is that some bishops, and some others of the Church, were determined to kill Bishop Pike. He, somehow, in his existence incarnated so much that threatened and frightened them as men that they conspired to murder him. I am speaking now theologically—their malice amounted to murder, as the Sermon on the Mount puts it —but I am equally speaking empirically—murder took possession of them. Some bishops, not all bishops; there were others: there were a few whose side was the same as Pike's on the issues, personalities aside; there were a lot of temporizers in between. What do you say of men who temporize when life is at stake? The Book of Common Prayer counts temporizers as accomplices. So does St. Paul. So did Bishop Daniel Corrigan, during the censure debate, when he described what he saw happening:

> I speak here against this statement, not as a Bishop, not even as a Christian, just as—just as a man. The substance I would not wish to argue. The whole process by which a man is publicly tried, excoriated really, and condemned—condemned in some deep sense to death—by God!—heresy is nothing . . . to what we say about this man!

Only Bishop Pike's death would satisfy them. Now he is dead, but they are confounded and in shame because their malice is not what killed him. He died in the wilderness in Judea, but the wolves had not hurt him.

> Let all those that seek thee, be joyful and glad in thee; and let such as love thy salvation, say alway, The Lord be praised.
> As for me, I am poor and needy; but the Lord careth for me.
> Thou art my helper and redeemer; make no long tarrying, O my God. (Psalm 40.19–21, Book of Common Prayer)

In a day when heroes are not heroic we turn to antiheroes to refresh our recollection of what heroes really are. By the same token, James Pike was an antibishop, embodying what other bishops are not to remind both the Church and the world of what bishops truly are.

It could not be expected, after so much tumult and controversy, that the Church in any official way would recognize that, not that it matters for Pike, though it matters profoundly for the Church. The days when Bishop Pike was missing in the Holy Land coincided with a general convention of the Episcopal Church held at Notre Dame University. A newspaperman tells me that he noted no prayer was said at the convention when the report of Pike being lost first reached South Bend. The journalist asked a dignitary—"Can't you guys even pray for Pike?" "We haven't had a chance to consult about it," was the reply. At the next session, my informant reports, there was a prayer—a "composite" prayer, he called it, mentioning in the same breath Bishop Pike and Ho Chi Minh. As the reporter concluded: "They prayed for all their enemies, all together."

The incident would have been a delight to Jim Pike. And surely the prayer was appropriate, for, wherever they can be said now to be, it is a moral certainty that Bishop Pike and Ho Chi Minh are in the same place.

In the Book of Common Prayer, the heading for the fortieth Psalm is *Expectans expectavi*, which is translated, variously, "I waited and waited," "I waited patiently," "I waited eagerly." I take that as a rubric for these remarks.

I commend to you James Albert Pike: he waited and waited, patiently, eagerly, for the Lord. The Lord did not tarry too long.

APPENDIX I

The Heresy Charges Against Bishop Pike

(Of the three occasions in which Bishop Pike was publicly accused of heresy, only one eventuated in a formal presentment requiring an official inquiry which could have resulted in an ecclesiastical trial. That was the presentment prepared by Bishop Henry I. Louttit in 1966. The earlier charges in 1961 by a Georgia clericus were in the form of a letter addressed to the Bishop of Georgia and to the press; and those in 1965, by some clergy in Arizona were in the form of a petition to the Bishop of Arizona, who referred the matter to the House of Bishops. The three sets of charges are repetitious; the Louttit presentment is reproduced here.)

(THE PRESENTMENT)

Whereas the Right Reverend James Albert Pike, J.S.D., S.T.D., D.D., J.U.D., LittD., LL.D., D.Hu.L., Hum.D., D.S.Litt., retired Bishop of California, has for the past several years held and taught publicly and advisedly (through both the written and spoken word) doctrine contrary to that held by this Church as set forth in the Creeds, the Catechism, the Offices of Instruction, and the Book of Common Prayer, and

Whereas this teaching has confused, not to say bewildered, many of the faithful laity of the Church, and

Whereas it becomes increasingly difficult to discipline the clergy who see one of their Right Reverend Fathers in God unwilling to discipline himself or to accept the kindly admonitions, criticisms, and suggestions of his fellow bishops given many times, both individually and corporately, and, moreover, see him continue to break his consecration and ordination vows by publicly proclaiming his erroneous and heretical views, and

Whereas this teaching jeopardizes our ecumenical conversations with our fellow Christians of the Eastern Orthodox, the Roman Catholic, and Conservative Reformed and Evangelical bodies,

THEREFORE the undersigned bishops of the Episcopal Church in the United States of America do herewith offer this presentment of charges to the Presiding Bishop under Article VIII of the Constitution of the Protestant Episcopal Church in the United States of America, and under Canons 53 and 56 of the General Convention of this Church, to wit:

1. Disloyalty to the Constitution of this Church;
2. Holding and teaching publicly and advisedly, doctrines contrary to that held by this Church;
3. Violation of the Constitution or Canons of the General Convention;
4. Any act which involves a violation of his ordination vows;
5. Conduct unbecoming a Clergyman;

To wit: In evidence of which is appended hereto information specified as necessary under provision of Canon 56, Sec. 3.

> THE BISHOP OF LONG ISLAND
> THE BISHOP OF TENNESSEE
> THE BISHOP OF MONTANA
> THE BISHOP OF GEORGIA
> THE BISHOP OF ALBANY
> THE BISHOP OF UPPER SOUTH CAROLINA
> THE BISHOP OF DALLAS
> THE BISHOP OF CHICAGO
> THE BISHOP OF KENTUCKY
> THE BISHOP OF NORTHERN CALIFORNIA
>
> THE BISHOP OF FLORIDA, and
>
> THE BISHOP OF SOUTH FLORIDA
>   *Co-Chairmen (Self-appointed) of the Committee of Bishops to Defend the Faith*

(*Specification of Charges*)

APPENDIX—PRESENTMENT OF THE RIGHT REVEREND
JAMES ALBERT PIKE, RETIRED BISHOP OF CALIFORNIA

CHARGE 1. That Bishop Pike has affirmed that this Church should *not* require belief in one God in three Persons as this Church has received the same; that in so saying, he has contradicted and denied the plain and inevitable meaning of Holy Scripture and the teachings of this Church.

The following Bishops make this presentment*

---

* The Bishop of Dallas later withdrew his signature. The Bishop of Long Island disassociated himself from certain parts of the presentment. The Bishop of Kentucky did not sign, though he promised to do so. The Bishops of Chicago and Montana are both recorded in Bishop Louttit's files as having reluctantly acceded to the use of their names after their names were published as signatories.

OFFENSE: Violation of Article VIII, Constitution of this Church.
Violation of Canon 53, Sec. 1, (2) (4) (6) (8).

GROUNDS: From his book, A TIME FOR CHRISTIAN CANDOR, (Harper and Row, 1964) Bishop Pike states: (P. 123, 124):

"Is a conceptualized doctrine of the Trinity in fact needed in order to preserve the essentials of the Christian Faith? If the answer is no, then the Church's mission would be relieved of a heavy piece of luggage . . . obviously, an essential of the Faith should not be abandoned or played down, even if it does make conversion to, or understanding of, Christianity more difficult . . . The Church's classical way of stating what is represented by the doctrine of the Trinity has in fact been a barrier with the well educated and less educated alike. AND IT IS NOT ESSENTIAL TO THE CHRISTIAN FAITH." (Bishop Pike has this last sentence in italics).

The following is from the farewell sermon at Grace Cathedral upon Bishop Pike's retirement, reported in the newspaper, ARIZONA REPUBLIC, Phoenix, September 5, 1966: "Bishop James A. Pike, in his final pastoral sermon at Grace Cathedral, declared yesterday that he could not affirm the existence of an "all-powerful . . . all-good . . . all-knowing God." The article goes on: "His faith is boiled down to what he himself observes and reads about." And it goes on to quote the Bishop, "Do you look at the data? Do you look at what is? There is only one breadth—the secular. There is no supernatural. If something is true, it is natural. If it is not natural, it is not true."

The following is from an article in the NEW YORK TIMES MAGAZINE, August 14, 1966, by John Cogley (p. 16): Pike acknowledges that he no longer thinks of himself as a Christian apologist, or as a defender of the faith. "I am," he said in a recent interview, "No longer primarily concerned with the question: Is it True or isn't it True? What I am interested in now is: How can I make it convincing?"

. . . . He says, however, that he no longer blesses "in the Name of the Father, and of the Son, and of the Holy Spirit," but simply "In the name of God." "Whatever is applied to One of the Three, even according to the classical theology, is the work of all Three," he argues. "So why complicate the issue by invoking the Trinitarian formula?"

"I have jettisoned the Trinity, the Virgin Birth and the Incarnation," he told an editor of LOOK Magazine in his Cambridge flat in England recently. Further references may be adduced by perusal of the article itself, in the February 22 issue of LOOK, p. 25ff; as well there is more of interest in the New York Times article in their Sunday Magazine, p. 16, issue of August 4, 1966.

*   *   *

CHARGE 2. That Bishop Pike has affirmed that Holy Scripture does *not* affirm the Person of the Holy Spirit, and that the Apostles and the early Church knew nothing about it; they "never heard of it". . . .

OFFENSE: Violation of Article VIII, Constitution of the Church.
Violation of Canon 53, Sec. 1 (2) (4) (6) (8).

GROUNDS: From his book, A TIME FOR CHRISTIAN CANDOR Pages
124, 125; Bishop Pike writes: (re the Trinity)
"These considerations support this conclusion: 1. The apostles and the
other first followers of the Way never heard of it . . . 2. All that can be
said of the Holy Spirit can be said of God without attribution to a distinct Person in the Godhead . . ."

*   *   *

CHARGE 3. That Bishop Pike has denied the doctrine of this Church and
of Holy Scripture as this Church holds the same, as regards the Second
Person of the Godhead, the Eternal Son, and has contradicted the same
doctrines of His Incarnation, and distorted the reasons for His being put
to death.

OFFENSE: Violation of Article VIII, Constitution of this Church Violation of Canon 53, Sec. 1 (2) (4) (6) (8).

GROUNDS: On pages 112, 113 of A TIME FOR CHRISTIAN CAN-
DOR, Bishop Pike Writes:

"So in the revelation of Jesus Christ the uniqueness lies not in the fact
of revelation or in the Source of what is revealed, but rather in the avenue of that Source's revelation—at the right time the right man related
aright to Him who is ever there and ready to be revealed. He was totally
open to the Source, the Ultimate Ground of all that is."
"His divinity is in the fullness of His true humanity, His total readiness to be a man, that is, the full, active vehicle of God's meaning and
love. But this possibility is in all men. . . . Some men had in a measure shown this capacity before; some have shown it since. It is ever a
possibility. But this possibility—in its fullness—would not have been an
actuality until the *kairos*—the right time, the time when men were ready
for God thus to be revealed, the time into which One could be born
who would be ready. Israel in that century was the right time and place,
and Jesus was ready. The one Source of all was recognized; the claim
had already been recognized; and He, with the authority of the source,
pushed the claim to the absolute limit. He did not deny the value of accepted rules in stating certain duties within the claim, but He honestly
declared that the codified law of His day was inadequate to encompass
the claim; indeed, He saw in the assertions of particular elements of the
law the minimization of the overall obligation. He in effect ordered His
own death."
(The reason for such a lengthy passage is that it encompasses all the
specifications of the charge it is appended to—i.e. the inherent adop-
tionist view in refusing the definition of God the Son as an infant in the
Incarnation; and related substitutionary matter in its place to explain
Jesus' "vocation"; and the obvious avoidance of the plain reason of the

account of His death, which was largely blasphemy, His being equated with God.) Cited also here as further grounds: from Bishop Pike's Book, WHAT IS THIS TREASURE, pages 60, 61, 62, where the Bishop not only distorts the reasons for Jesus being put to death, but assigns interpretation or contradictions to Holy Scripture that they do not bear: the several passages from pages 60–62 on who Jesus is: the declaration that St. Paul's passage in Philippian's 2ff is "apparent adoptionism"; and on page 63 his assertion: "in contrast to the Virgin Birth narratives which presuppose adoption at the time of conception or a prior status thereto."

On page 65, WHAT IS THIS TREASURE: "Therefore we should endeavor to rethink and restate the answer to the old question, "What think ye of Christ?" in a way which preserves three things: (1) The fact of Jesus' full humanity and individuality as a human being (2) the fact that in the experience of the Christian Community Jesus is sensed as belonging to the ultimate dimension of reality, and (3) the fact that God Himself, as the Ultimate Ground of all being, is unchanging and universal in His reality and ways, and though He is through the teaching and lives of many, many human beings—and very conspicuously in some, and though each of these manifestations is special, nevertheless God *is not acting 'specially' at any time."* This obviously is the Bishop's conclusion after examinations in the context of this chapter "Early assessments of Jesus," which examines the Holy Scriptures as to who Jesus is . . . and is his version of the doctrinal necessity of believing in "Incarnation." This obviously affects the possible operations of the Father, Son and the Holy Spirit.

To clinch the matter, on the next page, 66, he refers to his point 3 again: "It would have to be consistent with a sound view of God, particularly . . . in regard to the point (numbered 3) at the close of the last chapter: "what we see of reality in the operation of God in the image of Jesus must not be arbitrary or 'special' on God's part, no matter how 'special' we may regard Jesus.

And other distortions of Scripture: page 69 of WHAT IS THIS TREASURE: "If we assume that the 'exclusivist salvation' notion from the Fourth Gospel (purportedly supported by words from Jesus) did not really represent the true Jesus (but rather an early—and persistent—unfortunate development in the Christian Church) we yet have to deal with what one of the commentators has called a "Johannine bolt from the blue" which appears in two synoptic Gospels: "Everything is entrusted to me by my Father; and no one knows the Father but the Son and those to whom the Son shall choose to reveal Him" (Matt. 11:27; Luke 10:22).

Already referred to has been the contradiction in Judaism, reflected in the books of the Old Testament between a forum for universal salvation and an ethnic club. While the conversation with the Gentile woman might seem to indicate Jesus had opted for the latter, this is not at all clear: and certainly as we have seen, early organized Christianity followed the first alternative. But in the words attributed to Jesus there would seem to be support for the other kind of exclusivist salvation which has been the prevalent motif in organized Christianity, AS WE INDICATED IN CHAPTER 4, IT IS BAD ENOUGH FOR THE CHURCH TO HAVE HELD THIS VIEW SO LONG AND SO WIDELY, WITHOUT HAVING IT ATTRIBUTABLE TO THE CHURCH'S LORD. SINCE THIS TEXT IS SUI GENERIS (John 14:6—"No one comes to the Father but by Me) SO FAR AS THE RELATIVELY RELIABLE ACCOUNTS OF JESUS' TEACHING GOES. ONE CAN INDULGE WITH PLAUSIBILITY THE HOPE THAT THE WORDS ARE NOT AUTHENTIC . . ."

Another, Page 82: "The Resurrection of our Lord presents no special theological question. The Basic question is, does the individual personality survive into eternity? If the answer is yes, then of course this is true of Jesus."

On page 63, (on discussing the early General Councils) "Meanwhile the *bishops* had given *Jesus* equal place in the *new* trinity with the Father and *a* personified Holy Spirit."

From the NEW YORK TIMES MAGAZINE, August 14, 1966, by John Cogley, Religious News Editor of the TIMES: "Joseph, Mary's husband, Pike holds, was actually the natural father of Jesus."

From an article in LOOK MAGAZINE, February 22, 1966, on page 25ff: "That Jesus was man, though so perfect that God 'adopted' him, is the heresy of "adoptionism," for it denies that Jesus was God Incarnate. "My position," says Bishop Pike, "is not even that traditional, for adoptionism presupposes a special act of God. I've rejected that God does special things. Jesus freely adopted the Messianic role. God was able to flow through because Jesus was more open" . . . Then how does Jesus differ from other good but mortal men, like Socrates or Buddha? The Bishop's distinction is in degree, not kind. "Jesus is still unique because God Who breaks through Him is unique, and Jesus is the standard by which all others are measured."

*   *   *

CHARGE 4: That Bishop Pike has further distorted or denied doctrines of salvation as regards the Son of God as taught by Scripture and the Book of Common Prayer of this Church.

OFFENSE: Violation of Article VIII, Constitution of the Church
              Violation of Canon 53, Sec. 1 (2) (4) (6) (8)

GROUNDS: In his book, WHAT IS THIS TREASURE Bishop Pike writes, on page 38:

"A few examples are sufficient, from the Bible: 'No one can come to the Father except by Me.' (John 14:6). 'God so loved the world so much that He gave His only Son, that everyone who had faith in Him may not die but have eternal life.' (John 3:16) 'Everything is entrusted to me by my Father; and no one knows the Son but the Father, and no one knows the Father but the Son and those to whom the Son may choose to reveal Him.' (Matt. 11:27; Luke 1:22) . . . 'None can enter into the kingdom of God, except he be regenerate and born anew of Water and of the Holy Ghost.' (Book of Common Prayer, Page 273); . . . 'there is none other name under heaven given to man, in whom, and through whom, thou mayest receive health and salvation, but only in the Name of our Lord Jesus Christ.' (Book of Common Prayer, page 314).

Bishop Pike continues on Page 39: "The alternatives for reaction are clear: either (a) The New Testament and the preponderance of the teaching of the Church throughout the centuries is flatly wrong, or (b) that the God thus taught about either does not exist or is subhuman in morality—with the moral consequence that belief in Him (or if perchance such a god does exist, HE) is to be opposed."

*   *   *

CHARGE 5: That Bishop Pike affirms that beyond the ultimacy of God and His mighty acts, there is nothing else that is to be considered as essential, including (apparently) all that is spoken of in the Chicago-Lambeth Quadrilateral as *essential* to the Church.

OFFENSE: Violation of Article VIII, Constitution of the Church.
Violation of Canon 53, Sec. 1 (2) (4) (6) (8).

GROUNDS: On page 24 of A TIME FOR CHRISTIAN CANDOR, Bishop Pike writes:

"There is only one *Ultimate* God as known and experienced in His overall claim, His mighty acts. To make anything else ultimate is idolatry. Anything else: whether a particular doctrinal formulation, a particular book or books, a particular scheme of church government, a particular office or person, a particular ethical rule, a particular way of worship. *None of these is an essential of the Gospel.* (note: none of these are ultimate, by Bishop Pike's Christology, especially, but the Bishop said none are *essential* as well. . . .)

APPENDIX II

Books by James A. Pike

The Other Side: An Account of My Experiences
with Psychic Phenomena
If This Be Heresy
You and the New Morality
What Is This Treasure
A Time for Christian Candor
Teen-agers and Sex
Beyond the Law
A New Look in Preaching
Our Christmas Challenge
Facing the Next Day
Doing the Truth: A Summary of Christian Ethics
If You Marry Outside Your Faith
Beyond Anxiety
Cases and Other Materials on the New Federal
and Code Procedure

CO-AUTHOR OF
Administrative Law
The Faith of the Church
Man in the Middle
The Church, Politics and Society
Roadblocks to Faith

EDITOR OF
Modern Canterbury Pilgrims

BASED ON HIS NOTES
The Wilderness Revolt
by Diane Kennedy Pike and R. Scott Kennedy

Photo Credits